KT-434-538

INSIGHT GUIDES

AUSTRALIA

NEXT 92 km

Discovery CHANNEL

APA PUBLICATIONS

Part of the Langenscheidt Publishing Group

ABOUT THIS BOOK

Editorial
Project Editor
Jeffrey Pike
Editorial Director
Brian Bell

Distribution

UK & Ireland
GeoCenter International Ltd
The Viables Centre, Harrow Way
Basingstoke, Hants RG22 4BJ
Fax: (44) 1256 817988

United States
Langenscheidt Publishers, Inc.
36–36 33rd Street, 4th Floor
Long Island City, New York 11106
Fax: (1) 718 784 0640

Canada
Thomas Allen & Son Ltd
390 Steelcase Road East
Markham, Ontario L3R 1G2
Fax: (1) 905 475 6747

Australia
Universal Publishers
1 Waterloo Road
Macquarie Park, NSW 2113
Fax: (61) 2 9888 9074

New Zealand
Hema Maps New Zealand Ltd (HNZ)
Unit D, 24 Ra ORA Drive
East Tamaki, Auckland
Fax: (64) 9 273 6479

Worldwide
Apa Publications GmbH & Co.
Verlag KG (Singapore branch)
38 Joo Koon Road, Singapore 628990
Tel: (65) 6865 1600. Fax: (65) 6861 6438

Printing

Insight Print Services (Pte) Ltd
38 Joo Koon Road, Singapore 628990
Tel: (65) 6865 1600. Fax: (65) 6861 6438

©2005 Apa Publications GmbH & Co.
Verlag KG (Singapore branch)
All Rights Reserved
First Edition 1992
Fourth Edition 1998
Updated 2004
Reprinted 2005

CONTACTING THE EDITORS
We would appreciate it if readers
would alert us to errors or out-
dated information by writing to:
Insight Guides, P.O. Box 7910,
London SE1 1WE, England.
Fax: (44) 20 7403 0290.
insight@apaguide.co.uk

NO part of this book may be reproduced,
stored in a retrieval system or transmitted
in any form or means electronic, mech-
anical, photocopying, recording or otherwise, without prior written permission of
Apa Publications. Brief text quotations
with use of photographs are exempted
for book review purposes only. Information has been obtained from sources
believed to be reliable, but its accuracy
and completeness, and the opinions
based thereon, are not guaranteed.

www.insightguides.com

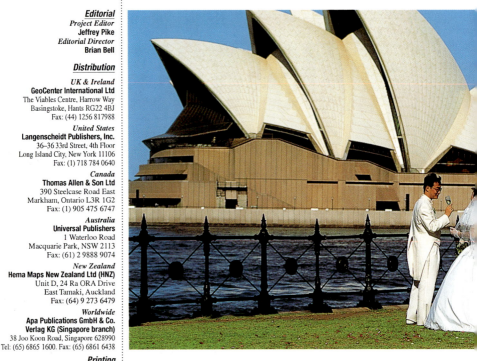

This guidebook combines the interests and enthusiasms of two of the world's best-known information providers: Insight Guides, whose titles have set the standard for visual travel guides since 1970, and Discovery Channel, the world's premier source of non-fiction television programming.

The editors of Insight Guides provide both practical advice and general understanding about a destination's history, culture, institutions and people. Discovery Channel and its website, www.discovery.com, help millions of viewers explore their world from the comfort of their own home and encourage them to explore it firsthand.

Insight Guide: Australia is structured to convey an understanding of the country and its culture and to guide readers through its sights and activities.

◆ The **Features** section, indicated by a yellow bar at the top of each page, covers the country's history, culture and people in a series of informative essays.

◆ The main **Places** section, indicated by a blue bar, is a complete guide to all the sights and areas worth visiting. Places of special interest are coordinated by number with the maps.

◆ The **Travel Tips** listings section, with an orange bar, provides a handy point of reference for information on travel, hotels, shops, restaurants and more.

The contributors

This edition was edited by **Jeffery Pike**, a London-based journalist and

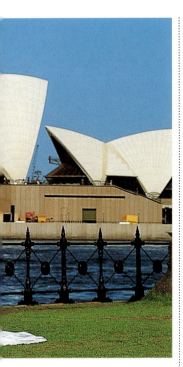

Map Legend

— ·· —	International Boundary
— — —	State Boundary
— · —	National Park/Reserve
— — —	Ferry Route
✈	Airport
🚌	Bus Station
P	Parking
ℹ	Tourist Information
✉	Post Office
✝	Church/Ruins
	Mosque
✡	Synagogue
	Castle/Ruins
∴	Archaeological Site
∩	Cave
★	Place of Interest

The main places of interest in the Places section are coordinated by number with a full-colour map (e.g. ❶) and a symbol at the top of every right-hand page tells you where to find the map.

photographer. Previous editors include **Tony Perrottet**, one of Insight's most experienced editors and the author of the chapter on his native Sydney; and **Cameron Duffy**, **Phil Jarratt**, **David McGonigal** and **John Borthwick**, all originally from Australia and widely travelled within their continent. Their contribution includes Borthwick's four chapters on Australia's remarkable history. Other writers whose earlier work appears are **A.D. Aird**, **Charles Perkins**, **Craig McGregor**, **Mungo McCallum** and **Lesley Thelander**.

For this book a team of experts was assembled from all corners of Australia – at least one in each state and territory – all with inside knowledge of their area and aspects of Australian life.

Amanda Burdon (who updated the Sydney and New South Wales chapters, and also wrote on Sydney's museums) was born in "country NSW" and has worked as a journalist in Sydney for over 10 years.

Victoria Kyriakopoulos (Melbourne and Victoria) is the Melbourne correspondent for Australia's weekly news magazine *Bulletin*. **Amanda Gryst** (South Australia) is a graduate of Adelaide University who has taught English in Bulgaria, managed restaurants in Britain and travelled extensively in her home state.

Paul Phelan (Queensland, the Great Barrier Reef) is an international writer specialising in air travel, who once piloted air taxis in the Outback.

Dennis Schulz (Northern Territory) is a Darwin-based photojournalist who covers Northern Australia and Southeast Asia for a wide range of Australian and international publications. He also wrote the pages on Aboriginal Art and Australia's Wildlife.

Victoria Laurie (Western Australia) is an ex-pat Brit who visited "three corners of the world", before making her home on Australia's west coast where she writes and broadcasts.

Finally, **Rick Eaves** (Tasmania) is a Tassie-born writer-photographer who is a regular contributor of stories and pictures to magazines in Australia and overseas.

Other new contributors are **Joe Rollo**, who describes Melbourne's buildings and **Robert Mayne**, who wrote about the wine industry. This edition was updated in 2004 by **Vic Waters, Paul Phelan** and **Robert James Wallace**, and edited by **Alyse Dar**. **Harriet Salisbury** edited the original Travel Tips. Thanks go also to **Sylvia Suddes**, **Naomi Everton**, and **Paul Burton**.

INSIGHT GUIDE
australia

CONTENTS

A map of Australia is on the inside front cover and a map of Sydney City Centre faces the inside back cover.

Lifesavers
at Bondi
Beach,
Sydney

Travel Tips

DOWN-UNDER

It's the world's largest island, or the earth's oldest continent. Either way, Australia is a place like no other

Australia is like an open door with the blue beyond. You just walk out of the world and into Australia. —D. H. Lawrence (1922)

Australia is the perfect place to suffer jet-lag. Waking up to the bush dawn, as the kookaburras begin their maniacal laughs and the golden light pierces the gumtrees, is one of the great outdoor experiences. Even in Sydney, a 6am stroll by the harbour as the first ferries roll past the Opera House will convince you that this may be the most gorgeous city on earth. This dawn beauty is just as well, since, even in the age of the jetliner, Australia's distance from almost everywhere else is the central fact of its existence – the source of its greatest strengths and weaknesses.

It always has been so, ever since a great chunk of earth broke off from Gondwanaland and Australia's landscapes and animals began to evolve into exotica. For 50,000 years the Australian Aborigines wandered these far shores, unmolested by the rest of the planet. In the 1780s the British knew exactly what to do with such profound isolation: take the dregs of their society, the criminals and the politically unsound, and expel them to the uttermost ends of the earth. For generations, settlers were overwhelmed by the "tyranny of distance" (as historian Geoffrey Blainey has called it). The remoteness from the Mother Country secretly convinced them that, as "transplanted Britons in another world", their lives were doomed to be second-rate. The strangeness of the landscape, the heat, the rain (or endless droughts), the prickliness and unwelcoming strangeness of it all… who would voluntarily choose to live in such a place?

All that has changed, of course. Today, Australians tend to be thankful for their distance from Europe and the United States, and embrace their (relative) proximity to Asia. The quirks of their homeland – the egg-laying mammals, the ghostly trees, the savage deserts, the spiders that can leap two metres, even the menagerie of deadly snakes – have become a source of endless fascination.

Thinking of their history, which was once considered dull and uneventful, Australians now agree with Mark Twain that it is a rip-roaring affair, so colourful that it might well have been invented. And culturally, Australians now look to their own resources – hardly indifferent to the rest of the world, but confident in their contributions. Indeed, Australian writers, film-makers, actors and painters have become ubiquitous.

How could it be otherwise? Living in this supposedly upside-down land – the Antipodes, "the exact opposite or contrary" – can hardly fail to provide a unique view of the world. ❏

PRECEDING PAGES: an island on the Great Barrier Reef; the coastline of the Great Australian Bight; the Three Sisters in the Blue Mountains; a sand-bottomed creek on Fraser Island, Queensland. **LEFT:** in the footsteps of *Crocodile Dundee.*

AUSTRALIA'S ANCIENT LANDSCAPE

Australia has been a continent for around 50 million years. But the history of the land can be traced back much further, to a time when the world was young

If there was ever a need to furnish an explanation of the strange and delightful contradictions in which Australia abounds, one might be found in the fact that a nation so young resides in a continent so old that its history almost defies comprehension.

For Australia's topography, so forbidding to the first European settlers who arrived over 200 years ago and now so compelling to more recent arrivals, takes us back to the earliest history of our planet. Certain rocks have been dated to 3,500 million years ago, while large chunks of the Australian landscape tell stories of earthly movements dating back more than 1,000 million years.

Whereas much of Europe and the Americas have the landscapes of youth – snow-covered peaks, rushing waterfalls, geysers, active volcanoes, giant gorges and mountain lakes – Australia's blunted, stunted, arid lands speak of an age which must be treated with respect. It is a land in which even the animals and plants, developed in isolation, are strikingly different.

The last great geological shifts in Australia took place some 230 million years ago, before the Permian Period. It was then that the forces of nature convulsed the earth's crust and created alpine ranges whose peaks extended above the snow line. Since then, modest convulsions on the eastern and western fringes have created low ranges (now known as tablelands), and volcanoes have occasionally erupted – but, generally speaking, Australia was already a sleeping giant when the rest of the world's landforms came into being. Barring unforeseen geological circumstances, it will also be the first continent to achieve equilibrium, a flattening of the land to the point where rivers cease to run, there is no further erosion, and landscape becomes moonscape.

Australia began to take shape some 50 million years ago when it broke away from the great southern continent known as Gondwanaland. This landmass at one time incorporated Africa, South America and India. Australia broke free and drifted north. This was a time when the dinosaurs, who had ruled the animal world for 120 million years, were fast disappearing, and the Australian landmass, which had already undergone great changes, was reshaping itself into a continent. The centre was rising from a

shallow sea to unite what had been a series of islands. One of these islands, the Great Western Plateau, had been the only constant during much of this change, sometimes partly submerged but always the stable heart of the continent.

Today that plateau spreads over almost half the continent, a dry and dramatic expanse of pristine beauty. It takes in the Kimberley and Hamersley ranges, the Great Sandy Desert, Gibson Desert and the Great Victoria Desert, and, although its topography has changed greatly, it houses the artefacts of ancient times.

A rock found near Marble Bar yielded the remains of organisms which lived 3,500 million years ago – the oldest form of life yet discov-

---

PRECEDING PAGES: Uluru (Ayers Rock), the world's largest monolith. **LEFT:** a dry lake at sunrise.
RIGHT: an electrical storm at Katherine Gorge, NT.

ered. A dinosaur footprint is frozen in rock near Broome, and in the Kimberley, once a coral reef in a shallow sea, landlocked ocean fish have adapted to fresh water.

The central eastern lowlands, stretching south from the Gulf of Carpentaria, form a sedimentary basin that has often been encroached upon by the sea. Although this is a catchment area of 1.5 million sq. km (600,000 sq. miles) for rivers running inland off the eastern range, much of the water is lost through evaporation or into the vast chain of salt lakes and clay pans. The largest of the salt lakes, Lake Eyre, is also the lowest part of the continent at 15 metres (50 ft)

below sea level. To our knowledge, it has filled completely only twice in history, but the abundance of dinosaur fossils indicates that it was once fringed with lush vegetation.

Much of the lowlands are so exceptionally harsh and inhospitable that it is difficult to imagine that beneath the surface lies the Great Artesian Basin, from which bores are tapped to provide water for livestock. The most ancient part of the basin area is the Flinders Ranges of South Australia, in which there are rocks and remains dating back 1,000 million years.

Because of its immense age, Australia can no longer boast a true alpine range. The Great Dividing Range that runs parallel with the east coast for more than 2,000 km (1,250 miles) is as diverse as any found on earth, tropical at one end and sub-alpine at the other. Mount Kosciusko, at 2,228 metres (7,300 ft), is the highest point, but equally majestic are the rainforests of the north and the moors of Tasmania. The Glass House Mountains in southern Queensland were formed by volcanoes about 20 million years ago, while the granite belt bridging the Queensland–New South Wales border and the Warrumbungle Mountains was born in similar circumstances a short time later.

In fact, Australia's last active volcano, in Victoria, died only 6,000 years ago – a few ticks ago, really, on the geological clock. In Tasmania the effects of volcanic activity and two ice ages have created a distinctive wilderness found nowhere else on the continent.

The coastline of Australia is as spectacular and as varied as the centre. It ranges from the limestone cliffs at the edge of the Nullarbor Plain to the jagged rock formations of Tasmania and western Victoria, from the mangrove swamps of the north to the spectacular beauty of the Great Barrier Reef – a lagoon which runs almost 2,000 km (1,250 miles) down the Queensland coast and contains more than 2,000 coral reefs.

Australia's vegetation is dominated by the eucalyptus, the humble gum tree, in its more than 500 forms. Across the length and breadth of the continent one cannot escape the smell, feel and sight of this tree, often stunted, knotted and offering little shade. While its hardiness is more notable than its beauty, some of its forms, such as the angophora, grow tall and attractive.

If the gum tree is the best-known example of Australian flora, the country's mammals are justly famous. The marsupials in particular have developed in isolation in extraordinary ways, and into 120 different species – from the red kangaroo and the gliders that fly between trees, to tiny desert mice.

The platypus and echidna are the world's only egg-laying mammals; the Queensland lungfish can breath both above and under water. Like the lungfish, which may be the fish that first stepped onto land – and ultimately became humankind – Australia has fascinating links to a time when the world was young. ❏

LEFT: sunset in the Outback.
RIGHT: Aborigines occupied caves like this for tens of thousands of years.

Decisive Dates

50 million years ago: Australia breaks free from the landmass that includes Antarctica, and drifts north.
50,000BC: The first Australians arrive, overland from New Guinea (some authorities place it earlier).
40,000BC: Tools from this period, found by Nepean River, are the oldest evidence of human occupation.
12,000BC: Tasmania and New Guinea are separated from the mainland as seas rise after the last Ice Age.
8000BC: Returning boomerangs are perfected and used for hunting for the first time, in South Australia.
2000BC: The dingo arrives in Australia.

AD**150**: Geographer Ptolemy decides there must be an unknown southern land *(terra australis incognita)*.

EARLY VISITORS

9th century: Seafarers from China possibly reach Australia's north coast.
11th century: Macassar fishermen regularly visit Australia in search of the sea cucumber, a valuable delicacy.
1290s: Marco Polo's journal refers to a land south of Java, rich in gold and shells.
1516: Portuguese establish colony on Timor, 500 km (310 miles) to the north; possibly visit north coast.
1606: Dutchman Willem Jansz, sailing east from Java, lands on the western side of Cape York Peninsula – the first verifiable European landing.
1642: Abel Tasman sees the west coast of Tasmania,

names it Van Diemen's Land. *Terra Australis Incognita* becomes *Hollandia Nova* (New Holland) on maps.
1688: English buccaneer William Dampier lands on the northwest coast.

COLONISATION AND EXPLORATION

1770: Captain Cook lands at Botany Bay, then sails north, charting 4,000 km (2,500 miles) of coast. He names it New South Wales and claims it for Britain.
1773: First picture of a kangaroo seen in Britain.
1788: First Fleet arrives in Sydney Cove, with a cargo of convicts. First white child is born in Australia.
1790: Second Fleet arrives.
1793: First free immigrants arrive in Australia.
1797: Merino sheep brought from Cape of Good Hope.
1803: Publication of *Sydney Gazette and New South Wales Advertiser*, Australia's first newspaper.
1801–3: Matthew Flinders circumnavigates Australia, proving it is a single island.
1811: Rev Samuel Marsden exports the first commercial cargo of wool to England.
1813: Australia's own currency is established. First crossing of the Blue Mountains.
1817: The name Australia is adopted (instead of New Holland). First bank is established in Sydney.
1829: First settlers land at Fremantle, and found Perth two days later. Western Australia becomes a colony.
1830: All Aborigines in Tasmania are rounded up and herded into reserves.
1831: Publication of *Quintus Servinton,* the first Australian novel, by Henry Savery, a former convict.
1836: Colony of South Australia established; Adelaide founded the following year.
1837: A year-old village on the Yarra River is named Melbourne (still part of New South Wales).
1838: Myall Creek Massacre: 28 Aborigines are butchered by white farmers.

GOLD RUSHES AND GROWTH

1842: New South Wales becomes a self-governing colony. Copper discovered in South Australia.
1850: Southern part of NSW becomes a separate colony called Victoria.
1851: Gold discovered, first in east-central NSW, then throughout Victoria.
1854: Battle at the Eureka Stockade between state troopers and miners protesting against licence fees.
1855: Van Diemen's Land becomes Tasmania.
1859: Northern part of New South Wales becomes a separate colony, Queensland. European rabbits introduced near Geelong; by 1868 they have eaten most of western Victoria.
1860: First south–north crossing of the continent

(from Melbourne to Gulf of Carpentaria) by the Burke and Wills Expedition.

1861: First Melbourne Cup horse race, watched by 4,000 people.

1863: South Australia takes over the administration of Northern Territory (formerly part of NSW).

1868: Transportation of convicts ends.

1880: Bushranger Ned Kelly is captured and hanged.

1882: Australian cricketers beat England for first time.

1883: Silver discovered at Broken Hill, NSW. Queensland takes possession of Papua (New Guinea).

1891: Delegates from the six colonies meet in Sydney to draft a constitution for Australia.

1893: Gold rush in Kalgoorlie, Western Australia.

1895: Banjo Paterson writes *Waltzing Matilda.*

1896: Athlete Edwin Flack represents Australia at the first modern Olympic Games.

A NEW NATION

1901 (1 Jan): The establishment of a federation of the six colonies into the Commonwealth of Australia (population 3,370,000).

1901 (May): The first Commonwealth Parliament sits in Melbourne.

1911: The federal government takes over the administration of Northern Territory.

1914–18: 330,000 Australians serve in World War I; 60,000 are killed, 165,000 wounded.

1915: Australian troops take a major part in the Gallipoli siege; more than 8,000 are killed.

1923: Chemist Cyril Callister creates Vegemite, Australia's national food.

1927: Parliament House opens in Canberra and the federal parliament moves there from Melbourne.

1928: Royal Flying Doctor Service founded by Rev. John Flynn in Cloncurry, Queensland.

1930: The Great Depression; 25 percent of the Australian workforce is unemployed.

1932: Sydney Harbour Bridge opens.

1939: Australia declares war on Germany. Australian Air Force is active in Britain, navy operates in Mediterranean, Australian troops fight in North Africa.

1941: Australia declares war on Japan.

1942: 15,000 Australians captured when Singapore falls to Japan. Japanese bomb Darwin.

1950: Immigration peaks at 150,000 new arrivals.

1954: Elizabeth II is the first reigning monarch to visit.

1956: Olympic Games held in Melbourne.

1959: Danish architect Joern Utzon wins the competition to design Sydney Opera House. Population of Australia reaches 10 million.

1965: Conscription re-introduced. First regular army battalion sent to Vietnam.

1967: Aborigines granted Australian citizenship and the right to vote.

1973: Sydney Opera House is finally completed. Australian Patrick White wins Nobel Prize for Literature.

1974: Darwin flattened by cyclone Tracy.

1975: Papua New Guinea is granted independence.

1983: The yacht *Australia II* wins the America's Cup.

1985: Uluru (Ayers Rock), Kata Tjuta (The Olgas) and surrounding desert are returned to Aborigines.

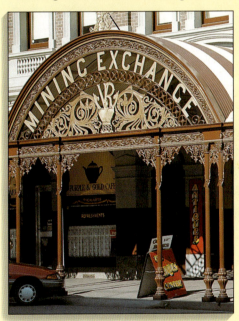

1986: Australian film *Crocodile Dundee*, starring Paul Hogan, grosses $116 million in USA.

1988: More than 2 million people visit Australia in its Bicentennial year. Queen Elizabeth II opens new Parliament House in Canberra.

1995: Australians protest strongly over French nuclear testing in the South Pacific.

1999: In a national referendum Australians narrowly vote against becoming a republic.

2000: Sydney is the first major city in the world to celebrate the millennium. Olympic Games are held in Sydney and IOC President Juan Samaranch declares the Games "the best Olympics ever".

2001: Centenary of the Federation.

2003: Australia's Liberal (Conservative) Government supports US military action in Iraq. ❑

LEFT: evidence of the earliest inhabitants – Namarkain spirits at Sorcery Rock in Arnhem Land, Northern Territory. **RIGHT:** Gold Rush memories – the Mining Exchange at Ballarat, Victoria.

50,000 YEARS OF DREAMTIME

Living in harmony with the land, Australia's Aborigines developed a culture rich and complex in its customs, religions and lifestyles

Long before the ancient civilisations in the Middle East, Europe and the Americas flourished, more than 50,000 years before European, Asian or Middle Eastern navigators recorded visits to the shores of "The Great South Land", Australian Aborigines occupied this continent – its arid deserts and tropical rain-

forests, and especially its major river systems and coastal plains and mountains. Estimates by anthropologists put the population of Aborigines, prior to 1770, at more than 300,000.

Their ancient traditions thrived in a kinship and close spiritual bond with every living thing and even with inanimate objects such as rocks, rivers and other geographical features. Each tribe recognises the local landmarks and links them with the rich mythology of the Dreamtime (or Dreaming). Various geological aspects are sacred sites with their own personality and significance. The Aborigine considers himself, nature and the land inseparably bound and interdependent. In this state of unity, he (and she) achieves a balance with the environment.

Dreamtime is the basis of all traditional Aboriginal thought and practice. It is the Aborigines' cultural, historical and ancestral heritage. In their mythology it is an age that existed long ago and yet remains ever-present as a continuing, timeless experience, linking past, present and future. Dreamtime was the dawn of all creation when the land, the rivers, the rain, the wind and all living things were generated.

Tribal elders, who possessed specialised knowledge of the community and the land, were responsible for maintaining the clan's group identity through its totemistic religion. Groups of people formed special bonds with a totem, usually an animal or a plant which acted as a protector and a symbol of group identity. Through special ceremonies and other social and religious practices, the elders transmitted their knowledge.

Although there were female elders and rituals, much of Aboriginal ceremonial life was secret and male-dominated. The sacred mythology that determined an individual's role in life and his tribal responsibility was passed on in complex initiation ceremonies. The tribal elders would entrust these secrets to the young boys, who in turn would become trustees of tribal lore as well as skilled hunters and providers. Political or religious power was rarely inherited; it had to be earned.

The Aborigines celebrated the adventures of

HUNTERS AND GATHERERS

Aborigines lived in clans of 10 to 50 or more people. Their life in the harsh landscape of Australia was based on hunting by the men and fishing and gathering by the women. A good hunter knew intimately the habits of the creatures he stalked, was an expert tracker and understood the seasons and the winds.

He took only what he needed to feed himself and his people and therefore kept in balance with his supply. Conservation was the Aborigine's way of denying starvation; in a country that would kill many white pioneers, the Aborigine was perfectly at home.

their Dreamtime spirit heroes through their paintings, songs and sacred dances. The heroes took both human and animal form; each had significance in the evolutionary cycle of the universe. The rock paintings were of special significance, bearing the strongest psychological and ritual values. As no Aboriginal language was written, these rock paintings, along with the oration of legends by tribal leaders, were responsible for passing the Dreamtime stories from one generation to the next.

The Aboriginal ceremony of

NATIVE TONGUES

Australia's Aborigines once spoke 500 different languages, grouped into 31 related language families, each as rich and complex as the languages of Europe.

dealt seriously with the procreation of life. Some tribes used a long, hollow piece of wood which, when blown, emitted a weird droning sound. This was the didgeridoo, whose sound was said to resemble the calling of the spirits.

Aborigines believed that a person's spirit did not die upon physical death, and that ceremonies were essential to ensure that the spirit left the body and became re-embodied elsewhere – in a rock, a tree, an animal, or perhaps another human form. Thus each person was the centre

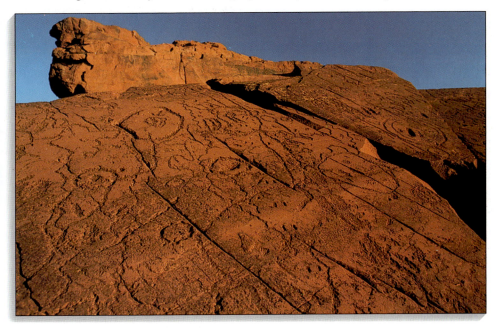

celebrating with song and dance was called *corroboree*. The male dancers were expert in mimicking the movements of animals; with these skills they reconstructed legends, heroic deeds or famous hunts. Bodies were elaborately painted, and songs were chanted to the accompaniment of music sticks and boomerangs clapped together.

Basic dance themes dealt with hunting and food gathering, or sex and fertility. Sometimes they took a humorous vein but more often they

PRECEDING PAGES: rock paintings at Nourlangie Rock, Northern Territory. **LEFT:** the didgeridoo was said to sound like the calling of the spirits. **ABOVE:** some rock carvings are tens of thousands of years old.

of an intricate web of relationships which gave order to the entire world and to all that might be included in it.

Totems and Dreamtime gave the individual his inherent link with the land, and thus his identity. So intricate was the Aborigines' relationship with the land that to remove them from it (and exile was indeed a punishment meted out to recalcitrants) was to kill them spiritually. Dispossession from the land meant dispossession from the Dreamtime.

Aboriginal culture had prepared the people for everything they might expect to face in life – everything, that is, except the coming of the white man. ❏

VOYAGES OF DISCOVERY

The first Chinese merchants may have reached Australia 700 years ago. But a string of accidents and misunderstandings left the continent largely unknown for centuries

When James Cook dropped anchor in 1770 in that east coast bay, so teeming with exotic new lifeforms that he decided to call it Botany Bay, he verified by flag and map an idea that Europe had craved.

"The Great South Land", "Greater Java", "Australia del Espíritu Santo", "New Holland", "Terra Australis Incognita" – this oldest of continents was known by many names.

The Greeks, the Hindus and Marco Polo had all speculated upon its location and nature. The Arabs, the Chinese and the Malays had probably come and gone, as had the Portuguese. The Dutch came, looked and left, disappointed at not finding "uncommonly large profit". At the end of the 17th century, the English explorer and privateer William Dampier saw the west coast as a barren reach inhabited by "the miserablest people on earth". The fertile east coast was, incredibly, missed by a matter of kilometres by both the French explorer Louis Antoine de Bougainville and the Spaniard Luis Vaez de Torres.

The continent's non-discovery was a history of such accidents. The land that the explorers did touch upon did not satisfy the European fantasies of gold, gods and glory. Had it happened otherwise, Australia might well be speaking an Iberian tongue, or Dutch, or French, or even in the Guringai words of Sydney's first inhabitants.

Finally, it fell to a small converted English coal ship, and to the humbly born genius who navigated her, to transmute the fantasies to fact and to put the stamp of Europe upon a continent which trade winds, tide and reefs had so far conspired to hide from these men of maps.

Pre-European visitors

Two thousand generations of Aborigines had roamed Australia since the first epic land and sea voyages of the Australoid migrations. The first possibly co-existed with two completely different races that preceded them. Earlier cave paintings show at least one of these was sophisticated, well-dressed and artistic. The other – from fossilised remains – was a prehistoric-looking figure, with thick bone and prominent brow ridges. But these populations were either wiped out or absorbed by the later waves of Aboriginal population. Chinese merchants seeking sandalwood

and spices may also have preceded the Europeans. During the 13th and 14th centuries their junks penetrated the Indonesian archipelago and sailed as far as East Africa. In 1879 a small Ming Dynasty statuette of Shou Lao, the god of Long Life, was unearthed in Darwin. It was embedded more than a metre below ground in the roots of a banyan tree, suggesting that Chinese sandalwood cutters from Timor, only 500 km (300 miles) away, may have been here.

Arab sailors, spreading Islam, had also reached Indonesia by the 13th century. They spread their influence as far as western New Guinea before being halted in the 16th century by Dutch Protestants. The Arabs, too, may have reached Aus-

LEFT: an early European impression of an Aboriginal camp. **RIGHT:** Captain Cook's *Endeavour*, a converted coal ship, rides out a South Pacific storm.

tralia's northern coasts only to find, like so many others, that it did not welcome them or their Allah.

The Bugis seamen of Macassar are known to have fared better. For at least a century before the white invasion of Australia, the Macassan praus were making annual excursions to the north coast in order to gather sea cucumbers, which they then sold to Chinese merchants.

By 1516 the Portuguese were spreading Catholicism and trade from their bases at Ambon in the legendary Spice Islands, the Moluccas, and at Timor. A set of documents known as "Dieppe Maps" shows that they were familiar with the whole eastern half of the continent at

of Austria, as "Austrialia del Espíritu Santo".

Upon realising his mistake, Queirós turned back to the Americas where he died a defeated dreamer. He had not found Australia but had unwittingly provided the beginnings of its name.

In 1607 his second-in-command, Luis Vaez de Torres, continued east towards the Moluccas and wrote another chapter in Australia's accident-prone history. Instead of navigating the north coast of New Guinea, he was forced to the south of the island, thus becoming the first European to pass through the strait between Australia and New Guinea which now bears his name. Slumbering just over the horizon was the Great South Land.

least 250 years before Cook's arrival. Because of the political jealousies of Spain, the absence of gold and spices, and the lack of souls agreeable to conversion, they probably suppressed the news of its location.

Pedro Fernandez de Queirós sailed west from the Spanish port of Callao in Peru in 1606. He was driven by the vision of finding the great southern continent and converting it to the "true faith" before the Protestant heretics and the Muslim infidels could taint it. Upon reaching what is now Vanuatu (known before 1980 as the New Hebrides), Queirós mistook it for his grail and, rejoicing, offered the region to the Holy Spirit and (by a Spanish pun) to Philip III

Dutch exploration

Torres had missed Australia, but already another European had taken the step that would stir the continent out of the morning of time and into AD1606. William Jansz had sailed east from the Dutch port of Bantam, Java, and had reached the western shore of Cape York Peninsula. Failing (once again) to find nutmeg, pepper, silver or gold, and having lost several crew in an altercation with the locals, Jansz reported Australia to be "for the greater part desert, with wild, cruel black savages... we were constrained to return finding no good to be done there."

For the next 35 years, Java-bound ships from Holland would round the Cape of Good Hope, drop into the nautical speedway of the Roaring Forties and then "take a left turn at Perth," so to speak. Because of difficulties in fixing longitude, they often bumped into the west coast, or overshot into the Great Australian Bight.

Dirk Hartog landed on an island in Shark Bay – halfway up the coast – and left a celebrated pewter plate nailed to a tree as his calling card. Peter Nuyts missed his turn and ended up 1,600 km (1,000 miles) into the Bight. The result of all this hitting and missing was that the

FIRST FOOTER

William Jansz was the first European known to have set foot on Australia. For this he is commemorated on an obscure street sign in Canberra.

from the Portuguese "open your eyes") off the west coast. The historian Geoffrey Blainey, in his book *The Tyranny of Distance*, tells how the ship *Batavia* "carried about 316 people, and some were drowned, and some died in the sand, and 125 were murdered by their own countrymen in a savage mutiny ashore. A few survivors reached Java in an open boat, and a ship was sent to rescue the remaining survivors, salvage treasure and cargo, and to punish the murderers." Two young mutineers were reprieved and

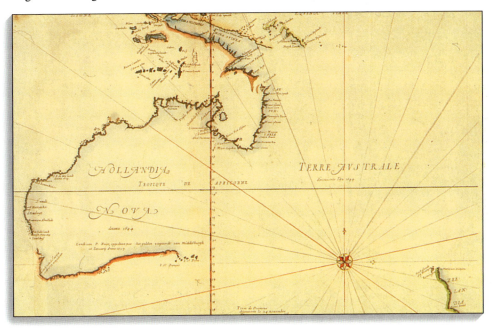

Dutch mapped almost two-thirds of the continent, its southern, western and northern perimeters, and yet – because it did not fit their dream of cloves and silk, gold and fruit groves, and because its "barbarians" knew nothing of metals or manners – they did not admit that this enormous territory *was* the Great South Land.

The lowest moment for the dreamers of a New Holland came in 1629, when one of their treasure ships, bound for Batavia (the old name for Jakarta), was wrecked on the Houtman Abrolhos Islands (ironically, the name comes

exiled on Australia's mainland near the present-day town of Geraldton; although nothing is known of their subsequent fate, they were no doubt Australia's first convict colonists.

The directors of the Dutch East India Company, still keen for their "uncommonly large profits", despatched Abel Tasman from Java in 1642, telling him to find the South Land. Voyaging anti-clockwise around Australia he discovered Tasmania (which he named "Van Diemen's Land" after the Governor-General of the Dutch East Indies), the Tasman Sea, the west coast of New Zealand and the Fiji Islands. This was the greatest voyage of discovery since Magellan, but the burghers in Batavia were not impressed.

LEFT: *Fishing*, portrayed by John Heaviside Clark.
ABOVE: a French map of New Holland, 1644.

They sent Tasman out again in 1644, but again he returned without satisfying their queries on the connection (if any) between Van Diemen's Land, the continent and New Guinea. Worse yet, he brought no news of mines or spices, nor of people who would barter or pray. His stories of beach-roving savages confirmed the Dutch despair. They simply gave up the search.

"A very unpleasing aspect"

In 1688, the much misjudged William Dampier was searching for new British trade routes in the Pacific. The idea of using New Holland (as it was still known) as a watering place appealed to him –

And so he mourned on. However, in his description there was the unheralded recognition of a practice more life-sustaining and, ironically, more Christian than the drives for glory, God and gold which fired so many of his predecessors and followers. Dampier was the first to note the Australian Aborigines' communality: "Sometimes they get as many fish as makes them a plentiful Banquet; and at other times they scarce get every one a taste: but be it little or much that they get, every one has his part, as well the young and tender, as the old and feeble, who are not able to go abroad, as the young and lusty."

The South Land lay undisturbed in its dream-

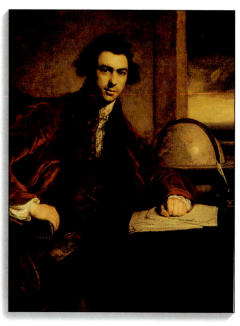

until he got there. Like the Dutch before him, he was appalled by the bleak landscape of the north-western coast, the fruitless trees and naked savages, and the disappointment of his well-spiced Arcadian fantasies. His account of the Aborigines epitomises the enormous cultural gap between European expectation and antipodean fact. He saw them as the most miserable people on earth "who have no Houses and Skin Garments, Sheep, Poultry, and Fruits of the Earth… setting aside their human shape they differ but little from Brutes… Their Eye-lids are always half closed, to keep the Flies out of their Eyes… They are long visaged, and of a very unpleasing aspect; having no one graceful feature in their faces."

time for another century. And then, on one of those bright autumn mornings when the westerlies blow offshore and the bush glitters euca-lypt-green, the small barque *Endeavour* rounded the bay on the southeastern coast, and things changed forever.

The coming of Cook

The ship's captain was a 41-year-old Royal Navy lieutenant by the name of James Cook. In

ABOVE: Captain Cook, as portrayed by Nathaniel Dance, and Joshua Reynolds' portrait of Joseph Banks.
RIGHT: an engraving from 1802 showing a kangaroo with two joeys in her pouch.

1768 he had been despatched by the Admiralty to Tahiti, at the request of the Royal Society, to observe a transit of the planet Venus. Among the company of 94 on his second-hand coal ship *Endeavour* were Daniel Carl Solander and Joseph Banks, two of the great botanists of the age.

Having fulfilled his duties in Tahiti, Cook sailed southwest to New Zealand and spent six months charting both islands. He was then free to return to England by either the Cape or the Horn. Instead, he and his officers decided upon a route that would lead towards the unknown, the then-fabled South Land. Cook had resolved to turn his ship "westward till we fall in with the East Coast of New Holland and then to follow that direction of the coast to the northward."

On 28 April 1770, *Endeavour* anchored in Botany Bay for one week. No naturalists before or since Solander and Banks have ever collected in such a short time so many new specimens of plant, bird and animal life. Meanwhile, the sailors ate their fill of seafoods, causing Cook at first to name the place Stingray Harbour Bay. He later changed it to Botany Bay because of Solander and Banks's discoveries.

Sailing north, Cook sighted and named (but did not enter) Port Jackson, Sydney's great harbour-to-be. On 22 August, at Possession Island off the tip of Cape York, he hoisted the British colours and claimed the whole of the eastern side of the continent under "the name of New South Wales" for George III.

Reflecting during his homeward journey upon the state of the Australian Aborigine, he took a far more enlightened view than had any of his European predecessors. He wrote the classic description of the noble savage: "In reality they are far more happier than we European; being wholly unacquainted with not only the superfluous but the necessary Conveniences so much sought after in Europe… the Earth and sea of their own accord furnishes them with all things necessary for life."

Upon reaching London in 1771, Cook reported to the Admiralty that he had found the east coast of New Holland, but not the Great South Land – if indeed such a place existed. During his voyage of 1772 to 1775, he destroyed the historical myth of the Great South Land by using the westerlies to circumnavigate the Antarctic. In 1779, he died at the hands of Polynesians in the Hawaiian islands, which he also discovered. ❑

CAPTAIN JAMES COOK

James Cook was stern and hot-tempered; physically, he was tall, dark and handsome. He was also, in the parlance of his time, a "tarpaulin", an officer who had advanced to his station without the boost of aristocratic or at least "gentle" birth.

Born in 1728, the son of a Yorkshire farm labourer, at 18 he had been apprenticed onto North Sea colliers. Enlisting in the Royal Navy in 1755, he distinguished himself as a navigator and a Master, particularly on the St Lawrence River in Quebec, Canada, during the Seven Years War with France. His secular egalitarianism, pride and loyalty to the Crown, and in particular his humble origins, seem appropriate traits for the founder of a nation which has often vaunted such characteristics as its own.

A courageous and proud man, Cook was driven more by a sense of duty and personal excellence than by greed or God. All supplies of fresh food which his crew obtained he "caused to be equally divided among the whole company generally by weight, so the meanest person in the Ship had an equal share with myself [Cook] or anyone on board." As for the soul-snatching men of the cloth, he would never permit a parson to sail on any of his ships.

COLONISATION AND EXPLORATION

In 1788 the British flag was raised and New South Wales was a colony. But it took the colonists more than a century to get to grips with this strange land

A dumping ground for rebels, poachers, prostitutes and murderers… A prisoners' island, its outlying cells founded by warders, whalers, escapees and anxious politicians… The auguries for Australia's future were not those of the Promised Land. Yet, from the little huddle of convicts and redcoats who in 1788 planted the cross and gallows of Europe's harsh order on this time-forgotten coast, a society of sorts soon took root.

With the loss of Maryland and Georgia in the American War of Independence, Britain was forced to find another place of exile for its unwanted convicts. The prisoners were temporarily stuffed into rotting river hulks around London, but these sinks of disease, depravity and escape soon became a source of public outcry. In desperation, the government took up Sir Joseph Banks's suggestion that Botany Bay in New Holland would be a suitable spot to house what the poet Les Murray has called "England's buried Gulag."

The First Fleet

In May 1787, 11 small ships of "the First Fleet" under Captain (later Governor) Arthur Phillip sailed from Portsmouth. Eight months later, the 1,000 passengers – three-quarters of them convicts – arrived at Botany Bay. A quick survey showed two things: Cook's description of the waterless place had been far too generous; and two ships of Comte de la Perouse were also there, possibly shopping for a new continent on behalf of Louis XVI of France.

Phillip hurriedly sailed 20 km (12 miles) up the coast to Port Jackson and (after a few toasts and a fusillade) raised the flag for George III on 26 January 1788. Officers, marines, transportees, sheep, goats and cattle were disgorged by these latter-day Noah's arks into a cove that's now overlooked by the Sydney Opera House.

The surgeon-general to the fleet rhapsodised

that Port Jackson was "the finest and most extensive harbour in the Universe." It is said that even the convicts, on sighting its fine blue bays and glistening headlands, raised a cheer of joy. It is also noted that two Aborigines shouted *"Warra! Warra!"* (Go Away!); no one heeded.

Thus the colony stumbled to life. And a hard

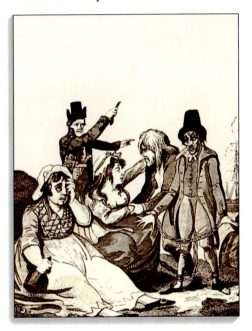

one it was at first. Marooned halfway around the world, these first New South Welshmen found that their seed-wheat, which had been damaged at sea, failed to germinate in the sandy soil. Their cattle grew wild, and the sheep fell foul of convicts, Aborigines and dingoes.

After 30 months of isolation and famine, locked in by the natural prison of this alien bush, the settlement was down to half-rations. When a ship finally appeared, to their despair, it was carrying not supplies but 222 elderly and ill female convicts. Fortunately, the supply ships of the Second Fleet were close behind.

The tents at Sydney Cove were replaced by brick and timber huts. Phillip tried to lay out a

LEFT: Sydney Cove soon after settlement.
RIGHT: the convicts who embarked for Botany Bay were a wretched lot, as this 1792 engraving shows.

town along orderly lines, but conformity was not in the nature of its inhabitants. Short cuts soon became streets and, despite later attempts at order, the convenient jigsaw that resulted can still be seen today as the ground plan of Sydney's high-rise pile-up.

Sydney Town expanded west towards the fertile farming lands of Parramatta, but was still hemmed in by the impenetrable escarpment of the Blue Mountains. Explorers fanned out by land and sea to open new pastures and farms, and to find even more isolated and savage prisons, such as Norfolk Island. This had originally figured in British strategy as a potential source of flax, hemp and masts for its Pacific naval and trade fleets. The plan failed, and the island's true "success" was as a hell-hole of sadism.

New South Wales was still costing London dearly (£1 million in the first 12 years), but it was turning a profit for its local landowners and the officers of the NSW Corps, otherwise known as "the Rum Corps". The Corps stood up against the extortionate demands of trading-vessel masters, while at the same time developing its own monopolies. The colony had become such a vat of drunkenness, and the demand for Bengal rum, which the Corps controlled, was so great that rum almost became the currency of the colony.

Hell on earth

Governor William Bligh (of *Bounty* fame) was despatched to clean up the Rum Corps' act, and to encourage free settlers to come to Sydney. However, the Corps, at the bidding of a farmer and officer, John Macarthur, pulled the second of the famous mutinies in Bligh's career, and in 1808 deposed him.

New South Wales and its satellite penal settlements at Moreton Bay (now Brisbane), Norfolk Island and Van Diemen's Land (Tasmania) entered the 19th century with a reputation as "hell on earth" – a reputation which the British hoped would function as a deterrent.

Irish rebels, Tolpuddle Martyrs and petty thieves caught for stealing buckles or loaves of bread were thrown together in Australia, when death at the end of a noose would often have been more merciful. In attempting to escape, some became the interior's first explorers. Pathetically, they fled into the bush, some believing that China lay beyond the Blue Mountains or that a colony of free whites dwelt inland. The only sure way of escape from the pathological violence on Norfolk Island was to commit murder in the hope of being hanged.

Yet these excesses were also tempered by the high-mindedness and reforms of Governor Lachlan Macquarie (1810–21), the hopes of some emancipists (freed convicts) that morality and dignity *could* prevail, and by a growing prosperity through trade. Macquarie, a paternalistic autocrat, stifled the Rum Corps' monopoly on the import of spirit, established the colony's own currency (1813) and first bank (1817), and encouraged the first crossing of the Blue Mountains (1813). His programme of public works

THE SEIZING OF SYDNEY

Sydney Town was named after Viscount Sydney, the secretary of the Home Department in London, which supervised colonial affairs.

The territory on which Sydney now stands was simply expropriated by Arthur Phillip from the local Aborigines. No treaty, no beads, no thanks offered. Thereafter Phillip, naively overlooking his own status as a gate-crasher, strove to foster friendly and fair relations between his tribe and the blacks.

For his pains he was speared in the shoulder at Manly Cove. An abyss of incomprehension continued to separate the two races.

and town planning (265 projects in 11 years) owes much to Francis Greenway, an emancipist transported to Sydney as a forger, who became the young colony's leading architect.

Transportation to Australia's various penal settlements had ceased by 1868. By then some 160,000 convicts had arrived; only 25,000 were women, a distortion which left its stamp in the harsh, male-dominated "frontier" society for decades to come.

Domestic exploration

A continent of 7.7 million sq. km (3 million sq. miles), much of it searing desert or dense scrub, colonial authorities into establishing settlements in Tasmania and Western Australia respectively. Once the Great Dividing Range had been penetrated in 1813, the drive for new lands, minerals and the glory of being "first there" – wherever "there" happened to be – lured men on.

Early explorers believed that the westward-flowing rivers of the NSW interior led towards a vast inland sea. In 1830 Charles Sturt and his party set out on the Murrumbidgee River, following its current into the Lachlan and Murray rivers, finally reaching Lake Alexandrina near the South Australia coast. After travelling more than 1,000 km (600 miles) they were within

could not be explored quickly or easily. The revelation of Australia's intimidatingly vast interior progressed sporadically over many years.

Before the crossing of the Blue Mountains in 1813, most significant exploration took place by sea. British sailors Bass and Flinders guessed correctly at the separation of Tasmania from the mainland. The French ships of Baudin in 1802, and later of Dumont d'Urville in 1826, scared the

---

LEFT: Bungaree, a celebrated Aborigine who could mimic officers, accompanied Matthew Flinders on his voyages around Australia.
ABOVE: Augustus Earle's painting of the Bathurst Plains, *circa* 1826, showing convicts breaking stones.

sight of the sea, but were unable to reach it. Instead they had to row against the current towards their starting point.

Their 47 days' rowing, on meagre rations and against flood tides, left Sturt temporarily blind, but is one of the most heroic journeys in Australian exploration. The myth of an inland sea had been dispelled.

By 1836, the vast river systems of the south-eastern continent had been charted. Tasmania had been explored, and the genocide of its natives had begun. A decade later most of New South Wales, half of Queensland, and the southern and northern coasts had been substantially explored.

A Tourist in the Colony

John Hood, Esq, a snobbish and ill-tempered old Scot, came to the colony of New South Wales in 1841 with no other purpose than to visit his son and enjoy himself. Arriving just after the suspension of convict transportation to Sydney, Hood may, in fact, have been Australia's first tourist.

But few who read the resulting travel memoir, *Australia and the East*, would have been encouraged to follow in his footsteps, for the colony was

wilder than Hood had bargained for. Apart from the rigours of bush life, the finicky Scot encountered tribal Aborigines, escaped convicts, horse thieves and lunatics – and was appalled by them all.

When Hood disembarked in Sydney, his delicate sensibilities were immediately offended. With 40,000 inhabitants, the town lacked sewerage. Convicts in chains clanked through the streets, which were lined with slab huts and 215 pubs. Worst of all, the colonists seemed to tolerate alcoholism. Indeed, he scoffed, they openly expressed their intention to "go out and get drunk."

Hood had a tearful meeting with his son Alexander who 10 years before had been packed off with the family servant to find fame and fortune. Now Alexander was a successful squatter near Mount

Connobolas, at the furthest frontier of settlement, and he took his father out for a visit. The journey turned into a nightmare. Crossing the Blue Mountains – a glorious drive today – was a gruelling ordeal on horseback. The convict-built road, which wound at absurd angles through the grey sandstone expanse, was "endless", Hood wrote. Soon it began to rain. His horse lost two shoes, and there was no hope of finding a blacksmith ("For the first time my spirits gave way"). His luggage was lost. The town of Bathurst was small and gloomy ("I was in despair").

When Hood finally saw his son's sheep property, near present-day Orange, he was mortified. The "gunyah" they were to live in "belonged to no recognised order of architecture," he wrote, being simply a bark hut with gaps in the walls that let in both light and insects. "You eat it, you drink it, you inhale it," Hood wrote of the ubiquitous bush fly. "Truly their name is legion!" They ate mutton for breakfast, lunch and dinner. Worst of all was the loneliness, no matter how many people were around.

Hood's adventures in the bush provide an entertaining slice of frontier life. With the nearest policeman, church or doctor many miles away, the Connobolas property was in constant danger of being attacked by bushrangers. Hood was so terrified that he buried all his valuables under the floor.

The Hoods took a journey towards Wellington – today a pleasant highway lined with towering ghost gums and green fields stretching beyond, but in 1841 drought-stricken and barren. They spent a night in Molong at "the worst managed inn I have ever entered," Hood wrote. "All the drunkards of the district seemed to congregate within its walls, allowing us no sleep, but annoying us through the night with all manner of low blackguardism."

The days on the frontier wore on in a tedious blur. Homesickness hit Hood worst at Christmas: "The sultry heat is a disagreeable contradiction to all our impressions of that happy season of frosts and snows and fireside comforts." He missed society life, books and letters, and complained of receiving newspapers only once a week, so he finally decided to head back to Scotland.

As Hood said farewell to Alexander in Sydney, knowing that they would never see each other again, he had serious misgivings about having sent his son to Australia. "I confess," he wrote, "that for me such a life has not charms to compensate for the disadvantages." ❑

LEFT: *The Landlord* by William Buelow Gould.

Leichhardt's vanishing act

In 1842, a 29-year-old Prussian draft dodger, Ludwig Leichhardt, landed in Sydney. He did not have good qualifications for an aspiring explorer: he could neither shoot nor see very well, and he also had a poor sense of direction. He did, however, know how to spot potential benefactors.

By 1844, he had found sufficient backers for an ambitious northwesterly thrust across Queensland and into the Northern Territory. His ambition was to open up the land from Brisbane to Port Essington (Darwin), a distance of 4,800 km (3,000 miles). With 10 companions, Aboriginal guides and a bullock team, he ran into innu-

seen again, and their fate was to become one of the great mysteries of the Australian bush. The first search parties could only report that the missing men had probably been speared by Aborigines in western Queensland. But the search continued for years, spurred on by finds of skeletons, relics and pack horses. Stories of a wild white man living among Queensland Aborigines in the 1860s suggested that one member, Adolf Classen, survived for some years.

Between 1852 and 1938, nine major searches were conducted for survivors or evidence of what happened to Leichhardt's party. These searches themselves were often occasions of

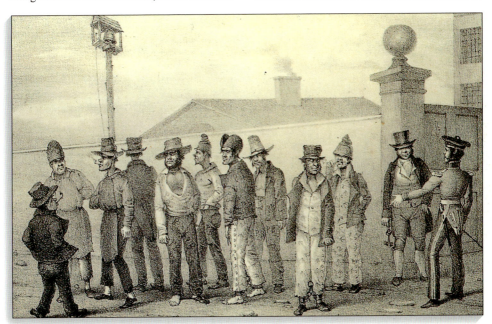

merable difficulties, lost his provisions, and saw three of his men speared (one fatally) by natives.

Fourteen months after their departure, and long after being given up for dead, Leichhardt and his party staggered into Port Essington. Returning by sea to Sydney these "men from the grave" were fêted as national heroes; the Prussian government even pardoned Leichhardt for his military desertion.

In April 1848, he set out again, this time on a proposed transcontinental trek from Roma in southern Queensland to the Indian Ocean. His party of seven men and 77 beasts was never

great courage, new discoveries and further deaths. For all these efforts, the desert has never relinquished the tale of Leichhardt's fate. The city of Sydney has, however, named one of its suburbs after him.

Heroes and villains

Aborigines played a major part in the European penetration of Australia, sometimes assisting and sometimes resisting it. Various accounts of loyalty and treachery have been recorded.

In 1848, Edmund Kennedy's party was exploring the interior of Cape York Peninsula. Difficulties with supplies, hostile natives and rugged terrain forced him to despatch his com-

ABOVE: a new barracks built to house the convicts.

panions to the coast, while he pushed on with his Aborigine guide, Jacky Jacky. Kennedy was speared by local natives, and died in Jacky's arms. The latter was also wounded, but struggled through the jungle to the Cape and informed the waiting schooner of the whereabouts of the other survivors who were stranded on the coast.

Edward John Eyre made an extraordinary journey in 1840, on foot, east to west along the coast of the Great Australian Bight. He began with an assistant, John Baxter, and three Aborigines. Some 4½ months and 2,000 km (1,250 miles) later, after an appalling journey mostly through desert, he and one Aborigine, called

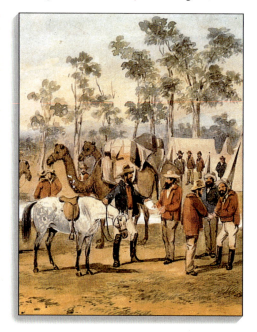

Wylie, walked into Albany on King George Sound. Baxter had been murdered by the other two, who had then run away. There are many such explorers' tales of courage and folly, some still carved as messages on tree trunks, or buried beside dried-up billabongs. Others are just blood on the sand of the inland deserts.

In August 1860, Robert O'Hara Burke and W. J. Wills left Melbourne with a well-equipped team and a camel train (imported from Afghanistan for the journey). Their intention was to be the first party to cross the continent from coast to coast. Their tale of misadventures is now deeply ingrained in Australian folklore.

Burke was brash, inexperienced, supremely

TERRA INCOGNITA

Although Australia was first settled in the 1780s, and first traversed from south to north in 1861, the surveying of the country was not completed until the 1930s.

confident and a glory-seeker. Too impatient to wait for the supply camels to keep up, he took Wills and other team members, Grey and King with him, and from Innamincka on Cooper's Creek, he forged ahead in 60°C (140°F) heat. They reached the Gulf of Carpentaria in February 1861 and immediately began retracing their footsteps. Grey died on the way.

The three emaciated survivors finally reached their earlier camp at Innamincka where they had left another companion, Brahe. But Brahe, who had waited four months for them, had departed only seven hours earlier. After rejecting the potential assistance of local Aborigines, Burke and Wills died soon after in the implacable Stony Desert. Only King, cared for by Aborigines, survived to tell the story.

Lasseter's Reef is another of the lodestone legends of Australia. Harry Lasseter claimed that in 1900, while travelling alone from Alice Springs to Carnarvon on the west coast, he discovered a reef of gold 1 metre (3 ft) deep and 16 km (10 miles) long. Few believed him, and the task of relocating the vein seemed impossible.

During the Depression, however, he again publicised his claims in Sydney. A search party was formed, and in 1930 it set out for the trove with Lasseter as guide. After months of fruitless searching, the scheme was abandoned and Lasseter was left with two camels to continue his search for the mythical gold. He was never seen again, but his diary was found and, some claim, his body. The diary tells of how he pegged the gold only to have his camels bolt, leaving him to wander, mad, and eventually die in the Petermann Ranges on the edge of Gibson Desert.

The controversy about his find, his death and his diaries lived on, and expeditions continued until as recently as 1970 to search for Lasseter's Reef. As with Leichhardt, the desert would give up neither the dead nor their stories. ❑

LEFT: John Wills, John King and Charles Grey set out on their ill-fated exploration of the interior in 1860. **RIGHT:** in a classic Tom Roberts painting, a squatter tries to stop his flock charging to water.

GOLD RUSHES AND BUSHRANGERS

The 1850s saw the discovery of gold, a sudden influx of immigrants set to make their fortune, and a similar boom in outlaws set to relieve them of it

The first half of the 19th century saw a clear change in European settlement in Australia. The transportation of convicts was phased out between 1840 and 1868. By 1860, the continent had been divided into five separate colonies, with each exhibiting at times more loyalty to Mother London than to its neighbouring siblings.

A major force within the colonies was the "squatocracy", the rich officers, emancipated convicts and free settlers who had followed the explorers into the fertile hinterlands. They had simply laid claim to or "squatted" upon enormous tracts of land, often 8,000 hectares (20,000 acres) and more. Like the merino sheep they introduced to their stations, the squatters both lived off and *were* "the fat of the land".

There were tensions between squatters and the new small farmers ("free selectors"), between the rural squatocracy and the urban bourgeoisie, and between "the Currency lads" (the Australian-born) and the immigrants. The tension between black and white also continued, with guns, poison and expropriation of lands achieving their sad ends. Yet, the continent and its new culture still seemed to be waiting for another awakening.

The discovery of gold

The awakening came in 1851. Edward Hargraves, an Australian forty-niner (a fortune seeker of the 1849 California gold rush) returned. He was certain, given the geological similarities he had observed, that gold must also exist in New South Wales. (Unbeknown to him, gold had been found 10 years earlier by a Rev. W.B. Clarke, but news of the discovery had been suppressed. Upon seeing the gold, the Governor, Sir George Gipps, had said: "Put it away, Mr Clarke, or we shall all have our throats cut!")

Having been roundly mocked in Sydney Town when he stated his intention of finding gold, Hargraves set out for the tributaries of the Macquarie River near Bathurst, 170 km (106 miles) west of

Sydney. Once there, he dug a panful of earth, washed it and announced to his companion: "Here it is. This is a memorable day in the history of New South Wales. I shall be a baronet. You will be knighted, and my old horse will be stuffed, put into a glass case, and sent to the British Museum!"

The announcement on 15 May 1851 of "Gold

Discovered!" sent shock waves through the Australian colonies. The rush of prospectors to Bathurst was so great that the economy and the population of Victoria went into an immediate nosedive. Melbourne employers offered a £200 reward for the discovery of gold near *their* city.

By July the prize had been claimed, and before the end of the year incredibly rich fields were in production in Victoria at Ballarat, Bendigo and Castlemaine. For the businessmen of Melbourne, the finds were a mixed blessing. While the prices of flour, blankets, bread, shovels and mining gear doubled and tripled, there was often no one to sell them. Melbourne and Geelong were almost emptied of men.

LEFT: *The Prospector* dreams of riches in an 1889 painting by Julian Ashton. **RIGHT:** the poet Banjo Paterson helped create the legends of bushrangers.

The Roaring Days

The scene in the goldfields was one of frantic activity, where teams of four or six men worked a claim, digging, shovelling, washing and cradling from dawn to dusk. In a lunar landscape of shafts, mullock heaps, shanties, tents and sly-grog shops they laboured for returns which ranged from nothing to nuggets such as the "Welcome Stranger" of over 78,000 grams (2,750 ounces) gross.

> **BOOM TIME**
>
> During the 1850s the lure of gold boosted Australia's population by over 600,000, to more than 1 million.

For all the chaos of the diggings, there was also considerable order, honesty, discipline and

Gold rushes flared like bushfire around the continent during the next two decades, and then sporadically for the rest of the century. The last great find was the Kalgoorlie-Coolgardie field in Western Australia in 1892–93. It was not only the shop assistants of Sydney and the sailors of Port Phillip whose imaginations were fired with gold fever. The rest of the world, on hearing tales of giant nuggets and creeks paved with gold, set sail. In 1852 alone, 95,000 new arrivals flooded into New South Wales and Victoria.

political solidarity between the diggers, contrasting with the lynch law of the California fields. But once the bright-shirted, bearded and booted miners returned to town, they let rip. Often blowing hundreds of pounds in a day, they regaled the city folk with wild tales and champagne, lit their cigars with "fivers" (£5 notes) and careened around the streets on horseback or in cabs.

At one Melbourne theatre, reported an eye-witness, the actors "were obliged to appear before the footlights to bear a pelting shower of nuggets – a substitute for bouquets – many over half an ounce, and several of which fell short of the mark into the orchestra."

The Eureka Stockade

To an Australian, the word "Eureka" does not evoke images of Archimedes' scientific breakthrough. Instead, it is coupled with the word "Stockade" and signifies armed insurrection against authority, and the first stirrings of an independent, republican consciousness in Australia.

At Ballarat, near Melbourne, the early gold diggers smarted under the imposition, whether they struck gold or not, of a £1 a month licence fee. Raids by thuggish police (often ex-cons from Tasmania, known as "Vandemonians") who enforced the licence fee *and* collected half the fine from defaulters added to their rancour.

In October 1854 a miner was kicked to death by a local publican, who (despite strong evidence against him) was cleared of the crime. Mass meetings attended by up to 5,000 miners railed against these injustices. The men demanded the granting of universal franchise and the abolition of licence fees. They formed the Ballarat Reform League and on 29 November made a bonfire of their mining licences.

The Lieutenant-Governor of Victoria, Sir Charles Hotham, sent in the "traps" (policemen) and troopers. Five hundred diggers built a stockade, swore to "fight to defend our rights and liberties," and hoisted the blue-and-white flag with leaders, and the licence fee was abolished. While the incident is replete with tragedy and some farce, the Eureka Stockade and its flag continue to evoke the ideals of revolt against colonialism and bourgeois authority. As Mark Twain commented, Eureka was "the finest thing in Australian history… another instance of a victory won by a lost battle."

Paradoxically, the monument erected in Ballarat in 1923 to mark the site takes a more ambivalent stance: "To the honoured memory of the heroic pioneers who fought and fell, on this sacred spot, in the cause of liberty, and the soldiers who fell at Duty's call."

the stars of the Southern Cross. No Union Jack for them. In the early hours of 3 December 1854, a force of 300 infantry, cavalry men and mounted police savagely attacked the sleeping stockade, whose defenders had dwindled to 150. Within 15 minutes it was all over. Six soldiers and 24 miners were dead. The rebel leader, Peter Lalor, had escaped, but 13 others were charged with high treason.

Eventually all charges were dropped, an amnesty was proclaimed for Lalor and the other

LEFT: a prospector and his family *On the Wallaby Track*, by Frederick McCubbin in 1889. **ABOVE:** troopers storm the Eureka Stockade in December 1854.

Bushranger boom

If the take-off point for the growth of Australia's population, its economy, and ultimately its sense of nationhood, came with the gold rush, it also created a new boom in bushranging – highway robbery. Many an "old lag" (ex-convict), as well as poor settlers, saw that gold need not necessarily be dug from the ground. The proceeds from "bailing up" a stagecoach or gold wagon could be good, and the work was a lot cleaner than digging. One Victorian gang in 1853 relieved the gold escort of 70,000 grams (over 2,400 oz) of gold and £700 in cash; three gang members were also sent to the gallows.

In the 1860s the most famous of the "Wild Colonial Boys" were the bushrangers Ben Hall, Frank Gardiner and John Gilbert. Well-armed and superbly mounted – often on stolen race-horses – they pulled off audacious raids. In November 1864, Hall's gang of three, working the Sydney–Melbourne road, rounded up 60 travellers at once. Then came the prize for which they were waiting – the armed mail coach. While one bushranger covered the 60 captives, Hall and Gilbert shot the police guard and robbed the coach. Several of the captives came out of the bush, not to aid the police but to watch the shoot-out.

The Kelly Gang

Ned Kelly was born in 1854 and grew up among impoverished Irish farmers near Benalla, northern Victoria. He first ran foul of the law in 1877 when he shot a constable in the wrist. Teaming up with his brother Dan and two friends, Joe Byrne and Steve Hart, he fled to the bush and turned outlaw. The following year, in a shoot-out at Stringybark Creek, Ned killed three of a party of four police who were hunting him. From then on, the Kellys became part of Australian folklore. Society became divided in its attitude to the outlaws: the upper classes and bourgeoisie saw Ned as a callous, blood-

BUSHRANGERS AND REBELS

Bushranging, the artful dodge of relieving travellers of their jewels, cash and other encumbrances, had been practised on the lonely bush roads of the colonies since the 1790s, usually by "bolters", runaway convicts. By 1820 it had become so prevalent that its practitioners increasingly found themselves with prices on their heads and then nooses round their necks.

From the time they first appeared on the scene, bushrangers were often sheltered by the rural poor, many of whom were Irish immigrants or the descendants of political transportees. They harboured strong republican sentiments, and regarded some of the outlaws as rebels against the same enemy – the British, Protestant landlords and authorities.

These colonial highwaymen often had names as colourful as their reputations. "Yankee Jack" Ellis, Black Caesar, Captain Thunderbolt, Captain Moonlight, the psychopathic "Mad Dan" Morgan, the Jewboy Gang and "Gentleman Matt" Cash (an ancestor of tennis champion Pat Cash) were among the many who rode out from behind a rock outcrop or a stand of gum trees and "bailed up" the Cobb & Co. stagecoach, the gold escort or the lone traveller.

thirsty ruffian, while the working classes in both town and country turned him into a hero.

Ned saw himself as a Robin Hood, a defender of the free against the oppressive British overlords. His escapades were always daring and dramatic. Instead of robbing coaches, his gang bailed-up whole towns, cutting the telegraph and robbing the bank before escaping.

The gang hid out in the Wombat Ranges in 1879, but in June 1880, on hearing that they had been betrayed and that a trainload of police was on the way to arrest them, they came out to fight. Having executed their suspected betrayer (an old friend), they captured the town of Glen-

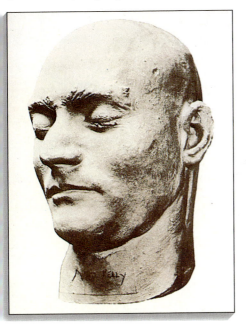

rowan, Victoria, held all the townsfolk prisoner in the pub and ripped up the tracks on which the police train was to arrive.

One captive, however, persuaded the sometimes compassionate Ned to let him go. He immediately fled and warned the approaching train. A furious shoot-out, which went on until dawn, erupted between the Kellys inside the Glenrowan Hotel and the traps outside. Wounded, Ned donned his suit of home-made armour and attempted to escape. Instead, he

ABOVE LEFT: *Bailed up*, painted by Tom Roberts at the end of the 19th century. **ABOVE:** the death mask of Australia's most famous bushranger, Ned Kelly.

YOUNG BLOOD

Ned Kelly's near-legendary career of mayhem and murder lasted a mere three years. He was only 26 years old when he was hanged.

stumbled into the police who at first thought they were seeing a ghostly apparition. Ned was shot down but not killed. The police torched the hotel and the other three members of the Kelly Gang died within it, rather than surrender.

Four months later in Melbourne, after one of the most celebrated trials in Australian history, Kelly was sentenced. The judge, Sir Redmond Barry, a prosperous free immigrant, represented the polar opposite to Ned and his impoverished, rebellious ilk. "Edward Kelly," he intoned, "I hereby sentence you to death by hanging. May the Lord have mercy on your soul." Ned, who was never one to miss his cue, replied in a clear, level voice: "Yes, I will meet you there." Kelly was hanged on 11 November 1880. Redmond Barry died a fortnight later of lung congestion.

The Chinese influx

The vast majority of diggers were British, but of the other nationalities the Chinese were the most numerous. In the five years from 1854, more than 40,000 Chinese flocked to the Victorian fields. The Chinese lived in their own communities and were usually diligent labourers. They sometimes wasted precious water, however, and this, along with the resentment of "Chinaman's luck", prompted resentment and occasional violent riots by white miners.

By 1887, Asian immigration had been stifled. Australia inaugurated "the White Australia Policy" with federation and nationhood in 1901. The Immigration Act allowed a dictation test in *any* European language (and one so chosen that the applicant was bound to fail) to be given to all non-European arrivals. It was not until 1966 that there was any genuine reversal of this race-based exclusion. In the face of such racism, it is comforting to know that there had even been one Chinese bushranger, San Poo.

Since the early days, Australia's gold-mining industry has developed into huge operations, both domestic and overseas. Some Australians believe that the spirit of the bushrangers still survives in small pockets, mainly in commerce and politics. ❑

FEDERATION AND THE WORLD WARS

*Six quarrelling colonies became a nation in 1901 – and spent the first half of
the 20th century redefining their relationship with the mother country*

I n September 1900, Queen Victoria regally proclaimed that, on 1 January 1901, not only a new century but also a new nation would be born. The table at which she signed this proclamation was then shipped from London to Sydney where, in Centennial Park on New Year's Day, the "indissoluble Federal Commonwealth" of Australia was inaugurated by the first Governor-General, Lord Hopetoun.

Nationhood and federation for the six Australian colonies was no revolt against the old God, queen and country of a distant culture. It was more the dutiful coming-out of an offspring who was "young, white, happy and wholesome." Also nervous. It had taken the adolescent since 1850 to decide whether leaving the shelter of Mother Britain's skirt was a good idea, what with the Russians and the increasingly strong Japanese prowling the Pacific.

With Australia not wishing to step too far out of line, its constitution was tame. The Queen remained head of state, retaining the power over all foreign affairs; her direct representative in Australia was the Governor-General. British parliamentary legislation could overrule any laws passed by the Commonwealth, and legal appeals ultimately were settled by the Privy Council in London. Few Australians objected to this arrangement, for each of the six colonies felt more at ease in its dealings with the motherland than with the other colonies.

For her part, Mother Britain did not let the new nation escape the interests of imperialism. She expected, and got, continuing support in her military involvements, and ample returns on her substantial investments in Australia.

Politics and war

Australia's first prime minister was Edmund Barton, a member of the Liberal Protectionist Party. His opponents in Parliament were the

Conservative Free Traders and the Labor Party. (The three parties were on an equal footing until 1910 when Labor achieved an absolute majority in the House of Representatives.) The names of the parties embodied the various political philosophies of the time – protectionists from Victoria versus New South Wales's free traders,

versus the labour movement. However, all three parties agreed that Australia was to be a white, European-style, liberal democracy, whose citizens were to be protected by trade tariffs and social-welfare legislation.

The nation needed a capital. Sydney and Melbourne each wished it to be in its own state, and neither of the longstanding rivals would permit it in the other's. After considerable backbiting, a separate Australian Capital Territory was established at a point between the two cities, 320 km (200 miles) from Sydney on the beautiful Monaro Tablelands. Some suggested naming the capital Shakespeare – hardly an appropriate choice considering the anti-intellectual cultur-

LEFT: *Flower Sellers* by Tom Roberts shows Sydney's King Street in the 1890s. **RIGHT:** a civic parade for the Governor-General, Lord Hopetoun, at the opening of the Federal Parliament in May 1901.

al cringers who formed a vocal part of the Australian population. In 1913 the Aboriginal word "Canberra" was chosen instead.

When Britain declared war on Germany on 4 August 1914 Australia, as a member of the British Empire, was automatically at war, too. The response by both Labor and Liberal parties was immediate. By the end of October the First Australian Infantry Force of 20,000 volunteers had been despatched to Europe via Egypt.

While the troops continued to train in Egypt, Winston Churchill (then First Lord of the Admiralty) conceived a plan that was intended to relieve Turkish pressure on Russia's troops by

forcing an entrance to the Black Sea. He wished to take the Dardanelles, and ordered the waiting Australian, New Zealand, French, British, Indian and Gurkha divisions to attack from the sea.

The Turks, who had been warned of these intentions, were entrenched in fortified positions along the ridges of the Gallipoli Peninsula. Their commanders, Mustafa Kemal and the German Liman von Sanders, were able safely to direct their fire upon the exposed beaches below.

From 25 April 1915, when they landed, until 20 December, when they withdrew, the British and Allied forces were pinned to the near-vertical cliffs and narrow coves. There was horrendous carnage and epic heroism upon the ridges and beaches of Cape Hellas, Lone Pine and Suvla Bay – names which remain on countless Australian war memorials.

The defeat at Gallipoli gave the Antipodes the legend of the Australian and New Zealand Army Corps (ANZAC). Thereafter, the two countries would remember their troops in terms such as those used by the poet laureate, John Masefield: "They were… the finest body of young men ever brought together in modern times. For physical beauty and nobility of bearing they surpassed any men I have ever seen; they walked and looked like the kings in old poems."

The Western Front

The Australian "Diggers" were deployed in France, on the Western Front, from April 1916. In the grisly attacks, through mustard gas and frozen winters, their losses were again appalling – 23,000 dead in nine weeks in the First Battle of the Somme, 38,000 at Ypres, 10,000 at Bullecourt. These places, along with others such as Pozières, Villers Bretonneux and the Hindenburg Line, saw much of a generation wiped out. If nationhood was being born, the nation itself was being cut down.

Many Australians were now openly expressing doubt at the sense of supporting Britain in what they saw as her own "sordid trade war". But a deciding factor was the presence at Australia's helm of a feisty and dogged little man who was loved and loathed with equal passion: William Morris ("Billy") Hughes, or "the Little Digger".

In 1916 Hughes had pledged a supply of 16,500 Australian troops a month. Such a number could be raised only through conscription – previously, recruitment had been voluntary. The

THE TOLL OF GALLIPOLI

During the eight months of fighting at Gallipoli, 78,000 were wounded and 33,500 killed on the side of Britain and her Allies. Of the dead, 8,587 were "Anzacs". Australians often overlook the fact that almost as many French died there, and twice as many Britons, Indians and Nepalis; also that 250,000 Turks fell.

Perhaps that forgetfulness is because those nations already possessed their own creation-destruction myths and Australia did not. Nevertheless, out of this baptism by mud, shrapnel and gallantry arose Australia's first coherent sense of nationhood and identity.

public outcry at the proposed legislation was bitter. Hughes's own Labor Party was firmly opposed to conscription. The proposal was defeated narrowly in a referendum, and Hughes was expelled from his party. He set about forming a national coalition government and held a second referendum in December 1917. Again he was defeated, but again he bounced back, and demanded a seat at the Versailles Peace Conference where, with characteristic showmanship and acerbity, he defended what most Australians then considered to be their national interests.

When America's president, Woodrow Wilson, objected to the Little Digger's noisy delays,

The Depression

Between 1929 and 1933 every government in Australia, both state and federal, was thrown out of office by an electorate voting on the principle of "Give the other mob a go – they couldn't be worse." But nor could they do any better, for the Great Depression had arrived. Thirty percent of the country's breadwinners were on "Susso" (sustenance benefits). Wearing war surplus greatcoats which the government had dyed black before distributing them free, hundreds of them were tramping the outback roads as "swagmen" looking for rural work.

Australia's economy was based heavily upon

Hughes replied crushingly: "Mr President, I speak for 60,000 dead. How many do you speak for?" He also fought, though not alone, to prevent the Japanese from inserting into the preamble of the League of Nations covenant a declaration of racial equality.

Billy Hughes returned home a hero. The nation needed one; of the 330,000 troops who had fought, 226,000 (68.5 percent) were casualties, a greater percentage by far than had been suffered by any other country among the Allies.

LEFT: a World War I poster encourages South Australians to enlist. **ABOVE:** in 1915 Allied forces were pinned down for eight months at Gallipoli.

the export of wheat and wool, and upon continued borrowings from Britain. When world prices for primary products slumped by 50 percent, and when Britain withdrew £30 million from the Australian economy, the result was traumatic, especially to those at the lower end of the social scale.

Sir Otto Niemeyer of the Bank of England was despatched to scold Australians for living at an unsustainably high standard, to advise wage cuts and retrenchments, and to make sure that the interest was still paid on his loans. Many Australians saw him as a British bailiff.

However, when New South Wales Labor Premier Jack Lang depicted Niemeyer as a Shylock and attempted to cut the interest repayments to England on his state loans, neither the establishment nor the electorate could go along with the revolt. Lang was dismissed in 1932, first by the governor and then by the voters.

World War II

When England again went to war against Germany in September 1939, Australia once more automatically entered the conflict. A Second Australian Infantry Force was raised and despatched to the Middle East.

In 1939 Australia's prime minister, the leader of the United Australia Party, was Robert Gordon Menzies, a clever, witty barrister and a deeply conservative Anglophile. He had earned the nickname of "Pig-Iron Bob" by selling pig-iron to the re-arming Japanese, of whom Australia had become increasingly nervous. Japan was now threatening Southeast Asia and had marked Australia for invasion.

While Australian air, land and sea forces fought in Britain, the Mediterranean, North Africa, Greece and the Middle East, Japan began to move south, first into French Indochina. Australian forces were sent to Malaya, the Dutch East Indies, Darwin and Rabaul (New Guinea) to try to stem the Japanese tide.

In Canberra, "Pig-Iron Bob" was being reviled for his Chamberlain-like pre-war appeasement of the Axis powers. His wit and skilful oratory could save neither him nor his party, and by October 1941 a Labor Government under John Curtin was in power.

A nation comes of age

The Japanese attack on Pearl Harbor confirmed Australia's great fear: to be isolated and white in an Asia at war. When Singapore fell on 15 February 1942, 15,000 of the 130,000 captured troops were Australian. The country was faced with the fact that a distant and beleaguered Britain could be of no real assistance against an imminent Japanese invasion. Curtin had already announced: "Without inhibitions of any kind, I make it quite clear that Australia looks to America, free of any pangs as to our traditional links or kinship with the United Kingdom."

Japanese planes bombed Darwin on 19 February and Broome on 3 March. Arms and food caches were established in the north of the con-

HEROES AND VILLAINS OF SPORT

During Australia's economic slump in the 1930s, much of the nation sought solace in sport. The 1932–33 England–Australia cricket Test Series was marred by "bodyline" incidents (a controversial and dangerous style of bowling aiming directly at the batsman). So great was the local ire at this English innovation that relations between the two countries were, for a time, severely strained.

On the racetrack, it was a brighter story. Australia's greatest galloper, Phar Lap, a horse which was actually born in New Zealand, was winning the hearts and minds of thousands of punters. Having won every race in Australia, including the 1930 Melbourne Cup, the "Red Terror", as he was called, was sent to California where, shortly after winning the world's richest horse race, he died. Australians have always suspected it was Yankee skulduggery.

Phar Lap now "lives on" in three different museums: his skeleton is in New Zealand, his stuffed hide is in Melbourne, and his treasured, huge heart is in Canberra.

As journalist Les Carlyon wrote: "It says something about Australia that the strongest strands in our folklore concern a military failure [Gallipoli], an outlaw [Ned Kelly] and a racehorse."

tinent. Australia faced the very real threat of invasion by Japanese troops.

The Australian war cabinet then outraged Churchill by diverting the 7th Australian Division from the defence of British Burma to the New Guinea and Pacific theatres. If it is true that the Australian nation was born at Gallipoli, it is no less true that with the fall of Singapore it finally came of age.

The tide began to turn against Japan in May 1942 when a combined American and Australian fleet checked a Japanese force at the Battle of the Coral Sea. The US victory at Midway in June assured Allied control of the Pacific, but

tember the Japanese were only 52 km (32 miles) from Port Moresby, but by November they had been pushed back by the troops to the northeast coast. As the threat of invasion receded, so another Australian male archetype, the Jungle Soldier, joined the Bushman, the Digger and the Lifesaver in the line-up of myths.

The tide turns

By the end of 1942, the tide had also turned in Europe. The Australian 9th Division had helped eliminate the Germans and Italians from North Africa at the decisive Battle of El Alamein; the Russian armies routed the Germans at Stalin-

on New Guinea, Japanese foot soldiers were closing in on Australia's main base at Port Moresby. Then, in August, a scratch force of Australians stopped the Japanese in a week of savage, hand-to-hand jungle fighting.

The Japanese continued to advance along a sodden, malarial mountain track which crossed New Guinea's Owen Stanley Ranges. This was the Kokoda Trail, scene of months of bloody guerrilla combat by the Australian 25th Brigade supported by the Papuan resistance (sometimes known as the Fuzzy Wuzzy Angels). In Sep-

grad. The Axis powers were on the defensive.

Of the 1 million Australian servicemen and women who had enlisted, almost 10,000 died in Europe and more than 17,000 in the Pacific. Of those taken prisoner by the Japanese, 8,000 did not survive the terrible privations and humiliations to which they were subjected.

Victory came too late for John Curtin, who died in office in May 1945. At 9am on Saturday, 15 August, the new prime minister, Ben Chifley, announced that the war had ended. All of Australia exploded in celebration. In Melbourne, more than 200,000 people attended a thanksgiving service at the Shrine of Remembrance; yet another "war to end all wars" was over. ❑

LEFT: food queues in the Hungry Thirties.
ABOVE: Sydney Harbour Bridge was completed in 1932.

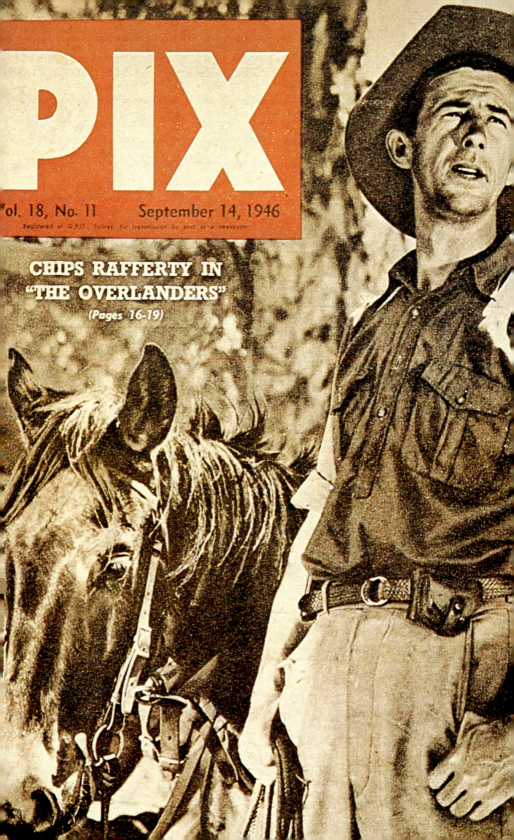

PIX

Vol. 18, No. 11   September 14, 1946

Registered at G.P.O., Sydney, for transmission by post as a newspaper.

CHIPS RAFFERTY IN "THE OVERLANDERS"

(Pages 16-19)

THE MODERN ERA

In the past 60 years, Australia has witnessed a trebling of the population, industrial booms and economic slumps, rigid conservatism and progressive liberalism

Australian history since World War II has been an up-and-down saga – a rise to undreamed-of affluence in the 1950s and '60s when the wool prices boomed, followed by unexpected cracks in the great suburban dream. At the dawn of the 21st century, the image of the country as a conservative, Anglo-Saxon society somehow finding itself lost in Asia has been completely recast. But the road towards a cosmopolitan, liberal, middle-class Australia has been long and tortuous. For a small country – population-wise – of which it was said "nothing ever happens", there has been a succession of booms, recessions, political crises, wars, culture shocks and social changes.

The 1940s were the most difficult years in Australia's history, the long war against Japan emphasising the country's vulnerability. The war also shook up Australian society internally; many women served in the armed forces, or worked in factories or office jobs that had previously been reserved for men, and were reluctant to go back to the old inequality between the sexes. Ex-servicemen didn't want to go back to the old order either. A year after the war ended, Australians voted an activist Labor government, led by Ben Chifley, back into power with plans for an expanded social welfare programme. In quick succession, Chifley set up a government-owned airline, took initiatives in housing and education (the Australian National University was opened in Canberra), and ordered massive work projects such as the Snowy Mountains Scheme, which would provide hydroelectric power for the whole of southeast Australia.

The most radical and revitalising change, however, occurred in immigration. The spectre of a Japanese invasion in World War II had convinced Australians that the country's population should be increased. Labor's immigration minister, Arthur Calwell, embarked upon one of the most spectacular migration pro-

grammes of the 20th century. Half of the assisted migrants were to be British, but the other half could come from anywhere – as long as they were white. More than 2 million migrants arrived between 1945 and 1965, and Australia's population leapt from 7 to 11 million.

The nation still clung to its White Australia policy, and Calwell himself was a racist. (He made the infamous wise-crack, when asked whether he would permit Asian immigration, "Two Wongs don't make a white.") The policy was modified slowly in later years until it was formally abolished in 1973. So rapid has been the overturning of these anachronistic attitudes that at the present time one-third of all immigrants are Asian *(see A Multi-Cultural Society, pages 75–79).*

The effect of this change in policy was to be far-reaching. In 1945 Australia had been a conformist, predominantly Anglo-Saxon country in which 98 percent of inhabitants had a British background. Suddenly it was confronted with massive contingents of Italians, Greeks, Ger-

LEFT: the actor Chips Rafferty specialised in playing archetypal bush characters. **RIGHT:** souvenir programme for a 1957 Bondi Beach carnival.

mans, Dutch and Yugoslavs who could hardly speak English and who set up their own communities, shops and newspapers, entered the workforce and schools, and very soon shattered the complacent, sterile mould of Aussie life. It all happened with surprisingly little friction, although with undeniably great hardship on the part of the so-called "New Australians". They were the workforce behind much of the intense development of the 1950s and 1960s, providing manual labour in steelworks, mines, factories and on the roads, as well as on major national projects such as the Snowy Mountains Scheme.

SALOON SYMBOL

In 1948, the American firm General Motors had set up Australia's first car manufacturing plant , which began producing the Holden saloon. The success of Holden automobiles was seen as a symbol of Australia's progress in the 1950s and '60s: it combined US finance, European migrant labour and an affluent Australian consumer market.

The subsequent eclipse of General Motors in the 1980s by Ford and the Japanese car makers similarly symbolised the decline of local manufacturing.

Into the modern world

Still, mainstream Australian culture changed slowly. In the 1950s, Australia remained a rigid society, one which had grown up in comparative isolation and was complacent and illiberal. It was still dominated by men, despite the postwar challenge from women: male rituals like sport, drinking and brawling predominated; homosexuals were persecuted as "poofters" and anyone with a beard or long hair was dubbed a "weirdo". Male values such as mateship were extolled while "the missus" was expected to stay at home and look after the kids. It seemed, visually and ethically, a very working-class society, a land of boots and felt hats, of men in dank pubs calling each other "mate" or "sport".

The churches, especially the Roman Catholic church, dominated morals; divorce was legal, but it was condemned and hard to obtain; abortion remained illegal, the province of seedy backstreet doctors. The nation was burdened with a suffocating puritanism which Australians labelled "wowserism". Censorship was strict (James Joyce's *Ulysses* and D.H. Lawrence's *Lady Chatterley's Lover* were banned, and had to be smuggled into the country). The language was stamped with prejudices, and the waves of migrants didn't escape: they were called reffos (refugees), Balts, wogs, dagos, Ities, Ikeys…

Politically, the decade is referred to as the "Boring Fifties". A revived conservative party – known as the Liberal Party, and led by the rabid Anglophile Robert Menzies, who proclaimed himself "British to his boot-straps" – was able to tap into the growing Cold War hysteria and attack the Labor Party for being riddled with Communists.

When rising unemployment threatened to turn the Liberals out of office, Menzies decided to plump for safe, middle-of-the-road policies that would disturb neither extreme of the electorate. The Labor Party split in 1955 on ideological lines and effectively kept itself out of power for another 17 years.

"Development" became the national slogan; there were posters everywhere stressing peace, prosperity and progress, and even the arrival of rock 'n' roll from the United States didn't seem to disturb the social equanimity. There were a few rebel groups, such as the bodgies (male) and widgies (female), who did such radical things as ride motorcycles and listen to Elvis, but it was hardly more than a milk-bar menace. Another nonconformist group was the Sydney "push", a group of freethinkers and libertarians who gathered at pubs and coffee shops and scorned the suburban coma ward which surrounded them. They wrote poetry and bawdy songs and, though mainly a male group, produced two remarkable women – Germaine Greer, author of *The Female Eunuch*, and the late Lillian Roxon, author of the first *Rock Encyclopedia*.

The newsreels of the time, seen now, are embarrassingly nationalistic, racist and sexist. The pubs closed at 6pm sharp each weekday, producing the infamous "six o'clock swill", when men crammed into pubs and guzzled as

London and other cities in Europe, seeking the excitement and the sort of mind-broadening experience which, despite the immigration programme, was unavailable at home. They could hardly be blamed.

Well into the 1960s, the district of Earls Court in London became an Aussie ghetto; Rolf Harris, the entertainer, started his climb to fame by singing *Tie Me Kangaroo Down, Sport* at the Down Under Club; unique talents like Barry Humphries, Clive James and Robert Hughes all fled Australia.. The nation's best artists and writers – Patrick White, Germaine Greer and Sidney Nolan among them –

much as they could between the end of work and closing time (women wouldn't have been allowed in even if they'd wanted to). Off-course betting was illegal, so SP (starting price) bookmakers flourished alongside sly-grog joints, where liquor could be bought after hours. On the positive side, during the 1950s Australia enjoyed the most even income distribution of any Western industrialised nation.

Every year thousands of young Australians left on their equivalent of the "Grand Tour" of

turned themselves into expatriates. At the time it seemed that little was happening back in Oz.

The affluent 1960s

Meanwhile, Australia had begun turning itself from a nation of primary industry (sheep, wheat and cattle) to one of manufacturing. Between 1940 and 1960 the number of factories doubled; refrigerators, washing machines, vacuum cleaners and cars became available to the great mass of the population for the first time.

By the mid-1960s, Australia was experiencing a period of unprecedented prosperity and its citizens were enjoying, after the North Americans, the highest standard of living in the

LEFT: prime minister Ben Chifley with his 1948 Holden, the first local mass-produced car.
ABOVE: Surfers Paradise on Queensland's Gold Coast.

world. They were also living in the most urbanised nation on earth, with three-quarters of the population in cities – more than half of that on the eastern seaboard.

Links with the Old Country were weakened when Britain joined the European Economic Community, leaving Australia out in the cold; trade with the US and Japan grew to fill the gap. The 1951 ANZUS defence treaty had brought Australia and New Zealand securely within the USA's sphere.

In the meantime, the shape of Australian soc-

OUTSIDERS

Before 1967, Aboriginal people did not have the right to vote – or even to become Australian citizens.

Lucky Country – a land that had squandered its opportunities and abandoned its best egalitarian traditions to wallow in complacency. The Australian social ideal of communality was changing and with it, apparently, the Australian character.

A time of change

Cracks began to appear in the bland facade of Australian contentment. In 1962 Australia had become involved in the Vietnam War and in the next 10 years sent 49,000 conscripts, chosen by lottery,

ity was being entirely changed. In the early 1960s the number of white-collar workers exceeded, for the first time, the number of blue-collar workers and then streaked far ahead. This booming group typically lived in comfortable suburban homes, owned cars and TVs, had bank accounts, and voted Liberal (Australian for "Conservative").

Australia, regarded for so long as a working man's paradise, had almost unnoticed transformed itself into one of the most middle-class nations in the world.

But, amid the prosperity, many were dejected over the fate of Australia. Donald Horne wrote a book called, with heavy irony, *The*

off to the jungles of Southeast Asia – where 499 were killed and 2,069 wounded. As in the United States, the anti-war movement breathed life into all forms of liberalisation, pushing Australia into an era of crisis and questioning.

Student power, the women's movement, black power and the sexual liberation groups began challenging the conservative consensus. The rigid censorship of books and films was slowly dismantled, allowing Australians to pore over *Lolita* and *Portnoy's Complaint*. Aboriginals had been allowed to vote in federal elections in 1967, but a "freedom bus" drove through Queensland and New South Wales in protest against the deep-rooted, systematic discrimination against black people. At the same time, it was found that 10 percent of Australians were living in chronic poverty; they included Aborigines, single parents, the sick and handicapped and the jobless.

At the same time, the migrants had begun transforming the staid British social customs of their host country. At an obvious level arrived the introduction of delicatessens, European food, open-air cafés, varieties of music and a hectic sort of cosmopolitanism hardly imaginable before World War II. More profoundly, the migrants also opened Australians up to new ideas and new ways of looking at the world.

Spurred on by the new spirit, a revived Labor Party was arguing for new policies on a grand scale and was being led by its most inspiring politician for years, the towering, bushy-browed, charismatic Gough Whitlam. When the Labor Party finally won office in 1972, under the slogan "It's Time", it seemed to many that a clean break with the past had occurred and a promising new, progressive era was about to begin.

Labor moved quickly to abolish military conscription, to end Australia's involvement in Vietnam, to recognise China and to begin the long process of reconstructing the social welfare system. Everything appeared to be happening at once, with plans underway for a universal health-care system, increased support for the arts (resulting in a spate of Australian films), and the formal end of White Australia.

But Whitlam didn't reckon on the economic and social impacts of big government spending. He managed to win another election in 1974 but was confronted with a sudden and unexpected world recession provoked by an oil price hike. Australians suddenly faced growing inflation and unemployment and the the government was beset by a series of scandals, including an attempt to borrow four billion petrodollars through a questionable intermediary.

Labor had been hobbled in its programme by a Conservative majority vote in the Senate. In 1975 the Liberal-National Country Party op-

position, led by Malcolm Fraser, used this power to deny the government its money supply. Whitlam refused to resign, and the nation was thrust into the gravest political and constitutional crisis of its history. This was resolved in a controversial manner: the Governor-General, Sir John Kerr, as the Queen's representative in Australia, dismissed Whitlam and called another election. It was an act that many considered illegal – in spirit, if not in the letter of the constitution.

Fraser won the subsequent election, consolidated his power and swore he would take politics off the front page.

Change is the constant

In 1983 a new Labor era began when Australians voted in a government led by Bob Hawke, an ex-union leader, ex-Rhodes scholar and ex-world champion beer drinker. The Labor Party had become more right-wing, economically liberal and in closer touch with increasingly powerful white-collar unions and business.

For the next 13 years, it ruled with little challenge (with the humourless Paul Keating taking over the prime ministership in the early 1990s). Consensus became the catchword, with the government brokering historic accords between business and unions, promising unprecedented industrial peace, and finally introducing a

LEFT: Gough Whitlam listens to the Governor-General's edict dismissing his government in 1975.
RIGHT: the Queen is a victim of pavement art.

national health care system for all, Medicare.

This new-look Labor government had to deal with an ever-sliding Australian economy, starting off with a series of devaluations of the Aussie dollar (the "Pacific peso", as it wryly became known). Keating warned that the country would turn into a Latin American-style "banana republic" if fundamental changes to the economy weren't made. Labor presided over a push towards free-market policies, yet was able to maintain some degree of social justice by keeping the welfare system intact.

Diplomatically and economically, Australia linked itself much more closely to Asia, while on taking on an international profile. Australians also began talking seriously about becoming a republic at last – an initiative driven by the news that Sydney would host the Olympic Games in 2000.

Despite the steady achievements of these years, Australian voters had wearied of Labor by 1996, and in 1999 voted in a more conservative government, led by its determinedly Liberal John Howard, with a large majority. In economic matters, Howard has been pushing for a freer market and smaller government, while also capturing swinging voters with economic support. Conservatism also held out in the 1999 status referendum, as Australia entered the new

the home front Asian immigration was stepped up. Women were admitted to more positions of power, and Aboriginal "land rights" (control over their native homelands) was put on the national agenda. The celebration of the Bicentennial of British settlement in 1988 was a landmark of Australian self-confidence, but also a cause for some soul-searching. A High Court ruling, known as the Mabo case, abolished the historical fiction of *terra nullius* – the colonial doctrine that said Australia was uninhabited when the British arrived – and opened the way to Aboriginal land claims *(see Aborigines Today, pages 81–85).*

The 1980s and 1990s saw a flowering of the Australian arts, with local film-makers and writers millennium voting against becoming a republic and opting to keep the Queen as head of state.

Australia's economic outlook has improved steadily with the "globalisation" initiatives of successive recent governments and the privatisation of costly and inefficient transport, energy and communications monoliths. In recent years the Australian dollar has regained considerable ground against the US "greenback". The country swept its economic woes aside in the euphoria of Sydney's successful staging of the 2000 Olympics. The IOC President dubbed it the "best Games ever". ❏

ABOVE: Prime Minister John Howard with wife Janette.

Green Australia

Beaches of all shapes and sizes, mountains of rugged grandeur, lush tropical rainforests alive with birdsong and dripping with humidity. Temperate eucalyptus forests, with towering mountain ash, karri and jarrah trees. Highland snow country, the epic sweep of the mallee plains. The endless desert expanses of the Outback.

With such geographical variety, Australia was always destined to be a major environmental player, and so it has become. From the inauguration in 1879 of coastal bushland just south of Sydney as the Royal National Park (second only in the world to America's Yellowstone National Park), to more recent issues like the Antarctica Treaty and a national biodiversity policy, Australia has solid "green" credentials. Queensland's Fraser Island had its two main industries, sandmining and logging, abolished before the damage was irrevocable, and the island is now a World Heritage Site, while the Great Barrier Reef – on the same list – has been spared the real threat of oil drilling.

Until quite recently, governments and industries (particularly logging, farming and mining) did pretty much what they liked with the environment, believing that there was so much land, such an abundance of natural resources, that degradation scarcely mattered. This attitude was part of an ambiguous Euro-Australian perception of the land: the place was simply too vast, too inhospitable, too different from ancestral homelands to be appreciated clearly. Welcome exceptions to this view came mainly in the form of bushmen of Irish extraction – great walkers like Paddy Pallin, Myles Dunphy and his son Milo – whose pioneering enthusiasm for and exploration of the NSW bush led to the designation of numerous national parks, such as the Blue Mountains and Kanangra-Boyd, in the mid-20th century.

Astonishingly, even today bush exploration remains an adventure. In late 1994, in the sprawling Wollemi National Park, not two hours' drive from downtown Sydney, a Park Ranger abseiled down a 600-metre (2,000-ft) gorge and discovered the oldest known surviving species of tree. The species, dubbed the Wollemi pine, is 160–170 million years old, a relic of a time when the continent was covered with the wet forests of Gondwana. Moreover, a month after this find, another occurred in northwest Tasmania – that of a 10,500-year-old Huon pine

tree, the world's oldest known living organism. If ever the case for conservation needed further justification, there it was.

Environmental activism took off in Australia in 1972, when the world's first green political party, the United Tasmania Group, was formed to save Lake Pedder. It lost that fight, and the lake was dammed and flooded, but since then, the tiny island state has been at the forefront of green issues, with activists battling over the Wesley Vale pulp mill, the Franklin River (a landmark victory, resulting in the declaration of the Southwest Tasmania World Heritage area) and the Tarkine Wilderness. Tasmania has the cleanest air and water in the inhabited

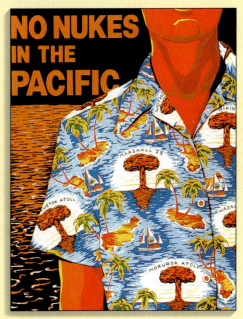

world, and Australia's highest proportion of national parks (roughly 25 percent of total land area).

All of the country's 12 World Heritage Sites are landscapes – or, in the case of the Great Barrier Reef, a seascape – indicating the value of the Australian environment. In late 1994 UNESCO identified 12 countries whose biodiversity was of the top order: Australia was one of the 12, and the only one in the "First World". This illustrious ranking places a big responsibility on the nation's shoulders, not only to get things right at home but also to act as a model for less well-off countries. Australia must show that conservation – on land and at sea – can be economically sustainable. Its track record is impressive. The nation's colours, green and gold, are beginning to assume a new meaning. ❑

RIGHT: a poster calls for a nuclear-free Pacific.

THE URBAN AUSSIE

Most of the population live in cities and suburbs, and most of them on the coast.

But that doesn't stop Australians dreaming of the wide open Outback

Accccording to myth, the "true Aussie" is a sun-bronzed stockman or jillaroo, riding the Outback range with a trusty sheepdog – which is like imagining all Americans to be tobacco-chewing cowboys, and Frenchmen going about in berets and striped shirts. Truth to tell, Australia is the most urbanised country on earth, with 80 percent of the population living in cities (66 percent in the state capitals). More precisely, it's the most suburbanised country on earth. The Great Australian Dream, still enjoyed by a huge portion of the population, is to live on your own plot of land, with a brick house, red tile roof, hoist washing line and a barbie in the backyard.

Most Australians now work in office jobs, and wouldn't recognise a trough of sheep dip if they fell in it. And although many still see the Outback as somehow embodying the most distinctive part of the country – and may even go about at times in a bushie's hat adorned with croc teeth, or the "Driza-bone" raincoat – relatively few have visited it, let alone considered living there. Even Patrick White, who set famous novels such as *Voss* in the furthest red-sand-and-spinifex deserts, never actually saw them (he got his images from his friend Sidney Nolan's paintings). White settled in Sydney's Eastern Suburbs, a stone's throw, relatively speaking, from the sea.

The fact is that Australians have clung to the coast rather naturally, shrugging off the priggish, cramped and tight-lipped spirit of the first British settlers and openly embracing the more sensual and hedonistic spirit of their Mediterranean environment. At least in the 21st century, the coast – and specifically the beach – has a far more powerful claim on Australian souls than the Outback. "How shall I put this delicately?" asks Sydney writer Robert Drewe. "Most Australians of the past three generations have had their first sexual

experience on the coast. So is it surprising that for the rest of their lives the sexual and littoral experiences are entwined in their memories; that most Australians thereafter see the beach in a pleasurable light?" It is to the sea that Australians return at each crucial stage of their lives: as lovers, on honeymoon, as parents. It is to the

sea that they were taken as children, and to the sea that they return in old age, to the endless retirement villages of the Queensland shores.

And how could it really be otherwise, in a country with such a climate and geography? It would take a serious effort of will not to lap up the perfect skies, the sea breeze, the glorious mounds of prawns and oysters, the bodies laid out on the sands and basted with oil like kebabs on a spit. Under the Antipodean sun, more austere national traits succumb to the easy-going, tolerant, obsessively casual Australian manner. It's no surprise to see a first-generation immigrant from Glasgow turn into a surfie overnight, or the daughters of black-shrouded Muslim

---

PRECEDING PAGES: locals at the Lion's Den pub in Helenvale, Queensland; Bondi Beach from the Pavilion. **LEFT:** Surfers Paradise, Queensland. **RIGHT:** lawnbowling on Sydney's North Shore.

women lolling bikini-clad in the outdoor beer garden of a pub, or the sons of Puritanical Germans dilute the work ethic so they can spend a few days each week windsurfing.

Leisure has become crucial to the Australian way of life – work is only a tedious interlude between stretches of spare time and long weekends. And few other places give people such opportunities to use their leisure well. Nature is close in Australia as nowhere else: in Sydney with its 70 metropolitan beaches, in Melbourne with one-third of its area devoted to parkland, in Darwin where 4-metre (13-ft) crocodiles are regularly fished from the harbour. Some visitors

right, mate". Politics is a matter to shake your head at ("The bastards are all the same" is the common refrain at election time). Economics, however, has become a matter of fascination, and cab drivers and supermarket clerks can talk with authority on economic rationalism, exchange rates and the balance of payments.

From convicts to democrats

Every country is shaped by its past, and few have had a stranger start than Australia's, as the dumping-ground for Britain's petty thieves. As Robert Hughes remarked in *The Fatal Shore*, it's one of the great ironies of history that a land

still arrive expecting kangaroos to hop across the tarmac. This may not be so, but even in the red-brick backblocks of suburbia a national park might begin at the end of the road, and residents may keep an eye out for funnel-web spiders, possums in the roof and snakes in the garden.

Despite the occasional natural menaces, relaxation now comes with the territory in Australia. It takes something truly grim to rouse most people to anger – and there's always a swim, or a beer, or a crisp Chardonnay to calm them down. From railway workers to restaurant waiters, the most common response to questions these days is a breezy "No worries" or "Not a problem" – the latest incarnation of the 1950s slogan "She'll be

BELIEVE IT OR NOT

Regardless of the diverse backgrounds of its citizens, religion is one topic that is unlikely ever to cause an argument in modern Australia.

As recently as the 1950s, the tension between Protestants and Irish Catholics was part of the very fabric of Australian life and politics. But the fervour has dissolved; today this is the most secular of societies, with the lowest church attendance records in the world.

There's an Aussie bumper sticker that sums up the prevailing agnosticism: "Everyone needs to believe in something. I believe I'll have another beer."

founded by felons should evolve into one of the world's most law-abiding societies. Few cities of equal size around the world are as safe, tidy and downright civil as Australia's.

Social commentators have tried to draw conclusions from the country's awkward origins: that the convict legacy instilled a disdain for authority, leading to its powerful union movement, or that it led to a blunt conformism, accepting serious curtailments of civil liberties for most of the 20th century. Hughes comes up with the formula "skeptical conformists": Australians like to think of themselves as rowdy rebels, talking big at the pub or behind authority's back, but obey with little question when it comes to the crunch, tugging the forelock while seething with contempt. Other, more jaded social commentators might say that Australia's beginnings as a penal colony have made it a corrupt place from day one. Many Australian officials, from police officers to immigration rubber-stampers, have a surprising arrogance; there is none more self-satisfied, it sometimes seems, than the petty Aussie clerk who is able to say "No".

Diverting as such theories are, the truth is that few modern Australians can really trace their lineages to convict times; most are the descendants of free English, Scottish and Irish settlers after the 1850s, or the wave of immigrants from the rest of the world a century later. Although the convict "stain" was once a matter of horror – an ignoble memory that any respectable society would excise, particularly from school books – the opposite is true in Australia today. Anyone who can dig up a convict ancestor now wears the fact as a badge of honour. In Sydney's Hyde Barracks Museum, schoolchildren eagerly type their names into a computer bank to see if they too bear the felon's mark.

Colonial machismo

The traditional image of Australians as sturdy bush workers may have little to do with modern life, but it has been potent nonetheless. It's the local version of the great frontier myth that crops up in the United States, parts of South America and South Africa. By the 1890s, writers, poets and painters were suggesting that a distinctive "national spirit" had been forged in the great empty wilderness, and that this "New Man" was

typified by a Kiplingesque mish-mash of colonial values: naturally democratic, excelling at sports, blunt in his language, sardonic, self-reliant, independent, not over-educated or burdened by musty traditions. Above all, an Aussie trusted his mates, who were bound to one another by an almost mystical bond. This image transmuted over the years from the miners of the gold rushes to the Outback drover and the ANZAC "diggers" of Gallipoli.

The one obvious drawback of this as a national myth was that it did not include women. The contribution of women on the frontier, or in the arts, or in the factories during wars,

tended to be brushed aside, so that by the 1950s, Australia had earned a reputation as one of the most sexist societies in the developed world. The worst manifestation of the crass male spirit was known as the "Ocker" – the beer-swilling, pot-bellied, narrow-minded, poofter-bashing, provincial redneck, who hung out watching footie at the pub while the sheila stayed at home minding the kids. Barry Humphries satirised the type with Bazza MacKenzie, the simple-minded tourist who was always ready for a schooner and a chunder. Paul Hogan started his TV career in stubby shorts and an Aussie Rules sleeveless shirt as an Ocker with a sense of humour, before elevating the image with more wit and irony in

---

LEFT: dining alfresco on Brighton Beach, Melbourne.
RIGHT: romantic interlude in Sydney Harbour.

Crocodile Dundee. Still, foreigners arriving in Australia hoping for the "last refuge of unself-conscious masculinity" will be disappointed.

Like the long-ingrained racism, sexism abated with the general loosening-up of society in the 1970s. These days, many Australians poke fun at the Ocker image. Others, such as those who perceive themselves as the "Urban Elite" with fashionable Inner Sydney or Melbourne addresses, simply cringe. Aussie women have always been strong characters – perhaps even more blunt, independent and self-reliant than the men so loudly proclaimed themselves to be, out of sheer necessity – so in recent years they have easily taken the

lead in many fields. Still, as in other Western nations, women remain sadly under-represented in politics and top management positions.

At the same time, the gay culture has exploded – especially in Sydney, which now has a higher concentration of gays than San Francisco. At the first Gay Mardi Gras parade in 1978, police blockades were set up and 53 marchers were taken into custody. Today, the annual parade is the highest-attended event in the country, usually luring 300,000 to watch floats of fabuously attired transvestites and lesbian nuns on Harley-Davidsons ("Dikes on Bikes"). In fact, Australia has turned into one of the most permissive and tolerant of societies.

POSTCARD FROM AUSTRALIA

Bruce Chatwin wrote to Paul Theroux: "You must come here. The men are awful, like bits of cardboard, but the women are splendid."

Australian dreams

Perhaps the myth dearest to the Australian heart is that this is the most naturally democratic of societies – the frontier past, and distance from the Old World, have naturally levelled Aussies to equals.

Certainly the outward signs are there. Waiters may still call you "mate" (and service can be a problem: diners must sometimes work hard, if they wish to be served, to convince waiters that they feel in no way superior). Taxi drivers can still get cranky if you sit in the back seat instead of up front (as a social equal supposedly would). Public officials, even prime ministers, are often known by their first names. The other side of the egalitarian coin is known as the "tall-poppy syndrome": a national resentment of high achievers and an inescapable urge to bring them down.

But is Australia a classless society? Patently not. There may be none of the rigid divisions of the British or the gross inequalities of the American system, but there are serious divisions of wealth and opportunity – and many think the gaps are increasing.

According to pessimists, the great settler's dream of Australia as the "millennial Eden" is being eroded. In a haphazard way, Australians have committed themselves to avoiding the errors of Europe and the US, and guaranteeing an unusual measure of social justice. But Australians are becoming increasingly materialistic, and less generous in their vision of society as a place where the weaker are protected. Australia's great narrative historian, Manning Clark, had a bleak vision of his compatriots before he died in the 1990s: "Mammon had infected the ancient continent of Australia," he intoned, in the manner of an Old Testament prophet. "The dreams of humanity had ended in an age of ruins."

Just don't try telling that to an Aussie on a sunny day. She'll already be at the beach. ❏

LEFT: dressed for partying in the heart of Saturday night Sydney. **RIGHT:** the urban Australian escapes to the great outdoors.

BUSH LIFE

The old stereotypes of rural Australia are disappearing fast, but there's still a distinct attitude of mind among those who live "out there"

Ten-year droughts, Biblical-style floods, bush-fires whistling through the scrub – the same natural processes that allowed the nomadic Aborigines to eke out an existence from the Australian countryside have made life an unpredictable hell for most farmers. Yet despite constant threats of bankruptcy, few ever give up. They stick to the land, aided by a peculiar brand of black humour and the solace of Saturday night at the Outback pub.

Rural Australia – sometimes referred to as West of the Divide, The Bush, Back o'Bourke, Beyond the Black Stump or The Mulga – is in some respects an Antipodean myth. While most Australians rise each morning to spend another city day at the factory or office, many harbour an obscure fantasy that they really belong on "the Wallaby Track" (the old sheep station shearing circuit), with belongings in a "swag" on the shoulder and a faithful blue-heeler cattle dog padding along beside them.

In ever-growing numbers they actually *are* taking to the bush, but in "Toorak tractors" – four-wheel drive recreational vehicles named after Melbourne's poshest suburb. And visitors from overseas wanting to abandon the delights of Sydney Harbour and "go bush" will be accommodated and rewarded by a growing number of specialised tourism operators catering for just that urge. Everything's available, from luxury air, coach and rail tours to motorised four-wheel drive backpacker parties with mega-decibel ghetto-blasters and huge refrigerators to keep the beer chilled.

The Outback also greets the adventurer with a great range of away-from-it-all resorts ranging from remote fishing camps to the accommodation conglomerates at Uluru (Ayers Rock) offering everything from camp sites to five-star luxury.

Schizophrenic attitudes

The Australian romanticising of the bush on the one hand and distaste for it on the other can be traced back to the turn of the 20th-century author and poet Henry Lawson, one of the country's literary folk heroes; and to another,

Andrew Barton (Banjo) Paterson, who had a different perspective.

After a wretched childhood on the western New South Wales goldfields, Lawson kept returning to the bush to reinforce his dislike of it. He hated the unrelenting grey-green of the eucalyptus, the monotony and hopelessness (his word) of the countryside. Lawson railed against the heat on the track to Hungerford, the "bloody flies", the thieving publicans, the greedy bosses, the arrogant squatters and the brutal police. He did, however, love the "bush battlers", the staunch early unionists and the great Outback tradition of mateship – male-bonding in the wild.

In his poems, such as *Past Carin' (see below)*, Lawson put the fear of God into city people about living "out there". But the bush people felt that Lawson was speaking truly for them. After all, his best writing was done when pioneer families were still living basic and often brutal lives in slab huts with no water. Paterson equally perpetuated the Aussie bushman's love of the "back country" and its people.

Lawson died drunk and destitute in Sydney in 1922, and Paterson passed away in a Sydney private hospital in 1941. The attitudes of both have permeated the nation's thinking. A genuine "swagman" (tramp) has not been seen on the Wallaby Track for many years; air transport has long replaced the bullock dray; refrigeration has meant that bush cuisine has gone beyond tinned beef and kangaroo-tail soup. Still, some urban Australians seem to believe that the Outback and its 170,000 farmers and graziers – there's

---

FROM *PAST CARIN'*

Now up and down the siding brown
The great black crows are flyin'
And down below the spur, I know,
Another milker's dyin';
The crops have withered from the ground
The tank's clay bed is glarin'
But from my heart no tear nor sound
For I have got past carin'…

HENRY LAWSON (1899)

an ideological difference – are stuck in an 1890s time warp. In fact, Aussie farmers are highly mechanised agribusiness people, mustering cattle by helicopter and trail bike, flying their own planes, and trying to figure out how to get the most out of their PCs and modems.

Another blind spot concerns the colour of cowboys. The best have always been black (although until the 1960s they were often paid only half of what white stockmen received). As jackaroos, boundary riders, shearers and trackers, Aborigines have contributed skill and labour to Australia's rural prosperity, particularly in the Northern Territory and Western Australia.

where the architecture is at least semi-colonial, which supplies a broad rural area, and where you can still believe that the inhabitants come out of the pages of Henry Lawson or Banjo Paterson.

Many of the old clichés about laconic, resourceful, friendly country people still have a good deal of truth. And there's a helpfulness in the bush that is not always immediately apparent to the visitor, thanks to a little bush mischief on the side. Any enquiry for directions, for instance, can be met with a slow "buggered-if-I-know" reply, followed almost immediately with an entertaining series of precise directions. Australians would never deliberately misdirect

With the recent granting of land rights, Aborigines in increasing numbers have taken over cattle stations and found a degree of independence.

The country mentality

Despite all the changes to the country lifestyle, it is still another world outside the Australian cities. And these days one doesn't have to pack a swag to find it. It is not a matter of tracking to the "dead heart"of the Outback, where the only establishment within 500 km is a lone pub with warm beer and a desolate emu in a chicken-wire cage. It can be found in any small country town

ABOVE: the best cowboys have always been Aborigines.

visitors, for, in the Outback, misdirection may result in death, by either starvation or thirst.

Given the continuing harshness of Outback life, little wonder that the bushie is pretty taciturn, or that, when he "spins a yarn" in a flat nasal monotone, it usually has nothing to do with success. Prominent themes are the stupidity of sheep, the cunning of the blow-fly and the idiocy of cattle dogs. In most stories, the anti-hero doesn't quite make it. "And then, stone the crows, after he'd got the mob of sheep across the river and saved the boss's daughter from the flood, the dopey bugger fell off his horse and broke his neck. Goes to show, don't it?"

Out Bush, some things will never change. ❏

A MULTICULTURAL SOCIETY

In the past 50 years the population has doubled and diversified. Immigrants have not always found it easy, but today's rich ethnic mix is seen as one of Australia's assets

When a survey in 1939 showed that the Australian population was comprised of 98 percent Anglo-Celtic stock, local newspapers proudly proclaimed that Australia was the most "British" country on earth. In this monochromatic society, the only unusual accents were those of the "new chums" from corners of Ireland or the Scottish highlands; foods were rarely more exotic than Yorkshire pudding; Christmas was a time for huge Dickensian meals of roast beef or pork, no matter how brutally tropical the weather.

All that changed after 1945, when Australia embarked on one of the most ambitious – and successful – immigration programmes of the modern era. The migrants were drawn first from the Mediterranean and Baltic countries of Europe, then in the 1970s from around the world. Since the programme began, more than 5 million settlers from almost 200 countries have made Australia their home. Four out of 10 Australians are migrants or the first-generation children of migrants, half of them from non-English-speaking backgrounds. More than 40 percent of settler arrivals now come from Asia, while British and Irish immigrants make up only 18 percent.

Just as the United States and Argentina were transformed by immigration in the 1890s, so the post-war influx has radically changed the structure and habits of Australian society. Take a seat on the Manly ferry and you're just as likely to be sitting next to the daughter of a builder from Athens as you are to a journalist from Naples, a car salesman from Thailand or a doctor from Lebanon. And the guiding principle of Australia's immigration policy, and of society in general, has become "multiculturalism" – tolerance and respect for all cultures and races.

But, although the multicultural society is now a *fait accompli*, just how to balance the demands of such a heterogeneous population can be a delicate task. Ethnic loyalties are encouraged, but the first loyalty must be to the Australian legal and parliamentary system; multiple languages are promoted, but English remains the official tongue; and any coercive cultural practices, such as arranged marriages, become illegal.

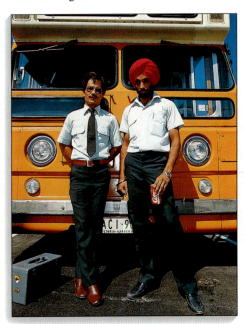

The closing door

Even as late as the 1970s, Australia welcomed almost anyone who applied as an immigrant, with the government even financially assisting the passage. But in the new century the country has become such a popular destination that relatively few applicants actually make it to Australia. On average, 1 million people make immigration inquiries every year. Of those, 400,000 apply officially. Only 75,000 or so are granted entry. Of those, 45,000 already have family in Australia; 17,000 are skilled workers and professionals whose skills are in demand on the Australian labour market; and 13,000 are refugees.

If the statistics are cold, the issue isn't. Immi-

LEFT: girls in traditional dress at Sydney's Greek National Day Festival. **RIGHT:** Vietnamese and Sikh – both bus drivers, both Australians.

gration is still a major point of debate in Australia, since it defines the very shape of society. Should there be more immigrants or fewer? More refugees? More from Asian countries? Scarcely a week goes by without a politician or an academic making a controversial addition to the discussion.

The process for a potential immigrant is now laborious, and the majority are family members of current immigrants or political refugees (since 1945, Australia has absorbed 435,000 refugees, a higher proportion per capita than any other industrialised nation). Other applicants are tested for their suitability to settle successfully, assimilate into the community and find work. Points are allocated for such categories as age, employability, English-language skill and so on.

Employability usually gets the highest weighting because of the greater contribution skilled migrants make to the economy. The programme is aimed at attracting "young, skilled and talented people" and does not discriminate on the basis of ethnic origin, sex or religion.

The New Australians

When Australia became a nation in 1901, there was no question that racial purity was top of the agenda; the notorious White Australia pol-

OLD ATTITUDES

In the 19th century, racism was as deep-rooted in Australia as in the Western world – and the "Asian hordes" to the north of the empty country were looked on with particular dread by the first British settlers. Imperialists were terrified that the Chinese would sweep down to occupy their near-empty continent; unionists feared that bosses would bring in cheap labour from Asia or the Pacific, destroying their workers' standard of living and creating a plantation economy. At the turn of the 20th century even the otherwise progressive Australian Labor Party stood on a xenophobic platform.

icy, instituted by the Immigration Restriction Bill, was one of the first measures to be passed by the new parliament. It would govern migration for decades, and would not be formally overturned until 1973.

Thus the first wave of non-British immigrants, brought over in the 1950s and 1960s, was drawn from Europe – mostly from Greece and Italy. Some 275,000 of these "New Australians" arrived in those years – although now, of course, they are Old Australians. Some 5 percent of the population is now of Italian descent, while Melbourne is often touted as the second-largest Greek city in the world.

This was not without its problems; many

Anglo-Australians feared that the "dagos", "wogs" and "Ities", with their garlic, switchblades and black-clad widows, would be the death of the pure, Arcadian, boiled potatoes-and-mutton Aussie way. How right the prophets were! Yet try denying Anglos their right to cappuccino, Gucci labels, lasagne or Greek restaurants, and they'll feel threatened indeed. The newcomers were also industrious to the point of exhaustion. By the 1960s, many entrepreneurs at the corner restaurant, milk bar or take-away food store were

HOME FROM HOME

There are probably more Greeks in Melbourne than in any city on earth apart from Athens and Thessaloniki.

divided; the elder children, including Teresa, went with their father, and the others followed with their mother about six months later.

The entire family paid only A$50 for the government-assisted passage, and were initially put up in a barrack-like hostel in Sydney. Teresa went to work in a factory three days after their arrival; she remembers some unpleasant name-calling at the time, the down-side of the immigrant experience. Poor conditions and low pay led her to seek another job, which she found in a nursing home.

from Southern Europe. This energy received mixed reactions: admiration from many, but also resentment from some traditionally relaxed Anglo-Australian "natives".

Typical of this wave of European immigrants is Teresa Cupri, who emigrated from Italy with her family as a teenager in 1970. It took her family two years to receive permission to migrate from Naples. When it was finally granted, there weren't enough places for all 10 members. The family had to be

LEFT: family celebrating Iranian New Year in Sydney's Observatory Park. **ABOVE:** Tiwi islanders outside an Aboriginal design shop in Nguiu, NT.

She stayed there for five years, learned English, and has been working steadily ever since.

With her husband Johnny – another Italian-Australian – Teresa now owns a popular pasta restaurant. The adult members of her family own their own homes; several of her siblings also have their own businesses. For them, hard work has produced the promised comforts, despite their impoverished beginnings. Although many Italian immigrants circulate amongst fellow countrymen, Teresa and Johnny do not have the time, and links with the community have grown weak. They have become integrated into Australian society: their children will not even speak Italian as a second language.

The polyglot nation

Even during the 19th century, there had been some exceptions to Australia's mono-cultural facade. There was a large Chinese population that had come to Australia during the gold rushes of the 1850s (and had survived the bitter resentment of Anglo miners, which occasionally erupted into violent attacks).

Several wine-growing valleys of South Australia, settled by Silesians in the 1840s, are still Teutonic in architecture, art and community festivals. Remote Broome at the top of Western Australia was full of Japanese pearlers. But these remained exceptions to the rule until the boom in different cultures that Australia received in the 1970s, once it truly opened its doors to the rest of the world, particularly to Asia. By the 1990s, one-third of all immigration was from Asian countries, and the proportion is expected to increase. The new arrivals do not always find it easy to adapt *(see the case histories below)* but their cultural influence is increasingly obvious in all regions of the country.

Other ways of settling

A number of immigrants now arrive under the Business Skills scheme. Applicants need at least $500,000 to invest, the ability and intent to

A TALE OF TWO ASIANS

John Lam arrived in 1979 from Vietnam to join an aunt and uncle. For his first two months he stayed in a migrant hostel, receiving A$36 a week in benefits, plus food and some clothing. After that, he moved in with his aunt and uncle, starting work in a kitchen, and then eventually became a barman. He now speaks good English, owns a house with his two brothers and sisters, and has become an Australian citizen.

Other Asian immigrants find the cultural transition more difficult. "The first two weeks, I was sick, totally homesick," recalls William Ho, originally from Hong Kong. "The country was new and I had no friends here. I had to start all over again."

A highly placed restaurant manager in Hong Kong, Ho arrived in 1981, having become interested in Australia through a friend, a chef. The friend knew that the owner of one of Australia's best Chinese restaurants was looking for a manager. Ho contacted the owner by mail and employer sponsorship was arranged. The entire process took about five months.

Despite a shaky start, he adapted and began to find bright spots in his changed life. Even so, Ho is not over his homesickness. He still thinks Hong Kong is the best place in the world to eat...

set up a business, and a good character. This category used to mean that people could virtually buy their way into Australia, and was often abused, but the government has redrawn the rules to stress business experience and the viability of the applicant's business plan.

Another booming area of migration activity might be called the "Eros visa". Thousands of Australian men have married women from foreign countries and brought them here. Often known as "mail-order brides" (because of the way introduction agencies used to advertise their Thai, Filipina, Fijian and Malaysian clients in Australian newspapers, to be brought over on the basis of a photo), these women join a long tradition of "imported spouses". Many ethnic groups, from Italians to Arabs to Indians, whose men or women may prefer to marry within their own community, have long arranged their own version of "mail-order" partners from "the old country".

Such a bride may find Australia, and her new mate, to be either heaven or hell. Often isolated in a rural area, or married to a partner with little capacity to manage cultural and language difficulties, the new arrival may find life brutal and lonely. Equally, she may find an affectionate husband, a local peer group of her own nationality and economic advantages unavailable in her homeland. One obvious group is the Filipino community. With their native English, outgoing personalities and strong work ethic, many Filipinas have found Australia to be a welcoming new homeland. In 1971, there were fewer than 1,000 Filipino-born women in Australia; today, there are more than 20,000.

Finally, for those for whom all legal avenues have failed, there is illegal immigration – often by arriving as a tourist and then staying on beyond the legal period. It is estimated that there are 70,000 illegal immigrants in Australia, many of whom remain undetected for years. They are often resented as "queue-jumpers" by other immigrants, who may wait years for their own family reunion approvals. When apprehended, they face the choice of rapid departure or mandatory deportation.

As a result of these immigration waves, 2 million Australians speak a language other than English when they are at home. An ethnic radio and television broadcasting network – Special Broadcasting Service (SBS) – began in the 1980s to transmit in a Babel of languages (with everything subtitled in English). Throughout the main cities, SBS Television's evening news is regarded as the most wide-ranging and balanced coverage on offer. Many viewers stay tuned to catch variety shows from Brazil, films from Israel, comedies from China. Today, SBS has become perhaps the most public manifestation of Australia's cultural diversity.

Overall, the Australian experience of immigration has been one of the most successful in his-

tory: the massive influx has been absorbed into society with remarkably little friction. Indeed, it has been widely accepted as the key to the country's vitality. As Professor Jerzy Zubzycki – himself a Polish-born professor at the Australian National University – recently summed up, immigration "has become the most dynamic and constructive and self-renewing feature of Australian society. We need to share our country with others, but also unashamedly want the talent, energy and industry of diverse groups of immigrants, to help us develop a potential which is plainly abundant. The tolerance of our ethnic diversity is the principal means available to us to reach this goal." ❑

LEFT: mingling in the sun at a Melbourne café. **RIGHT:** three New Australians celebrate on the beach after completing the citizenship ceremony.

ABORIGINES TODAY

An understanding with Aboriginal Australia is seen as essential to the spiritual wellbeing of the country – but there is still some way to go

Captain Arthur Phillip reported that the first words the Australian Aborigines said to his men were *"Warra! Warra!"* (Go away!) Their first reaction was not mistaken.

After more than 200 years of European settlement, Aboriginal Australians are the country's most disadvantaged group. Statistics show the sad results of the colonial experience: the average life expectancy for Aborigines is 15 years shorter than that for other Australians; they have three times the infant mortality rate and a far higher incidence of both communicable diseases, such as hepatitis B, and "lifestyle" diseases such as heart failure; an unemployment rate six times the national average; half the average income level; and a large proportion living in sub-standard housing or temporary shelters. Aborigines are also 16 times more likely to be imprisoned than other Australians.

But, despite two centuries of cultural attrition, the 300,000 Aborigines – including 27,000 racially distinct Torres Strait islanders, with whom they are generally grouped – have held on to a strong sense of identity and a fierce pride in their heritage. Aborigines today also have a keen political consciousness, born of years of struggle to attain the basic rights and freedoms denied them until the early 1970s.

The colonial curse

From 1788, the first British settlers to arrive on Australia's remote shores could not understand the Aborigines' nomadic lifestyle or the profound connection they had to their tribal lands. It seemed that the Aborigines came and went without reason across the sparse landscape. Terra Australis was conveniently declared a *terra nullius* – effectively, an uninhabited void that could be occupied without further thought.

The results were devastating to Aboriginal culture, which had survived and adapted to other profound changes for 50,000 years. As white settlers arrived by the boatload, Aborigi-

nal communities were systematically pushed from their homes, leading to the disruption and destruction of their traditional culture and communal life. Massacres of the indigenous population became common; whole peoples disappeared, their languages remembered only in place names. Introduced diseases swept

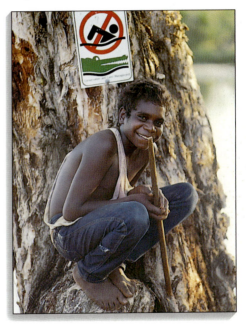

through the hinterland: by the beginning of the 20th century the Aboriginal population, estimated to be in excess of 300,000 in 1788, had been reduced to 60,000.

The colonial governments had little interest in allowing the Aborigines to determine their own future. In the mid-19th century bureaucrats and missionaries – well intentioned but believing in innate Aboriginal inferiority – sought to "protect" them from the expansion of what they saw as the superior Anglo-Saxon civilisation. The most dramatic case was the removal of the Tasmanian Aborigines to Flinders Island in the Bass Strait in the 1830s. The move was organised by the well-intentioned George Augustus

LEFT: the traditional *corroboree* is still performed.
RIGHT: after-school croc-spotting in Northern Territory.

Robinson in an effort to save the Aborigines from brutal farmers and soldiers, who were inclined to shoot them on sight as pests. But taken from their native homes to a barren and unfamiliar island outpost, forced to wear European clothes and eat starchy British food, the Aborigines simply, one by one, expired. All over Australia, similiar tragedies were acted out, as Aborigines were taken from their lands and grouped with other peoples with whom they shared neither language nor traditions.

With the booming cattle and sheep industries in the mid-19th century, the demand for land became more acute and the forms of "protec-

tion" stricter. A quasi-apartheid system was established in the Outback, with Aborigines segregated on reserves and given inferior legal status. When Australia became a federation in 1901, Aborigines were not allowed to vote: they were considered a "dying race" with no future.

Yet by the early 1930s it became apparent that they were not dying out. Their numbers were, in fact, increasing. Policies of assimilation were developed to integrate "half-caste" Aborigines into the lower strata of society, at the same time maintaining the strict segregation of "full-bloods" who, it was still felt, would disappear.

The Aborigines were not passive victims. Political activity began, to obtain basic freedoms.

LOST FOR WORDS

Of the hundreds of different languages spoken by the 500 or so Aboriginal peoples in 1788, only 30 have survived.

And despite their enforced marginalisation, many Aborigines had adapted to European society. As early as the 1860s, Aborigines had successfully engaged in farming enterprises, while the development of the cattle industry in Outback Australia would not have been possible without Aborigine stockmen and boundary riders (paid, of course, considerably less than their white counterparts).

Aboriginal political awareness grew steadily from the 1930s, culminating in the Freedom Rides of the mid-1960s, when young activists rode in buses through Outback Queensland and New South Wales bringing their message to the remotest communities. An "Aboriginal Embassy" was set up in front of Parliament House in Canberra; demonstrations resulted in violent clashes with police, pushing the Aboriginal plight on to the front pages and into white middle-class homes on television. The activists demanded that discriminatory legislation be repealed and that Aborigines be awarded basic freedoms enjoyed by other Australians.

Towards self-determination

By the early 1970s, this new-found political consciousness forced the Federal Australian government, led by the then Prime Minister, Gough Whitlam, to come up with a new policy: "self-determination". This allowed Aborigines to make decisions affecting their own future, retain their cultural identity and values, and achieve greater economic and social equality.

The Department of Aboriginal Affairs was established in 1972, followed by the Aboriginal Development Commission (ADC) in 1980. The underlying concept was to develop programmes that would bring increasing economic independence to Aboriginal people by fostering the development of business enterprises.

It didn't happen overnight. In 1988, while the rest of Australia celebrated 200 years of white settlement at the Bicentennial, Aborigine activists took the opportunity to stage peaceful protest marches. As the international media carried their message around the world, white Australians were forced to admit that, indeed,

Aborigines had very little to celebrate: from their perspective, the colonial "invasion" had been an unmitigated disaster. In many ways, the events of 1988 pushed Aboriginal issues into the forefront of the national political agenda.

Since the 1970s, Aborigines have become involved in the development of government policies that affect them and in the delivery of services. More importantly, a wide range of organisations, from community-based medical and legal services to Land Councils (which govern the affairs of different regions), have been established; there are now over 1,200 Aboriginal community organisations.

vast swathes of the Outback on the basis of traditional ownership. The act also gave them significant control over mining and other activities on their land. Royalties from mining operations were distributed to Aboriginal groups throughout the territory.

Land rights acts have been passed in various states, and in 1985 the federal government attempted to introduce national land rights legislation. There was strong opposition – particularly in Queensland and Western Australia, where mining lobbies are powerful – and Canberra backed down, agreeing that a state-by-state approach was more appropriate.

Land rights

For all Aboriginal groups, "land rights" have always been the top priority. The land is a crucial part of their being, and the responsibility for protecting significant sites is central to their spiritual life. It has been a source of profound distress that they have been pushed from their traditional homes, and seen sacred sites mined, built on, flooded or otherwise destroyed. The Northern Territory Land Rights Act, passed in 1975, allowed Aborigines to make claims to

HANDING BACK

In the early 1990s, the federal government in Canberra agreed to "hand-back" ceremonies of Aboriginal sacred sites: Uluru (Ayers Rock) and Kakadu in the Northern Territory, and the southern part of Jervis Bay in New South Wales were restored to their traditional owners. Aboriginal groups now help run these national park areas, and the local clans derive a good income from their management.

The federal government has encouraged the other states to make similar "hand-backs" of sites with traditional significance to Aborigines, but none has yet done so.

LEFT: Aborigines were shoehorned into Western ways of living. **ABOVE:** a new Aboriginal cultural centre is declared open.

Perhaps the most symbolic change occurred in 1992, when the High Court of Australia overturned the legal fiction of *terra nullius* that had been the basis of Australia's settlement. The judges agreed that "native title" had always existed for land that had been continuously occupied by Aborigines, and in 1993 the government set up a Native Title Tribunal to regulate claims.

As time went on, however, it appeared that the tribunal would achieve little in practice: since 19th-century missionaries had moved Aboriginal peoples around, often splitting up clans by force and lumping them together again in remote areas, few Aboriginal groups could

rivers of cash flowing from government aid and mining rights, and some decisions were made that brought no long-term advantages to Aborigines at all.

In the early days, the commission acquired or helped establish a large number of businesses, but the optimum strategy was often seen as one of pouring cash, rather than training and professional guidance, into such high-profile projects as the operation of hovercraft, large grazing properties, a fully stocked outback pub purchased as a going concern, and a holiday resort. ADC Chairman Charles Perkins once admitted in public: "We've funded over

prove continuous occupation of their lands. The lack of progress has been frustrating for many Aborigines, and the emotional land-rights debate remains one of the most contentious issues in Australia today.

Dealing with problems

Inevitably, the growth of an "Aboriginal industry", comprising politicians, city-based do-gooders and opportunistic Aboriginal leaders, had been nurtured by the uneasy communal guilt that sprang from the endless reiteration of old injustices against Aborigines. These groups began competing with genuinely committed people and organisations for control of the

150 projects, and they've all gone broke."

After 20 years of financial outcomes that would shock any investor, the futility of such misdirection became apparent. What is more, welfare dependency was increasingly seen as a corrupting influence. The prominent and popular Aboriginal lawyer, Noel Pearson, said in 1999: "Welfare is a resource that is laced with poison and the poison present is the money-for-nothing principle. Welfare is a parasitic exploiter." Pearson is now advocating that money alone, even if effectively administered, cannot solve the problem. He insists that the "welfare mentality" and the downward spiral of alcoholism and substance abuse must be dislodged by people taking their own destinies into their own hands, building up their self-respect and self-discipline from within. Believing that blaming society lets people off the hook for their own behaviour, he is urging Aborigines to leave behind them what he calls the "victim mentality" and set about standing on their own two feet.

Pearson and his views are winning growing acceptance in both communities. He is still urging that viable businesses be established in Aboriginal homelands, to avoid the social dysfunction that springs from moving into largely European-controlled communities. Pearson may have discovered a better foundation on

which to build such businesses. Following the failures of earlier endeavours and under more comprehensive guidance, a number of successful Aboriginal businesses have been established throughout Australia, from shopping centres and cattle stations to craft shops.

The Aboriginal and Torres Strait development Commission (ATSIC), which replaced the ADC, helped some communities buy their native lands (thus circumventing the land rights arguments), to build adequate housing and to take out home loans. However, following an endless

ABOVE LEFT: chopping a tree for bush honey, Bathurst Island, NT. **ABOVE:** Olympic track star, Cathy Freeman.

TRADITIONAL NAMES

Most Aborigines in New South Wales and Victoria now prefer to be called Kooris; they are Murris in Queensland, Nungas in South Australia and Nyoongahs in Western Australia.

series of scandals over financial mismanagement and apparent nepotism, the government began to disband ATSIC in early 2004.

In the past, cultural accommodation has often ended tragically. Albert Namatjira, for example, was the first Aboriginal painter to interpret the rugged landscapes of central Australia in Western-style watercolours. While his work received international acclaim, Namatjira couldn't cope with the huge cultural differences between Aborigine and European societies. In the 1950s, official Australian citizenship and the accompanying right to drink alcohol were granted to him at a time when Aborigines were not normally afforded these privileges. His white patrons bestowed on him the trappings of the European world but refused to recognise his tribal obligations. While his money was shared among his kin, Namatjira went from alcoholism to jail in a decline that saw this man of dignity and great skill die prematurely, a disillusioned fringe dweller.

Success stories

Many Aborigines, however, have successfully entered Australian society on their own terms. Neville Bonner became a Senator of the Commonwealth Parliament and pastor Sir Doug Nichols was appointed Governor of South Australia. Evonne Goolagong-Cawley became a Wimbledon tennis champion, and Oodgeroo Noonuccal (formerly Kath Walker) remains one of Australia's most prominent artists and authors. Writers such as Herb Wharton and Evelyn Crawford are immensely popular.

There have been numerous Aboriginal sports stars, such as the "flying Ella brothers" in Rugby Union, and Olympic gold-medal winner, Cathy Freeman. In the arts and entertainment, there are actors such as David Gulpilil; the television and film comedian and actor, Ernie Dingo; an Aboriginal and Islanders' Dance School; contemporary painters such as Trevor Nickolls and Danny Eastwood; the part-Aborigine photographer Tracey Moffatt; and the outstanding music group, Yothu Yindi, led by a former Australian of the Year, Mandawuy Yunupingu. ❑

THE ARTS

In music, drama, literature, film and the visual arts, Australia has absorbed
influences from around the world – and has at last found its own voice

The first century of Australian European culture was, unsurprisingly, entirely derivative. The white convicts and their white jailers took little notice of the black Aboriginal culture that had been in existence for at least 50,000 years before their arrival. It was Georgian English art, vision and aspirations that were transplanted to Australian soil at the same time as European crops. There is little in the painting or poetry of the time that reflects an indigenous approach; in early colonial landscapes even the trees look European.

The first great turning point in Australian cultural history was the 1890s, which saw a tremendous upsurge in Australian nationalism. This was reflected in the arts, especially in literature. This was the period when *The Bulletin* magazine's school of balladists and short-story writers got under way, helped by balladists such as Banjo Paterson, who wrote *The Man From Snowy River*, and Henry Lawson, Australia's finest short-story writer. Many of them celebrated the bush, and its male traditions such as mateship, Aussie nationalism and the underdog, at the expense of the ruling Anglophile "bunyip aristocracy". Joseph Furphy wrote his novel

PRECEDING PAGES: studying a contemporary sculpture in the Art Gallery of South Australia, Adelaide. **LEFT:** outdoor sculpture in Capt John Burke Park, Brisbane.

Such Is Life (which were said to be the last words of Ned Kelly, the bushranger and folk hero, before he was hanged) at this time.

At a more popular level, Steele Rudd began writing his *On Our Selection* series, about life on poverty-stricken bush properties, which led many years later to a decade of Dad and Dave comedy serials, radio shows and jokes. A little later, C.J. Dennis started celebrating city larrikins in his poems about Ginger Mick and The Sentimental Bloke.

This creative leap was the start of a distinctive Australian literature, which continued strongly in the 20th century through the novels of Henry Handel Richardson, Miles Franklin, Christina Stead and Eve Langley, the short stories of Barbara Baynton, Gavin Casey and Peter Cowan, and the poetry of Christopher Brennan, Kenneth Slessor, R.D. Fitzgerald, Douglas Stewart and Judith Wright, to the writers of the present day.

A similiar nationalistic burst could be seen in the other arts in the 1890s. Louis Esson began writing plays in self-consciously Australian idiom. A recognisable Australian school of landscape painting emerged and crystallised later in the work of Sir Arthur Streeton, Tom Roberts and the "Heidelberg School" (named after the Melbourne suburb, not the German town). Dame Nellie Melba, the first of a line of Aus-

ARTISTS IN EXILE

For much of the 20th century, Australia was regarded as a cultural wasteland – by the rest of the world and, oddly, by many Australians themselves. In the 1940s, '50s and '60s, local artists often went overseas – almost always to London – to make a name for themselves: opera singer Joan Sutherland, novelist Patrick White, painters Sidney Nolan and Albert Tucker, ballet dancer Robert Helpmann, sculptor Clement Meadmore, and many others.

Australian audiences at that time, the expatriates lamented, showed a general lack of sophistication and appreciation for the "high" fine arts.

The artistic scene changed dramatically in the 1970s, with a flowering of all forms of creativity that lured many of the expatriates home. In the early 21st century, most Australian artists prefer to remain in their own country.

This is partly because their audiences have grown tremendously, to the point where it is now possible to make a living in Australia (at least with government arts subsidies, from the Australia Council). Partly it is because mass communications have made it possible for them to stay in Sydney or Melbourne and still, quite often, reach an international market.

tralian opera divas, made an international name singing French arias in Italian in British concert halls and gave her name to an ice-cream dessert, the "Peach Melba". Low, May and Hop began drawing for *The Bulletin*. Australians made *Soldiers of the Cross*, which is said to be the world's first feature movie, and the film industry flourished.

By the time of federation in 1901, Australian architecture had developed an indigenous style based upon the bush homestead, with high-pitched galvanised roofs and shady verandahs. By about 1910, however, most urban Australians were living in the rows of terraced

distribution networks. American movies, pop songs, radio shows and, later, television shows, took over much of the media. American slang crept into the language, American idioms slipped into advertising, business and finance, and American ideas influenced house design, shops, advertising, motels, supermarkets and much else. American writers topped the best-seller lists, American comics took over the newsstands, and American movie stars became the nation's cultural icons.

The result is the odd sensation that Australia often gives today, of being part British, part American and part Australian. It is.

houses, decorated with cast-iron balconies, that still predominate in the inner suburbs of Melbourne and Sydney, or in the suburban red-brick or fibrocement bungalows that were to become the dominant local architectural style.

In the late 1920s and early 1930s, an important change took place. At the very time that Australia was beginning to break free politically and culturally of British domination, it came under the influence of the United States. In doing this, Australia was taking part in the internationalisation of an immensely influential American culture.

The Australian film industry virtually disappeared as the US took control of the local film

VOICES ON THE AIR

For nearly 50 years, Australian broadcasting displayed symptoms of cultural confusion. Radio became a tug-of-war between Australian Broadcasting Commission (ABC) announcers, who kept to impeccable British accents, and commercial disc jockeys who adopted phony American accents and became known as "Woolloomooloo Yanks" (Woolloomooloo is a district of Sydney).

Not until the 1970s did a genuine Australian accent become acceptable over the airwaves, and then only after the horse-racing announcers had paved the way.

An Australian cultural resistance

Despite this, a vernacular Australian culture continued to develop and strengthen itself. In a sense, it had merely added the American to the British, European and Asian ingredients already stirred into the local mix. There was considerable resistance to some of the American input: the traditional arts, especially music, drama, opera and ballet, kept very close to their British and European sources. American culture was regarded as inferior. On a popular level, there was some

KING OF COUNTRY

Country music legend Slim Dusty received a state funeral at Sydney's St Andrews Cathedral in 2003.

country and western music (or hillbilly music, as it was then called) became popular in country towns. Aussie hillbilly singers began imitating the Americans. They adopted names like Tex Morton, Buddy Williams and Slim Dusty… and then began writing their own songs about Australian rodeos, outlaws, bush picnics, pubs, bushrangers, yarns, tall tales, and country myths.

Before long, Australia had developed its own hybrid style of country music, along with its own travelling music-and-rodeo shows and its

resentment left over from World War II, when large numbers of US soldiers were stationed in the country and there were open fights between Australian and American servicemen. Things American had a certain glamour about them, but they met with scepticism as well. Large US cars were known as Yank Tanks; there were a lot of anti-American jokes around.

Sometimes cultural resistance took strange forms. For example, many of Australia's 19th-century bush songs and ballads had either died out or faded into the background; American

LEFT: the Sydney Symphony Orchestra.
ABOVE: a rehearsal at the Sydney Opera House.

own country music stars, records and radio stations. Slim Dusty's *The Pub with No Beer* became a smash hit in the late 1950s and has been a perennial bestseller ever since. Slim's real name was David Gordon Kirkpatrick. Born and bred in the bush, he learned to yodel by listening to American records, and churned out country and western songs right up until his death in 2003.

The next big bang

The late 1960s and 1970s were the next great period of Australian cultural growth, and the reasons are complex. The perils of World War II gave a clear boost to Australian nationalism;

the 1960s and early 1970s were a time of steady economic growth and growing self-confidence. Meanwhile, the nation's isolation seemed to have come to a decisive end; a massive immigration programme brought millions of migrants from Britain and Europe, including a hefty influx of Italians, Greeks and other Southern Europeans.

There was a sense of the old, stale moulds, which had contained Australian life for so long, being broken open. Australians suddenly learnt about salami, white wine, pizza, rock 'n' roll, hippies, women's lib and student power. The traditional connection with British high

Adamson, who adopted a freer, more vernacular approach to their verse and concentrated more on specifically Australian themes. Murray has borrowed from Aboriginal techniques to celebrate his "roots" in the mid-north New South Wales coast.

In the novel, progress was steadier, perhaps because it was dominated for so long by the late Patrick White. The 1974 Nobel Laureate influenced younger novelists, especially through his poetic prose style. A new generation of writers, including David Ireland *(Woman of the Future)*, Thomas Kenneally *(Bring Larks and Heroes, The Chant of Jimmie Blacksmith, Schindler's*

culture was weakening, and the American input seemed to have been partly absorbed. Phrases like "crisis of identity" and "the Australian character" were in the air. In retrospect, all the right ingredients seemed to be there for a cultural take-off.

The poets, as usual, led the way. At first they were dominated by academics such as A.D. Hope and James McAuley. Professor Hope's erotic yet intellectually disciplined poetry, in particular, has had a profound impact on Australian literature. These were followed by a loose collection of poets, such as David Malouf, Tom Shapcott, Bruce Dawe, Les Murray, Gwen Harwood, John Tranter and Robert

SHORT CUTS

The 1970s saw a boom in short-story writing. Earlier writers such as Hal Porter and Peter Cowan led the way, but they hardly prepared Australia for the sudden burgeoning of writers such as Frank Moorhouse, a cool ironist; Peter Carey, concocter of bizarre and eerie fables (who won the 1988 Booker Prize for his novel *Oscar and Lucinda* and has since gone on to international fame); Morris Lurie, Murray Bail, and Robert Drewe (whose wonderful collection *The Bodysurfers* became a bestseller). Women short-story writers include Judith Wright, Helen Garner, Thea Astley and Inez Baranay.

Ark), Elizabeth Jolley *(Miss Peabody's Inheritance)*, Glenda Adams *(Dancing on Coral)*, David Malouf *(Remembering Babylon)* and the Boston-based Jill Kerr Conway *(The Road from Coorain)*, have taken their own idiosyncratic approaches, as have Tim Winton *(The Riders)*, David Foster *(Moonlite)*, Kate Grenville *(Lillian's Story)* and Fotini Epanomitis *(The Mule's Foal)* and a string of Aboriginal writers.

Centre stage

At the same time, a revived Australian film industry has drawn, in part, upon the work of these writers. *The Chant of Jimmie Blacksmith,*

to the old Australian male traditions of mateship and sympathy for the loser or underdog).

Melbourne's experimental theatres of the 1970s, La Mama and The Pram Factory (both in Carlton), provided the artistic focus. Among the playwrights they encouraged were Barry Oakley, Jack Hibberd (author of *Dimboola*, about a country wedding – the most successful piece of restaurant theatre ever staged in Australia) and David Williamson. Williamson has written a series of highly successful topical plays such as *Don's Party*, *The Club*, *Travelling North* and *Emerald City* (all of which have sbeen made into films) and scripts for movies such as *Gallipoli*.

for example, took director Fred Schepsi to Hollywood. But the film makers have drawn more heavily upon the dramatists who emerged in Melbourne and created a lively, radical, political theatre in Australia for the first time.

There had been, once again, harbingers – Ray Lawler's *Summer of the Seventeenth Doll*, and Alan Seymour's *One Day of the Year*. The latter dealt with the Anzac Day celebrations, in which Australia ritualistically celebrates its defeat at Gallipoli in World War I (a remarkable act of catharsis closely linked

LEFT: *Dirty Deeds* and **ABOVE:** *Rabbit-Proof Fence,* two of Australia's international movie successes.

In Sydney, Bob Ellis, Stephen Sewell, Michael Gow and Louis Nowra have written equally successful, though less political, plays. Such are the film and stage possibilities in Sydney that Williamson and Oakley have both moved there, confirming the view of some artists that Sydney is an Antipodean New York, annexing the country's best work through its cultural (and financial) power.

With the burst of dramatic talent and new government incentives, the film industry became Australia's biggest cultural export. Sales figures in 2000 showed the business generated $1.5 billion.

Many of the best-known films can be rented

in video stores around the world: everything from the brutal post-apocalpytic *Mad Max* series starring Mel Gibson to period pieces (Gillian Armstrong's 1979 version of the Miles Franklin classic, *My Brilliant Career*; Peter Weir's atmospheric *Picnic at Hanging Rock* in 1975); from Jane Campion's suburban *Sweetie* (1989) to George Miller's 1996 talking-pig, *Babe*. Baz Luhrmann's dance comedy *Strictly Ballroom*, the drag queen frenzy of *Priscilla, Queen of the Desert* and the kitschy vision of *Muriel's Wedding* rounded off the eclectic 1990s. Contemporary Australian actors including Nicole Kidman, Cate Blanchett, Toni Col-

lette, Geoffrey Rush, and Hugh Jackman have become Hollywood success stories with their path to Tinseltown paved by established stars such as Judy Davis and Mel Gibson.

Recently Australia has been bringing the world's stars to Sydney's Fox Studios (where Luhrman's 2001 blockbuster *Moulin Rouge* was filmed). At the same time there are numerous local film-makers endeavouring to export uniquely Australian-style movies to the wider world. There are also actors and directors, such as Leah Purcell, who, inspired by the love of their homeland, are content to work within the confines of a smaller market. Another is director Philip Noyce whose 2003 film *Rabbit-Proof Fence* traced the Outback odyssey of three half-Aborigine girls.

Images on canvas

Painting and sculpture enjoyed such popularity in the mid-1970s that it was commonplace to talk of an "art boom", with buyers and business investors paying very high prices for local works. This activity was partly reflected in the construction of the new National Art Gallery in Canberra and spectacular million-dollar purchases.

Once again, Melbourne was the early focus; after World War II, a group of figurative painters emerged which for a long time was identified as "the Australian school". Its practitioners included Sidney Nolan, whose series on Ned Kelly the bushranger became national icons; Albert Tucker, whose gnarled Aussie faces on the cover illustration helped make Donald Horne's *The Lucky Country* a bestseller; Arthur Boyd, Lloyd Rees and Clifton Pugh.

In the early 1970s Sydney became the centre for an abstract expressionist movement which drew upon earlier painters such as Ian Fairweather and Godfrey Miller, and was soon experimenting with hard edge, colour field and lyrical expressionist modes. John Olsen painted a landscape series called *The You Beaut Country* which summed up the optimism of the time. Eric Smith, William Rose, John Coburn and Stanislaus Rapotec were followed by younger painters such as Brett Whiteley (who became the most famous before he died of a heroin overdose in 1992), David Aspden, Michael Johnson and Tim Storrier.

In Melbourne, Fred Williams established himself as the most important landscape painter of the post-war years – possibly in the history

SOAP STORY

The export of Australian cinema was paralleled by a boom in home-grown television. If the films represented the cultural equivalent of fine Hunter Valley wines, a good few ordinary *vins de table* made it abroad too, in the form of an endless stream of television daytime soaps.

Most of them served to fill off-peak slots in the schedules of the world's burgeoning television industry, but a few – notably *Neighbours* and *Home and Away* – became cult viewing in the UK, particularly among schoolchildren and students.

of Australian painting – with his haunting, semi-abstract depictions of the Outback. Williams always joked that he was wary of the bush, but his re-creations of it have given Australians a powerful image of their own country to replace the earlier visions of Streeton and Drysdale.

Probably the best-known contemporary Australian artist is Brisbane-born Tracey Moffatt whose painterly films and photographic works have attracted international critical acclaim.

Antipodean rhythms

Classical music in Australia has always been a matter of performance rather than composi-

Anne Boyd and Moya Henderson frequently have their work performed here and in other countries. Ballet has shared in the recent growth in the "high" arts, helped by the work of such dancer-choreographers as Graeme Murphy and Kai Tai Chan.

In recent years, Australia has become as well known for its rock bands as its films; the local pub music scene, especially in Melbourne and Sydney, is extraordinarily healthy. Performers such as Spiderbait, Nick Cave, The Whitlams, Powderfinger and The Cruel Sea started off on the pub circuit. Older groups that made it big overseas included The Easybeats, the Seekers,

tion. The nation has several well-established symphony orchestras, chamber groups and opera companies, including The Australian Opera. A tradition of local music-making at eisteddfods and concerts has been strong; the diva Joan Sutherland (sometimes known in Australia as "Wonderlungs") made her way to the top from exactly that background. Despite the limited opportunities, contemporary composers such as Richard Meale, Peter Sculthorpe, Nigel Butterley, George Dreyfus,

the BeeGees, Skyhooks, Mental as Anything, AC/DC, INXS and Men at Work. Midnight Oil became a self-consciously Australian group, politically committed to an independent, nuclear-free country. The Aboriginal band Yothu Yindi, with didgeridoos and tribal dancers, is unmistakably Northern Territory. One of Australia's best-known exports is Kylie Minogue, now a pop icon.

As in any art scene, the best way to find real Australian music is to do the rounds of the pubs and clubs; there are literally thousands of local groups, some aiming for stardom, others just having a good time performing their music. Both attitudes reflect the real Australian spirit. ❏

LEFT: multi-talented performer, Leah Purcell.
ABOVE: Aboriginal band Yothu Yindi blends traditional instruments with rock music.

WHERE THE PAST MEETS THE PRESENT

From Dreamtime to polymer paints...the artworks being created by modern Aborigines carry within them thousands of years of myth and tradition

It's contemporary yet traditional. It's today but it's timeless. Attaching a label to modern Aboriginal art can be as difficult as establishing the meanings behind the symbols. But it does provide us with a unique cultural vision of Australia, as deep and enduring as any on earth. The international explosion in Australian Aboriginal art began in the early 1970s as a spark in Northern Territory, first in various groups in Arnhem Land and in the desert community of Papunya, west of Alice Springs. In Arnhem Land, missionaries encouraged tribal people to paint their designs, derived from traditional rock art and body decoration, on bark panels stripped from trees. Meanwhile in central Australia, teacher Geoffrey Bardon introduced polymer paints to desert-dwellers, producing an entirely new genre of art: the strongly symbolic dot style was born. Today the National Gallery in Canberra, the state galleries and private galleries in all the major cities feature desert and Top End art.

THE EXPLOSION SPREADS

More recently, other northern Aboriginal communities have also earned distinguished reputations for their artisans: Tiwi islanders for their carving and distinctive painting *(the picture above shows a Tiwi decorating a shell)*; representations of WA's Kimberley region, as characterised by Rover Thomas and Paddy Carlton; blazing acrylics from Eubana Nampitjin of Balgo Hills. Works by the recently deceased Emily Kngwarreye put the central Australian community of Utopia on the map; her niece Kathleen Petyarre continues that tradition.

▷ **ALTERED ALTAR**
St Theresa's church on Bathurst Island, Northern Territory, is a strictly Tiwi version of Roman Catholicism. The cross is still prominent, but highly decorated in Tiwi designs.

◁ **TRIBAL INSPIRATION**
Muntja Nungurayai, from WA's Balgo desert community, is recognised Europe as a living master. Though virtually unknown home, her paintings draw their inspiration from the r of ritual in her lifestyle and the secret nature of tribal "women's business".

▽ **PAINTING ON WOOD**
On the Tiwi Islands, carving and painting wooden sculptures is a natural extension of the production of Pukamani burial poles.

▷ **CORRUGATED COLOUR**
Art is omnipresent on Bathurst and Melville Islan Modern icons decorate pu buildings, from the local primary school to the fabr showroom of Tiwi Designs Corrugated iron, the classi Australian building materia remains a favourite texture display Tiwi graphic desigr

△ **A NEW DEVELOPMENT**
Though dots remain prolifi paintings from Balgo Hills, colourful design element ha recently emerged, as characterised by this tryptic by the Tjakkamarra brother

▷ **ANCIENT AND MODERN**
A painting in the dot style, c display in Fremantle, emplo traditional elements such a the tortoise and lizards, and also alludes to the ancient hand silhouettes found in Aboriginal rock art.

A PICTURE BOOK OF HISTORY

Aboriginal rock art is recognised as the world's oldest and longest continuous living tradition. The ancient art is found all across Australia in the form of paintings or engravings on rock. Archaeologists continue to argue over their age, but some of the earliest paintings, in red ochre in northern sandstone shelters, could be 50,000 years old. In 1996 in the Kimberley region of Western Australia, an engraving site was dated at over 110,000 years old, sending archaeologists back to the drawing board and rewriting the history of modern human movement.

Arnhem Land and neighbouring Kakadu National Park in the Northern Territory provide the finest Aboriginal rock art experiences. At Ubirr shelter in Kakadu, many of the paintings were made well before the last Ice Age, 8,000 years ago. A layer of animal depictions (some of species now extinct) lie beneath red dynamic figures racing across the shelter. Over them are splashed X-ray paintings of barramundi fish, their internal organs accurately detailed. Over them are sailing vessels, documenting the European arrivals in Australia. Each layer reads like a page in the history of the continent.

▽ **FUNERAL POLES**
Pukamani burial poles are still carved today as an enduring gesture of respect for the dead. The number of poles produced reflects the individual's standing in the community. A plethora of poles are erected at the funeral of an important elder.

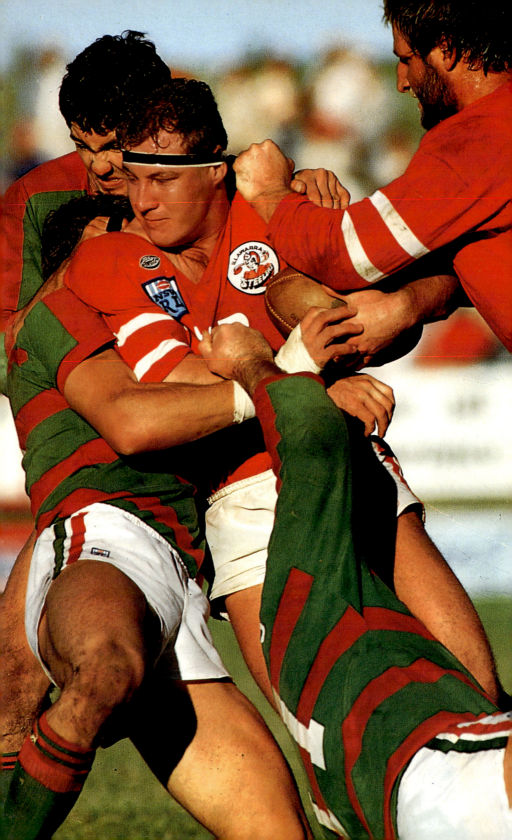

WHERE SPORT IS SUPREME

If you want to join in the local conversation – especially with Australian males –
you need to know how the local team is getting on

In Australia, sport is more than an outlet for excess energy. The 19th-century macho physical culture has transmuted into competition on the game field. Last century, sport was the language in which Australians first shouted: "Hey world, here we are!"

Although the grip of sport has loosened – these days, success in the arts brings more attention to Australia than physical exertion – a working knowledge of any major sport still offers the easiest entry to the often male-dominated Aussie pub. In fact, wherever males gather – in pubs, clubs or the workplace – sport tends to be the major topic of conversation. They bet on it and brag about it, they eulogise or verbally crucify its performers, analyse its conduct and speculate about its future. One thing they never do is tire of it.

The golden 1950s

This sports fixation might seem a giant charade if it weren't for an Australian sporting tradition based on real achievements. The 1950s was a period of Australian dominance in world swimming and tennis, plus its arrival as a force to reckon with in track and field, cycling, boxing, sculling and golf. Unlike the British Commonwealth games of cricket or rugby, these sports were truly international and established Australia's place on the world podium. To the Europeans and Americans of the day, Australia might have been a remote cultural wasteland; but, boy, could its people run, swim and play.

The world got to know Aussie athletes like John Landy, Herb Elliott, Marjorie Jackson and Betty Cuthbert (track); Murray Rose, Dawn Fraser, John Henricks, Lorraine Crapp, John and Ilsa Konrads (swimming); Frank Sedgman, Lew Hoad and Ken Rosewall (tennis). Culled from a tiny population, they created a tradition for generations to follow. The climax to this golden era came in 1956: Australia dusted the

United States 5–0 in the Davis Cup tennis final, while at the Melbourne Olympic Games, Aussie athletes won 35 medals – 13 gold, eight silver and 14 bronze – an astonishing number for the small population.

Yet, as much as sport has been a unifying factor in Australian society, it can also be strangely

divisive. The problem is that Australians are preoccupied with a vast range of different and often conflicting sports. Football, for instance, is by far the largest spectator sport; but "football" itself is really a broad term that covers the codes of soccer, Australian Rules, Rugby League and Rugby Union.

The cricket mania

It is only in summer, when cricket grabs the public's imagination, that Australians are more or less united in their sporting focus. Spectator interest settles squarely on the national team in its Test Match encounters with the West Indies, India, Pakistan, New Zealand, South Africa and,

LEFT: the macho confrontation of Rugby League.
RIGHT: Australian Rules football, unknown outside the country, attracts a fanatical following.

most crucially, the traditional rival, England.

A Test Match normally takes five days to complete and even then it frequently finishes in a draw. To the detached observer, cricket's tactical intrigue is less than evident. But to many Australians raised on the exploits of Don Bradman, Ray Lindwall, Keith Miller, Dennis Lillee or Greg Chappell, the game is followed with religious zeal. Radios blare the ball-by-ball commentary at the beach; pub discussions focus on the latest catch in the slips; and cricket receives extra TV coverage, day in, day out, making armchair experts of millions of Aussies.

In the more than 100 years since Australia

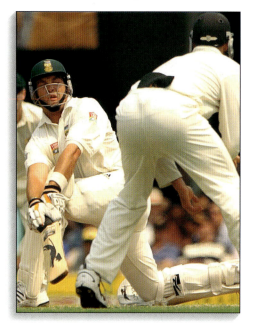

played its first Test series against England, nobody has been better at the game than a slightly built fellow by the name of Donald Bradman. "The Don", as he was known, was the greatest batsman ever, racking up century after century in matches with apparently effortless ease. During the 1930s and 1940s, Bradman was to cricket what Pelé later was to football or Babe Ruth had been to baseball. It was unfortunate that the age of television didn't arrive soon enough to show the man in his prime.

A Test series is played over three, four, five or sometimes six matches, with the battlegrounds moving between Sydney, Melbourne, Adelaide, Brisbane and Perth. Ground capaci-

TOP SCORE
Don Bradman's 452 scored at the Sydney Cricket Ground in 1929 remained the highest score in first-class cricket for over 60 years.

ties range from 30,000 to 90,000; lovers of the game say there are few greater sporting moments than to experience the opening "over" of an England v Australia Test before a capacity Melbourne or Sydney Cricket Ground crowd. Despite one local writer's opinion that cricket is a "high-speed version of croquet", a test match is never as boring as it sounds: the combination of sun, partisan passion and beer can make cricket crowds boisterous, humorous and sometimes downright dangerous (at least if you take a spot on the SCG's notoriously raucous and abusive "Hill").

If a five-day test sounds too much to take in, consider watching a "limited-over" or one-day game. As the name implies, these are wham-bam affairs that come and go in a heated rush and often wring participants and spectators dry with their tension and drama. These games often continue into the evening, under floodlights. Given the right circumstances and participants, a limited-over match at the Sydney Cricket Ground can be a day and night of pure theatre with all the prescribed elements of tragedy, tension, climax and triumph.

While international test cricket is the top of the pyramid, the game is also played at multiple levels, from the Sheffield Shield (interstate matches) down through district ranks to the junior and social levels. On any summer Sunday you'll find the social plodders, with their attendant picnics and barbecues, enjoying the game at an entirely different and less frenetic pace, some of them no doubt fuelling and foiling their Bradman fantasies with a can or four of the amber fluid (beer).

Aussie Rules footie

On the surface it seems incongruous that a country so fond of cricket, with all its esoteric customs and traditions, could have given birth to a game as apparently anarchic as Australian Rules football. The sport may be virtually

LEFT: Australia v. South Africa at Sydney Cricket Ground. **RIGHT:** Cameron Ling handballs clear in the Australian Rules Wizard Cup Final

unknown beyond Australia's shores, but in Melbourne it is a passion: the city may have only 3 million inhabitants, yet "Aussie Rules" ranks among the most popular football leagues of any codes anywhere in the world. It is estimated that, each winter Saturday in Melbourne, one person in 16 attends an Australian Football League game and thousands more follow the saturation TV coverage. Crowds of almost 80,000 have attended premiership games while 121,696 was the official attendance record for the 1970 grand final between Collingwood and Carlton. September's AFL grand final is one of the great sporting experiences, rivalling an Eng-lish FA Cup Final or an American Super Bowl for colour, passion and atmosphere.

The power and wealth of the AFL clubs draws star players from other districts and states such as South Australia, Tasmania, Western Australia and, occasionally, New South Wales and Queensland. While Victoria is the showcase of Australian Rules football, the other states get a chance to flex their might during the State-of-Origin games. These are inter-state representative games in which each state picks its best players, including those who have departed for the glory and lucrative semi-professional pay packets offered by interstate AFL clubs.

AUSSIE RULES OK?

The game now known as Australian Rules football originated from a crude brand of Gaelic football played by miners on the Victorian goldfields in the 1850s. In 1858 H.C.A. Harrison and T.W. Wills formed Melbourne Football Club, after drawing up a set of rules borrowed liberally from other football codes.

In 1866 the game's first official rules were established, although they were altered over and over again in subsequent years. The spectacular series of kicks and catches at the heart of the game have led its detractors to dub the game "aerial ping-pong".

The popularity of "Aussie Rules" in Melbourne is truly an enigma, for it cuts across sex, age, and class barriers. Sydneysiders, perhaps spoiled by their beach and harbour lifestyle, cynically claim that Melburnians have nothing better to do than go to the football. It's a comfortable put-down, but there's more to the appeal of the code than that. Even a first-time spectator can see that the game tears along at a rush with high scoring and spectacular play.

The art of non-compromise

In Sydney and points north, footy of a different kind is the winter preoccupation. Rugby League started as a professional alternative to Rugby

Union. It's played in a half-dozen provinces of a half-dozen countries, and to that degree qualifies as an international sport, although 80 percent of the world's best League players live within 30 km (20 miles) of Sydney Town Hall. League attendances are nothing like as large as those of the AFL, but the Sydney clubs – such as St George, the Western Suburbs, Manly and Parramatta – keep their players fabulously well-paid through the revenue of their slot machines and licensed clubs. In Brisbane and Sydney, the game found its roots in the inner working-class suburbs and, despite media overkill, hasn't significantly broadened its social base.

As in the Australian Football League, in the 1990s teams from beyond Sydney have risen to the top, with the Canberra Raiders and Brisbane Broncos removing the Winfield Cup trophy from Sydney. The Aussie national side, known as the Kangaroos, regularly hops through tours of France and Great Britain unbeaten.

God's own game

According to its devotees, Rugby Union is "the game they play in heaven" – which is remarkable considering its relative popularity in New South Wales and Queensland, where angels are in short supply. The game's popular interest is

Rugby League is a physical rather than cerebral game. Modern strategy is based on an uncompromising masochistic style of defence that prompted one American football coach to observe: "Our guys could never stand up to that sort of constant punishment." You don't have to play this game to feel how much it hurts. The game's appeal rests in its strong gladiatorial image and macho confrontations as pairs of teams slam into one another head-to-head – although fans believe that a dazzling backline movement resulting in a try (touch-down) is one of the real joys in sporting life (and TV advertisements relentlessly proclaim League to be "the greatest game of all").

at state rather than club level. Two or three times a year, the New South Wales and Queensland teams engage in a brutal battle that makes the Eureka Stockade seem like a church tea party. If you enjoy football, take the opportunity to see the Wallabies (the national side) in action. The Aussies are acclaimed for combining the best of the combative spirit with a creative flourish that can make the game a joy.

At club level, Rugby Union projects a social spirit often lacking in the professional codes. Compared with League, the game has a "silver-tail" (upper-crust) image based partly on its strength in the universities and private schools. The "flying Ella brothers" of the 1970s were a contradiction to the class rule, three gifted Aboriginal athletes from Sydney's inner southern suburbs who all wound up wearing the gold shirts of the Australian team. Mark, the most disciplined of the three, captained both his club and his country. His home club was Randwick, known internationally as one of the world's finest – plundering successive Sydney premierships in a style that has earned its teams the title of the "Galloping Greens".

Great individualists

Many of Australia's greatest sports heroes have been loners. The 1950s and '60s brought forward a rash of tennis talents, including Rod Laver, John Newcombe, Evonne Goolagong-Cawley and Pat Cash. More recently, world-famous golfers have included Bruce Devlin, Graham Marsh, Peter Thomson, Jan Stephenson and Greg Norman. Johnny Famechon, Lionel Rose, Jimmy Carruthers, Jeff Fenech and Jeff Harding punched portholes in the fabric of world boxing. The spartan long-distance runners include Herb Elliot, Robert de Castella, Steve Monaghetti and world triathlon champion Michellie Jones.

But it has been those sports which pit the individual against the elements which have brought out the best in Australians. With such a vast coastline and fine summers, it's not surprising that swimming has been a top sport: kids are tossed into the pool almost as soon as they can walk. In the 1950s, Dawn Fraser became Australia's darling as much for her cheeky anti-establishment attitude as her victories. In the 1970s, Shane Gould followed in her wake, with a slew of Olympic medals. Australia's latest swimming hero is Ian Thorpe, who won three gold and two silver medals in the 2000 Olympics, and in 2003 became the first swimmer ever to win three consecutive world titles in one event, the 400 metres freestyle.

Aussies have ruled international surfing almost since its inception as a competitive sport, with Mark Richards' four world titles marking him as the greatest-ever competition surfer. Names like Nat Young and Tom Carroll have permanent niches in a notional "surfing hall of fame". In surf lifesaving, nobody has epito-

mised the breed better than multiple Iron Man champions Grant Kenny and Trevor Hendy, the former also an athlete of Olympic calibre in kayaking. Australia has some of the world's best gliding conditions, so it's not surprising that Ingo Renner and Brad Edwards have been sailplane world champions. Hang gliding and sailboarding are two relatively new sports in which Aussies have also excelled.

Australian motor racing has produced Formula One world champions in Jack Brabham (three times winner) and Alan Jones, plus motorcycle champs Wayne Gardner, Daryl Beattie and Michael Doohan. Yet the real local heroes of the

HIGH STANDARDS

In the Olympic Games of 1992 and 1996 Australia raised its tally of gold and silver medals to levels that hadn't been recorded since the heady days of the 1950s. In Sydney 2000 Australia achieved its greatest medal haul yet, with 16 golds.

To maintain sporting standards, and to bring Australia in line with modern coaching, psychology and medical techniques, the Australian Institute of Sport was established in Canberra. The AIS caters for athletes from a wide range of sports, taking students on either a part-time or a full-time basis.

LEFT: taking a curve at the Australian Formula One Grand Prix in Melbourne. **RIGHT:** shiny, happy tennis fan at the Australian Open.

track are the touring car drivers. The class attracts heavy sponsorship and wide television coverage for its championship series, the highlight of which is the Bathurst 1000 held in October, an endurance event that attracts an international field of drivers. The Formula 1 Grand Prix is held on Melbourne's Albert Park circuit in early March.

Basketball has also made a run on the public imagination and its hip pocket. The National Basketball League has bolstered club standards and established the national team's rating in the world's top 10. The NBL has also rocked the local cradle by restricting the intake of imported

players per team. As a result, basketball has earned itself a clean administrative image which is the envy of other sports.

The history of soccer in Australia bears little comparison to other forms of football. The game first kicked off more than a century ago among earnest British migrants, then more or less stagnated until post-World War II, with the arrival of migrants from Southern Europe. Now most clubs in the National Soccer League are dominated by players from the Italian, Greek, Croatian, Slavic, Maltese, Dutch and Macedonian communities. Australia's national team, the Socceroos, continue to edge their way up the international ladder.

A nation of punters

It's often said that Aussies would gamble on just about anything – including which of two flies crawling up a wall would reach the top first. All year round, the punter can risk money on horse, harness or greyhound racing, but there's only one race in the year that captures the imagination of all and puts millions of dollars through the bags of bookmakers and the agencies of the Totalizator Agency Board (TAB). That race is the Melbourne Cup.

At 3.30pm Melbourne time on the first Tuesday in November, the whole of Australia stops for the running of this classic horse race. The (3,200-metre) two-mile event has become an international thoroughbred classic since it was first held at Melbourne's Flemington course in 1861. No other race, including the Kentucky Derby and the English Derby, exercises so strong a hold on the public. Only the most miserable wowsers (killjoys) refuse to have a punt on the Melbourne Cup, or at least go in a betting "sweep". It's a public holiday in Victoria, and even the process of government is suspended so that the nation's decision-makers can watch the live telecast.

The Cup has been dominated by horses bred in New Zealand, with perhaps the most famous being the mighty Phar Lap. The "Red Terror", as he was known, was Australasia's greatest racehorse, and included, among his greatest wins, the 1930 Cup. He started 51 times for 37 wins, his last being a record time in the Aguas Caliente Handicap in America.

Phar Lap died under mysterious circumstances soon after and, although an autopsy failed to reveal the cause of death, it was widely believed

STARS OF THE TURF

Australia's greatest jockey was George Moore, whose career stretched over 22 seasons; he rode 2,278 winners in seven different countries. In 1967 he went to England and won the first three classics of the season – the 1,000 Guineas, the 2,000 Guineas and the Derby. Ironically, he never won a Melbourne Cup.

Besides the "Red Terror", Phar Lap, other horses who have retained the affection of Australian punters are the great Kingston Town, Manikato (who died in 1984 and is buried at Moonee Valley racecourse), the gutsy grey Gunsynd, and Luskin Star.

that he was poisoned by "the Yanks". Phar Lap became a symbol of hope and courage in Depression-hit Australia. His heart was 1½ times the size of a normal thoroughbred's, and veterinary surgeons claimed that this was the explanation for his strength and valour. The expression "a heart as big as Phar Lap" remains an Australian accolade for a human or animal with more than its share of courage.

Breeding and betting

The Australian thoroughbred industry is one of the world's most sophisticated. International owner-breeder Robert Sangster rates Australian

to relieve the punter of cash; and if you have a phone account, you can take on the TAB without having to step outside your front door.

The real punter, of course, goes to the track and takes on the bookmakers. The "track" could mean a night harness meeting at Sydney's Harold Park, a country greyhound venue, or something as exotically Australian as the Birdsville Picnic Races; one of many country horse races, this is held every September in the utterly remote Outback town of Birdsville in Queensland; overnight the population leaps from 30 to 3,000 for the event, with many spectators arriving by light planes from all over Australia to watch.

brood mares among his best stock and bases part of his racing empire on the Australian racing calendar, which operates in opposite seasons to that of the Northern Hemisphere.

Capital city racetracks are superbly planned and appointed, offering a wide range of on-course betting. There are no private betting shops in Australia – although illegal or starting price (SP) bookmakers run flourishing telephone services. The TAB is the national agency and offers a multiplicity of computerised ways

At the racetrack you'll observe a different slice of Australiana. It's big on brash and cash and thrives on a level of street savvy you will not encounter anywhere else. At Sydney's Royal Randwick or Melbourne's Flemington, the atmosphere on race day is electric, regardless of whether you've wagered five bucks or fifty grand. Here the colourful character is commonplace and the battle of wits with the bookmakers is never-ending. The sight of thoroughbred horseflesh parading among the manicured lawns and gardens, jockeys in their brilliant silks and the well-shod punters in the latest fashions makes a trip to the races an exhilarating day out. ❑

LEFT: Australasia's most famous racehorse, the New Zealand-born Phar Lap. **ABOVE:** taking on the bookies at Melbourne's Flemington Racetrack.

MODERN AUSTRALIAN CUISINE

It took a long time to happen, but food in Australia is now distinguished for its quality, imagination and a truly multinational diversity

Not so long ago, the term "Australian cuisine" conjured grisly images of meat pies, boiled beef, Vegemite sandwiches and sausage rolls. Then, almost out of the blue, Australia transformed itself into a paradise for foodies (antipodean gourmands). Few places in the world have restaurants that can compare with

the variety, quality and sheer inventiveness of Australian ones. From formal dining rooms to tiny beachside cafés, creations such as "seared kangaroo fillet with wilted beetroot greens and roasted onion" pop up on menus; even the most basic corner diners, which once served up hamburgers and chips, dish up focaccias with fresh King Island cheeses and exotic fruits.

In fact, the culinary art in Australia has emerged as possibly the most adventurous in the world. Each capital city has seen a swarm of new restaurants within the genre "Modern Australian" cuisine, with inventive chefs at the helm and an audience of willing epicures at the ready.

This culinary renaissance is due to two factors: the wealth of superlative Australian produce – including native foods – and the plethora of international cuisines brought to Australia by its immigrants, in particular, those from Asia. The mix of traditional flavours from around the world has provided an astonishing flurry of innovation.

Slow start

But the Australian palate, like the nation, is relatively young, and the current sophistication follows a bleak culinary history. The early settlers struggled to maintain their stolid British or Irish diets, subsisting on salted meats – either roasted, stewed or baked into pies. Various early recipes indicate that native animals were eaten but, apart from kangaroo (whose tails make a fine soup), were rarely appreciated. The unfamiliar harshness of the Australian bush bred tough bellies used to tinned beef and damper (the most basic bread of flour, water and a pinch of salt).

During the Gold Rush days of the 1850s, Chinese immigrants recognised the potential for cultivation and grew a great variety of herbs and vegetables (on some occasions, their industry saved white mining camps from starvation). Even the tiniest country town still has its Chinese restaurant, which for decades saved the citizens from complete culinary deprivation.

Even by the 1960s, the only things approaching an Australian cuisine were a couple of bizarre confectioneries – pavlova (meringue pie shell filled with fruit and cream) and lamingtons (sponge cubes covered with chocolate and coconut). Of course, there was always Vegemite – the black, salty yeast spread that most Aussies were weaned on, abhorred by most others – but this hardly made up a culinary identity. Thanks to the climate, the "barbie" (barbecue) did become an Australian institution, but English roast dinners were turned out every Sunday; and on Christmas Day, in steaming hot summers, the hot roast turkey graced every table. Yet even then local fruits and vegetables might be slipped into the meal, to leaven the heavy Anglo mix.

From famine to feast

Today, the acknowledged basis of Australian cuisine is the quality of its ingredients. Aussies were slow to recognise the wealth of seafood in their tropical waters, but now a range of fresh fish is on every menu. Small farms devote themselves to gourmet beef and poultry, while the quality of everyday vegetables tends to be better than anything grown on organic farms in Europe or the United States. And far from pining for imports of French cheese, Greek olives

HARD TIMES

An early settlers' recipe for galah (cockatoo) soup: "Place galah and large stone in pot. Bring to boil. When stone is tender, discard galah and serve."

succulent reef fish, mudcrabs and Moreton Bay Bugs (shellfish, not insects). The Northern Territory can add the white-fleshed barramundi and Mangrove Jack to the list of tropical fish, while in Darwin, buffalo and crocodile are regularly served as steaks and burgers. New South Wales has Hunter Valley wines, Balmain Bugs and perfect Sydney rock oysters (the acknowledged top of the oyster line). Victoria produces some of the tenderest meats, such as Gippsland beef and Meredith lamb, Mallee squab and corn-

or Italian wine, for example, Australians are now producing their own – and often finding the results to be of superior standard.

Like Italy and France, Australia can be divided into regions that are known for particular produce: King Island cream, Sydney rock oysters, Bowen mangoes, Coffin Bay scallops, Tasmanian salmon, Illabo milk-fed lamb. Each state has its acknowledged specialities, which travellers should take advantage of. Tropical Queensland produces a wealth of exotic fruits (try Bowen mangoes and papaya in season),

LEFT: Asian cooking has made an impact on Australia.
ABOVE: Sydney's world-famous rock oysters.

fed chicken. Tasmania is one of the least polluted corners of the globe, and has gained national attention for its salmon, trout, cheeses, oysters and raspberries. South Australia is home to the Barossa Valley wine industry, Coffin Bay scallops, olive oils, tuna and cultivated native foods. Finally, Western Australia has received rave reviews for its superb new wines from the south-west and for goat cheeses.

The massive migration from Mediterranean countries after World War II made the first real dent on Australia's monolithic Anglo-Saxon or Celtic palate. Italians in particular helped revolutionise cooking, introducing wary Aussies to the wonders of pasta, garlic and olive oil. Today, each capital city has its concentration of Italian restaurants – Melbourne's Lygon Street and Sydney's Leichardt being the most famous – serving authentic, well-priced food. Meanwhile, classic French methods became the undisputed basis of fine cooking.

This was only the beginning. The extension of immigration in the 1970s added myriad new cuisines. The great "melting pot" – or perhaps more appropriately "salad bowl" – of Australian society meant that restaurants were suddenly opened by Lebanese, Turkish, Balkan, Hungarian and Spanish chefs. But the biggest impact by far has been made by the Asians.

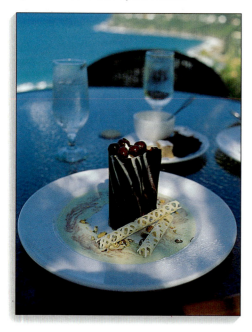

Regional Chinese, Thai, Vietnamese, Japanese and Indian restaurants are now Australia's biggest success stories, with Korean, Sri Lankan, Singaporean and Indonesian cuisines waiting in the wings. Every capital city offers pristine teppanyaki Japanese dining rooms, and take-away lakhsa stalls. Singapore-style "food courts" have sprung up everywhere; even local supermarkets now stock the required pastes and condiments for everyone's favourite Thai or Indian dish.

Not that Australia has tossed off its British heritage altogether – just spruced it up a bit. Your fish 'n' chips might still come in folded newspaper, but inside is the freshest grilled barramundi instead of battered shark. And although pies 'n' peas are now thankfully low on the food chain, you can still get a version at the occasional retro-chic diner.

Towards a modern cuisine

With the sudden wealth of new ingredients from all quarters – including "bush tucker" *(see facing page)* – enterprising chefs in the 1990s proceeded to defy the rules by mixing flavours from completely different ethnic traditions. Modern Australian cuisine was born, and names like "Pacific Rim" and "fusion" are bandied with ease.

Potent Asian flavours such as lemongrass, coriander, chilli and cardamom can be added to many essentially European dishes. By the same token, a Modern Asian cuisine has emerged as Asian chefs substitute traditional ingredients for unusual local ones: Cantonese stir-fried kangaroo meat, perhaps, or barramundi in a Thai green curry. And with the added options from the Mediterranean, young Australian chefs are currently afire with their own powers of invention, turning out dishes like:

◆ Angel-hair pasta with Balmain Bugs, prawns and lime mascarpone
◆ Ocean-trout tartare on potato rösti with wasabi
◆ Kangaroo tenderloin and emu fillet with bush-tomato chutney, yam (sweet potato) pancake and native pepperleaf glaze
◆ Tandoori marinated buffalo fillet with curried spinach and beetroot relish and a roasted pear and saffron polenta
◆ Schnapps and star anise-cured Mangrove Jack with basil aioli
◆ Pan-fried marlin with olive and caper ratatouille.

Some young chefs have acquired celebrity status, and restaurants' fortunes rise and fall depending on which big name is currently in the kitchen. These are fickle times, so chefs will move from place to place as fast as their powers of transformation can take them.

Meanwhile, the Australian dining public has become increasingly adventurous – experimenting at home, and openly demanding to be surprised and titillated at restaurants. Chefs are often struggling to keep up with the challenge, so not all the unique combinations are successful. But there's always another meal.   ❑

LEFT: imaginative dessert at a Whale Beach eatery.

Bush Tucker

In one of Sydney's finest restaurants, you may come across a dish called "Anabaroo, Mango and Burrawong Soup". It's a blend of three foods from the Northern Territory: water buffalo, roasted in an elastic net to keep the high water-content meat intact; the tropical mango; and burrawong, a native nut that was first mentioned in the journals of the 19th-century Outback explorer Ludwig Leichardt.

Next on the menu might be reef fish served in a tart sauce of green billyoat plum – an Aussie fruit found by researchers to have 5,000 times the vitamin C content of an orange per gram. Or quandong-rowbumba – a duck cooked in a sauce made from the South Australian peach quandong, orange extract and brandy. And you may start off with emu pâté, smoked possum or witchetty grubs...

It's all part of the new Australian fascination with "bush tucker" – or, in its more gourmet incarnation, "native cuisine". Restaurants are now merrily discovering ingredients from the great storehouse of the Outback and mixing them with European and Asian traditions.

Of course, Aborigines have been using the same ingredients for 50,000 years. Europeans first tasted many Aboriginal recipes in the earliest colonial days, when the members of the First Fleet in Sydney were on the brink of starvation, waiting for food from Britain. Some settlers turned to Aborigines for help, and learned ways of surviving in the bush. But once the supply lines were established to the Mother Country again, most settlers turned back to their porridge and stodge.

Only the bushmen on the frontiers of settlement kept up the cooking traditions using native Australian materials – at least up to World War II, when supermarkets and frozen foods made it to the Outback. Even in the 1930s, a cookbook written by an Englishwoman included recipes using everything from possum and rosella to kangaroo meat.

Until the early 1990s, the only native plant food harvested commercially was the macadamia nut (which even most Australians thought was Hawaiian). The native spinach, or samphire, had been taken back to Europe by Sir Joseph Banks on Captain Cook's voyage in 1770 and was common in French cooking – but could not be found in the markets of its homeland.

Today it is known that, of Australia's 20,000 plant species, some 20 percent are edible. A vast untapped reserve of native flora now turns up on menus: riberries, bunya nuts, wild rosellas, Kakadu plums, lilipili, bush tomatoes. New herbs include native pepperleaf, aniseed myrtle and wattle seed – a flavouring agent for ice cream and cakes.

Although some three million kangaroos are shot each year in the Outback, the sale of kangaroo meat was only recently legalised in Australia (despite the fact that for years it was exported to Europe and the United States). It has become extremely popular, partly because of its low fat content: the flesh can be as low as 1 percent fat,

compared with 25 percent in marbled red meat.

Along with crocodile, possum and emu, the list of new ingredients includes baby eels, freshwater yabbies and witchetty grubs. The latter are often pan-fried and served on a bed of alfalfa sprouts, in a curved Aboriginal plate *(coolamon)*. The correct way to eat the grub is by hand, holding the head between the fingers. It tastes like a cross between prawns, peanuts, pork crackling and chicken skin.

Few other dishes are quite so exotic as witchetty grubs. In fact, most dishes are based on familiar culinary ground – seducing nervous palates with more Western, time-honoured favourites. Which is why your emu pâté will probably come with a compote of mango, and lamb, barramundi and prawns still feature prominently on the food line-up. ❑

RIGHT: locally grown produce on the menu in an Alice Springs diner, Northern Territory.

MORE THAN 200 YEARS OF WINEMAKING

It's only comparatively recently that they have attracted international attention, but Australians have been making wine for a long time

Australia's wine industry dates back to the First Fleet, which arrived in Sydney Cove in January 1788 bearing grape vines from the Cape of Good Hope and convicts from Britain. The vineyards spread from Sydney and today grapes are grown and wine is made in all six States and two Territories. Most of the European varieties are grown by some 7,000 grapegrowers in 158,549 hectares (352,331 acres) of vineyards. Riesling, Chardonnay and Semillon are the most favoured white varieties; reds include Cabernet Sauvignon, Shiraz and Pinot Noir. Climatic conditions provide excellent ripening, with an abundance of flavour and comparatively high alcohol levels.

Winemakers use stainless steel and temperature control to retain flavour and purity and maintain consistency. Imported oak, mainly American and European, is used for dry reds and some dry whites for maturation. The harvest is from January to May.

Australian wine exports reached a staggering $2.4 billion in 2003, led by surging demand from the USA. There are now 1,625 wineries in Australia, many of them small family operations. But around 80 percent of all wine production comes from the Big Four conglomerates – Southcorp Wines, which owns Penfold, Lindeman, Seppelt, Leo Buring and Rouge Homme brands; BRL-Hardy, a public company controlling Chateau Reynella, Leasingham, Berri, Renmano and Hardy's; Orlando Wyndham, owned by France's Pernod Ricard; and Mildara Blass (owned by Fosters Brewing) with Mildara, Wolf Blass and Rothbury Estate.

◁ **WHERE TO GET A DRINK**
The Hunter Valley's wineries, 160 km (100 miles) from Sydney, are popular with tourists.

▷ **HIGHER AND COOLER**
Mountadam's vineyards are at High Eden, several hundred metres above the Barossa Valley, SA. The purple flowers are Salvation Jane – a weed.

△ **NO WOOD, NO GOOD**
The ancient art of coopering is alive in the Barossa Valley. Penfolds' chief cooper Bob Butler uses fire to shape staves of American oak.

▽ **SUNSHINE IN A BARREL**
Clare Valley winemaker Neil Pike takes a sample of red wine. Australian winemakers put a lot of time into individual barrel selection and blending.

▷ **EXPORT DEMAND**
Demand for Australian wines has been growing so fast that many winemakers have had trouble coping. Shiraz (known as Syrah when it's grown in France's Rhone Valley) is the most popular red wine grape, and is the variety used in Penfolds famous Grange.

FLYING WINEMAKERS

Australia's vintage takes place at the opposite end of the year to the European and North American harvests – which allows talented Australian winemakers to visit the northern hemisphere's winemaking areas to share their new-found expertise.

High temperatures during the Australian summer, when the grapes are ripening, are both a blessing and a problem. The sunshine means higher sugar levels, which in turn translate into high alcohol content and plenty of ripe flavours in the finished wines. But hot weather during the December–February period can also stress and damage ripening grapes. Many big vineyards are harvested by machines at night, so that the fruit can be taken to the crusher while cool.

Aussie winemakers have had to develop special skills in high-technology wineries – such as Lindeman's big Karadoc winery in Victoria (above) – to keep ferments under control and retain the high fruit levels of their wines. Many of these techniques are now being exported, mainly to France, Italy and Spain, by Australians (nicknamed "flying winemakers") during the European vintage.

◁ **FROM BUST TO BOOM**
Barrel cellars at Yeringberg winery in the Yarra Valley, east of Melbourne. The winery was established in 1862, when the area was enjoying a wine boom. Tragedy struck a few decades later when the vine louse Phylloxera, imported from Europe, nearly destroyed the Victorian wine industry. Today Victorian wine is flourishing again.

FORTIFICATIONS
rels of sherry age at Morris Wines, herglen, Victoria. Morris is e of the best producers of tified wines, including azing muscats. Although Austrailan industry was nded on fortified es, they have ned in popularity.

UNIQUE FLORA AND FAUNA

Not surprisingly in a continent that has been so remote for so long, Australia has a range of plants and animals that are found nowhere else on earth

Australia's splendid isolation has had a profound effect on the evolution of animals and plants in the southern continent. The sheer age of the landmass and its division by sea from other continents allowed Nature to have her way, independent of what was happening elsewhere. Consequently, Australian wildlife took on a unique character that prospered until the arrival of the white man and the onset of the technological age.

There are no better examples than the Australian mammals. Mammals are warm-blooded and furred, and almost all give birth to their young alive and suckle them. There are three groups: monotremes, marsupials and placentals. In Australia, marsupials are by far the most prominent. Their young are born not fully developed, and so are kept securely in a pouch until they are strong enough to move around independently. Kangaroos, possums and wallabies are examples of Australian marsupials.

Monotremes are probably the most exotic type of mammals. Rather than giving birth to live young, they lay eggs. However, they do suckle their young and display many other mammalian traits. The amphibious duck-billed platypus is a monotreme, as is the echidna (also known as the spiny anteater).

The placental group comprises all the familiar large mammals that exist on earth. While they proliferate on most continents, very few examples can be found among the native Australian fauna. The native dog, the dingo, is a member of the placental group but it was only introduced into Australia by Aboriginal immigrants sometime within the past 20,000 years.

Scientists have found examples of marsupials in fossil form in many parts of the world, but Australia provides the only opportunity to study live marsupials in large numbers in their own habitats. Most marsupials are herbivorous, but there are some that include insects, small rep-

tiles or smaller mammals in their diets. The larger members of the carnivorous group are the native "cats" and "wolves".

In fact, these animals have no relation to the cat or dog families but their names do suggest some sort of confusion on the part of the early white settlers who attempted to classify these

SAVING AUSTRALIA

In the second half of the 20th century, the conservation movement in Australia gathered such impetus that the continent's environmental future is starting to look more secure.

Notable victories by the conservationists include the rescue of large sections of the southwest Tasmanian wilderness from the threat of dam construction, the official protection of endangered plants and animal species, restrictions on logging in the shrinking rainforests of the eastern seaboard, and the acceptance by all political parties of the growing power of the conservationist movement.

PRECEDING PAGES: pandanus trees in the Outback. **LEFT:** kangaroos really do box in the wild. **RIGHT:** the dingo arrived with Aborigines comparatively recently.

strange creatures in northern hemisphere terms.

Examples include the Tasmanian devil and the Tasmanian tiger (Thylacine). The latter is a wolf-like carnivorous creature thought to be extinct – except by a few die-hards who occasionally report uncertain sightings in wilderness areas.

The herbivores abound and represent the cuddly postcard image of Australian wildlife. The shy, tree-dwelling koala is an example, as are the many varieties of possum, including

LOCAL RODENTS

When Europeans first landed in Australia there were already more than 50 species of rodent, including fruit bats, rats and mice. They had not evolved on the continent but arrived with earlier immigrants.

times of plenty the kangaroo population increased. However, this fine balance was altered when artificial irrigation of the grasslands created more food for the 'roo troops. While the kangaroos grew in number and competed with sheep and cattle for the available food, farmers sought ways to keep the 'roos off their properties – no small task when you consider a kangaroo's ability to jump fences.

Now licences are issued to professional shooters to cull the

the ringtail and the sugar glider. But undoubtedly the best known are the macropods, or hopping marsupials, such as the kangaroo, wallaby, wallaroo and kangaroo rat. The familiar kangaroo profile is the greatest Australian symbol of them all, which makes foreigners wonder just why some Aussies seem bent on hunting the breed to extinction.

Before the arrival of the white man and his sophisticated agricultural techniques, the kangaroo population was controlled by the climate and environment. In times of drought, female kangaroos intuitively did not come into season, thereby putting restraints on the expansion of the herd. This helped preserve food supplies. In

creatures. Ironically, much of the kangaroo meat finishes up in the food bowls of family pets, a rather pathetic conclusion seeing that the woes of the noble native creature were caused by the introduction of "foreign" animals.

Today, the kangaroo populations are carefully monitored and, although many of the tinier or more specialised species have been steadily losing out to such introduced species as rabbits and cats, there is little risk that the great bounding macropod will be disappearing.

The retiring koala, despite its often misused title, is not a bear but is yet another exotic example of Australia's herbivorous marsupials. Its habit of sleeping openly in the forks of gum trees made it an easy target for hunters seeking its fur. So great was the slaughter that urgent steps were taken to save the koala in the 1920s. This shy marsupial is now completely protected.

The wombat is related to the koala, but instead of making its home up a tree and dining on gum leaves, it uses its powerful digging paws to make burrows under stumps, logs or in creek banks. It lives on roots, leaves and bark.

Reptiles figure prominently in Aboriginal legend and diet, but whites do not hold them in such

THE "SALTIE"

The saltwater crocodile – a fierce and dangerous predator – is found not only in the sea off Australia's north coast, but also far inland in fresh water.

prickly spines. Many city dwellers welcome the presence of the blue-tongued lizard in their gardens. It hunts snails and insects, and while it is not as faithful as a dog, it is cheaper to keep.

Australia has more than its share of frogs and toads, many similar in appearance to those of Europe and North America, and many peculiarly Australian. One type found in the drier climes of central Australia is known to inflate itself with water and burrow underground to survive long, dry periods. Sadly, the most

regard, particularly the venomous snakes such as the taipan, tiger snake, death adder and brown snake. Non-venomous varieties such as the carpet snake and green tree snake abound.

Lizards, ranging from the tiniest of skinks to goannas more than 2 metres (6ft) long, proliferate in Australia. The most exotic is the frill-necked lizard, which has a frock of skin around its neck erected into a broad collar when confronted with danger. It should not be confused with the bearded dragon, named for its mane of

LEFT: koalas in the Lone Pine Sanctuary, Brisbane.
ABOVE: Australia's national bird, the emu.
ABOVE RIGHT: the blue-tongued lizard is found in cities.

infamous amphibian is the Queensland cane toad. This giant was introduced to eradicate a cane parasite but has become such an unwelcome intruder in its own right that environmentalists are searching for ways to eradicate the species. It's yet another example of the destabilising effect that introduced species have had on the local environment.

The Great Barrier Reef is a natural wonderland blessed with numerous fish, shell and polyp species peculiar to Australian waters (*for more on the Reef's ecosystem, see 7s 270–1*). But one doesn't have to go snorkelling in the Reef to sample the coastal wildlife. A scramble over any coastal rock platform will reveal shellfish, starfish, anemones, crabs and even the occasional octopus.

Australia's early explorers were almost as intrigued by the strange birdlife as they were by kangaroos and koalas. Here was a land where the swans were black instead of white, where a relative of the kingfisher that the Aborigines knew as a kookaburra pealed off a manic laugh, and where the great flightless emu could almost outrun a horse. There were elegant magpies who would signal the start of day with their peculiar call, and strutting lyrebirds with their silver tails, exotic mating dances and an ability to mimic the sounds of other animals, including human beings.

On the east coast in particular, flocks of raucous parrots plundered the fruit trees. They included brilliantly plumed rosellas and lorikeets, displaying such colours as suited their precocious personalities.

The eccentric bowerbird builds a structure or bower on which he performs to win the attention of a female. He adorns his court with brightly coloured trinkets (preferably blue) such as stones, glass or objects collected from gardens or houses. The mallee fowl places her eggs under a mound of sand that acts as an incubator. By varying the level of sand, the bird can keep the eggs at a regular temperature according to the heat of the day.

DEADLY SEA CREATURES

The seas around Australia contain several hidden perils. The blue-ringed octopus, a small coastal variety, is known to be extremely venomous, but little has been learned about its toxin. It is not known, either, why it can sometimes be handled without risk but very, very rarely might claim a victim.

And always take heed of any warnings you see about the box jellyfish, another potentially fatal hazard. It swarms in great numbers along northern coastal beaches for six months of the year, making it dangerous to swim in the sea between October and May.

Eagles, hawks, crows and cuckoos of native origin can all be observed. The opening up of the southern continent helped Europeans to map the migratory habits of numerous northern hemisphere species which were known to "fly south for the winter".

The size of the continent and the variety of habitats allow for numerous species of waterfowl. Some were hunted by the early settlers, and development consumed coastal habitats, but protective measures have saved many from the threat of extinction.

Visitors to Australia expecting to see kangaroos bounding through the streets of the cities and koalas scuttling up the nearest telephone pole will be disappointed. Like most wildlife, Aussie animals are generally shy of man. Of course, you can go to any of the city zoos such as Sydney's Taronga Park or the Melbourne Zoo and see most forms of local wildlife from platypus to black snake. If you don't have the time to spend weeks in the bush studying creatures in their natural environment, a suitable compromise is a visit to any of the larger nature reserves that exist on the fringes of the cities. Here, in natural surroundings and often under

PLANT PARADISE

Captain Cook renamed Botany Bay (he originally called it Stingray Harbour Bay) after Joseph Banks's many discoveries there.

The first European to appreciate Australia's unique flora was the great botanist Sir Joseph Banks, who sailed with Cook on the *Endeavour*. Not only was Banks intrigued by the incredible variety of new plant life he encountered, but he and his assistants went to extraordinary lengths to collect samples, to log descriptions and to make detailed drawings of their finds. For Banks, it was a labour of love, and it is fitting that he should hold such an important place in Australian history. The

the guidance of a park ranger, you can observe examples of Australia's wondrous animals.

As for the flora: well, it's almost everywhere. From a stroll through the leafy outer suburbs of Sydney or Melbourne, to a bushwalk in the jarrah forests of Western Australia or a camping trip in the Tasmanian wilderness, you can easily expose your senses to the great Aussie bush. You will find many of the species are those that qualify as rare exotica in Europe or America.

LEFT: a rainbow lorikeet, pretty and precocious.
ABOVE: coastal banksia (one of the many species named after Joseph Banks) on a Fraser Island beach.

eye-catching banksia trees that proliferate along the coastline are sturdy reminders of the botanist's interest.

The range of Australian eucalyptus is immense, ranging from low, stunted, scrub-like bush to the great towering varieties of the highland forests. There are ghost gums, so named because under the light of the moon they appear silvery-white, and rock-hard ironbarks, capable of blunting the toughest timber saws. The name "eucalyptus" includes a very wide range of trees in all climates and terrains.

It is from the gold and green of the acacia, or wattle, that Australia draws its national colours. So hardy is the wattle that it is usually one of the first varieties to rejuvenate after a season of bushfires. In season, wattles bathe the bush in gold with their blossoms.

Unlike the softwood varieties of Europe and North America, most Australian trees have very hard timber. This made clearing the land an extremely arduous task for the early settlers. When the pioneers encountered softer timber, they were often ruthless in their zeal to fell it. The virtual disappearance of cedar from the rainforests of the coastal hinterlands is witness to their efforts.

In Tasmania, the mighty Huon pine was found to be one of the best building timbers in

the world. It is especially prized by boatbuilders. The jarrah forests of south Western Australian are currently under threat from mining and from culling. Jarrah and the tough karri are also superb building timbers, and foresters are exploring ways to guarantee their proliferation by combating a disease called "die-back".

A concerted drive to replant some of the tree life laid waste in the name of agricultural development is currently in process. As shade for stock, protection against soil erosion, enrichers of soil and friends of man, trees are making a comeback.

The Australian deserts might appear to be vast infertile wastes in the dry season, but it only takes a good downpour to turn them into paradises of wild flowers. The seeds can lie dormant in the soil for years, waiting for moisture to bring them to life.

One section of Australia noted for its variety of wildflowers is the southern corner of Western Australia. The area has become so famous that commercial growing of some of the more exotic types has become a minor local industry. The best-known plant of the area is the kangaroo paw, appropriately named for its resemblance to the hind paw of the kangaroo. Among the semi-desert plants is the Sturt desert pea, which proliferates with the slightest hint of moisture.

An understanding of Australia's vast climatic and geographical differences provides an insight into the wealth of plant life. From the tropical growth of northern Queensland's steamy jungles, to the delicate blossoms of New South Wales's cool southern tablelands, there is seemingly no end to the variety of plant life.

There are some types of plant that thrive almost anywhere in Australia, regardless of climate, soil type or mankind's presence. The most abundant of these is the acacia, or wattle. And visitors might note the presence of grass-trees in almost all areas. These are sometimes called "black boys" because of the spear-like vegetation that juts from the centre, often to a height of 5 metres (16 ft).

Like many of the continent's animals, Australian flora has been affected by the introduction of foreign trees, grasses, shrubs, and plants. In some instances these types have flourished unchecked, completely altering the ecological balance of entire regions. However, many city- and country-dwellers are becoming aware of the importance of native plant life.

In the cities, the replanting of native trees has encouraged bird and insect life to return to these areas with the resultant re-germination process for which the birds and the bees are so celebrated. More than 200 years after Joseph Banks went into raptures about this botanical wonderland, teachers are leading Australian children out into the wild to experience and appreciate the beauty and uniqueness of their local wildlife. ❏

LEFT: the grass tree, or "black boy". RIGHT: red river gum trees in the Flinders Ranges National Park.

WILD, WONDERFUL AND ONLY FOUND HERE

Australia has been an island long enough for evolution to take a unique path. The result is a population of strange animals like no other

Few countries on the planet possess a more bizarre and distinctive array of native fauna than Australia. Down Under we can find mammals that lay eggs, rats that eat pythons, spiders that eat birds and crocodiles that eat crocodiles. It's a scenario that is due, of course, to epochs of evolutionary seclusion, Australian species divorced from the world's zoological mainstream.

Australia has mammals so specialised that they occupy their own classification – monotremes. They're the duck-billed platypus and the spiny echidnas who lay eggs to produce offspring, then suckle them from abdominal ducts.

But it's the marsupials that rule the bush – from tiny rodent-like nocturnal hoppers and rabbit-eared bilbies *(pictured above)* to 2-metre (6-ft) tall red kangaroos and subterranean wombats. They all give birth to their tiny young in an embryonic state. Naked and undeveloped, following the scent of its mother's milk, the newborn finds sanctuary in the maternal pouch.

THEN CAME MAN

Marsupials were successful because Australia knows few predators. That was until man arrived about 50,000 years ago. Marsupials were bigger then: the megafauna – kangaroos as big as grizzly bears and rhino-sized wombats – were easy prey for men with spears.

Humankind also imported Australia's first canine – the dingo – which wiped out many species and, in the process, adapted itself to Australia, as did those that came later: the domestic cat, the pig, the fox, the cane toad and even the camel. These imported species are now breeding out of control at the expense of natives. Feral animals today provide Australia with one of its greatest ecological headaches.

△ **MYSTERY DOWN-UNDER**
A blind, burrowing desert-dweller, the marsupial mole swims through the sand, leaving no burrow behind it. The young are nurtured in the pouch – but how they survive once they leave remains a mystery.

▷ **SIDEWINDER**
The southern side-neck tortoise does not draw its neck straight back into its shell but tucks it in sideways.

◁ **TASMANIAN DEVIL**
This noisy, carnivorous marsupial enjoys a ferocious reputation beyond its means. It's unable to kill a rat and even a small dog will scare it off. Extinct on the mainland, it thrives in Tasmania, often venturing into the suburbs.

▽ **MOTHER'S BOY**
The joey of the eastern grey kangaroo lives in its mother's pouch for over a year. It leaves for short spells at nine months, but does not vacate completely until 18 months old. By then the female has produced another joey.

OZ'S NATURAL-BORN KILLERS

Australia is a land where lethal killers abound…or crawl or slither or float or dive. Scorpions hide beneath rocks across the continent, great white sharks devour the occasional abalone diver off South Australia, saltwater crocodiles stalk fishermen (as do box jellyfish) in the Northern Territory, the poisonous blue-ringed octopus waits on the reefs, and the venomous funnel-web spider lurks in the gardens of suburban Sydney.

And as if that weren't enough, Australia possesses more species of venomous snakes than any other country on earth. It is home to 30 varieties of fanged killers – 16 of them, like the stunning copperhead *(pictured above)*, more deadly than the king cobra. The inland taipan takes the prize as the world's deadliest snake: it is 50 times more venomous than the cobra.

This rich reptilian diversity is not limited to the mainland: there are also 32 known varieties of poisonous sea snakes residing in offshore waters.

However, dangerous liaisons between humans and these creatures are rare, with most sightings of killer animals confined to city zoos. When you do encounter them in the wild, most animals prefer escape over confrontation with mankind – a species with an equally lethal reputation.

AGGRESSIVE ARACHNID
The lethal Sydney funnel-web spider, despite its name, is found throughout the eastern coastal region, preying on frogs, insects and lizards.

△ **EGGSTRAORDINARY**
The uniquely Australian duck-billed platypus is an agile swimmer, propelling itself with webbed forefeet. It is found from Queensland to Tasmania, competing with man for its habitat.

▷ **INTERIOR DECORATOR**
To impress its mate, the regent bowerbird builds two high walls of sticks and decorates the floor between with shells, bottletops and colour-coordinated glass.

PLACES

*A detailed guide to the entire country, with principal sites
cross-referenced by number to the maps*

The world's largest island, or its smallest continent – whichever way you look at it, Australia's vastness is inescapable. In area it matches Europe or the continental USA. And, just as a traveller might not plan to journey from London to Moscow or from New York to Los Angeles in a week or two, travel in Oz takes a little time – and some judicious selection.

With only 20 million inhabitants, almost all living in eight major cities, Australia is also one of the world's emptiest corners. Nowhere else is it so easy to escape the crowds as in Australia: there are more than 540 national parks, a dozen World Heritage areas, vast swathes of countryside where you could pitch a tent for six months and never see another soul. Indeed, in much of the Outback the sheer loneliness can be the greatest danger.

The way to see Australia, therefore, is by choosing your destinations thoughtfully, flying across the greatest distances and dipping into the wilderness with care. Almost every international traveller arrives in Sydney – Australia's biggest city and, despite the protestations of rivals Melbourne (the old financial centre) and Canberra (the official seat of government), fast becoming its *de facto* capital. Number two on any list of "greatest hits" is Cairns and the Great Barrier Reef – the world's largest living organism, sprawling along the Queensland coast. Next comes Uluru, or Ayers Rock – the world's largest monolith, looming mysteriously in the middle of the Outback plains. Finally, there's Darwin in the wild, monsoonal "Top End", jumping-off point for the Kakadu, with its Aboriginal carvings, tropical swamps and giant saltwater crocodiles.

These high-profile attractions are so rare and wondrous that the outside world is only now taking a look at the rest of Australia. This book divides the country into its official states and territories – the arbitrary lines set up by British colonial administrators in the 19th century remain the divisions today. In New South Wales, consider a trip beyond Sydney to the Blue Mountains or the northern beaches. Victoria is the most mountainous and rugged state, with the most British flavour. In South Australia, visit the wine-country of the Barossa. Queensland may have the Reef, but it also has the world's oldest rainforests and the wilderness of Cape York. The red-earth Outback is most famous in the Northern Territory, but Western Australia has the breathtaking Kimberley and 3,000 km (1,800 miles) of virtually uninhabited coastline. Or you can pop "overseas" to the island of Tasmania, the most pristine corner of Australia, with the finest bushwalking and the most spectacular ruins of the convict era. ❏

PRECEDING PAGES: the Pinnacles, Nambung National Park, Western Australia; a Pacific surfer catches the wave; Sydney Harbour, seen from McMahons Point. **LEFT:** Weano Gorge in the Hamersley Range National Park, WA.

Australia

0   400 km
0   400 miles

Timor Sea
Melville I.
Gurig N.P.
Bathurst I.
Cartier I.
Darwin
Kakadu N.P.
Adelaide River
Litchfield N.P.
Browse I.
Katherine
Nitme
Wyndham
Kununurra
Kimberley Plateau
Victoria River Downs
KING LEOPOLD RANGES
Derby
Purnululu N.P.
Broome
Windjana Gorge N.P.
Fitzroy Crossing
Halls Creek
Newcast Wate
Port Hedland
Great Sandy Desert
Tanami Desert
Te
Barrow I.
Marble Bar
North
Millstream Chichester N.P.
Exmouth
Wittenoom
Lake MacKay
Territ
Cape Range N.P.
Ashburton
Hamersley N.P.
Newman
Rudall River N.P.
Gibson Desert
MACDONNELL
Tropic of Capricorn
HAMERSLEY RANGE
Lake Disappointment
West MacDonnells N.P.
Lake Amadeus
Spri
Carnarvon
Gascoyne
ROBINSON RANGES
Western
Uluru (Ayers Rock)
867
Dirk Hartog I.
Murchison
Lake Carnegie
Australia
South
Kalbarri N.P.
Meekatharra
Wiluna
Austral
Northampton
Mt. Magnet
Great Victoria Desert
Houtman Abrolhos
Leonora
Geraldton
Nambung N.P.
Moora
Coolgardie
Kalgoorlie
Indian Pacific Railroad
Forrest
Cook
Northam
Perth
Johnston Lakes
Norseman
Nullarbor Plain
Nullarbor N.P.
Eucla
Penong
Fremantle
Cocklebiddy
Strea
Bunbury
Wagin
Cape Arid N.P.
Great Australian Bight
Stirling Range N.P.
C. Leeuwin
Fitzgerald N.P.
Esperance
D'Entrecasteaux N.P.
Albany

INDIAN   OCEAN

SYDNEY AND BEYOND

Map,
page 136

The glittering harbour with its coat-hanger bridge, the pearly sails of the Opera House, the bronzed lifesavers at Bondi Beach… most of the symbols that define Australia are located here

Sydney is where Australian hedonism finds its most spectacular backdrop, a city where leisure has been elevated to an art form. Yet Australia's largest metropolis, with over 4 million people, can still baffle expectations. The natural beauty of the harbour and beaches often stands in stark relief to the man-made landscape: the narrow, traffic-clogged streets, the lacklustre architecture of its inner city, the endless orange-roofed expanse of its suburbia.

To its critics – who mostly live in the traditional rival, Melbourne – Sydney is all glitz, obsessed with superficial show, appearances above substance. But none of this seems to matter to most Sydneysiders, and even less to visitors. The city continually lures the wealthiest, smartest and most artistically talented from the rest of Australia, while real-estate values go through the roof. Everybody wants to live in "the capital of the Pacific Rim" or the "Best Address on Earth", as Sydneysiders modestly think of their home.

Yet few of the world's great cities have had such an unpromising start. On 26 January 1788, a fleet of 11 ships under the command of Captain Arthur Phillip landed a seasick gaggle of male convicts and their jailers – an unsavoury group of naval recruits well schooled in rum, sodomy and the lash – while the local Aborigines let out furious howls and threw stones to drive them away. The officers pitched their tents east of the freshwater Tank Stream at Sydney Cove, the prisoners and their guards to the west (creating a social division that lasts to this day, with the wealthier suburbs of the east versus the have-nots of the west). Two weeks later, the women convicts disembarked with the many children that had been born on the voyage. An extra rum ration was handed out, a violent storm began, and the 736 felons of the young colony – along with not a few of their randy guards – embarked on a drunken orgy.

The site of this Hogarthian display is now ground zero for tourist Sydney: **Circular Quay Ⓐ**. This is the gateway to **Sydney Harbour** and the place where everyone should begin a visit. Ferries, Jetcats, water taxis and tour boats of every stripe plough in and out of its docks, taking passengers up and down the grand waterway of Port Jackson, described by Phillip as "the finest harbour in the world, where a thousand ship of the line may ride with the most perfect security". To get a feel for Sydney, hop on a ferry, take a seat outside and, for the first trip, don't get off at all; all ferries return to the Quay. Breathe in the sea air, and gaze on the sandstone bluffs, the cityscape and Australia's twin symbols of modernity.

First to be constructed was the **Harbour Bridge Ⓑ**. The longest (and widest) single-span bridge in the world, it was erected during the depths of the 1930s Depression as a symbol of hope in the future. It became dubbed the Coathanger, the Toast Rack and the Iron Lung (the latter

LEFT: Port Jackson and Sydney Harbour from the air.
BELOW: the Central Business District.

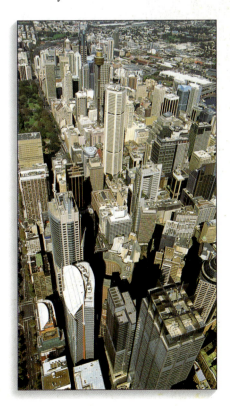

or the number of people given work on its construction, which kept Sydney breath-
ng). These days, despite dire predictions that rust is rotting it away from the inside,
he bridge is still the major link between Sydney's northern and southern suburbs
an underground tunnel provides some less picturesque assistance). The south-
astern pylon on the Harbour Bridge (daily; entrance fee) contains a museum and
iewing platform with superb views of the harbour and city.

The second symbol, begun in 1959, is the **Opera House** ⓒ – without a doubt
ne of the world's most spectacular buildings (or, as art critic Robert Hughes
would have it, "the biggest environmental site-specific sculpture south of the
quator"). It was designed by Jørn Utzon, a Dane, after an international compe-
tion – although nobody at the time quite knew how it would be built. It was the
rst large-scale project to make extensive use of computer technology but, even
o, the construction was fraught with difficulties. Costs escalated. Utzon became
aught up in the petty-minded moneygrubbing of Australian politics, and resigned
disgust in 1966 (he has never returned to Sydney, although he did act as adviser
n a $70-million renovation in 2003). A state lottery raised the necessary cash,
nd by the time the completed building was opened by the Queen in 1973, it had
ost $102 million – 15 times its initial budget. But few have ever complained
bout the price since. The Opera House became an immediate icon for Australia's
ew-found cultural independence. Today, Sydney without it is unthinkable.
Guided one-hour tours daily, every half-hour 8.30am–5pm; entrance fee.)

trolling into the past

part from the docking ferries, Circular Quay is a lively scene, packed with
skers, pedlars and relaxing office workers. Just around the waterline lies the

Map,
page 136

*At the opening of the
Harbour Bridge in
1932, a zealous
right-wing royalist,
Francis Edward de
Groot, rode up on a
horse and cut the
ribbon before the left-
wing premier Jack
Lang had the chance.*

BELOW: Sydney's
spectacular
Opera House.

Cadman's Cottage was built in 1816 to house the crews of the governor's boats, and was occupied from 1827 by John Cadman, a former convict who was boat superintendent.

squat yellow **Museum of Contemporary Art**  (MCA; daily 10am–5pm) whose outdoor café is the ultimate lunch address on a sunny day. Behind begins Sydney's most historic district, known as **The Rocks** ❷ after the sandstone bluffs from which the first convicts cut golden bricks for public buildings (take a look up the **Argyle Cut**, which slices straight through the cliffs – the pick marks are still easily identifiable).

Next to the MCA is the tiny stone **Cadman's Cottage**, believed to be Sydney's oldest building, now housing an information centre. The Argyle Cut passes the **Argyle Centre**, a convict-era storehouse that is now a boutique shopping centre, the **Garrison Church**, and eventually leads up a steep path to **Observatory Hill** ❻. This was originally a fortress for officers in case of a convict uprising; today it is a picnic spot, with fine harbour views. Further towards Millers Point lies a network of narrow streets that have traditionally been home to wharf workers. The **Hero of Waterloo** and **Fortune of War** compete for the honour of being Sydney's oldest pub, with the **Palisades** one of the most atmospheric.

Following the waterline in the opposite direction from the Quay leads you past the Opera House to the **Royal Botanic Gardens** ❼ (daily sunrise–sunset; free), a vast, voluptuous collection of Antipodean flora, including some truly majestic Moreton Bay figs. Hidden amongst the sculpted lakes and exotic fronds is an excellent café-restaurant. From **Mrs Macquarie's Point** ❽, one gazes out at the tiny island of **Fort Denison**.

BELOW RIGHT: old warehouses have become new restaurants.

Paths continue through the gardens to the **Art Gallery of New South Wales** ❾ (Tues–Thur 10am–5pm, Wed 10am–9pm; free). This imposing edifice is crowned with the celestial names of Leonardo da Vinci, Michelangelo, Botticelli and the like, although not one of these artists is actually represented

THE ROCKS

Today the pubs, restaurants and terraces of The Rocks are glossily painted and polished, full of upmarket stores selling Aboriginal art, opals and tourist souvenirs. But until comparatively recently The Rocks was one of Sydney's most squalid and dangerous quarters, a Dickensian warren of warehouses, grog shops and brothels, where the rum was laced with tobacco juice and the larrikin "razor gangs "preyed on the unwary. An outbreak of bubonic plague in 1900 was a particular low-light in The Rocks' sordid history.

The whole area was due to be levelled for redevelopment in the 1970s – but there was fierce resistance from residents and academics, and the project was thwarted when the construction unions, led by activist Jack Mundey, refused to start work.

This was the beginning of the green movement to preserve whatever was atmospheric about Old Sydney.

d in the collection. What the gallery does contain, however, is the finest
rouping of Australian art in the country.

Sydney's **Central Business District** – the "CBD" as many refer to it – is an
ddly anonymous hodge-podge of glass skyscrapers and architectural styles
rom the past two centuries, all squeezed onto a street plan drawn up in Georgian
mes. It is best seen by strolling up Young Street from the Quay, past the 1846
lassical revival **Customs House** (now a bar and restaurant) – evoking the period
•hen Sydney was turning into one of the great imperial ports – and the new
Museum of Sydney ⦿ (daily 9.30am–5pm), which has entertaining sight-and-
ound exhibits from the city's earliest days to today *(see pages 140–1).*

Cut over to Macquarie Street for a view of official Sydney: in quick succession
ome the **State Library** (Mon–Fri 9am–9pm; Sat, Sun 11am–5pm), **Parliament House** ⦿ (Mon–Fri 9am–5pm), **Sydney Mint** and **Hyde Park Barracks**
•. The Barracks now houses one of Sydney's most popular museums (daily
.30am–5pm). Designed in 1817 by convict architect Francis Greenway and
ompleted in 1819, the building was first used to house hundreds of prisoners.
xhibits relating to the convict system include a re-creation of the cramped can-
as-hammock sleeping quarters.

At the end of Macquarie Street lies **Hyde Park**, with the powerful art deco
nzac War Memorial. To the east of the park on College Street stands the
ustralian Museum ⦿ (daily 9.30am–5pm; entrance fee), the oldest (1827)
nd still the largest in the country. It is the foremost showcase of Australian nat-
ral history, and also includes an extensive Aboriginal section.

Cut back across Hyde Park towards Pitt and George streets, the two main ar-
ries of the CBD. The controversial needle of **Sydney Tower** ⦿ is regarded as a

Map,
page 136

*You can spend the
night in Hyde Park
Barracks, sleeping
on a hammock in the
dormitories built
for transported
convicts. For details
of bed and breakfast
convict-style, call
(02) 9223 8922.*

BELOW: Fort Denison
was built during the
Crimean War to
defend Sydney
against Russia.

SYDNEY ON DISPLAY

From the depths of archaeology and shipwrecks to the heights of modern aviation and architecture, Sydney's museums offer a range of experiences both traditional and contemporary

Although it's built on the site of Australia's oldest building – the first Government House – the experience offered by the Museum of Sydney (opened 1995) is thoroughly modern in its exploration of Sydney life. You can still look down into the remains of Governor Arthur Phillip's 1788 house, but state-of-the-art technology is a key feature. Hologram-like ghosts speak to you of colonial times, and a 33-screen video display and soundtrack delivers towering vistas of Sydney's natural environment. The culture of the region's indigenous people, the Eora, is widely recognised, and the museum also tells stories of trade, art, architecture and everyday life – but without relying on boring interpretive panels. Instead, each exhibit is accompanied by excerpts from private journals and literary works, to encourage you to make your own connections with Sydney's rich character.

THE CALL OF THE SEA

For a more traditional museum experience, navigate around the National Maritime Museum at Darling Harbour. Designed by Sydney architect Phillip Cox to resemble billowing sails, the museum charts the relationship Australians have had with the sea over 50,000 years. It contains a permanent Aboriginal gallery (Merana Eora Nora) and also covers early European exploration, trade, Australia's naval history, immigration, sport and leisure. You can see the America's Cup-winning yacht Australia II, a naval destroyer and the world's fastest boat, among many others.

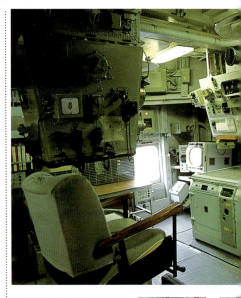

△ **MISSION CONTROL**
The operations room, hub of navigation and defence on board *HMAS Vampire* ("The Bat"). Decommissioned in 1986 after 27 years' service, the destroyer is docked at the Maritime Museum.

▷ **SILENT SAFEGUARD**
The uncrewed *Carpentaria* served as a lightship in the Gulf of Carpentaria for most of its working life before finding a new home in Darling Harbour in 1991.

▷ **ASTOUNDING EXHIBITS**
These Crazy Crooners, in a Museum of Sydney exhibit on city sights, are from an early Lunar Park amusement game.

POWER TO THE PEOPLE

Australia's largest and most popular museum, the Powerhouse, contains more than 30,000 objects in 25 galleries on the themes of science, technology, decorative arts and social history. Since opening in 1988 on the site of the old Ultimo power station, it has become home to one of the country's largest transport collections: visitors can travel in time from the industrial revolution to the frontiers of space, through exhibits that include 12 operating steam engines and a life-size model of NASA's space habitation module.

Some of the museum's rare decorative art work includes Thomas Hope's Egyptian suite (*circa* 1800), a stunning Wedgwood collection and a model of the Strasbourg clock. There are also impressive recreations of a bush hut and the interior of a country pub.

For a more hands-on experience, children and adults alike are encouraged to sample more than 100 interactive demonstrations on topics as diverse as the chemistry of smell, lace-making and computer animation.

◁ **SHADOWS OF TIME**
The Edge of the Trees sculpture outside the Musuem of Sydney represents human memory and experience, drawing on Eora culture and the many layers of Sydney occupation since 1788.

△ **COMMERCE COLLECTION**
The Trade Wall in the Museum of Sydney maps the varied items available in the 1830s and today, from Malayan raisins and New Zealand manganese to Turkish figs and West Indian rum.

◁ **SUBMARINE'S SOUL**
Surfacing and diving commands were executed here in the control room of the Russian submarine *Foxtrot*, on temporary display at the Maritime Museum. Visitors could step through its cramped interior and hear authentic Russian commands.

▷ **ANCIENT MARINER**
The 180-year-old giant wooden figurehead from the battleship *HMS Nelson* passed from the Royal Navy to the Victorian Colonial Navy to the Royal Australian Navy, and was restored in 1988 for display in the National Maritime Museum.

phallic eyesore by many locals, but it has great views from the summit, plus th inevitable revolving restaurant. Covering an entire city block is the **Quee Victoria Building** 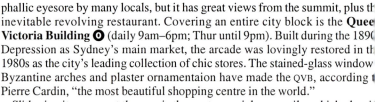 (daily 9am–6pm; Thur until 9pm). Built during the 189(Depression as Sydney's main market, the arcade was lovingly restored in th 1980s as the city's leading collection of chic stores. The stained-glass window Byzantine arches and plaster ornamentaion have made the QVB, according t Pierre Cardin, "the most beautiful shopping centre in the world."

Slithering its way past the QVB is the controversial monorail – which, despit protests that it turns Sydney into a Disneyland, and promises by politicians that will be torn down, shows no sign of slowing. This is the easiest way to get to **Dar ling Harbour**, largest of the city's modern developments. In the 1800s, this wa the "back door" to Sydney, where most trading ships docked. It is now a shiny an touristy collection of shops and restaurants, with a **Maritime Museum** 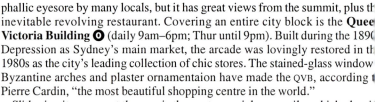 (dai 9.30am–5pm; *see pages 140–1*), **Aquarium** 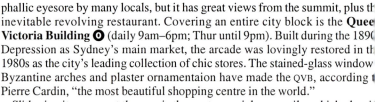 (daily 9.30am–7pm; entrance fee **Exhibition Centre** and **Chinese Garden** thrown in for good measure.

Next stop on the monorail leads to the **Powerhouse Museum** 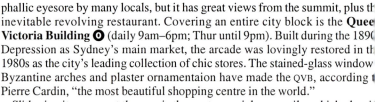 (dail 10am–5pm; entrance fee), a huge space devoted to science and technology, wit lots of interactive displays (*see pages 140–1*). From there, it is a short stroll bac into Sydney's **Chinatown** 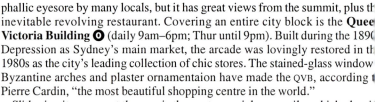, with its wall-to-wall Asian food.

Away from the centre

In many ways, it is the assortment of "inner-city suburbs" (as they are oddl called) that show Sydney at its most genuine. In the late 19th century, row afte row of terraced houses were thrown up as cheap accommodation for workers usually with small gardens, tight porches and elaborate iron-lace decoration In the early 20th century several families at a tim would squeeze into these places, and as soon as the could most moved out to the more spacious outer sub urbs in search of the Aussie dream. But from the 197C gentrification began apace, turning many dismal old ad dresses into the very height of fashionable living.

In the inner west lies **Glebe** 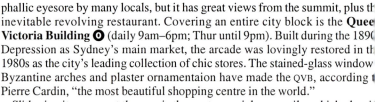, whose main thor oughfare, Glebe Point Road, is now lined with boutique and cafés – many catering to students and academic from the nearby **University of Sydney**, a leafy have which was built in a self-conscious Oxbridge style. Har bourside **Balmain** was once the raunchiest of working class suburbs, with industrial dockworks and 41 pubs one for every 366 residents. There are still 24 pubs, bu the leafy ambience is decidedly more upmarket. It ca be reached by regular ferry from the Quay, and is a ideal spot for a Sunday stroll (the 19th-century wate front residences are particularly impressive – they fea tured in Peter Carey's novel *Oscar and Lucinda*).

The inner east is more of a mixed bag. In Victoria times, **Kings Cross** 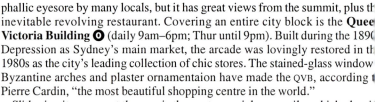 was an elegant, tree-lined sub urb; in the 1920s and 1930s "The Cross" was Sydney' bohemian mecca, but the Vietnam War and the dru boom turned it into the city's sleazy red-light strip. Th recent addition of a horde of backpackers' hostels ha hardly lifted the atmosphere. A jaunt up **Darlinghurs Road** late on a Friday and Saturday night past th smack-addled prostitutes, drunken yobbos, cheap stri

TIP

Duty-free and tax-free shopping can save you up to 30 percent on jewellery, watches, electrical goods, alcohol, etc. Look for the duty-free shops in central Sydney, and be prepared to show your passport and onward ticket.

BELOW: chic shopping in the Queen Victoria Building.

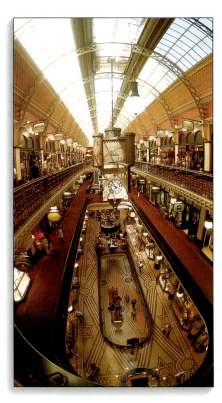

ints (with mottos like "point yer erection in our direction") and fast-food
rlours is without doubt Sydney's least attractive tradition. For a change of
ce, down **William Street**, hordes of transvestites cluster outside car deal-
ships. Yet, curiously, to either side of these promenades lie some of Syd-
y's most delightful streets. **Victoria Street**, in particular, has turned into a
ic centre for fashion.

Running out to the eastern suburbs, **Oxford Street** has become another cru-
al promenade. It begins in the suburb of Darlinghurst, now the centre of Syd-
y's gay culture, a thriving society that has outstripped San Francisco's in
ze and energy. This is the Antipodean version of New York's East Village,
here you'll find the hippest bars, cheapest restaurants, coolest attitudes and
ost fashionable haircuts. It's also the epicentre of Sydney's gay scene. Every
bruary, the **Sydney Gay and Lesbian Mardi Gras** lures hundreds of thou-
nds of Sydneysiders from all corners of society to watch a flamboyant parade
million more Aussies catch it on TV). In this tolerant city, the Lord Mayor
d MPs make sure they're in on the act, and even the climactic party – ticket-
ly, for 17,000 revellers – is a respected institution.

As Oxford Street enters **Paddington** ❸ it becomes more self-consciously
endy. The terraced houses here are the most impressive in Sydney, the iron-
ce more intricate, the back streets the most leafy and picturesque. Tiny art gal-
ries crop up next to ritzy cafés, friendly pubs and expensive furniture stores.
'addo" is at its best on a Saturday, when the **Paddington Bazaar**, Sydney's
dest market, sets up in the grounds of the Uniting Church. Half of Sydney
ems to turn up in search of bargain clothes from young designers, hand-made
wellery or objets d'art.

Maps,
pages
136 & 146

*Sydney's Gay and
Lesbian Mardi Gras
culminates in a
spectacular
sequinned parade in
early February.*

BELOW: the terraced
houses of "Paddo".

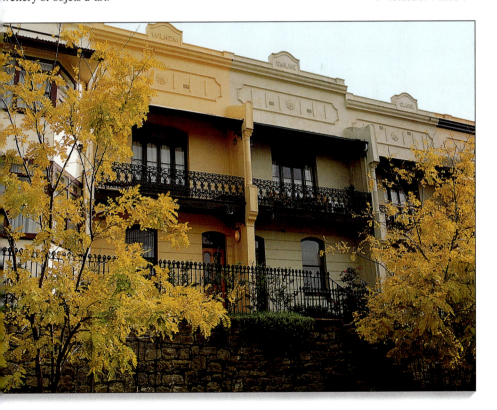

Harbour-hopping

Sydney's green-and-yellow harbour ferries are perhaps the world's most pleasant form of commuter transport, and should be taken whenever possible. A surprising amount of the city can be seen by hopping from wharf to wharf.

A five-minute ride directly opposite Circular Quay (the main ferry terminal) leads to the North Shore suburb of **Kirribilli**, where the Prime Minister and Governor-General have official residences (and both are known to pop in to the legendary Kirribilli fish-and-chip shop for a meal beneath the Bridge pylons).

On the other side of the Bridge, **McMahons Point** is held to have the best view in Sydney (the Opera House is framed beneath the Bridge); running up to North Sydney, **Blues Point Road** is a string of cafés much favoured by yuppies, ostentatiously barking into their mobile phones.

Only slightly longer is the ride to **Cremorne Point**, a dramatic promontory with a leafy harbourside walk to Mosman (considered by aficionados to be one of the best hikes in Sydney), where a ferry can be caught back to the Quay.

Also accessible by ferry is **Taronga Park Zoo** (daily 9am–5pm). Surrounded by virgin bush, this must be one of the most beautiful zoo sites on earth (taronga is an Aboriginal word for "view across the water"). There are more than 5,000 animals in the collection, including the full panoply of local critters (this is your best chance for seeing a platypus, for example, and many a snake that you would rather not encounter in the wild). In summer, classical, jazz and swing concerts are held in the zoo's gardens.

Around half of Sydney's beaches are actually within the harbour (nets are set up to keep the sharks at bay). One of the best, near the entrance to Middle Harbour, is **Balmoral**, which also has the famous Bathers Pavilion restaurant on its shores. **Nielsen Park** at Vaucluse is a favored picnic spot, while **Lady Jane** allows nude bathing. **Camp Cove**, on the southern side near the Harbour entrance permits topless bathing and is popular with families.

The most famous ferry ride of all is to **Manly**; it crosses through the open sea between the Heads, and on a rough day waves can dwarf the boats. The name was given by Captain Phillip in 1788 when he was struck by the "manly" bearing of the Aborigines he met there. In the 1930s, the isthmus became Australia's favourite holiday resort "seven miles from Sydney and a thousand miles from care". The family atmosphere has lingered, with a bustling pedestrian mall and reasonably priced eateries. There is an 11-km (8-mile) harbourside walk to the Spit from here (catch a bus back). On West Esplanade are **Manly Art Gallery and Museum**, with a good selection of Australian paintings, and **Oceanworld**.

From Circular Quay a high-speed catamaran now speeds down the river to **Parramatta** ("where the eels lie down", in the original tongue) – technically a city in its own right, although Sydneysiders persist in regarding it as a suburb. Parramatta still has several colonial buildings scattered through it, including Old Government House; an Explorer bus meets the River Cat at the docks and transports passengers to the attractions. ❑

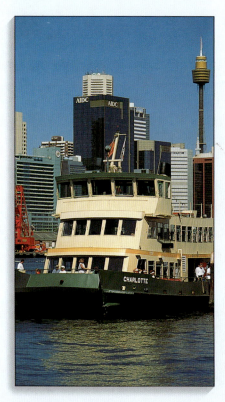

LEFT: one of Sydney's harbour ferries.

Sydney's beaches

From Paddington, it is a short bus or taxi ride to any of the eastern beaches – of which the most famous is certainly **Bondi ❹** (pronounced *Bond-eye*). It was from this great arc of sand in the late 1880s that the first Sydney "cranks" braved the ocean – breaking an old law that forbade swimming during daylight hours as indecent. The breakthrough came in 1902, when Manly newspaper proprietor William Gocher defied the ban and invited arrest. A similar challenge to the ban came the following year from a Waverley clergyman and a respectable bank clerk, and crowds of Sydneysiders soon followed suit. In 1906, the world's first lifesaving club was set up, and twenty years later, crowds of up to 100,000 people were reported at Bondi on summer days. With its wide golden sands, ragged sandstone headlands and reliably fine rollers, Bondi had become another potent Sydney icon. This iconic status was added to during the 2000 Olympics when Bondi beach played host to the beach volleyball competition.

The place is at its best, not surprisingly, in summer. Activity kicks off at dawn, with the joggers on the promenade, bodybuilders by the shore and surfies catching a few waves before work. Sun-worshippers arrive early, closely followed by busloads of Japanese tourists. The Bondi Pavilion opens up, selling ice-creams and souvenirs, picnickers arrive with their fish and chips, and the activity continues until well after dark, when lovers take over the sands.

Bondi is also a suburb. **Campbell Parade**, the main beachfront thoroughfare, is a motley string of 1930s-era storefronts that seems to resist all improvement ("one of the great disappointments of Sydney," according to the writer Jan Morris). In the mid-1990s, talk of a "Bondi Renaissance" began as the suburb leapt to new heights of fashionability, and strings of "New Australian" restaurants

Surfing – which has long been a way of life for many Sydneysiders – was introduced to Australia in 1912, by Duke Kahanamoku of Honolulu.

BELOW: Bondi lifesavers minding the sea in queues.

For those worried about swimming in the sea surrounded by surfers and sharks, Bronte has a saltwater swimming pool.

opened on the North Bondi end. But still, the Parade hangs on to its raffish, sand-gritted personality – and most Sydneysiders really would have it no other way.

Even in winter, Bondi is well worth a visit, not least for the hour-long walk from the south end of the beach, along the sandstone headlands to **Tamarama** and **Bronte** (this latter with a string of cafés to reward the persistent). Looming over another wind-battered headland, the **Waverley Cemetery** is worth a look; the poet Henry Lawson is buried here. Further south lie **Clovelly** and **Coogee** beaches, the latter being a favourite for families now that it has been given a major facelift.

North of Bondi, New South Head Road runs to **Watsons Bay**, whose pub has the finest outdoor beer garden in Sydney, with views across the yachts to the city skyline. Next door is Doyle's, Sydney's oldest and best-known fish restaurant. It's a stiff hike up to **South Head** at the mouth of Port Jackson, but worth it. The sheer cliffs of The Gap are still a favoured suicide spot.

The route back to the city goes through one of the most exclusive suburbs, **Vaucluse**. It centres around a magnificent mansion, **Vaucluse House** (Tues–Sun 10am–4.30pm; entrance fee), built in 1827 for the statesman, poet and explorer William Charles Wentworth. The tea rooms are charming, as are the garden picnic grounds. Swanky **Double Bay** is synonymous with Old Money, although there is also a large central European contingent that has made the grade.

The Blue Mountains

Just 65 km (40 miles) west of Sydney lie the **Blue Mountains**, the range that divides the populous, beach-fringed coastal plain from Australia's notoriously flat, harsh interior. It was an effective barrier to the colony's first explorers, whose efforts to conquer this section of the Great Dividing Range were thwarted

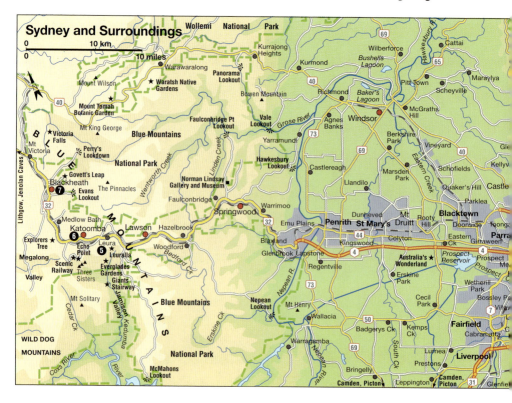

y the rugged sandstone cliffs. The footsteps of the trio who in 1813 success-
ully found the narrow passes are now followed westwards by the main route
ut of Sydney, the **Great Western Highway**. Today those three pioneers – Blax-
and, Wentworth and Lawson – are remembered in the names of towns along
he highway as it winds up into the mountains. It was not until the 1920s that
his "rude peculiar country" took off as a holiday destination for fashionable
ydneysiders. Small European-style guest-houses sprang up, catering to hon-
ymooners and families escaping the summer heat. In 1932, a group of bush-
valkers came across a farmer about to cut down a gorgeous blue gum forest in
he Grose Valley. They begged him to stop, and in the end offered to buy the
and. It was the beginning of a movement that has since protected almost 1 mil-
on hectares (2½ million acres) of Australia's most magnificent wilderness.

Despite the almost impenetrable barrier the Blue Mountains presented to early
avellers, they are in fact a sandstone plateau reaching a height of only about
,100 metres (3,600 ft). Erosion has let the stone fall away to form sheer cliff
aces punctuated by picturesque waterfalls. The **Blue Mountains National
ark**, totalling 247,000 hectares (950 sq. miles), is well served by bushwalk-
ig tracks and picnic and camping spots. Like backwoods New England in the
JSA, its small towns are riddled with fine restaurants, old-style cafés and an-
que stores catering to wandering urbanites who drift through at weekends.

As you drive up from Sydney, first stop should be **Leura** ❺, a classic Blue
Mountains hamlet; it's a tidy, picturesque railway town that makes an ideal lunch
reak. The region's main town, **Katoomba** ❻, is perched on the edge of the
amison Valley, and shows off its natural wonders to the best advantage at **Echo
oint**, which overlooks one of the state's most photogenic rock formations, the

Map,
pages
146–7

TIP

The best time of day to
view the Three Sisters,
near Katoomba, is late
afternoon, when the
bus tours have moved
on and the three
sandstone pillars are
bathed in golden light.

BELOW: viewing
Grose Valley from
Govett's Leap.

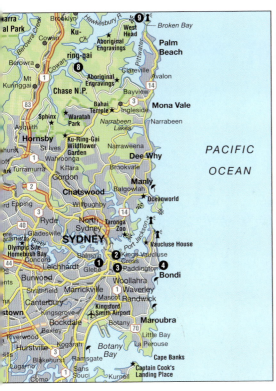

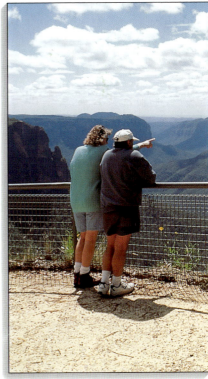

Three Sisters. Around the corner, on Panorama Drive, is the guest-house Lil ianfels where "high tea" by the fireside is a coveted Mountains experience.

High on the list of breathtaking experiences is the **Scenic Railway** that shaft down into a tree-clad gorge and is claimed to be the world's steepest railway There are many footpaths for one-day walks in the area – an excellent choice is hiking down the "Golden Stairs" to the rock formations known as the **Ruined Castle**. Katoomba has a giant Maxvision cinema with a screen as tall as a six storey building; its feature on the Blue Mountains is quite stunning.

Some 10 minutes' drive further west along the highway looms the **Hydro Majestic Hotel**, an art deco former casino that catered to high society in the 1920s and is now slowly being restored. **Blackheath** ❼ has some of the bes guesthouses and restaurants. Follow the signs to **Govetts Leap**, a spectacular lookout over the Grose Valley.

As the road drops from the mountains down the steep **Victoria Pass**, it nar rows to cross a convict-built bridge that was part of the first road through to the rich wool, wheat, cattle and sheep country. A little way on, and 46 km (29 miles south of the highway, are the magnificent **Jenolan Caves**, a mighty series of underground limestone halls encrusted with stalactites and stalagmites. In the 1920s, this was the premier honeymoon spot for young Australians, who regarded the arduous journey and difficult conditions as a badge of honour.

On the highway, 12 km (7½ miles) past the Jenolan Caves turn-off, there is a monument to the ingenuity used in solving one of the 19th century's greatest engineering problems at **Lithgow**. It is the railway line which originally conquered the steep descent out of the Blue Mountains, known as the **Zig-Zag Railway** – so named for its unique method of overcoming the almost sheer

The blue haze that often hangs over the Blue Mountains, and gives them their name, is produced by vaporised eucalyptus oil from the leaves of countless gum trees.

BELOW: intrepid climbers on the Three Sisters.

Map, pages 146–7

mountainside. The zig-zag line was finished in 1869, but was abandoned in 1910 for a more modern descent. Dedicated train buffs have eventually restored the line to give day excursions travelling back into railway history (for details tel: 6353 1795).

Between Sydney and the Blue Mountains lie several historic towns. In 1805 John Macarthur was granted nearly 2,000 hectares (5,000 acres) to raise sheep in **Camden**, the beginning of the nation's great wool industry. His wife Elizabeth carried out important experiments in the breeding of Merino sheep. The Camden-Campbelltown-Picton region is still known as Macarthur Country, and **Camden Park House** (1835) is still owned by descendants of John Macarthur; it is open by appointment only – tel: 4655 8466 . Today Camden (pop. 8,000) is the centre of a dairy region focused on the Nepean River Valley.

Sixteen km (10 miles) southwest of Camden, tiny **Picton** also has numerous remnants of 19th-century settlement. Upper Menangle Street is listed by the National Trust as "representing a typical country town street" of 100 years ago. It is a fine base from which to explore the scenic surrounding region.

An hour's drive north of Sydney lie some of New South Wales' most beautiful national parklands, at **Ku-ring-gai Chase National Park** ❽. Hundreds of Aboriginal carvings dot the cliffs here, which often give sweeping views of the countryside and Cowan Creek: the easiest to reach are on the **Basin Trail** off West Head Road. At the mouth of the Hawkesbury River is **Broken Bay** ❾, a favourite recreational area, where boaters and picnickers flock at weekends.

Palm Beach, home of international Aussie soap *Home and Away*, is one of Greater Sydney's smarter neighbourhoods, and its beach is rated highly by surfers. If you're short of time, consider visiting this area by seaplane; these leave regularly from Rose Bay in the city, landing in Pittwater. ❏

BELOW: the start of the Zig-Zag Railway, Lithgow.
FOLLOWING PAGES: windsurfing in Pittwater.

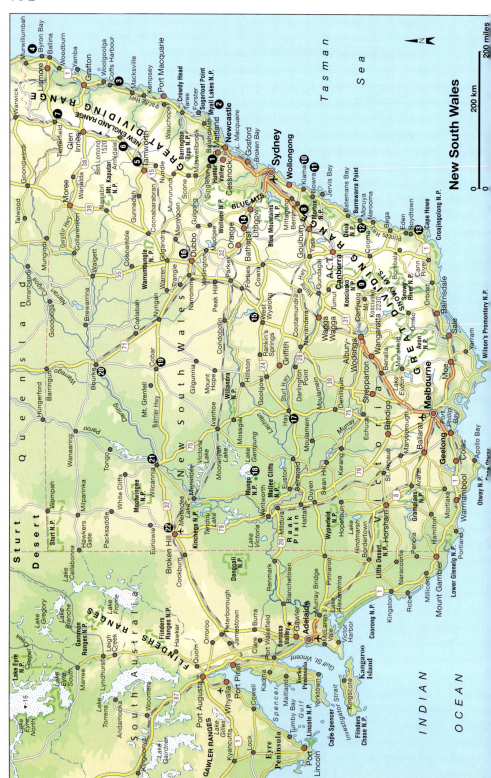

New South Wales

NEW SOUTH WALES

*NSW has something of everything. Head north from Sydney
for tropical banana plantations, south for snow-capped mountains or
west for the vast expanses of the Outback*

Map,
page 152

New South Wales is a state of baffling contrasts, both culturally and geographically. On a day when it's snowing on the Southern Alps, spiralling dust storms may be striking the west and monsoons could be flooding the northeast. Similarly, while crowds are pouring into the Sydney Opera House, others will be heading for the pub, bringing in the cattle for the evening or turning on the radio to catch the latest sheep and cattle prices.

We have divided the state (usually written as "NSW") into six separate regions. These are: the Pacific Highway to the North Coast (with a detour to the Hunter Valley), New England, the Southern Highlands, the Snowy Mountains, the South Coast, and the western slopes and plains.

The Pacific Highway

In the minds of Sydneysiders, "up the coast" symbolises a track of dreams. It was always "up the coast" where one escaped to from the tedium of a Sydney winter. Travelling north, moving by degrees up the longitude towards the sun, one passed hick settlements and hiccup pubs. The people-to-land ratio inverted until the bush and breezes did most of the talking; words were left to billboards and the neon tics of motel signs.

Naturally, development has come to the coast. Going north now up National Route One, the Pacific Highway, is still a flickering parade of gum trees in the late afternoon light and occasional glimpses of the Pacific Ocean's white-lace hems (despite its name, the Pacific Highway is usually several kilometres from the coast). It is also increasingly a ribbon development of motels, expanding coastal towns and sea-front subdivisions.

This bitumen river of country pubs, milk shakes, potholes, surfers and farmers is best approached with a little time up one's sleeve. You can roar up the Pacific Highway to Queensland in 12 hours, see nothing, collect a load of speeding tickets and risk life and limb on the highway's fatal curves – but if speed is so important, it's probably easier to fly. Three days is the minimum needed to experience the coast.

The trip north starts at Sydney Harbour Bridge. Northbound traffic soon throttles down into the four lanes of the Pacific Highway; at peak hours, this artery is clotted every few minutes at stop lights and suburban intersections, although at other times it flows freely. After negotiating past the Volvos and Saabs of the upper middle-class upper North Shore, you finally hit the beginning of the Newcastle Freeway at **Wahroonga**.

Where the highway crosses the **Hawkesbury River** at **Brooklyn**, a vista of ridges, valleys and arms of open water spreads east and west. This is a popular weekend playground for many Sydneysiders, who travel here to

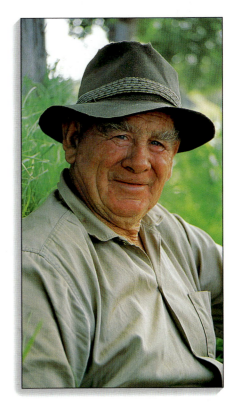

BELOW: a New South Wales farmer.

Newcastle, NSW, failed to impress Mark Twain when he spent a few hours there in 1895. He described the town as consisting of "a very long street with, at one end, a cemetery with no bodies in it and, at the other, a gentlemen's club with no gentlemen in it".

rent cabin cruisers and drift among the bays and inlets. If you have time, spend half a day on this glorious body of water, either in a runabout or on the unique "Riverboat Postman" ferry, both found at Brooklyn.

The commercial hub of this Central Coast region (a mixed bag of retirees, new industries and Sydney commuters) is a detour away at the not-terribly-alluring **Gosford**. But beyond the urban sprawl are the orchards and forests of the **Mangrove Mountain** area, plus a string of beautiful beaches to escape to. Nearby is the **New Australian Reptile Park**.

At **Doyalson**, the Pacific Highway heads along a ridge between the ocean and **Lake Macquarie**. Frequently overlooked by tourists, the lake (particularly its western shore) is a fascinating relic of a past age, when working folk could afford water frontages. The mining village of **Wangi Wangi**, for many years the retreat of the artist Sir William Dobell, is a classic example of lakeshore charm.

The second-largest city in New South Wales, **Newcastle**, is a sprawl of heavy industry and spread-out suburbs of the Australian Dream (the squat brick bungalow on a quarter-acre block). Because of the preponderance of steelworkers and miners, Newcastle was once considered a blue-collar town of little sophistication. Travellers who have just struggled out of Sydney may be tempted to bypass the city in favour of the warmer north. "Novocastrians" are used to this. But nowadays, the "Steel City" has developed both aesthetically and culturally. Stately homes are perched high on a hill that runs down to an industrialised but picturesque harbour at the mouth of the **Hunter River**.

Newcastle is regarded by residents as a perfect compromise between city and country living. Within easy reach are the boating and bushlands of Lake Macquarie to the south and expansive, wild Myall Lakes to the north, plus a ribbon

BELOW:
camping on the
Hawkesbury River.

f fine surfing beaches. And, as a bonus, there are the prosperous wineries of
he lower **Hunter Valley** ❶, a region that contains some of NSW's most beauti-
ul pastoral land.

Many of its hillsides were originally settled in the pursuit of coal; today, wine
s the source of the region's fame *(see page 156)*. Turning off from Newcastle
ast the city of **Maitland**, the route leads through one winery after another. Some
f the old mining villages of this area retain echoes of their 19th-century ori-
ins, but most of the lower Hunter has undergone a metamorphosis which has
ropelled it into the 21st century. Aluminium smelters, giant open-cut mines
nd power stations are turning the area into a compact "Ruhr of New South
Vales", despite earlier opposition from conservationists, the influential wine
ndustry and many residents.

As the highway heads deeper into the valley, the pace of life slows down. **Sin-**
gleton is a mixture of modern and old civic buildings and private homes. It is a
delightful place to while away a few hours.

The town of **Scone** (rhymes with *own*) is pretty but unremarkable save for its
horsiness". This is the home of thoroughbred stud farms, horse shows and the
port of polo. Much of New England is "squatter" territory, where the sons and
aughters of the landed gentry (or aspiring "wannabes") continue the traditions
f Mother England – political conservatism, good riding skills and bad dress
ense. Scone hosts major polo tournaments, at which champagne flows freely
etween the chukkas.

While the Hunter Valley is very pleasant to visit, its scenery is not that spec-
acular; in high summer, its low hills can become unbearably hot. Many Aus-
ralian wine buffs now prefer to head an hour's drive further east to visit the

Map,
page 152

BELOW: Segenhoe
Stud Farm, Scone.

The Hunter Valley wine industry

Although the state of South Australia produces more than half of Australia's fine domestic wine, New South Wales's Hunter Valley is the next most important wine region in terms of both size and quality. In the past, the area specialised in particularly dry red and white wine, but with the expansion of the vineyards to the upper Hunter, Rieslings and fine full-bodied reds are also produced here. There are now more than 60 wineries in the lower Hunter at Pokolbin and seven in the upper Hunter near Denman.

The Australian wine industry actually had its beginnings 160 km (100 miles) to the south. By 1827 the Macarthur family was making wine in considerable quantities at Camden, west of Sydney, but real commercial production of Australian wine did not begin until the later 1830s – in the Hunter Valley.

In the past few decades, local winemakers

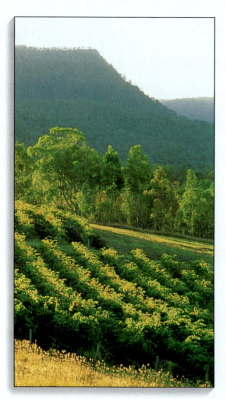

have embraced new technology with enthusiasm, enabling them to combat the heat at vintage time and produce wines of a remarkable consistency – an essential requirement of supermarket buyers in Europe and the USA. They may not always be subtle but, because the grapes ripen in hot, sunny, rain-free conditions, where the wines acquire more fruit, more flavour, more alcohol and less acidity, they do have a wildly exuberant flavour.

Semillon does especially well in the Hunter Valley. With about five years' ageing, it offers great oak-infused flavours, plus a rich, honeyed lime-like fruit. Shiraz also produces strong, spicy reds here and, being a less fashionable grape than Cabernet Sauvignon, can offer good value for money.

The wineries are spread over quite a large area around **Pokolbin**, and 80 km (50 miles) further up the valley near **Muswellbrook**. Most offer tasting facilities and some, such as the Rothbury Estate in Pokolbin and Black Hill Cellars at Muswellbrook, have restaurants. The wineries differ considerably in size, from the internationally famous names such as Lindemans and Rosemount Estate to small boutique wineries which offer distinctive, limited-edition wines. Many of the latter are available only by a personal visit, during which you might buy your bottle from the person who tended the vines, picked the grapes, supervised the fermentation and stuck on the labels.

The most tourist-oriented winery is Hungerford Hill Wine Village near Pokolbin, which has a restaurant, adventure playground for children, barbecue facilities and wine tastings.

A pleasant way to discover the valley is to tour the wineries of the lower Hunter, spend the night at Pokolbin or **Cessnock**, and drive on for a second bout of liver and brain damage at Muswellbrook the next day. Alternatively, you can do your exploring by bicycle (rentable at Pokolbin). The table wines of the region are uniformly good, and an ideal lubricant for your picnic lunches in the rolling hills. The prices may be higher than those in discount bottle shops in Sydney, but the surroundings are infinitely more relaxing. There is plenty of very good accommodation in the Pokolbin region at places like **Peppers**, **Casuarina Country Inn** and **Kirkton Park**. ❑

LEFT: vines were first planted here in the 1830s.

esser-known vineyards around **Mudgee**. The picturesque village of **Gulgong** makes an ideal base; it was the childhood home of the poet Henry Lawson, and has a centre devoted to him, and a pioneer museum.

Back on the Pacific Highway, north of Newcastle the road crosses the Hunter River at Hexham and skirts the western shore of **Port Stephens** (whose resorts such as **Nelson Bay**, **Tea Gardens** and **Hawks Nest** offer great fishing, swimming, boating and oysters) before reaching **Bulahdelah**, the gateway to the beautiful **Myall Lakes ❷**. Preserving the blue pearls of Myall Lakes was an early victory for conservationists. Here paperbarks, palms and other wetland vegetation crowd the shores, while the waterways are filled with birdlife said to be the most exotic in the state. Surrounding the chain of lakes is national park – and where nature lovers may camp in the wild. A week or a weekend spent dawdling down these waters on a rented houseboat is one of the east coast's loveliest offerings. The beach at the tiny community of **Seal Rocks** is one of the most scenically exquisite along the whole NSW coast.

Seal Rocks is the first of a string of beaches at the northern end of the lakes leading to the holiday resort of **Forster**, the southernmost of the North Coast beach towns. Travelling north also entails crossing river after river, for the NSW coast is crenellated with the mouths of waterways which carry run-off from the Great Dividing Range. The further north you go, the rivers become more and more romantic, their shores wilder, their bars and tides more spectacular.

Taree, about a two-hour drive from Newcastle, is a thriving market town in the dairy-rich **Manning Valley**. The beautiful Manning River runs through the middle of town and, if you follow it west to **Elands**, after an hour's drive you find yourself at **Ellenborough Falls**, one of the highest single-drop falls in Australia.

The Manning and other valleys of the mid-North Coast are timber centres providing native woods and pine from vast forests which stretch westwards onto the New England Plateau. Here the highway winds through miles of forest, and it is worth a detour along the well-made coast road from Kew to **Port Macquarie**. These are some of the prettiest beaches in the state, with rocky outcrops and golden sands. On the western side of the road there is yet another chain of ocean lakes, ideal for fishing and boating.

However, North Coast tourism has taken its toll on the landscape at Port Macquarie (a former penal settlement, founded in 1821, and still full of historic sandstone buildings). Garish motels, retirement villages and timeshare resorts dot the headlands, and red-brick suburbia has taken over the flatlands to the west. But, for all its superannuated qualities, there is still much to like about "Port" – good restaurants, top-quality accommodation and easy access to uncrowded beaches. At **Wauchope**, a few miles up the Hastings River, there is a replica of an old sawmilling village, **Timbertown**.

The highway again snakes inland and through the forests. It is worth making the 24-km (15-mile) detour to take in the resort of **Crescent Head** – a pretty, peaceful town with fine surf and good golf. For a real escape, head south from Crescent on the old dirt coast road for 10 km (6 miles) to a grassy headland and beach known as **Racecourse**. There's no sign, but a ranger appears

Map, page 152

The little town of Mudgee was laid out in 1838 by Robert Hoddle, who later planned Melbourne.

BELOW: heading north on the Pacific Highway.

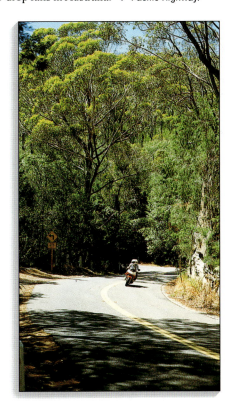

The giant concrete banana on the Pacific Highway north of Coffs Harbour marks the entrance to a plantation that welcomes visitors.

BELOW: the rolling hills of NSW known as "Bananaland".

from nowhere after a day or two to collect a modest camping fee. Given the joys of an empty beach, uncrowded waves and occasional dolphin sightings, the fee is a gift.

Kempsey, another major dairy and timber centre, is almost as old as Port Macquarie. Its position 32 km (20 miles) inland, and the industrialisation that has occurred around it, have largely dissuaded tourists. Still, if you're sick of resort life and you want to sample rural normality, this town is for you. It is also a handy setting-out point for **South West Rocks** and **Trial Bay**, to the northeast, home of an historic jail that held convicts and, later, German war internees.

Beyond Trial Bay a distinctly tropical feel begins to permeate the air and from **Macksville** north, banana plantations are a common sight. Houses are built on stilts, Queensland-style, in order to catch the cooling breeze and keep things dry in the wet. Everywhere the dominant colour is a lush green, and the roadside signs tell you this is paradise. It isn't, but it's a step in the right direction. While you're filling the tank in Macksville, pop around to The Star pub, which sits right on the banks of the Nambucca River, as pretty and profane an ale house as you'll find anywhere. Out on the coast, just south of Macksville, is the small town of **Scotts Head** with a long, clean beach and a caravan park.

The timber port of **Coffs Harbour** ❸ is reputed to have Australia's best climate and has developed into a major centre of North Coast tourism. Unfortunately, most motorists know Coffs only as the city of the Big Banana, another manifestation of Australia's bizarre tourist gigantism. Upmarket resorts in the area include **Pelican Beach Travelodge Resort**, **Quality Resort Nautilus**, **All Seasons Pacific Bay** and **Opal Cove**, while those with a taste for adventure can join whitewater professionals for a day of rafting action on the nearby **Nymboida River**.

Map,
page 152

Coffs is more or less the midway point between Sydney and Brisbane – around even and six hours' driving distance, respectively. Travellers often plan to stay ere overnight only, but end up staying a week. The town is alive with restaurants and pubs, bars and discos, particularly in the strip from the jetty to Park Beach. While it poses no threat to the nightlife supremacy of Queensland's Gold Coast, Coffs is a pleasant holiday mix: more upbeat than a country town, more mellow than the bright lights. Parasailing, 4WD tours into the surrounding forests, the beach, golf and galleries fill the days.

Inland, the Bellingen Valley and the beautiful village of **Bellingen** (which features dramatically in the climax of Peter Carey's novel *Oscar and Lucinda*) offers scenic pleasures quite different from the coast. This and **Nimbin** to the north are the heart of alternative culture in NSW, although concessions have been made to capitalism since the real-estate boom hit and idyllic communal farms became worth millions. Some parts of this valley, particularly the pebbled river banks, look more like the northern hemisphere than east-coast Australia. And as the valley gives way to the inland ranges nearer Dorrigo, there is excellent trout fishing.

The Pacific Highway swings inland yet again through the forests, this time emerging at **Grafton**, a lovely old town shaded with jacaranda trees (a wonderful sight in late October and early November) and situated on a bend of the Clarence River, 65 km (40 miles) from its mouth. Grafton has some delightful 19th-century architecture enhanced by its wide, tree-lined streets. This is flood country, and the houses close to the river are tropical bungalows on stilts. Like several towns away from the coast, Grafton has been bypassed in the tourist boom, and prices for food and lodging are still reasonable.

North of Grafton, the highway follows the line of the Clarence River across flatlands to the coast, with rambling old houses peering out from behind fields of sugar cane. The village of **Maclean**, built on several hills a few miles upriver from Yamba, is quaint, quiet, and a great spot from which to view the workings of the Clarence with its fishermen and cane haulers. Fifteen minutes down a straight bitumen road is the resort of Yamba, once a sleepy hollow and now filled with shoddily built "weekenders" and more garish motels. But the pub on the headland and the beaches spread below are first-rate. Down the coast a few kilometres from Yamba is the village and famous surf point of Angourie, with its rocky coastline and "Blue Pools".

Across the Clarence, just up from its mouth at Yamba, the river divides into channels around a series of islands linked by the highway. Here, amid the sugar cane, is one of the few gourmet restaurants between Sydney and Brisbane, the Chatsworth Island Restaurant, a visual and culinary delight that makes full use of the abundant local seafood delicacies.

After a stretch of alternating river and cane scenery, the Pacific Highway clips the coast again at **Ballina**, the southernmost beach town in a string reaching to the Queensland border, collectively known as the Summerland Coast. Ballina, the scene of a minor gold rush in the 19th century when the precious metal was found in beach sand near the mouth of the Richmond River, has

Just north of Coffs Harbour, at the ocean-front town of Woolgoolga, a large Sikh community has put its unique stamp on the landscape with a lavish temple and a superb curry restaurant.

BELOW: surfing at Angourie.

Two Pacific gems

Two of Australia's tiniest tourist areas are also among the most attractive. Although Norfolk and Lord Howe are South Pacific islands, these are not atolls of palm trees and corals. Rather, they are lush green specks on the vastness of the ocean, rather like a bonsaied version of Tasmania.

A rich and fascinating cultural heritage, relaxed lifestyle and rolling green pastures characterise **Norfolk Island**, 1,700 km (1,050 miles) northeast of Sydney. No one lived here until a British penal settlement was established in 1788.

The most bizarre event in Norfolk's history occurred after the British government decided, in 1852, that the settlement was too expensive to maintain and evacuated all the inhabitants. At about the same time, on remote Pitcairn Island the descendants of the Bounty mutineers and the Polynesian women they took with them from Tahiti in 1789 (after dumping Captain William Bligh) were finding it difficult to grow enough food for their increasing population. So they were relocated to Norfolk Island in 1856, although a few later returned to Pitcairn.

Today there are fewer than 1,800 people on the 3,500-hectare (8,750-acre) island, but many of them share the same set of Bounty surnames. Indeed, so many Christians, Quintals, Youngs, McCoys, Adamses, Buffetts, Nobbses and Evanses crowd the telephone book that it's the only one in the world to publish subscribers' nicknames.

Norfolk is a self-governing territory within Australia. The tourist clutter of **Kingston** is the island's only town. Surprisingly, tax-free shopping here is very cheap, especially for fashionable wool and cashmere sweaters.

Down by the waterfront, the buildings of the early settlements are still in very good condition – some are still used as government offices. The evening sound and light show along these buildings, remnants from a savage time, is well worth your while.

Norfolk Island isn't the place to come in expectation of a wild time. However, you feel close to history here, and there is enough to do to warrant several days' stay on the island. Diving is a popular activity, and Fletcher Christian's descendant Karlene Christian, at the Bounty Dive Shop, takes daily diving groups.

Accommodation on the island ranges from basic and cheap to quite upmarket. There are regular flights from Sydney and Brisbane, and Norfolk can be a very pleasant interlude on the way between Australia and New Zealand.

Much smaller than Norfolk Island, crescent-shaped **Lord Howe Island** is only 11 km (7 miles) long and 2 km (1¼ miles) wide, with a population of about 300 and only a couple of cars. Visitors usually travel on bicycles.

This heavily forested and partially mountainous isle often has a cap of cloud on top of the highest peak, Mount Gower (875 metres/2,870 ft), at the southern end. There are numerous walking trails, many birds and some unique vegetation. As on Norfolk, there are also facilities for diving, snorkelling and, of course, holidaying.

Lord Howe, which is part of New South Wales, is only 700 km (430 miles) off the NSW coast, about level with Port Macquarie. ❑

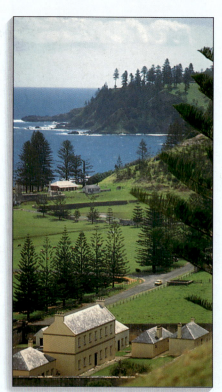

LEFT: Norfolk Island is a World Heritage area.

ow found more consistent treasure as a bustling tourist centre and fishing port. The Pacific Highway heads due north through magnificent rolling hills, but the alternative coastal route takes in some equally breathtaking coastal scenery, including the village of **Lennox Head** and the delightful resort town – and the easternmost town in Australia – of **Byron Bay ❹**. In the 1960s, Byron took off as a quiet rural/alternative community; today, thanks to its magnificent setting, it has become a mecca for the rich and famous. *Crocodile Dundee* star Paul Hogan is among those who own property here. Still, Byron's a wonderful place to spend a week or two relaxing in the sun or bodysurfing (one reason why it has lured so many unemployed youths).

The border town of **Tweed Heads** has only recently emerged from the shadow of its flashier sister across the Queensland border, Coolangatta, but the tourist boom now proceeds apace. The end of one journey is the beginning of the next. As you cross the Tweed River, the North Coast of NSW falls behind, and what opens ahead is a very different beast: the Queensland Gold Coast.

New England

At **Murrurundi** the New England Highway climbs up, leaving the Hunter Valley to enter the Great Dividing Range, the vast upheaval which separates the coastal plains from the tablelands along the entire length of New South Wales. The town itself is set in a valley of the Liverpool Ranges, and seems constantly shrouded in mist.

The road winds further into the ranges and onto the New England plateau, eventually reaching the city of **Tamworth ❺**. This pretty centre, surrounded by hills, is the largest in the northwest, with a population of 50,000 and a thriv-

Map, page 152

Captain Cook named Byron Bay after Commodore (later Admiral) John Byron, grandfather of the poet.

BELOW: Cape Byron, the easternmost point of Australia.

*The 10-day Country
Music Festival
staged in Tamworth
in January attracts
more than 40,000
visitors and adds
millions of dollars to
the local economy.*

ing local economy based on sheep and cattle. Tamworth's role as a commercial centre for outlying farms and ranches prompted a local radio announcer to establish a promotion on the cowboy theme. In the early 1970s he organised a country music festival and started calling Tamworth "the country music capital of Australia." At first, most residents were appalled at the thought of being typecast as hillbillies, but the annual festival is now the town's major tourist drawcard.

Not far from Tamworth, along a road that follows the bends of the Peel River, is the old gold-mining town of **Nundle**. Abandoned diggings and the ghost town atmosphere make it well worth a detour. North of Tamworth the New England Highway passes through spectacular country, with rugged peaks and long plains dotted with quaint old mining towns. **Uralla**, once a thriving gold centre, houses the grave of the legendary bushranger Captain Thunderbolt, shot during a battle with police at nearby Kentucky Creek in 1870.

As its name suggests, the **New England Tableland** bears striking similarities, in both topography and climate, to "the old country", England. Its altitude gives it frosty mornings nine months of the year, occasional snow and a year-round freshness. The graceful charm of the towns is also very English.

Nowhere is this more evident than in the city of **Armidale** ❻, a university town greened by parks and gardens, with two cathedrals and tree-lined streets. As well as the University of New England, Armidale has one other college and three boarding schools, establishing it as the major NSW seat of learning outside Sydney. The student population has given Armidale an air of youthfulness in contrast to its stately Victorian architecture, and the downtown area is a schizophrenic mixture of refined clothing stores and stock agents on the one hand, and health-food bars and funky bookshops on the other.

BELOW: dawn in New England.

The highway out of Armidale leads along a ridge to the watershed of the Great Dividing Range, 1,320 metres (4,330 ft) above sea level, at **Guyra**, then on to the junction with the Gwydir Highway at **Glen Innes**, famous for its fine gemstones. Almost a third of the world's sapphires are mined in this area and, although most of the good spots are on commercial lease, you can search for sapphires, garnets, jasper, agate and numerous other stones at many places. The town itself features magnificent ornate buildings and is fringed by five lovely parks. The mist-shrouded **New England National Park**, east of Armidale, is beautiful.

Tenterfield ❼ is the next major town along the route, once chiefly famous as "the birthplace of Federation" (because Sir Henry Parkes first called for the Australian colonies to unite in a speech made in the School of Arts here in 1889), but now more famous as the birthplace of Peter Allen's grandfather. The late, expatriate Aussie singer topped the charts in the early 1980s with a soapy eulogy to his grandfather called *Tenterfield Saddler*. For all that, it is a rather ordinary country town in which there is not a great deal except memories.

The Southern Highlands

The Hume Highway is the main road running south from Sydney to Melbourne, along the inland route. **Mount Gibraltar**, a denuded volcanic plug known locally as "The Gib", rises above Mittagong and the surrounding terrain, marking the gateway to the Southern Highlands. **Mittagong**, home of Australia's first iron smelter (Fitz Roy Ironworks, 1848–80), is one of several interesting towns in the district.

Five km (3 miles) further on is **Bowral**, a fashionable tourist resort for Sydneysiders in the 1880s and back in favour today as the site of a well-attended

Map, page 152

The numerous Scottish settlers in New England tried (and failed) to have the region known as New Caledonia.

BELOW: New England drovers.

Tulip Festival in September–October. The town offers access to the **Moun** **Gibraltar Reserve**, noted for its wombats and brush-tailed possums.

But the gem of the Southern Highlands is **Berrima** ❽, a small village pre served just as it was in the first half of the 19th century. It is off the Hume High way, about 8 km (5 miles) west of Bowral, and most of it is protected by historic trusts. The township was established in 1831, and today many of its impressive old sandstone buildings have been converted to antique and craft galleries; mos of those with historical artefacts are open from 10am to 5pm daily. These includ the Surveyor General Inn (1834), said to be the oldest continuously licensec pub in Australia (and still serving draught beer); the Court House (1839), now the information centre and museum; the Gaol (1839), now a prison rehabilitatior training centre; the Church of Holy Trinity (1849); and St Francis Xavier's Ro man Catholic Church (1851).

The big country town of **Goulburn** (pop. 22,500) is located 200 km (12(miles) southwest of Sydney, about midway between the Southern Highlands and the national capital of Canberra. For most of its life Goulburn has been a staging post for travellers along the Hume Highway. In 1992 that period ended when the extended freeway skirted the town, and Goulburn today is a much more relaxed place since the semi-trailers stopped rumbling through. Livestock wool, wheat and potatoes provide the economic foundation for the town, whose peaceful Georgian homes and two classical cathedrals belie its 19th-century his tory as a centre of police action against the bushrangers who plagued the sur rounding roads for decades. **Towrang Stockade**, 10 km (6 miles) to the north, is sparse ruins today; outlaws like Ben Hall and Frank Gardiner gave this once- formidable penal settlement a wide berth.

Goulburn is home to another of NSW's giant oddities: the Big Merino, on the western outskirts, is a 15-metre (50-ft) concrete sheep that houses a shop and wool museum.

BELOW: a farm in the Southern Highlands.

Iron hitching posts still stand outside some of the graceful commercial buildings on the main street of **Yass** (pop. 5,200). Hamilton Hume, the explorer after whom the Hume Highway is named, spent the last 40 years of his life here; his **Cooma Cottage** can be inspected (daily except Tues and Wed, 10am–4pm; entrance fee) and his tombstone can be visited in the local cemetery.

Gundagai, where the Hume crosses the Murrumbidgee River, has such an evocative name that several songwriters have used it in their titles – *The Road to Gundagai*, for example, or *When a Boy from Alabama meets a Girl from Gundagai*. The town still contains reminders of a devastating flash flood in 1852, the worst disaster of its kind in Australian history. Eighty-nine people in the community were drowned.

Map, page 152

The Snowy Mountains

Although the gentle slopes of **Mount Kosciusko** (pronounced *koz-ee-oss-ko*), the highest point in all Australia, rise to only 2,230 metres (7,315 ft), the expansive southern Alps are well worth a visit. With 6,900 sq. km (2,664 sq. miles) of territory, **Kosciusko National Park ❾** is the largest protected area in the state. In winter the ski resorts of **Thredbo**, **Perisher-Blue** and **Charlottes Pass** cater for skiers of all abilities (although the runs are relatively short), and in summer the region has many beautiful walking routes. This is the best area in Australia to observe that the continent really did have a glacial past.

Tumut, on the Snowy Mountains Highway, is a timber town known for its autumn colours and its May Festival of the Falling Leaves. It's the northern gateway to the Snowy Mountains Hydroelectric Project, a 25-year, $820 million scheme to provide energy for Sydney, Melbourne and the rest of southeastern

The hydro-electric project completed in 1974 in the Snowy Mountains includes 145 km (90 miles) of tunnels, 80 km (50 miles) of aqueducts and 16 major dams, with a total storage capacity 13 times the volume of Sydney Harbour.

BELOW: Blowering Reservoir in the Snowy Mountains.

Australia while diverting water to irrigate vast stretches of the Riverina district west of the mountains.

South of Tumut, the highway enters the national park and skirts the eastern shore of **Blowering Reservoir**, venue of numerous water-ski and speed-boat records including the fastest (510 kph/317 mph) and longest (1,673 km/1,040 miles) runs. Further on, the **Yarrangobilly Caves** have become one of the Snowy Mountains' leading attractions. About 260 caves have been discovered in a 2.5 by 12 km (1½ by 7½ mile) limestone belt around the 300-metre (1,000-ft) deep Yarrangobilly River valley. Few caverns anywhere can rival the variety and beauty of their calcite formations. Six caves are open to the public for inspection, five of them by guided tour only.

The road climbs rapidly into **Kiandra**, 90 km (56 miles) from Tumut. Now a desolate road-junction, it has two 19th-century claims to fame: it was the site of Australia's highest goldfield (1,414 metres/4,639 ft), and the location of its first ski club. In fact, the 15,000 miners who lived in tents and shanties on these slopes around 1860 were holding competitive ski races before anyone in Europe. They strapped fence palings – "butter pads" – to their boots to move around the surrounding countryside in the winter months. The Kiandra Snow-Shoe Club, established in 1882, numbered among its members the poet Banjo Paterson.

Travellers proceeding towards Melbourne should turn west at the Kiandra junction. The road climbs to **Cabramurra**, the highest town (about 1,500 metres/4,900 ft) in Australia. From this point, it's downhill 63 km (39 miles) to the park's western gateway of **Khancoban**. From January to April, this road is a delightful trail through fields of wildflowers, forest stands of mountain ash and snow gum, a number of lovely blue lakes, and frequent herds of kangaroos.

BELOW: the Snowy Mountains are the state's most popular winter sports area.

The South Coast

NSW's South Coast is a wildly diverse land of fishing ports and resort towns, steel mills and cheese factories, primal forest and coal country. Those travelling **Highway One** (the Princes Highway) are only a short detour away from a windswept peninsular national park and an island whose best-known denizens are fairy penguins. Because the highway south stays close to the coast, it is more scenic than the better-known Pacific Highway north from Sydney.

Departing the metropolis, the Princes Highway spectacularly skirts the rim of the **Illawarra Plateau** until descending suddenly to **Wollongong**, a major industrial city in an impressive natural setting. Some may argue that the smokestacks of the nation's largest steel works provide an unsightly backdrop to the otherwise pristine scene of surf and sandstone cliffs, but the heavy industry is the bread and butter for 10 percent of Wollongong district's population of 255,000.

That population is spread along 48 km (30 miles) of coastline from Stanwell Park in the north to Shellharbour in the south, but is mostly concentrated in the southern Wollongong and **Port Kembla** townships, where the steel works, a copper smelter with a 198-metre (650-ft) chimney, engineering plants and an artificial harbour are located. In 1996–97, mines in the south Wollongong district produced 15,784,800 tonnes of raw coal.

Back in 1797, explorer George Bass anchored in tiny **Kiama Bay** and remarked on a "tremendous noise" emanating from a rocky headland. Today, the **Blowhole** is the most popular attraction of the fishing and market town of **Kiama ⑩**. When seas are sufficiently high to force water geyser-like through a rock fissure, the spout can reach an amazing 60 metres (200 ft) in height. Beware – visitors have been swept to their death off these rocks.

Map, page 152

The hamlet of Mount Kembla, on the west side of Wollongong, was the site of one of Australia's worst mining disasters. In 1902 an explosion deep in a coal mine split the mountain and buried 95 men.

BELOW: hang-gliding over the South Coast.

Southwards, a short distance of 20 km (12 miles) west of **Berry** ("The Town of Trees"), is **Kangaroo Valley**, a lovely historic township set in an isolated vale among heavily forested slopes. Established in 1829, today it is a favourite haunt of picnickers, bushwalkers and spring wildflower lovers. The **Pioneer Settlement Museum** at Hampden Bridge contains a reconstructed 1880s dairy farm, a settler's hut and pioneering farm equipment. Kangaroo Valley is the gateway to the magnificent **Morton National Park**, which encompasses a large part of the Shoalhaven escarpment.

Nowra ⑪ (pop. 23,000) is the hub of the Shoalhaven district, 162 km (101 miles) south of Sydney. A regional farming centre and an increasingly popular focus of tourism, this riverbank city is 13 km (8 miles) from the mouth of the Shoalhaven River. Regional attractions include *HMAS Albatross*, Australia's last naval air training station; **Greenwell Point**, where fresh oysters can be purchased directly from local growers at the co-operative; and the **Nowra Raceways**, three separate modern tracks for horse racing, trotting and greyhounds. The horse-racing track is known as Archer Raceway after the home-bred winner of the first two Melbourne Cups (1861 and 1862). Archer's stall is still maintained as a veritable shrine at Terara House, a private property east of the town.

Jervis Bay once rivalled Sydney Harbour (Port Jackson) in importance as a colonial port. Surrounded on all sides but the southeast by 50 km (30 miles) of headlands and beaches, it was first sighted and named by Captain James Cook in 1770. In 1915, some 7,200 hectares (17,800 acres) of the bay's southern headland were annexed to the Australian Capital Territory (ACT) under an act which stipulated that the capital must have access to the sea. This ACT land is the present-day home of the Royal Australian Naval College, *HMAS*

Hyams Beach on Jervis Bay claims to have the whitest sand in the world.

BELOW: farmhouses in Kangaroo Valley.

reswell, the **National Botanic Gardens Annexe**, and the popular picnic eas of Green Patch and Illuka.

Ulladulla is a rapidly growing beach resort and fishing port which supplies uch of Sydney's fresh fish daily. The importance of its fleet can be credited to lian immigrants of the 1930s who created the town's artificial harbour.

Batemans Bay, another 85 km (53 miles) south, is a tourist, crayfishing and *stering centre at the mouth of the Clyde River. Offshore are the **Tollgate Is-nds**, a wildlife refuge frequented by penguins. Mogo, 12 km (7½ miles) south Batemans Bay, was struck by gold fever in the 1860s. At **Old Mogo Town**, st of the Princes Highway near Mogo, an old mine, a steam engine and a ntury-old stamper battery (ore crusher) attract modern-day fortune-seekers.

Moruya ⑫, like Nowra to the north, is established several kilometres inland the tidal waters of a river mouth. Its first home, Francis Flanagan's Shannon ew (1828), is still occupied, and the Uniting Church (or Wesleyan as it was own in the past) was built in 1864 of local granite. The 130-year-old granite *arry on the north side of the Moruya River once supported a town of its own. nong its notable "clients" has been Sydney Harbour Bridge.

As the Princes Highway winds through the hills into **Bodalla**, 38 km (23 les) south of Moruya, it's hard to miss the little town's **Big Cheese**. Some 4½ etres (15 ft) high and equally wide, it was sculpted from metal in early 1984 to lster the community's image as a cheesemaking centre and to generate extra urist revenue. The region's two largest cheese manufacturers produce almost ,000 tonnes of fancy and cheddar cheese annually.

The waters off the Eurobodalla area, around the small coastal resort towns of arooma and **Bermagui** – especially those around **Montague Island**, 8 km (5

Map, page 152

Bodalla's success as a cheese-producing centre was largely due to Thomas Mort (1816–78) who not only established a huge farm and factory but was also the first cheesemaker to use refrigerated cargo ships.

BELOW: Rosedale Beach, near Batemans Bay.

miles) off Narooma – yield record tuna, shark and kingfish catches. **Centra Tilba**, 29 km (18 miles) southwest of Narooma, is a community in which time ha stood still. Each of the two dozen wooden buildings in this village, classified an protected by the National Trust, is as it was in the late 19th century. The ABC Cheese Factory is open (daily 9am–5pm) for cheese tasting, and ancient equip ment is on display in the souvenir shop. Central Tilba was established in th 1870s when gold was discovered on Mount Dromedary. There are fine coasta views from the 825-metre (2,700-ft) mountain top, reached by a walking track

Bega (pop. 5,000) is generally regarded as the "capital" of the far South Coa of New South Wales. Settled in the 1830s, it lies about 435 km (270 miles) b road south of Sydney. The Bega Cheese Heritage Centre welcomes visitors fo factory tours, cheese tasting and sales (daily 9am–5pm), while the Brogo Valle Rotolactor Dairy, 23 km (15 miles) north of Bega, offers milking demonstra tions on a revolving platform from 2pm–5pm Mondays and Wednesday an daily during school holidays.

Merimbula and its sister town of **Pambula**, on the so-called "Sapphir Coast", offer fine surfing, boating, fishing, prawning and oystering. **Eden**, th last sizeable town before you cross the Victoria state border, is located on **Two fold Bay**, once a thriving whaling port and now host to whale-watching tour The **Whaling Museum** on Imlay Street recalls those 19th-century days. Twofol Bay – the world's third-deepest natural harbour – is home to a fine fishing flee a fish-processing factory and the controversial Japanese-sponsored Harris Daishowa woodchip mill on the south shore of the bay.

During its whaling era, Eden had stiff competition as a port fron **Boydtown** , established in 1842 by banker-adventurer Ben Boyd on the sout side of Twofold Bay. Boyd dreamed aloud that his set tlement would one day become the capital of Australia He established a steamship service to Sydney an erected many buildings, but in 1850 his empire col lapsed. Boyd went bankrupt, fled Australia to the Solo mon Islands, and was never heard of again.

BELOW: the fishing fleet at Eden.

All that remains of the grand scheme today are th **Seahorse Inn** – a magnificent building with stone wall a metre (3 ft) thick, Gothic arches and hand-carve doors and windows – and **Boyd's Tower**, a 31-metr (102-ft) sandstone lighthouse built in 1846 but never li The 8,950-hectare (22,110-acre) **Ben Boyd Nationa Park** encompasses the coastal headlands north an south of Twofold Bay. Its highlights include stunnin red sandstone cliffs, rich animal and bird life, and lovel wildflowers.

Western slopes and plains

The route due west from Sydney, along the Great West ern Highway, passes through the Blue Mountains (se pages 146–9) and enters the vast grazing land tha begins where the mountains end. The city of **Bathurs** ⑭ (pop. 31,000) was a major pastoral centre ever before it boomed with gold discoveries in the 1850s. I importance is once again based on rural production although to the visitor its main interest is its link wit the romantic gold-rush days. There's a packaged Gol Rush experience at **Bathurst Goldfields** on the city'

Map, page 152

nic **Mount Panorama**, where old-time diggings have been set up, and gold-
nning demonstrations are given. A bit more authentic is do-it-yourself pan-
g at **Hill End** or **Sofala**, ghost towns north of Bathurst. Take a drive around
town and inner suburbs to see the civic buildings and grand mansions built
m the profits of Australia's first gold rush.

In Bathurst, the scenic drive around Mount Panorama becomes a world-class
tor-racing circuit for the 1,000-km (600-mile) touring car race and V8 race in
ptember and October. Just over 50 km (30 miles) from Bathurst is the photo-
nic and intensively photographed village of **Carcoar**, where more than 20
stored colonial buildings with National Trust classification nestle in a pictur-
que little valley.

The highway runs through mainly sheep and wheat country to **Cowra** (pop.
00), a prosperous agricultural centre on the Lachlan River. Cowra has strong
ks with Japan. During World War II, Japanese prisoners of war were interned
a camp there, and in 1944 it was the scene of a suicidal mass break-out attempt
which nearly 231 prisoners were killed. The care local people gave to the
ves of the dead prisoners impressed the Japanese, who later repaid them with
gift of a classically laid-out Japanese garden, a colourful Oriental showpiece
the gold-brown central west of New South Wales.

At Cowra, the highway becomes a basic two-lane blacktop, running fairly
aight for 1,000 km (600 miles) or so, until the approaches to Adelaide. This is
true "sunburnt country" and "land of sweeping plains" of Dorothea Mackel-
's evocative poem. The kangaroo warning signs aren't there just to provide
al colour or target practice for frustrated shooters. Postcard-cute though they
y seem, kangaroos are a serious driving hazard, especially at night.

The city of Bathurst was founded by Governor Macquarie in 1815 – which makes it Australia's oldest inland town.

BELOW: mustering sheep near Cowra.

The harshness of the elements is burnt into the wild-west appearance of **We**
Wyalong 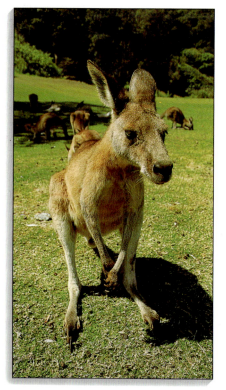, 161 km (100 miles) west of Cowra. Motorists should spurn the by
pass and drive down the main street of the former gold-mining town. The quai
town of **Orange** (pop. 36,000) is, predictably, a fruit-growing centre – but, n
so predictably, the crops are apples and cherries rather than citrus fruits (it wa
named after the Duke of Orange). The extinct volcano **Mount Canobolas**, 1
km (9 miles) southwest of Orange, is a 1,500-hectare (600-acre) flora and fau
na reserve with walking trails, picnic areas, waterfalls and a 360-degree view
of the countryside from the summit.

The **Ophir Goldfields**, 27 km (17 miles) northeast of the city, were wher
Australia's first payable gold was discovered in 1851 and are now an offici:
fossicking area. Banjo Paterson's birthplace is marked by a memorial 3 km (
miles) off the highway on the Ophir Road.

The Mitchell Highway runs through undulating terrain around **Wellingto**
The **Wellington Caves**, 8 km (5 miles) southwest of the town, have huge sta
lagmite formations in their limestone caverns. The last truly productive agricu
tural area is around the thriving city of **Dubbo** (pop. 38,000), in the middle c
the wheat belt, with large sheep and cattle properties and irrigated farms.

Dubbo's main attraction for tourists is the **Western Plains Zoo**, which is a
excellent wildlife park associated with Sydney's Taronga Park Zoo. Animal
are placed in settings as near as possible to their native conditions, and penne
by moats rather than cages or fences. Australia has an inordinate number of jai
as tourist attractions, and Dubbo is no exception: the **Old Dubbo Gaol**, whic.
was closed in 1966 after almost 80 years, has been restored, complete with gal
lows, and is open for self-guided inspection tours.

BELOW: an
inhabitant of the
Western Plains Zoo.

Narromine, 39 km (24 miles) on from Dubbo and o
the edge of the western plains, is a major citrus-growin
area, and the local Citrus Packers Co-operative will le
visitors have a look around. The terrain here provide:
thermal air lifts, making the area ideal for gliding. I
the **Macquarie Valley Irrigation Area**, the town o
Trangie is the centre of a large cotton-growing industry
and visits can be arranged to the nearby Auscott Cotto
Farm. Harvesting and ginning take place from late Apri
to June, the best time to visit.

The scenery starts to turn dry brown at **Nyngan** o
the Bogan River, where the Barrier Highway begins
Here motorists should only press on if they have confi
dence in their vehicles, and should start keeping ar
eagle eye on the fuel gauge. There's only one fuel sup
ply (at Hermidale) over the 128 km (80 miles) to Cobar
only one stop (at Topar) between Wilcannia and Broken Hill; and few service stations from there to Yunt:
in South Australia.

It's a desolate drive on to **Hay** (pop. 3,000). Banjc
Paterson's bitter poem *Hay, Hell and Booligal* was inspired by the almost treeless horizons and the sun-
parched tedium, broken only by the sight of ar
occasional emu, goanna or flock of budgerigars. The
town, about halfway from Sydney to Adelaide, is a well-
watered oasis on the banks of the Murrumbidgee River.
For many years it was an important river crossing or
the stock route to Victoria; it also served as a major link

he legendary Cobb and Co. passenger coach network and is now the centre of
extensive horticultural and wool-producing area. An old Cobb and Co. coach,
d on one of the runs through the town until 1901, is on display at the coach-
se, corner of Lachlan and Moppett streets, and Hay's Gaol Museum has a
at array of pioneering memorabilia.

alranald is another spot of green on the Murrumbidgee. About 150 km (93
es) north of Balranald are the **Walls of China**, a geological phenomenon of
metre (100-ft) high walls of white sand running for 30 km (19 miles) across
ngo National Park ⓲. This dry lake is also the site of archaeological excava-
s that have recovered the world's oldest evidence of cremation – a first sign
ivilisation – from 26,000 years ago. Tools, ancient hearths and middens show
t Aboriginal peoples were inhabiting this site over 40,000 years ago. Mungo
he most accessible section of the **Willandra Lakes World Heritage Site**, a
,000-hectare (950,000-acre) system of Pleistocene lakes that was put on the
rld Heritage list in 1981. Formed over the past 2 million years, they are pro-
ted on the eastern shore by a lunette, or dune, formed by the prevailing winds.
obar ⓳, on the fringe of the Outback, typifies the resilience of the area's
ple as well as its hardy flora and fauna. From being a rip-roaring town of
000 people and 14 hotels not long after copper mining began there in the
70s, its fortunes have fluctuated: 100 years later its population was less than
00 and only one mine was operating; today the figures are 7,000 people and
r mines. The Eleura lead, zinc and silver mine (which was opened in 1983)
sted the town's population and economy. The **Great Cobar Outback**
ritage Centre, in an old two-storey mining company office, gives a fasci-
ing insight into the area and its people.

Map, page 152

BELOW: Walls of China in Mungo National Park.

The hand-stencil paintings you can see at Mount Grenfell, and at many other Aboriginal sites, were produced by holding a hand against a rock wall and blowing a mouthful of pigment around it.

BELOW: viewing rock art in Mottwingee.

Cobar's Great Western Hotel is the epitome of country hotels with its massive first-floor verandah. It gives a chance to sample the character of the ubiquitous two-storey pub, found on at least one corner of any large town, but without the inconvenience of the old-style sagging bed and bathroom down the corridor. Classification by the National Trust means that the exterior retains original timberwork and iron lace but, on the inside, accommodation has been transformed into modern motel-style units. It didn't need the National Trust to keep history alive in the Great Western's public bar, where the regulars lining the counter are always ready for a yarn with strangers.

North of Cobar, the Mitchell Highway meets the Darling River at the small and pleasant township of **Bourke ㉒** (pop. 3,500), once an important port. The colloquial expression "out the Back o' Bourke" signifies a place so remote that it is exceeded only by going "beyond the Black Stump". But the prettiness of the town is set off by the sheer emptiness that extends so far around it.

About 40 km (25 miles) along the highway from Cobar to Wilcannia is the turn-off to the **Mount Grenfell Aboriginal cave paintings**. Drive 30 km (19 miles) along a good dirt road to the cave, a shallow overhanging rock shelter, for rare examples of the techniques of pigments applied by finger, in human, bird and animal outlines, and hand stencils.

The highway continues on with long, straight stretches to the sleepy town of **Wilcannia ㉑**, where a number of historic buildings and wharf remnants are reminders of the days when its position on the Darling River made it a major inland port and earned it the title of "Queen City of the West". The lift-span bridge on the approach to the town is an interesting relic of those days: machinery lifted the roadway straight up to allow paddle-steamers to pass beneath.

Travelling into **Broken Hill** , you find a symbolic recognition of the city's individuality: although it's in New South Wales, watches and clocks are turned back 30 minutes to South Australia's time zone. Broken Hill (pop. 23,500) lives in NSW geographically and administratively, but conducts most of its trade and communication through the much nearer capital, Adelaide.

The city looms large in Australia's industrial history, with legendary unions eventually dominating the city with the Barrier Industrial Council. Its mineral wealth played the largest part in changing the nation from a strictly pastoral outpost to a more industrial base.

It all began in 1883 when a boundary rider and amateur geologist, Charles Rasp, stumbled across a lump of silver ore on a rocky outcrop he described as a "broken hill". From the claim that he and his syndicate pegged grew the nation's largest company, the Broken Hill Proprietary Co. Ltd. Although it diversified widely and had completely moved out of Broken Hill by 1939, BHP is still spoken of with distaste in the city for its abrasive attitude to the workforce.

"The Hill" turned out to be the world's largest silver, lead and zinc lode and, while other mining towns have tended to peter out over the years, this one is still going strong. It has yielded more than 147 million tonnes of ore from its 8-km (5-mile) long lode. **Delprat's Mine**, BHP's original dig, an almost black hill that dominates the city, gives the non-claustrophobic a chance to don a hard hat, lamp and boots for a guided tour. The route heads 120 metres (390 ft) underground in pits that were started in the early, dangerous days of hand drilling. With former miners as guides, visitors will get a feel of the terrible hardships faced by miners of the past and the still difficult conditions of today's underground workers. There are also surface tours

Broken Hill is a centre for the School of Distance Education (formerly School of the Air), providing daily lessons by radio for children who live far from any school. You can visit the centre at the airport and listen in to the on-air classes; book via the Visitors Information Centre.
Tel: 08 8087 6077.

BELOW: the source of Broken Hill's wealth.

Map, page 152

Map, page 152

of **South Pasminco Mine**, and you can see reproductions of mine working at **White's Mining Museum**, off the Silverton Road.

But not everything in Broken Hill is related to the great black hill. This Outback town has become an unlikely font of the arts, and is now home to several locally famous painters including Pro Hart, Jack Absalom and Hugh Schulz. Among the 27 galleries in the city, Pro Hart's is the most exotic. Besides a wide range of paintings by Hart himself, it also houses much of his private collection which includes works by Monet, Rembrandt, Dali, Picasso, Dobell, Drysdale, Lindsay, Arthur Boyd and Tom Roberts.

Broken Hill has also become a centre for one of Australia's unique institutions – the **Flying Doctor Service**, which carries medical attention across the vast distances of the Outback by aircraft.

At night, head for the licensed clubs to play the "pokies". A good deal of the city's social life revolves around the Musicians, Sturt, Legion and Social Democratic clubs, which welcome visitors and have good dining and bar facilities.

In red, rocky country it may be, but Broken Hill still has its beach resort at **Lake Menindee**, 110 km (68 miles) away. This is the city's part-natural and part-artificial water-supply system. The lake and a system of other lakes and channels cater for yachting, power boating and swimming; it combines with the adjacent **Kinchega National Park** to provide a home for a wide variety of water birds.

The restored ghost town of **Silverton**, a mining centre 23 km (14 miles) from Broken Hill, is not just an attraction for tourists; it's becoming a regular star in Outback movie epics. With repainted shop and hotel signs, it has appeared in *A Town Like Alice*, *Mad Max II* and *Razorback*. The predictable result is that an Outback Hollywood is evolving. Also in the Silverton area is the 100-year-old **Day Dream Mine**, where inspections include walking down into the workings the way the pioneer miners did.

For the braver traveller with a bit more time, it's possible to drive right off the beaten track from Wilcannia to Broken Hill, with a detour through the opal fields. It's a rewarding diversion, but not one to be taken lightly because of its lack of sealed roads, fuel and water.

White Cliffs, 98 km (61 miles) north of Wilcannia, is a lunar landscape of craters created by opal diggings, and fossickers with permits can have a scrounge around. Many residents live underground to escape the scorching winds and extreme temperatures, and some of them don't mind showing off the interiors of their white-walled subterranean settlements, which can be surprisingly luxurious. The best accommodation at White Cliffs is, of course, an underground motel or subterranean bed-and-breakfast.

Looping around about 160 km (100 miles), a road leads to **Mootwingee**, a surprising patch of greenness in the barren Bynguano Ranges. Strange and colourful rock formations surround ancient Aboriginal campsites, tools, engravings and paintings, which are explained in films shown at the visitor centre. Visitors must check with the resident ranger on arrival. There are camping facilities, but no power, and ranger-guided tours are available during the cooler months. ❑

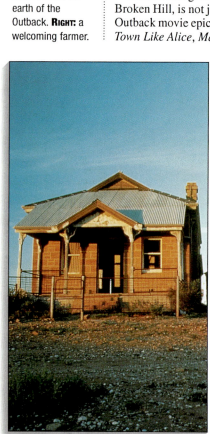

BELOW: ochre tones reflect the earth of the Outback. **RIGHT:** a welcoming farmer.

CANBERRA

*The capital of Australia is a place conceived by accident,
built by bureaucrats and located on a compromise.
Considering all that, it's a remarkably pleasant place to visit*

Map,
page 182

S ome years ago, during one of his visits to Australia's national capital, the Duke of Edinburgh declared that **Canberra** (pop. 322,000) was "a city without a soul" – a royal snub the citizens of Canberra have not forgotten. January 2003, raging bush fires spread into the city, destroying 530 homes d 30 farms, and killing four residents. The community spirit in the aftermath monstrated that even if Canberra were "a city without a soul", its residents ll had hearts. But it is not a soul that Canberra lacks – it is more a sense of pur-se. Like many administrative capitals, it is an artificial city, constructed not und any existing settlement, but simply out of thin Monaro air.

The reason it was built at all can be traced to colonial jealousy: in 1901, at e time of the federation of the six Australian colonies, there was intense alry (which still exists) between Sydney and Melbourne over which was the ief city of Australia. After some wrangling, the founding fathers solved the oblem by the compromise of inventing a new capital at an equally incon-nient distance from both. Thus a small and hitherto undistinguished valley in e southern tablelands of New South Wales was selected as the site.

Visitors to the city often complain that they can never find the centre – even hen they are actually standing in it at the time. Canberra, the political, diplo-atic and administrative capital of the Commonwealth, simply not built as a commercial city, and so far it has bbornly refused to look or act like one. In fact, what looks most like, apart from a spread of pleasantly ooded suburbs, is a kind of semi-dignified Disney-d, complete with a **Captain Cook Memorial Water t Ⓐ** which flings water 140 metres (460 ft) into the . Visitors are either impressed or bemused by the y's uncluttered, circular road system that tends to d the unwary around in circles. Of equal wonder is e absence of external TV antennas and the lack of nt fences – both of which were decreed aesthetical-incompatible with Canberra's image.

Similarly, new homes are supplied with young native es in order to promote the city's reputation as a leafy burbia. In contrast to the absence of planning in other ustralian cities, the zeal with which the bureaucracy s monitored and moulded this city's character does press. As a result, Canberra is a city of showcase chitecture.

Parliament House Ⓑ, which cost more than $1 lion and is adorned with many art and craft works, as opened in 1988. It's built into the side of Capital ll, its roof grassed in order to blend in, and exten-ve areas can be visited (daily 9am–5pm). Its pre-cessor, **Old Parliament House Ⓒ** on King George rrace, now houses exhibitions and events run by e **National Museum of Australia**, the **Australian**

PRECEDING PAGES:
Parliament House.
LEFT: view of the
city across Lake
Burley Griffin.
BELOW: the Captain
Cook Memorial
Water Jet.

TIP

Visit the Royal
Australian Mint south
of the lake, in Deakin
(open Mon–Fri
9am–4pm; Sat–Sun
10am–3pm), where
you can not only
watch the production
of the country's
coinage but also have
"coins" and tokens
minted to your
specifications.

Archives and the **National Portrait Gallery** (daily 9am–5pm).

On the lakefront are the **National Library** ❿ (Mon–Thur 9am–9pm; Fri–Sa
9am–5pm, Sun 1.30am–5pm, free guided tour at 12.30pm Thur only) which ha
4½ million books and whose displays include a model of Captain Cook'
Endeavour; the **National Gallery** ❶ (daily 10am–5pm), which has a fine col
lection of Aboriginal art and a Sculpture Garden; the **High Court** ❷ (dail
9.45am–4.30pm), grandiose enough to echo a Moghul palace; and the **Ques
tacon National Science and Technology Centre** ❸ (daily, 9am–5pm; entranc
fee), which has many enjoyable hands-on displays. On Aspen Island, the **Car
illon** tower, a 53-bell gift from Britain, plays muzak-like selections to the res
idents at weekends.

North of the lake, the **Australian War Memorial Museum** ❹ (daily 10am
5pm) looks oppressive but has a collection of relics, weapons, documents an
photographs said to be one of the best of its kind in the world. The **Australian
American War Memorial** ❺ on Kings Avenue is known to local people a
"Bugs Bunny" because the winged eagle that adorns its summit bears a resem
blance to the rabbit. West of the lake, the **National Aquarium** ❻ on Lad
Denham Drive, (daily 9am–5pm; entrance fee) is worth a visit and includes
wildlife sanctuary.

In the midst of all the high-minded architectural efforts, Canberra retain
considerable charm. It remains one of the few cities (as opposed to towns) i
Australia where it's still possible, occasionally, to see kangaroos in the streets
For those who miss out on this spectacle, the nearby **Tidbinbilla Natur
Reserve** offers a range of Australian flora and fauna.

Nature lovers should also visit the **National Botanic Gardens** ❼ (daily

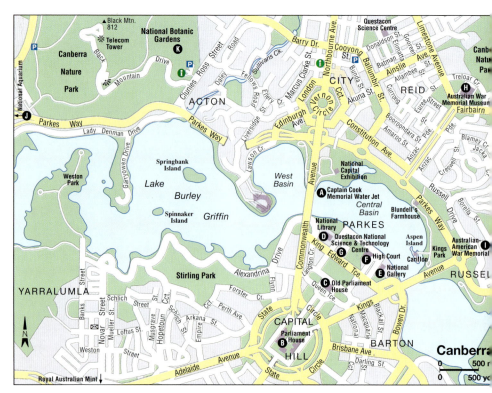

am–5pm) at Black Mountain Reserve, which contain a huge range of Austral-
in plants, the best of its kind in the country. The surrounding bush is one of the
ty's great attractions; indeed, to its residents, Canberra has all the advantages
f life in a leisurely country town, but comparatively few of the disadvantages.

The city has acquired an impressive range of restaurants of many national
uisines, and several international-class hotels (such as the fabulous Art Deco
yatt). Nightlife is improving, too: there are 200 bars (including some 24-hour
nes), a variety of cinemas and theatres, a casino, and some good music, rang-
g from classical to rock. For half the year you can watch the Australian par-
ament in session – which, when the "pollies" go at each other hammer and
ngs, is the best free show in town.

Canberra is a good jumping-off place for outdoor entertainment. There are
asy day-trips to old mining and farming towns such as **Captains Flat** and
ungendore. A few hours' drive to the south, along the Kosciuszko Alpine
/ay, are the **Snowy Mountains**, Australia's best ski area in winter and the
etting for spectacular bushwalking in summer. About the same distance east is
e **South Coast** of New South Wales, with some of the prettiest and least-
poilt beaches. A number of sheep stations welcome visitors. There is a bonus
r astronomers, as Canberra is surrounded by optical and radio telescopes and
deep-space tracking station. Many of the telescopes were destroyed in the
003 bush fires but will promptly be rebuilt.

Although the city is Australia's capital, it can seem surprisingly casual, with
w-key security. The best times to visit are spring, when it's fresh and green
d covered with blossom and wattle; and autumn when the weather is balmy
d the yellowing leaves of the deciduous trees are strikingly beautiful. ❑

Map, page 182

After the Aboriginal place name was adopted for the new capital, there was some embarrassment when it was discovered that the word "canberra" actually means "woman's breasts".

BELOW: a Remembrance Day ceremony at the Australian War Memorial.

MELBOURNE

*The capital of Victoria is Australia's financial and commercial heart.
It is also Australia's most "European" city, a 21st-century
metropolis with an abundance of 19th-century charm*

L egend has it that when you arrive as a visitor to Perth, locals first ask where
you are from; in Adelaide which church you belong to; in Sydney how
much money you make; and in Brisbane or Darwin simply if you would
like a beer. In Melbourne they want to find out what school you went to.

Melbourne has long enjoyed a reputation as the seat of Australia's Establishment, where background and connections still have their relevance in its corridors of power. In the Queen City of the South, stockbrokers, lawyers, bankers
and company directors are more often than not the product of the city's elite
grammar schools and colleges. Think of old clock towers and quadrangles,
school blazers, playing fields and cricket pitches – the legacy of the great schools
of Britain – and you're beginning to get the picture. The Melbourne Club, the last
mothballed bastion of archaic tradition and WASP power in Australia, still does
not admit women as members.

Along with this thick conservative gloss, Melbourne has always been Australia's capital of genteel, refined, European tastes. One has always come here for
fashion and theatre, art galleries, restaurants and shops; Melbourne has wide,
leafy streets, public gardens and gorgeous fountains, and is crowded with Victorian architectural gems erected when gold was the cornerstone of its prosperity.

While Sydney has a sense of the rough diamond
about it, Melbourne is considered more as a cultured
pearl: lots of class, but not much sparkle. This has provoked some odd responses. In the 1950s, evangelist
Billy Graham dubbed Melbourne "the most moral city
in the world". (Little did he know!) And, in the 1960s,
the actress Ava Gardner, in Melbourne working on the
film of Nevil Shute's *On The Beach*, was quoted as saying that it was the perfect place to make a film about the
end of the world.

But, as even Sydneysiders grudgingly admit, Melbourne has changed a lot since Ava Gardner's visit: it's
now a vibrant, exciting, sophisticated city with a thriving arts scene, a pub music circuit that has produced
some of Australia's most famous bands, and a disproportionate number of the country's best restaurants. And
the evidence of history demonstrates that the capital of
of the State of Victoria has never been the dowager she's
painted to be, more like a spirited woman who periodically kicks up her skirts and enjoys life to the full. But
let's go back, for the genesis of Melbourne's odd reputation is woven into the city's beginnings.

Free men from the start

Unlike Sydney, Melbourne was not founded as a penal
colony. Instead, the city's early settlers were free men
intent on building a new and prosperous life for themselves. In June 1835, John Batman, a land speculator

Map,
page 188

PRECEDING PAGES:
the Victorian
grandeur of the
Windsor Hotel.
LEFT: striking South
Bank café sculpture.
BELOW: Parliament
House.

from Tasmania, sailed his schooner into Port Phillip Bay, rowed up a broad river and declared: "This will be the place for a village." With a payment of goods including blankets, mirrors and axes, he persuaded the local Aborigines to "sell" him 600,000 acres (240,000 hectares) of prime land and drew up a document to legalise the purchase. This was later discounted as a farce by the British government, which accused Batman of trespassing on Crown Land.

A year later, the settlement beside the Yarra River was officially named in honour of Lord Melbourne, Britain's prime minister. The first land sales took place soon after, and small properties at the centre of the settlement sold for £150. Two years later the same properties were changing hands for £10,000, a good indication of Batman's keen sense of speculative real estate.

If it was these auspicious beginnings that laid the foundation for Melbourne's establishment and the city's continuing role as Australia's financial centre, it was the discovery of gold at nearby Ballarat in 1851 that propelled the sudden growth in population and prosperity which determined its true character. The finds, 115 km (70 miles) from Melbourne, drew thousands of fortune-seekers from Europe, the USA and China. Gold fever swept the country: it was the greatest gold rush the world had seen. But in time the alluvial gold ran out, and thousands of diggers left the goldfields to make Melbourne their home. The population more than quadrupled in 10 years, and the gold revenue financed new development in a rapidly expanding city determined to grow in a grand style.

When Mark Twain visited Melbourne on a lecture tour in 1895, he was entranced by what he saw: "It is a stately city architecturally as well as in magnitude. It has an elaborate system of cable-car service; it has museums, and colleges, and schools, and public gardens, and electricity, and gas, and libraries, and

One of Australia's most famous exports was born Helen Mitchell in 1861 in the Melbourne suburb of Richmond. She changed her name to Nellie Melba in honour of her native city and became a world-famous operatic soprano.

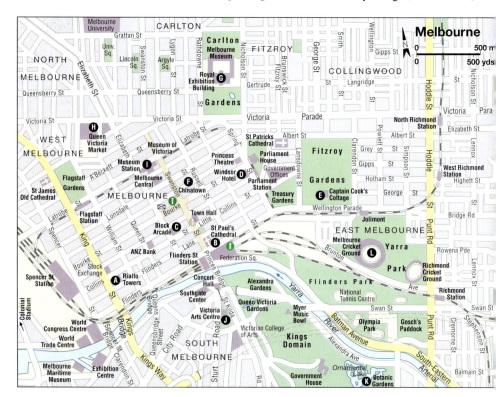

heatres, and mining centres and wool centres, and centres of the arts and sciences, and boards of trade, and ships, and railroads, and a harbor, and social clubs, and journalistic clubs and racing clubs, and a squatter club sumptuously housed and appointed, and as many churches and banks as can make a living. In a word, it is equipped with everything that goes to make the modern great city."

A cosmopolitan centre

Over one hundred years later, Melbourne is no longer the largest Australian city, but it is still growing steadily – often with escapees from Sydney looking for a less hectic lifestyle and more affordable real estate. With a sizeable migrant population from Europe and Asia (it's the largest Greek city outside Greece), Melbourne is a melting pot of cultures, friendly and understated.

True, it is not one of those spectacular, assertive cities that confronts the visitor with its visual impact or its energy. Rather, it insinuates itself into your subconscious, playing Boston to Sydney's New York. Melbourne's streets are wide and unhurried, rather like a vast country town; old trams still rattle along the streets; and Melburnians have a fondness for conversation and dinner parties quite lost in the more bustling, glitzy rival to the north.

Melbourne nestles comfortably on the banks of the **Yarra River** – a rather unimpressive sight, and the butt of many a cruel joke (it is said, for example, that it is the only river on earth that flows upside-down, with the mud on top). Still, it is spanned by ornate bridges, and one can watch the precisely coordinated movements of the rowing eights that train in the shadow of the skyscrapers.

The city's 3½ million inhabitants mostly live in the suburban sprawl that fans out from the bay towards the Dandenong Ranges. Most visitors will stay in the

Map, page 188

TIP

About one-third of Melbourne's 2,000 restaurants are not licensed to sell alcohol, but they are allowed to serve liquor that you have bought elsewhere. Look for the "BYO" sign (bring your own).

BELOW: a medley of facades at Federation Square.

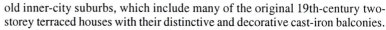

The most famous plant in the Botanic Gardens is the "Separation Tree", an old river red eucalyptus around which a great public party took place in 1851 to celebrate the independence of Victoria from New South Wales.

BELOW: the 1887 Windsor Hotel.

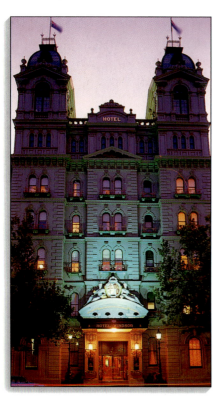

old inner-city suburbs, which include many of the original 19th-century two-storey terraced houses with their distinctive and decorative cast-iron balconies.

Melbourne is laid out on a convenient grid system that makes it easy to find your way around. In **Collins Street** and **Bourke Street**, among the soaring office towers of glass and steel, you can find fine examples of late 19th-century and early 20th-century buildings. The banking chamber of what was the CBA bank at 335 Collins Street is a masterpiece of baroque imagination. Other interesting buildings nearby are the Gothic-styled ANZ **Bank**, the **Rialto** complex Ⓐ (observation deck on the 55th floor open until 8pm; entrance fee), and **St Paul's Cathedral** Ⓑ, located on the corner of Swanston and Flinders streets. The small area bounded by Collins, Bourke, Swanston and Elizabeth contains seven of the finest shopping malls; the most impressive is the **Block Arcade** Ⓒ, with a high domed ceiling and mosaic-tiled roof. Nearby, a significant addition to the skyline is the architectural eyesore known as the **Federation Square Complex**, built over the site of the former Princes Bridge railway station, whose gaudy, pseudo-modern façades give the appearance of an uncompleted aquarium.

At the other end of town on **Spring Street** lies the stately **Windsor Hotel** Ⓓ. Opened in 1887, the Windsor is Melbourne's *grande dame*, and has been restored to its 19th-century opulence. High tea is served every afternoon from 3.30pm to 5.30pm, and is one of Melbourne's more distinctive Anglophile pleasures. Nearby are the **Princess Theatre** and the Victorian **Parliament House**, both of which have guided tours.

Melbourne has 680 hectares (1,700 acres) of landscaped parks and gardens that surround the city proper and are one of its great joys. The **Treasury Gardens**, with avenues of giant trees, extensive lawns and rock pools, almost reach into the Central Business District (CBD) at the top of Collins Street. At lunchtime on warm days the lawns are dotted with sunbathing office workers, while sweat-glistening joggers drum along its paths. In summer these and the adjoining Fitzroy Gardens are the main site of the City Council's free "Summer Fun in the Parks" programme, which includes lunchtime and twilight concerts, star-gazing and fairy stories.

The **Fitzroy Gardens** are the location of **Captain Cook's Cottage** Ⓔ, the home of the great mariner who put Australia and New Zealand on the map. It was brought to Melbourne piece by piece from its original site in Yorkshire.

For a taste of Melbourne's migrant legacy, head for **Chinatown** Ⓕ on Little Bourke Street. It has been a distinct ethnic area in Melbourne ever since Chinese prospectors joined the gold rush in the 1850s. Today you'll find dozens of restaurants and the intriguing **Museum of Chinese History**.

In the Carlton Gardens on the northern edge of the city is the **Royal Exhibition Building** Ⓖ, a domed stucco palace on the site of Australia's first Federal Parliament. Next door is the new **Melbourne Museum**, the largest museum in Australia, featuring among other things a Forest Gallery and Aboriginal Centre.

Melbourne likes its markets. The biggest is **Queen Victoria Market** Ⓗ on Victoria Parade, right on the northwestern edge of the CBD. On Tuesday, Friday and

Saturday morning it is essentially a food market – a sprawling collection of fruit and vegetable stalls that seem to go on forever. But on Sunday the food is replaced by purveyors of every imaginable item, and shopping becomes even more of an adventure. For a more bohemian flea market, don't miss the one at Camberwell Junction on Sunday mornings.

Shopping of a very different kind is to be found in **Melbourne Central ❶**, a striking new development stretching from Lonsdale Street to La Trobe Street and containing no less than 300 stores. Among them is the Japanese **Daimaru**, with six floors of the finest merchandise from Asia and the Pacific region. It's an extraordinary architectural melding, built around a ancient brick shot tower.

Melbourne is the only city in Australia that still has a wide-ranging tram network. A ride down St Kilda Road on a No. 8 tram is a must for the visitor who really wants to get the feel of the town. There's also the maroon "Colonial Tram-car", a fine restaurant on wheels, which makes for a great sightseeing tour.

Many trams stop outside the imposing **Victoria Arts Centre ❶** on St Kilda Road, which includes the state Art Gallery, three major theatres, the circular Melbourne Concert Hall and a Museum of Performing Arts. You may spot this colony of culture by its 115-metre (350-ft) white webbed-metal spire, laser-lit at night. Adjacent, on the banks of the Yarra, lies the **Southgate Center**, a pleasant dining, shopping and entertainment complex; on a sunny afternoon, hordes of Melburnians converge here and outdoor tables provide the best people-watching in town. The Sunday market is excellent for local art, craft and souvenirs.

Melbourne's supreme park, and surely one of the finest in the world, is the **Royal Botanic Gardens ❸** (open daily; guided tours at 11am and 2pm Sun–Thur, 2pm Fri). About 15 minutes by tram from downtown, these undulat-

Map, page 188

One-third of the total area of Melbourne is parkland or gardens.

BELOW: a picnic in the Royal Botanic Gardens.

TIP

A convenient way to see Melbourne's main sights is to take the City Circle Tram, a free service using old-time tramcars (look for their maroon-and-gold livery). Daily 10am–6pm, every 10 minutes.

ing gardens beside the Yarra River offer a tranquil breathing space where visitors can get lost in fern grottoes and cactus gardens, watch black swans cruise regally over the lake, or explore its 40 hectares (88 acres) of green lawns and thousands of native and exotic plants.

At weekends you'll find a great potpourri of Melburnians doing their thing in the Botanic Gardens: Greek families with mountains of food and bouzouki music, promenading lovers, nature freaks, sunbathers, elderly couples taking a stroll, martial-arts experts practising their movements, and kids allowing their adventurous spirits to run free. In summer there are outdoor theatre performances, and a moonlight cinema showing the classics (Birdwood Avenue entrance).

Toorak Road, which is serviced by trams, runs through South Yarra and Toorak, Australia's finest and richest suburb. Here affluence and the flaunting thereof is the common denominator. Boutiques, bookshops, restaurants and beauty salons beckon. European sports cars and the occasional Rolls-Royce cruise with panache. If you are image-conscious, this is the place to be.

At its South Yarra end, Toorak Road is bisected by **Chapel Street**, renowned as the best designer shopping strip but also accommodating everything from the avant-garde to the mundane. It's a real resource centre for the many ethnic communities (particularly Greeks) and flat-dwellers living in the Prahran area. It also gives access to **Prahran Market**, one of Melbourne's great Saturday morning experiences if you respond to exotic foods and equally interesting people. The **Jam Factory**, a cinema and restaurant complex of award-winning design, deserves special mention, as does the new **Como Centre**, part of the swanky designer Como Hotel. Nearby is **Greville Street**, a small and quirky strip of antique bookshops and fashions of the new wave and second-hand variety.

BELOW: Lygon Street is the heart of Little Italy.

Map, page 188

rahran's High Street runs off Chapel Street; if you travel east on it you will enture into a wonderful world of antique shops and markets at **Armadale**. The starting point for Melbourne's coolest crowds is **Brunswick Street** in itzroy and Collingwood, only 10 minutes by tram or five by cab from the cen-e. In the evenings, Melburnians drift here from around the city with bottles of ine tucked under their arms, looking for the latest BYO restaurant. There are fghani, Thai, Greek and South American places, as well as Modern Australian. ine bars, pubs with local bands and comedy nights, hip designer clothes stores, ny retro fashion shops, gay and lesbian bookshops, artists' cafés of the type opular in the 1950s and '60s, full of confused-looking characters who look as they've escaped from a Camus novel… the whole bohemian shebang. Inter-cting with Brunswick Street, **Johnston Street** is Melbourne's Spanish quarter, ned with tapas bars that pulsate at night with salsa and flamenco dancing.

Or, for a different cultural take, visit **Lygon Street** in Carlton, just 10 min-es by tram from the city centre, sometimes known as **Little Italy**. It was this ea that the waves of post-war Italian migrants adopted as their own. Today ygon Street is quite touristy and often filled with cruising young Italians. Still, lively community of professional people and entertainers, plus academics from ljacent Melbourne University, gives the place an ambience all its own. Cof-e bars, bistros, trattorias, noisy pubs and pool rooms, as well as anxiously up--date fashion boutiques, contribute to a lively atmosphere; at night, visitors roll from one end of Lygon Street to the other, choosing a restaurant.

A recent addition to Melbourne's skyline and culture is the controversial $1.6-llion **Crown Casino** and entertainment complex, a monolithic structure with re-belching columns on the Yarra riverfront. Open since 1997, it has changed e focus of the city, with 24-hour gambling (its 350 mbling tables and 2,500 gaming machines make it e of the world's biggest casinos), Australia's only 24-ur cinemas, nightclubs, restaurants, designer shops ch as Armani, Prada and Versace, an All Star Café and anet Hollywood theme restaurant.

Melbourne was the centre of a brewing revolution 100 years ago. In the 19th century most Australian beer had been made like British ales, until lighter Continental-style lagers were brewed in Melbourne by immigrants from Germany.

BELOW: a Fitzroy and Collingwood café.

ootie fever and the Cup

winter a strange malaise infects Melburnians. They ll it "footie fever". Aussie Rules football was invented Melbourne in 1858 *(see page 100)* and has been an psession ever since. It was once suggested that the city s no summer, only a period of hibernation between otball seasons. Don't fight it. Give in and join the cal crowds at a Australian Football League Saturday atch at the **Melbourne Cricket Ground** (MCG Sta-um) ❶. It's a fast, sometimes violent, always skilful, yle of football. The game was played mainly in the uthern states but has become a national competition. In elbourne, its spiritual home, the Grand Final match to cide the premier team of the year is played at the MCG fore 100,000 screaming, beer-drinking fans.

The only day of the year to rival the Grand Final is e first Tuesday in November, when the Melbourne up horse race is held, bringing Australia to a standstill. t 3.20pm, office workers produce transistor radios om their filing cabinets, schoolkids surreptitiously lm earplugs into place, pedestrians crowd around car

TIP

Melbourne's night life offers something for all tastes. To find out what's happening in the pubs and clubs, check *Beat* magazine, available free in cafés, or the EG section (Entertainment Guide) in the Friday edition of *The Age*.

BELOW: St Kilda's fashionable Stokehouse restaurant.

radios and shop-window televisions. In Canberra politicians break from their acerbic debating, and in Victoria the whole state takes an official holiday.

Almost everyone in Australia has a bet on The Cup – around $100 million is wagered on the race. Its fate is decided in three minutes as the horses strain round the two-mile (3,200-metre) course at **Flemington Racecourse**. But the Melbourne Cup is more than just a race: it is a key social ritual. The rich and famous set up private marquees or enjoy the traditional chicken-and-champagne picnic luncheon from the boots of their cars. The bonhomie lasts all day and rolls across Flemington in a way that casually transcends the usual social barriers.

Towards the beaches

Not so long ago, Sunday in Melbourne was a metaphor for existential boredom, death-in-life. No longer. **Acland Street**, St Kilda, is a busy Sunday shopping centre which the Jewish community has made its own. Famous for its cafés and cake shops, it displays the palate-delighting influences of Vienna and Warsaw, Budapest, Prague and Tel Aviv. Men in hats stand in little groups on the footpath and debate with restrained passion. Families crowd into the cafés, and plump women amble home with boxes of creamy delights. Recently, Asian-style cafés have sprung up in Acland Street, to add to the ethnic mix.

Walk towards the beach along **Fitzroy Street**, once a sleazy row of derelict hotels and now one of Melbourne's most fashionable addresses. On sunny days, the restaurants here take over the footpaths with their tables and umbrellas, creating a Mediterranean atmosphere. Further along, past Luna Park's gap-toothed grin and clattering roller coaster, lies the **Upper Esplanade** and the Sunday arts and crafts market. Here stallholders offer all manner of jewellery, leatherware,

paintings, ceramics and glass work. Keep going down to the seashore. There may not be surf to speak of, and few would brave a dip in the water, but the sand is clean and the beachfront on weekends is rather like Los Angeles' Venice Beach: rollerbladers and cyclists speed past, models preen themselves in the sun, body-builders work out on the grass. Fight for an outside table with the fashion-conscious crowd at the Stokehouse restaurant, or walk along the jetty for a distant view of the city skyline (there's a seafood café at the end).

On the other side of the bay, over the Westgate Bridge (or take a ferry from St Kilda or Southgate), is **Williamstown**, with the atmosphere of a bayside town, plenty of cafés, restaurants and great views back to the city.

Excursions from Melbourne

Some Melburnians like to live closer to the bush and commute to the city. In the **Eltham** area, 30 km (19 miles) along the Yarra River, people have built homes using natural materials and designs influenced by the old squatter homesteads. Mud-brick walls and slate floors, heavy wood and beams, wide all-round verandahs to ward off the sun and large landscaped gardens of gum trees and native plants have created some uniquely Australian homes.

About 50 km (31 miles) east of Melbourne lie the **Dandenong Ranges**. Here, the mountain bluffs are riddled with fern gullies and art galleries, while small towns like **Belgrave** and **Olinda** make lovely destinations for day trips, offering antique shops and cafés serving cream teas. Attractions include the **William Ricketts Sanctuary** (in a forest setting, where Aborigine spirit figures have been carved from wood by an elderly white sculptor) and **Puffing Billy**, a narrow-gauge steam train that plies a track from Belgrave to Menzies Creek. ❏

Map,
page 188

There's a glorious view across Melbourne (especially at sunset) from the Sky High restaurant on top of Mount Dandenong.

BELOW: St Kilda Beach is Melbourne's Bondi.

CLASSICAL AND CONTEMPORARY

Australia's second city arguably takes first prize for architecture, with some elegant 19th-century survivors amid striking modern buildings

Melbourne grew on the back of the great wealth created by the 1850s gold rush. By 1880, when the population stood at 250,000, the city was illuminated by more than 1,000 gaslights. The following 10 years saw a building boom on a scale unprecedented in Australia. This period, known as "Marvellous Melbourne", was heralded by the International Exhibition of 1880, for which the splendid Melbourne Exhibition Building was created. By the turn of the century Melbourne was regarded as one of the major cities of the world, rich in theatres, churches, arcades, rows of terraced houses and magnificent gardens.

Collins Street, Melbourne's best-known thoroughfare, still contains a number of grand buildings from the Victorian era. The street's development began around 1849, when doctors and dentists began building residences and consulting rooms. At the eastern end, near Parliament House and the Treasury, the impressive stone buildings and trees on the footpaths led this area to be called the Paris End. The dignified 19th-century buildings still standing on Collins Street include banks, offices, theatres, churches and the Melbourne Club, the oldest of its kind in Victoria.

TALL STOREYS

The face of the city began to change in 1959 with the construction of Melbourne's first skyscraper. The skyline is now dominated by modern glass and concrete towers, although many grand Victorian buildings remain at their feet. The 1990s saw a return to city living, with the renovation and conversion of warehouses and historic buildings for residential use.

△ **HIGH AND MIGHTY**
The ornate facades of the Rialto and Winfield buildin on Collins Street are dwarf by the Rialto Towers, Australia's tallest building.

◁ **FIVE-STAR RATING**
The Windsor Hotel, opened 1887 and still popular, has memorable facade, staircas and domed restaurant.

▷ **BATH TIME**
The City Baths, splendidly restored in 1990, were built in 1903–4 and originally contained separate men's and women's swimming pools, slipper baths, spray baths, Jewish Mivka baths and Turkish baths.

◁ **ANGEL DELIGHT**
An angelic feature of the Princess Theatre, completed in 1886. The theatre retains its classical facade, although the interior was remodelled in 1922.

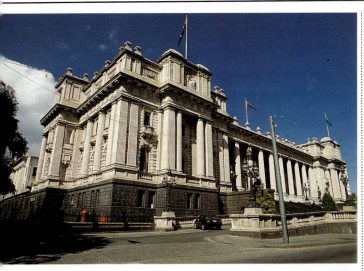

THE ADVANCE OF THE MODERN

4 YEARS IN THE MAKING
e building of Parliament
use began in 1856 but was
finished until 1930, and a
ne in the original design
s never completed. The
nd interior is one of the
st in Australia.

▽ PURE EXHIBITIONISM
The Melbourne Exhibition
Centre opened in 1995. Its
main hall measures 84 x 360
metres (275 x 1,180 ft);
outside, a stunning 60-metre
(200-ft) cantilevered steel
blade proclaims its presence.

△ END OF THE LINE
Flinders Street Station has
been the hub of Victoria's
railway system since it was
completed in 1911.

With many of Australia's leading architectural firms based in Melbourne, it's not surprising that the city is rich in modern architecture. The lattice-work laser-lit spire of the Victorian Arts Centre *(far left)* is not just a beacon for the impressive arts precinct it adorns, but a symbol of modern Melbourne.

The rejuvenation of the south bank of the Yarra – including the Southgate Center, the Crown casino and entertainment complex with its elegant ovoid tower, and the Melbourne Exhibition Centre – has completed one of the most exciting waterfront developments in Australia.

Melbourne has many modern office towers worthy of note, among them Rialto Towers (Australia's tallest); 101 Collins Street, with arguably the city's most impressive foyer; the former BHP House at the corner of William and Bourke streets, which uses expressed steel on its exterior; the AMP building on the opposite corner; the twin towers of Collins Place; the Melbourne Central shopping precinct, which houses the historic Coop's shot tower and factory inside a glass cone *(above)*; and Melbourne's first skyscraper, ICI House in Nicholson, built in 1959 and one of the first curtain-wall buildings in Australia.

VICTORIA

ll the destinations in Victoria are within a day's drive of Melbourne – alpine mountains, desert plains, pristine beaches, historic wineries, gold-mining villages and quaint spa towns

Map, page 202

The southeastern state of Victoria is Australia at its most civilised. Although its founding was basic, Victoria developed during the gold-rush days when the supply of money seemed endless, and the countryside is still littered with colonial mansions. The Victorian influence on Australia's society and politics continues; it's no coincidence that Victoria has Australia's most prestigious schools and has produced a high proportion of its prime ministers.

For a small state, Victoria packs in a lot of attractions. The range of scenery is wide: from the coastal resorts of the east coast to good ski resorts, the stunning spectacle of the Great Ocean Road to the picturesque valleys north of Melbourne or the old inland port of Mildura. Whereas motor touring in much of Australia is an adventure and a battle against rugged roads, Victoria has an excellent highway system and a scale small enough to ensure you see a great deal along the way.

Northeast Victoria

Many visitors enter Victoria via the Snowy Mountains in NSW. Below Khancoban, the road crosses the headwaters of the Murray, Australia's greatest river, and wanders into **Corryong**. This little town features the **Man From Snowy River Folk Museum**; its collection includes mid-19th century skis from Kiandra. A few miles south is the village of **Nariel Creek**, where folk-music festivals are held on an old Aboriginal corroboree ground on New Year holidays and Victorian Labour Day weekend. Northwest of Corryong, with access from Cudgewa, is the **Burrowa Pine Mountain National Park**. The gently rolling countryside is left for cattle grazing and some pine plantations.

Tallangatta, at the eastern tip of **Lake Hume**, is a new town, built in 1956 to replace the former community flooded by the damming of the Murray River and the creation of the lake. Traces of the old township – lines of trees, streets, even some buildings – eerily reappear at times of low water. The lake, four times the size of Sydney Harbour, is now a playground for swimmers, water-skiers, fishermen and bird-watchers. It widens as it arcs from Tallangatta toward Wodonga, 38 km (24 miles) west by highway.

Wodonga is the Victorian half of Australia's fastest-growing inland metropolis. Its big brother, **Albury ❶**, across the Murray River in New South Wales, gives the twin cities a combined population of about 85,000. Hub of the Riverina district, which produces prodigious quantities of grain, fruit and livestock, Albury marks the site where the explorers Hume and Hovell discovered the Murray in 1824 after trekking south from Sydney. Drage's Historical Aircraft Museum in Wodonga contains the nation's largest collection of biplanes.

All towns here have one thing in common – a history

PRECEDING PAGES: Mount Buffalo National Park. **LEFT:** a dramatic way to view the Grampian Ranges. **BELOW:** the Queenscliff Hotel.

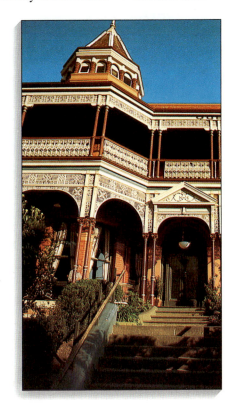

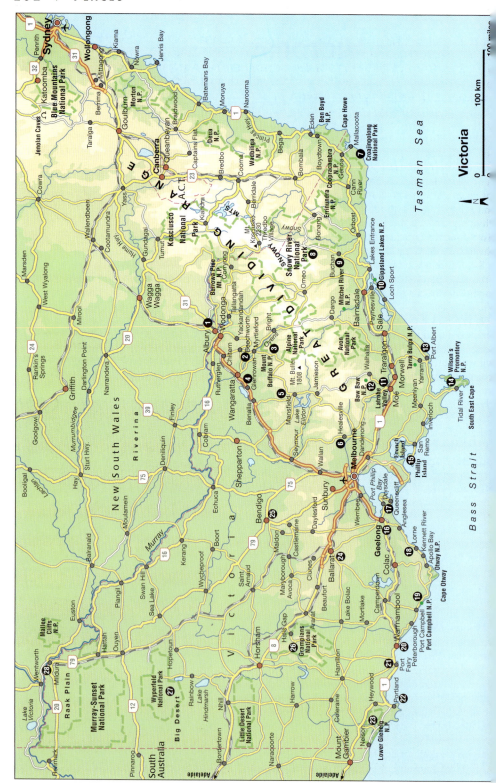

Map, page 202

nked to gold. In 1853, when gold was discovered in the valley of the Ovens iver, dozens of prosperous mining settlements sprang into life almost over-ght. By 1870, most of them had folded as the precious mineral became harder find, but some of the towns survive as vital reminders of a thrilling history in valley better known today for its wines.

Chiltern was originally established in the 1850s as Black Dog Creek. With its ide streets flanked by shops with Old West-style facades, the town has proved popular film set. Today its main claim to fame is Lake View, the childhood ome of novelist Henry Handel Richardson *(The Fortunes of Richard Mahony).*

Sixteen km (10 miles) northwest of Chiltern is **Rutherglen**, centre of Austral- 's oldest vine-growing district and still the foremost producer of fortified ports, kays, muscats, sherries and frontignacs. This region exported wine to England nd France in the 19th century, but few vineyards survived an invasion of the hylloxera mite at the turn of the 20th century. Some vintners stubbornly per-sted, finding the soil and climate ideal for sherries and dessert wines – they dis-overed they could ripen their grapes late in the season to a high sugar level.

The entire township of **Yackandandah** has been classified by the National rust. Miners who came from California and the Klondike in the 1860s helped give the town a lingering air of the American West. Today it is the centre of ictoria's largest strawberry industry.

Nestled in the midst of rolling hill country is northeast Victoria's best-reserved gold town, **Beechworth ❷**. No fewer than 32 of its buildings have een classified by the National Trust, including the towered Post Office (1867) ith its Victorian stone construction, Tanswell's Commercial Hotel (1873) with s handsome facade and wrought-iron verandah, and the **Robert O'Hara Burke**

Australia's only strawberry wine is produced at Allan's Flat Strawberry Farm, a short distance northeast of Yackandandah on the road to Baranduda.

BELOW: wrought iron adorns Tanswell's Hotel in Beechworth.

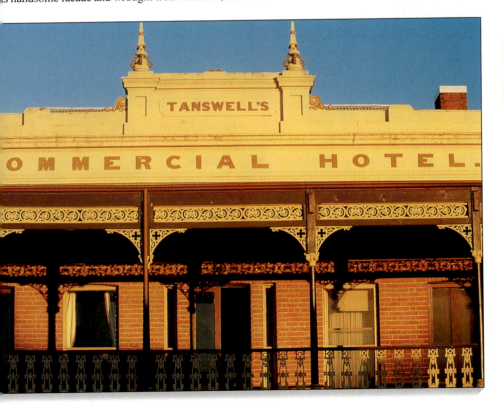

TIP

With the desert on one side and the sea on the other, Victoria is notorious for its changeable and unpredictable weather. Be prepared for cold winds, rain and searing heat all in the same day.

Memorial Museum (1856). This museum exhibits the finest provincial collection in Australia. Myriad relics and memorabilia of the gold-rush era – when million ounces of gold were garnered in just 14 years – are displayed with other pioneer objects, and there is even a life-sized recreation of Beechworth' former main street. During its heyday the town had 61 hotels and a theatre which hosted international acts.

South from Beechworth is a region of considerable natural beauty. **Myrtle ford** is also the thriving centre of a walnut, tobacco and hop-growing region **Mount Buffalo National Park ❸**, comprising a vast plateau at 1,370 metre (4,495 ft) elevation, becomes a huge snowfield in winter, a carpet of wildflower in spring, and a popular spot for bushwalking in the summer and autumn.

Bright, a town of 5,000 famed for its autumn colours, is a short distance away Oaks, maples and other hardwoods give the town a serene feeling which belie its violent gold-rush days, including the notorious 1857 Buckland riots when white prospectors brutally ousted Chinese miners from their claims.

Wangaratta is a skilfully planned agricultural centre with a population o 17,500 on the Ovens River. Today it is noted for its wool mills, two interesting 19th-century churches, and Byrne House, a fine art gallery which displays indig enous Australian talent.

This is the heart of "Kelly Country", the stamping grounds of the legendary Ned Kelly, Australia's most infamous bushranger. The site of Kelly's last stand was the **Glenrowan Inn**, 16 km (10 miles) southwest of Wangaratta. Kelly' comrades were killed in a shoot-out with police as the inn burned to the ground and Ned himself was brought to trial in Melbourne, where he was hanged in No vember 1880. Today, travellers on the Hume Highway through **Glenrowan ❹**

BELOW RIGHT:
Australians' favourite criminal lives on as a tattoo.

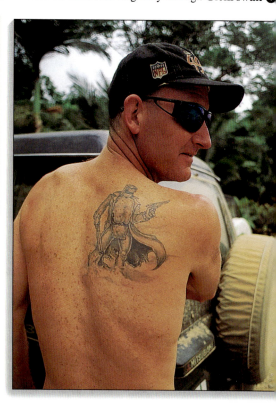

THE MAN IN THE IRON MASK

Edward "Ned" Kelly, the son of an Irish ex-convict, was a thief and a murderer whose legend has been immortalised in poems, plays, paintings and a 1970 movie starring Mick Jagger. Even when he was alive, his daring exploits and defiance of the law captured the imagination of Australians. During the three short years (1878–1880) when he was terrorising townships, robbing and killing people, the larcenous Kelly and his gang gained an almost legendary reputation. His superb horsemanship and his famous metal suit of armour, fashioned by hand from the mouldboard of a ploughshare, helped to create his charismatic image. But spare some pity for his poor horse: the armour, including the helmet, weighed 44 kg (97 lb).

Map, page 202

n't miss the tourist tat, try as they might. An armed, larger-than-life techni-
olour Ned Kelly looms over a block of tacky shops pushing Kelly kitsch. Next
oor, the shoot-out is re-enacted several times each day. More reminders of the
elly days are on display in two museums in **Benalla**, which calls itself the "Rose
ity" after the thousands of bushes that bloom from October to April. These add
olour to the unusual **Benalla Art Gallery** overlooking the Broken River.

Mansfield ⑤, at the junction of the two highways, is an important grazing
nd timber centre and the gateway to **Mount Buller** (1,808 metres/5,932 ft),
ictoria's largest ski resort. It lies just 3 km (2 miles) from **Lake Eildon**, a 130-
l. km (50-sq. mile) body of water formed from the damming of five rivers to ir-
gate thousands of square miles of farmland. Today the lake is a year-round
aradise for water-skiers and fishermen angling for trout, perch and Murray cod.

Only 61 km (38 miles) from Melbourne is **Healesville ⑥**, best known for the
Healesville Sanctuary. This world-renowned open-air zoo, established in 1934
o study and breed native fauna, is a very popular tourist attraction. The sanctu-
ry has played a key role in replenishing some of Australia's endangered wildlife.

ast coast

t the hamlet of **Genoa** near the NSW border, a sealed side road turns south
owards **Mallacoota Inlet**. This tiny resort town, much beloved by fishermen
nd nature lovers, is at the end of a 24-km (15-mile) journey off the Princes
ighway at Victoria's southeasternmost tip. It is surrounded by **Croajingolong
ational Park ⑦**, 86,000 hectares (212,500 acres) of rocky cliffs and open
eaches, rainforest, open woodland and health, stretching some 100 km (60
iles) from the NSW border to Sydenham Inlet. Numerous nocturnal mammals

For a rare chance to see the extraordinary duck-billed platypus in a fairly natural environment, visit the Healesville Sanctuary, the first place to breed this shy creature in captivity.

BELOW: near Mallacoota on the east coast.

In some of the limestone caves near Buchan (not those open to visitors) explorers have found tools and rock engravings dating back 17,000 years.

(including possums and gliders) and many snakes – some venomous – make their homes in the park; birdlife includes lyrebirds, oystercatchers, pelicans, sea eagles and kingfishers. The pub at the charming village at **Gipsy Point** over looks the inlet between Mallacoota and Genoa.

West of Genoa, the Princes Highway winds through its most remote stretch 208 km (129 miles) of mountains and rainforest to Orbost. Logging trucks seem to congregate at **Orbost**, a prosperous town of about 3,000 people near the banks of the lower Snowy River. **Snowy River National Park ❽**, in the mountains above Orbost, is popular with whitewater canoeists.

Another timber town, 93 km (58 miles) northwest of Orbost by winding rugged road, is **Buchan ❾**. It hosts a rodeo over Easter, and a lumberjacks' contest in May. But its main attraction is its limestone caves, unquestionably the finest in Victoria. There are 350 caves here, but only three are open to the public, including the Fairy Cave, whose numerous honeycombed chambers are embedded with ancient marsupial bones.

At **Lakes Entrance**, the Princes Highway offers its only ocean glimpse west of Eden. The resort is situated at the narrow man-made inlet to the Gippsland Lakes, a long string of interconnected lagoons stretching west along the inner shore of the Bass Strait for some 80 km (50 miles). They are separated from the sea only by a narrow band of dunes and hummocks called **Ninety Mile Beach**

The year-round population of Lakes Entrance (about 3,000) increases to more than 20,000 in summer as holidaymakers pack the motels and caravan parks. Fishing, boating and swimming are the main draws; cruise boats offer regular sightseeing tours of the lakes, which cover 388 sq. km (150 sq. miles). Sometimes called the "Victorian Riviera", the area has consistent temperatures of

BELOW: autumn comes to the Victorian countryside.

out 20°C (68°F) in the middle of winter. The **Gippsland Lakes Coastal** **ark**, a reserve of dunes and heath along the lakes' seaward edge, and the **akes National Park** ⓾, a bird-filled woodland on a sandy peninsula between **ake Reeve and Lake Victoria, help protect natural features.

Map, page 202

The commercial centre of East Gippsland is **Bairnsdale**, 285 km (177 miles) st of Melbourne via the Princes Highway. A sheep, dairy and timber centre, is best known for its fine botanic gardens and the "Sistine Chapel" murals in t Mary's Catholic Church. Nearby **Paynesville**, a boating resort, features the zarre yet interesting Church of St Peter: a sailors' house of worship, it has a ire like a lighthouse, a pulpit shaped like the bow of a boat, and a sanctuary ghting fixture that was once a ship's riding lamp.

A 45-minute drive northwest of Bairnsdale is **Glenaladale National Park**, ythical home of an Aboriginal monster called Nargun. This demon had an appetite for young children, whom he enticed to his den and then devoured. The en of Nargun, hidden behind the mist of a waterfall, has formations of stalactes and stalagmites.

Sale proudly bears the title of "Oil City". Since oil and natural gas were discovered in the Bass Strait in 1965, the industry has developed rapidly in this egion, with processing plants and supply ports, and numerous rigs offshore. he major processing plant is near **Longford**. Public visits can be arranged.

The string of small cities along the Princes Highway from Sale comprises the atrobe Valley ⓫, whose coal produces about 90 percent of the electricity for Melbourne and Victoria. The valley sits upon the world's largest deposit of rown coal – about 60 km (37 miles) long, 16 km (10 miles) wide, and 140 etres (460 ft) thick. Open-cut mines and the steaming towers of power sta-

BELOW: the Italianate interior of St Mary's Church, Bairnsdale.

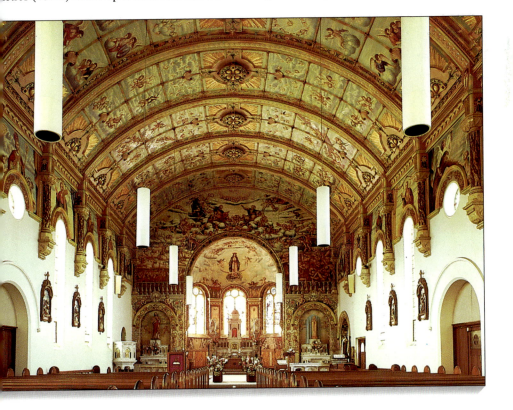

On the Bass Highway, near the turn-off for Phillip Island, there's a museum dedicated to Megascolides Australis, the largest worm in the world, which grows to 3.5 metres (11 ft) long and 2.5cm (1in) thick. You can't miss the Wildlife Wonderland – it's shaped like a worm. It also includes Wombat World and other wildlife.

BELOW: lush ferns in the Tarra Valley.

tions are everywhere. Public mine tours are offered at **Morwell** and the mode town of **Yallourn**, built by the State Electricity Commission.

Moe, the valley's largest and most modern city, is the site of the Old Gipps town open-air folk museum and also the gateway to the mountain communitie of **Walhalla** (a veritable ghost town that once boasted Victoria's richest gold mine) and **Mount Baw Baw** (the nearest ski resort to Melbourne).

About 30 km (19 miles) northwest of **Yarram**, in the heart of the dense and rugged Strzelecki Ranges, the tiny twin national parks of **Tarra Valley** and **Bulga** feature primeval fern gullies, waterfalls and a plethora of plant species South of Yarram are the historic townships of **Port Albert** and **Tarraville** The Port Albert Hotel (1842) may be the oldest continuously operating licensee hotel in Victoria, while the old timber jetty – at which eager 19th-century Chi nese gold miners once disembarked – is now crowded with yachts and motor boats. The **Port Albert Maritime Museum** is housed in the old Bank o Victoria. Tarraville was Gippsland's largest town in 1851, with 219 breweries Perhaps it is divine justice that the Tarraville Anglican Church, a wooden struc ture held together without the use of nails, should have outlived all of them.

Wilsons Promontory , a huge granite peninsula that represents mainland Australia's furthest thrust towards Antarctica, is the most popular national park in Victoria. "The Prom", as it is affectionately called by regular visitors, fea tures more than 80 km (50 miles) of walking tracks to long sandy beaches forested mountain slopes, and heath and marshes packed with bird, animal and plant life. An estimated 100,000 people visit the park each year. Environmental ists are concerned with the impact they may have on the fragile ecology; for tha reason, most of the park is inaccessible even by footpath. The most frequent

emory taken home by visitors is of the huge flocks of flamboyantly coloured
sellas and lorikeets that mischievously invade campsites in summer.

For many travellers, the most interesting stop in this final stretch to Melbourne
Phillip Island ⓑ. Seven km (4½ miles) off the Bass Highway southwest of
orumburra, it is connected to the mainland fishing community of **San Remo** by
bridge. In an area about 104 sq. km (40 sq. miles), most of it cleared for grazing
d chicory growing, is a bewildering array of tourist attractions. Phillip Island
as the site of Australia's first motor-racing circuit (1928), which was rebuilt
the late 1980s. Today it hosts the Australian 500cc Motorcycle Grand Prix in
ctober. Among other attractions are koala and bird sanctuaries, scenic offshore
ck formations, historic homesteads, pottery shops, and sports from surfing,
ving, sailing and fishing to golf, tennis, bowling and croquet. Tourist accom-
odation is centred at the north coast summer resort town of **Cowes** – named
ter the main port of England's Isle of Wight.

Unquestionably the biggest regular attraction for Phillip Island visitors is the
lony of fairy penguins at Summerland Beach. Around dusk each day of the
ar, hundreds or even thousands of these little birds, apparently tuxedo clad,
arade from the waters of the Bass Strait to their protected burrows in the sand.
ings outstretched, they waddle in small groups up a concrete ramp past throngs
curious human onlookers. This has developed from being a haphazard event
enormous charm to a tourist spectacle, with a great loss of atmosphere.

About 1.5 km (1 mile) off the western tip of the island are the **Seal Rocks**,
e breeding ground for Australia's largest colony of fur seals. Early December
the peak of the breeding season – is the best time to watch the 5–6,000 seals
rough coin-operated telescopes in the kiosk on the clifftop at **Point Grant**.

Map,
page 202

BELOW LEFT: "The
Prom" – Wilsons
Promontory.
BELOW: two of
Phillip Island's fairy
penguins.

The black lighthouse at Queenscliff, still guarding the treacherous entrance to Port Phillip Bay, was prefabricated in Scotland and shipped to Australia in 1863.

BELOW: some of the Twelve Apostles.

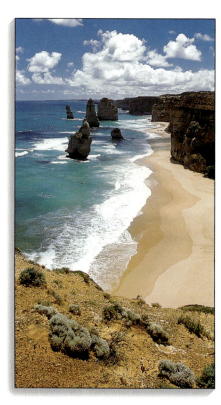

The coast west of Melbourne

From the fringe of **Melbourne** the Princes Freeway speeds through the fla plains along the northern shore of **Port Phillip Bay**. Melbourne's favourite sea side precinct, the **Mornington Peninsula**, lies at the bay entrance, with beache vineyards and hobby farms (smallholdings). For a glimpse of an era of opuler elegance, take the exit to **Werribee Park**. In a 60-room Italianate mansion buil in 1877 by the Chirnside family, who migrated from Scotland and created a pas toral empire, visitors can see a vivid example of flamboyant wealth.

Another half-hour's drive, with the volcanic You Yangs dominating the sky line, brings you to the heart of Victoria's second city. In its early days **Geelong ⓰** rivalled Melbourne as an outlet for the wool of the Western District and the star ing point for thousands who tramped northwards to the goldfields at Ballara From Ceres Lookout you have a view of a park-filled city curving around **Cori Bay**. A drive along the waterfront shows Geelong past and present – the old man sions, wool stores and piers and the new industries, wharves and container term nal; the fishing boats and the palm-treed lawns and pools of Eastern Beach. Alon the Barwon River are fine homes such as the National Trust's **Barwon Grange**, re furnished in the style of 1855, when it was built by a merchant ship-owner.

For a whiff of nostalgia, take the Bellarine Highway out of Geelong and joi the coast at **Queenscliff ⓱**. This was "Queen of the Watering Places" in th 1880s when the great paddlesteamers brought the fashionable to stay at the hand some turreted hotels. The Queenscliff fort, with red-brick walls and cannor was built in the 19th century to defend Melbourne against a possible Russia invasion. Now it is the Australian Army Command and Staff College.

The road from Queenscliff to Anglesea meanders through small seaside settle ments, sleepy in winter and pulsing with life in summe Below the lighthouse at **Point Lonsdale** is the cave c William Buckley, an escaped convict who lived with a Aboriginal tribe for 32 years. He was the only white ma in an Aboriginal world until the first settlers arrived i 1835. Near **Torquay**, the surf centre of Victoria, is Bel Beach, internationally famed for its Easter surf contest

Beyond **Anglesea**, where kangaroos share the gol course with the players, is the start of the **Great Ocea Road**, one of the world's great drives, built by returne soldiers after World War I. It opened up 200 km (12 miles) of the state's most spectacular coastal scenery.

A favourite spot is **Lorne ⓲**, set on a picturesque ba with a bush backdrop and plenty of restaurants an shops. Its annual Pier-to-Pub Swim in January attract entrants from all over Australia. In the **Lorne Fores Park**, tracks wind through eucalyptus forest and fer gullies to waterfalls and lookouts. Walks vary from gentle stroll along the St George's River to rock-hoppin along the craggy Cumberland to the Cascades. A three hour hike up the Erskine River to the falls can be stren uous. The less energetic can reach the site by car.

Along the coast at Kennett River, a 6-km (3½-mile drive leads to the **Grey River Scenic Reserve**. It's short walk (1½-km/1 mile round trip), one of the bes in Victoria, up a fern gully amid towering blue gums.

From Apollo Bay, the Great Ocean Road leaves th coast to wind through the forest behind **Cape Otway** where the lighthouse has watched over the hazardous entrance to the Bass Strait since 1848, until it was decommissioned in 1994.

For an alternative panoramic view of the ranges, turn inland at Skenes Creek and drive up into the hills. After 15 km (9½ miles), turn left into the delightful fern and mountain ash forest along Turton's Track. When the country opens out again you are on a high ridge. On the left, wooded spurs reach down to the sea; on the right are the volcanic lakes and plains of the Western District.

Beyond Princetown lies the spectacular coastline of **Port Campbell National Park** 🅙 where breakers have battered the soft limestone cliffs, creating grottoes and gorges, arches and sea-sculptures rising from the surf. The clifftop road gives only occasional glimpses of the drama below, which includes the stark rock stacks of **The Twelve Apostles** and the spray billowing through the collapsed arch of **London Bridge**. Take the time to stop at all the vantage points: they overlook Victoria's most dramatic array of sights.

Beyond Peterborough and the dramatic Bay of Islands, the road turns inland to **Warrnambool** 🅩, once a busy port and now a progressive pastoral and holiday centre. Around the original lighthouse is the **Flagstaff Hill Maritime Museum**, a recreated 19th-century port with its ships' chandlers, shipwrights and sailmakers. Near Warrnambool is **Tower Hill**, a volcanic crater containing smaller cones and lakes. Once a lush oasis of bush life, it was destroyed when the land was cleared for grazing and cultivation, but is being restored to its original beauty. A one-way road takes you through the centre of the crater, where ducks again nest on the lakes and emus enthusiastically share your picnic.

Along the coast is the fishing-village charm of **Port Fairy** 🅩 where brightly painted boats tie up at the jetty with their catches of lobster and crab. Tradition-

**Map,
page 202**

TIP

From May to August you can watch Southern right whales at play in the waters around Warrnambool. There's a special viewing platform at Logan's Beach.

BELOW: the jetty at Port Fairy.

ally the birthplace of Victoria, Port Fairy was named by Captain James Wishart who brought his tiny cutter, the *Fairy*, into the Moyne River to find shelter during a sealing expedition in 1810. Sealers and, later, whalers built quaint stone cottages which still nestle under the tall Norfolk Island pines shading the streets. You can still drink at the Caledonian Inn which opened in 1844 and is said to be the oldest continuously licensed hotel in Victoria.

Griffiths Island, at the mouth of the river, was a whaling station, but is now a rookery for thousands of mutton birds that return in September from the north Pacific. The young hatch in January, and every evening till they leave in April you can watch the adult birds swoop in from the sea to feed their chicks.

On the way to Portland look in at **The Crags** with its unusual rock scenery and a view of flat-topped **Lady Julia Percy Island**, where a colony of fur seals breed. **Portland ㉒** – big wharves on a broad bay and solid 19th-century bluestone buildings – was a whaling station when Edward Henty arrived in 1834 and ploughed the first furrow in Victorian soil. Around Portland, gentle beaches contrast with surrounding rugged rockscapes. Take the cliff walks at Cape Nelson and view the moonscape bluff of Cape Bridgewater, where wind and water have fashioned a petrified forest from scrub.

The coast road to South Australia skirts **Mount Richmond**, a sand-covered volcano ablaze with wildflowers in spring. It borders **Discovery Bay Coastal Park**, with its vast rolling sand dunes and stretches of unspoilt beach, and runs along the southern margin of **Lower Glenelg National Park ㉓**, known for its gorge and delicate limestone cave formations.

You can drive or take a guided boat tour from Nelson up the gorge to the caves. The park is nature-rich with 700 species of native plants, but most of it can be explored only by river or on rough, sandy tracks.

Gold-rush memories

Ballarat ㉔ is within an hour's drive of Melbourne, a far cry from the jolting day-long journey along potholed tracks that faced the miners bound for the gold-diggings in the 1850s.

On the way into Ballarat, a signpost points to **Eureka**, a name etched into Australian history. At the site, a diorama brings to life the day in December 1854 when the diggers, angered by government oppression, stood up for their rights at the Eureka Stockade. When troops stormed the stockade, 22 diggers lost their lives. Their sacrifice gained a new deal for their mates and provided a pivotal point for Australian republicanism which still burns strongly today. The Eureka flag remains a strong Australian trade-union icon.

The rambunctious life of those times is recreated in the gold-mining town of **Sovereign Hill**. In the main street, resembling Ballarat in the 1850s with its old-fashioned wooden shops, apothecary and confectioners, you can watch blacksmiths, tinsmiths and potters at work; have your own Wanted poster printed by the old press in the *Ballarat Times* office; sample a digger's lunch at the New York Bakery; or have a drink at the United States Hotel next to the Victoria Theatre where Lola Montez danced her famous and risqué "spider dance". Take a ride on a Cobb & Co. coach and pan for

Australia's foremost folk and roots music festival is held in Port Fairy in March, attracting major national and international practitioners of folk, country, bluegrass, blues, jazz and world music.

BELOW: the bar of Craig's Royal Hotel, Ballarat.

Map,
page 202

TIP

Buy a Gold Pass at
Sovereign Hill for
admission to all the
sights, including the
Gold Museum and
an underground mine
tour. There's also a
son et lumière show
twice nightly,
recreating the Eureka
Stockade battle.

BELOW: Maldon's
well-preserved
main street.

ld in the creek. After a look around the Red Hill gully diggings, slake your
irst at the "lemonade" tent – the sly-grog shop where diggers celebrated their
ck or drowned their sorrows. Then walk along the underground tunnel of the
uartz Mine, typical of the company mines where, in the later years, the real
oney was made.

Today's Ballarat was born in the boom time, and its wide streets, verandahs
nd iron lace, towers and colonnades give it grace and charm. The fine-art
allery is renowned for its Australian paintings, and the Botanic Gardens be-
de Lake Wendouree sport Italian statues and a blaze of begonias, at their best
uring the Begonia Festival in March.

Worth exploring are the other "golden" towns to the north of Ballarat, where
nce thousands of men dug into their 7.4 sq. metres (8 sq. ft of dirt) with ant-
ke ardour. **Clunes**, the scene of the first Victorian gold strike on 1 July 1851,
as an ornate town hall, elegant banks and bluestone churches standing beside
acant shops. **Daylesford**, a picturesque town on Wombat Hill, is known (along
ith its neighbour **Hepburn Springs**) as the spa centre of Australia. In **Castle-
aine** the Greek temple-style market (now converted to a museum) and other
ne buildings date from an era of promise never quite fulfilled. **Maldon** was
elected as the National Trust's first "notable town in Australia" for its well-
reserved gold-rush era streetscapes.

In **Bendigo** ㉕, some of the richest quartz reefs in the world created a Victo-
an extravaganza. The scarlet Joss House is an interesting reminder of the many
ousands of Chinese who came to the "Big Gold Mountain", bringing with
em their temples, tea-houses and festivals. Their colourful Chinese dragon,
un Loong, is 100 metres (328 ft) long and the star of the Bendigo Easter Fair.

Visit Seppelt's winery at Great Western, 16 km (10 miles) north-west of Ararat; the guided tour includes lengthy underground galleries (originally dug by gold miners) where millions of bottles of champagne-style wines are maturing.

The road west from Ballarat passes **Lake Burrumbeet** and **Beaufort**, notable for its beautifully preserved iron-lacework band rotunda topped with a clock tower, then continues past forested hills to **Ararat**. The town's first settler named a nearby peak Mount Ararat "for like the Ark, we rested there." Two French settlers, who saw that the soil and climate between Ararat and Stawell resembled that of France, planted the first vines here in 1863. Wines, both red and sparkling white, have been produced at Great Western ever since.

Towards **Halls Gap** the ranges of the **Grampians National Park** 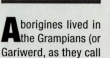 rise abruptly to dominate the surrounding plains. These craggy mountains, named after the Scottish Grampians, are a series of rocky ranges thrown up by the folding of a sandstone mass into an uncommon cuesta formation – spectacular escarpments on the east side and gentle slopes to the west. Erosion has shaped bizarre rock sculptures, and waterfalls cascade over the sheer face.

Motoring mountaineers can drive to many other scenic points, but there is wilderness aplenty for the more adventurous and walking tracks to suit all grades of hiker. You can drive past **Lake Bellfield**, where koalas feed in the manna gums, to the highest peak in the ranges, **Mount William** (1,167 metres/3,827 ft). A 1½-km (1-mile) walk takes you to the summit. Return to Halls Gap via the Silverband Road to take in some of the highlights of the Wonderland Range.

More than 40 Aboriginal art sites have been found in caves and rock shelters in the Grampians. Some of the more accessible are in the Victoria Range, where you can see hand stencils in red ochre in the **Cave of Hands**, and a variety of paintings including animals, human figures and a kangaroo hunt in the Glenisla Shelter. This site was found in 1859 by the owner of **Glenisla Station**, a sheep run established in 1836 that once covered most of the Western Grampians. Today guests can stay at the century-old stone homestead and at several other farm properties around the district.

On the Mount Victory Road, short detours lead to **Reid Lookout**, high over the Victoria Valley, and a home of kangaroos and emus. A 15-minute walk along the clifftop brings you to **The Balconies**, outcrops of sandstone that hang like giant jaws over the precipice.

As the road winds through the forest, stop at the viewpoint for the **McKenzie Falls** or take the walking track to the falls along the river, before going on to **Zumsteins**. Walter Zumstein, the beekeeper and bushlover who pioneered this valley, befriended the kangaroos, and each afternoon their descendants still come from the forest to be fed; they can seriously disrupt a picnic.

The highway travels through the heart of the **Wimmera**, the granary of Victoria, a sweep of golden wheat fields as far as the eye can see. This area, the size of Wales, stretches from the Grampians west to the South Australia border and north to the sand dunes and dry lakebeds of **Wyperfeld National Park** . It is dotted with small townships, soaring silos, and populated by more sheep than people.

Horsham, a small town with an art gallery and botanical gardens, is its hub, and here, on the banks of the Wimmera River, one of the largest and richest fishing competitions in Australia takes place. On Labour Day in March, thousands of fishermen line the river bank to try their luck at catching the biggest redfin.

DREAMTIME IN THE GRAMPIANS

Aborigines lived in the Grampians (or Gariwerd, as they call the area) at least 5,000 years ago. It was a land of plentiful resources, where the people did not have to spend all their time hunting and gathering – which explains the abundance of rock paintings in the area. You can visit sites of rock art at Gulgurn Manja (Flat Rock), Billimina, Larngibunja and Ngamadjidj. Many of the geographical features of the region are woven into the Aborigines' Dreamtime legends. One of them tells of Tchingal, the monstrous emu, who chased War, the crow, from her home in the Mallee. When War took refuge in a tunnel under one on the Grampian ranges, Tchingal struck it with her foot, splitting it in two and so forming Roses Gap.

he northwest

he city of **Mildura** ㉘ is the veritable Riviera of the northwest. While many
ustralian centres claim the biggest of something, Mildura aims for the long-
st bar in the world – 91 metres (298 ft) long, at the Workingman's Club; the
argest fruit juice factory; and the largest deckchair ever built (in front of a main-
treet motel). It is soon to be the site of the world's tallest man-made structure;
1-km (3,300-ft) convective solar tower as wide in diameter as a football field,
osting $1 billion and generating enough electricity to supply 200,000 homes.

Mildura is an exceptionally pleasant and friendly city, and its tourist orienta-
on combines well with its great climate and inherent water pastimes of fishing,
wimming and boating. Irrigation has given the district a wealth of orchards
nd vineyards, and among the places offering tours and tastings are the Mil-
ura and Capogreco wineries. The town and irrigated farms were established by
vo American brothers, George and William Chaffey. W B. Chaffey's imposing
omestead is now a museum within a city park. His other legacy is that, in the
JS style, Mildura has streets with numbers rather than names.

The **Murray River**, of course, is the dominant attraction, and it's easy to re-
ve the days when the mighty paddle-wheelers, laden with cargo and passen-
ers, made the river a busy thoroughfare before the railways made them
bsolete. You can get a taste of this stately cruising along the lazy Murray, lined
vith tall red gums, and through one of the river's series of locks. There are two-
our trips on the steam-driven *Melbourne*, day cruises on the *Rothbury* which
ncorporate local wineries and the zoo, lunch and dining cruises on the 1877
intage *Avoca*, and five-day, fully catered cruises on the *Coonawarra*. For the
nore independent, there's a wide range of houseboats for hire. ❑

Map,
page 202

BELOW: winter
comes to the
Grampians.

SOUTH AUSTRALIA

South Australia, with its multinational culture, is renowned for food, wine and festivals. It is also blessed with a Mediterranean coastal climate, great beaches and awesome stretches of Outback

AUSTRALIA

Perth · Sydney ·
Adelaide ·

Try a word-association test on most Australians: say "South Australia". The first response is likely to be "wine". The second could be "Adelaide Festival", and the third might be "Flinders Ranges" or "Nullarbor Plain". The mix suggests the unlikely variety of this remote corner: the state covers the gamut of Australian landscapes and culture, from the lush pastures of the coast, with its intensely civilised capital city, to the subterranean lifestyle of Coober Pedy and the barren beauty of the Coorong. No other Australian state has such a high proportion of classic Outback desert to arable land, and this vast hinterland has seen some strange sights. At the far-flung base of Woomera, the state once hosted Australia's early forays into the space age (*woomera* is the Aboriginal term for a spear launcher). The remotest corners were the sites of British atomic testing after World War II, the full story of which didn't leak out until the 1980s (many Aboriginal people were affected by the testing, and reparations from the British weren't agreed until the 1990s). And the expansive salt pan of Lake Eyre was used by Sir Donald Campbell to set a land-speed record in 1964.

PRECEDING PAGES:
art in downtown
Adelaide.
LEFT: the cellars of
a Barossa vineyard.
BELOW: Adelaide
has more
restaurants per
capita than any
other Australian city.

A user-friendly city

In the world's most urbanised country, South Australia is the most urbanised of states: the vast majority of its inhabitants live in the capital, **Adelaide**. Yet, of all Australian cities, Adelaide is perhaps the most gracious. Mark Twain was one of the first tourists to pronounce himself thoroughly captivated. During his Australian visit in 1895, he praised its orderly layout, graceful parklands and distinctive bluetone architecture and declared that "if the rest of Australia or any small part were half so beautiful, it was a fortunate country".

Situated roughly one-third of the way from Sydney to Perth, this city of 1.2 million people is ideally placed to ignore the rest of the world – which, for most of its history, it did quite happily. Among Australians, Adelaide used to epitomise conservatism with a small "c". A certain implacable smugness was evident, especially among its "Establishment", which was convinced this was one of the last truly civilised corners of the globe. There was some truth to this: by a combination of letting the world pass it by and judicious planning, Adelaide has avoided the worst excesses of modern social upheaval, pollution and urban blight.

Adelaide should be savoured slowly. It is possible to rock around the clock in Adelaide, if you know where to go, but it can be done better elsewhere (except at festival time, when no other Australian city can compare – see page 222). For most of the year, to get the most out of Adelaide you should shift down a gear or two, move at a leisurely pace and meet it on its own terms.

TIP

A convenient way of visiting Adelaide's sights is the Explorer Tram, which leaves the Travel Centre (corner of King William Street and North Terrace) at 9am, 12.15pm and 3pm. Catch one of the earlier ones, so that you can hop off and explore, then board the next tram.

No less than in Mark Twain's day, one's first impression of Adelaide is its sheer prettiness. This isn't an accident of nature. The city was laid out in a choice location according to the grand design of a British Army engineer, Colonel William Light, who founded the city in 1836. He came with a bevy of free settlers who had the express idea of founding a Utopia in the Antipodes. Sadly, Light – who was suffering from tuberculosis – was given a breakneck two-month deadline to choose a location and survey it. He managed the feat, choosing an inland site that was controversial at first, but his health collapsed; he had to retire, and died soon after.

The "City of Light" still follows his original design. From the air the original city resembles a lopsided figure eight, with residential North Adelaide on one side of the Torrens River and the central business district on the other.

North Adelaide has some of Australia's grandest homes. It was intended as an exclusive enclave for the transplanted English gentry, who shipped out grand pianos and chandeliers to put in their colonial salons. Despite the prevailing local opinion that many were the "idiot sons" for whom there was no room in the old country, the gentry more or less thrived, in spite of itself, on the mineral and agricultural wealth of South Australia. On this side of the Torrens is **Adelaide Oval**, the most beautiful cricket ground in the country, and well worth a visit during the summer cricket season. At the northern end of the Oval stands the neo-Gothic **St Peter's Cathedral**.

South of the river, the central business district was designed for walking; it measures one imperial square mile and is surrounded by extensive parklands, studded with majestic gum trees, which act as a scenic buffer between the city centre and the suburbs. This leafy "moat" means it is quite impossible to enter or

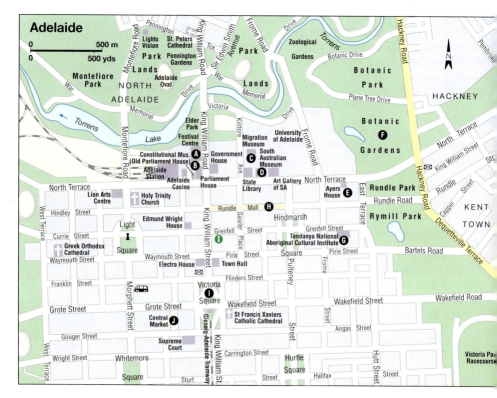

Map, page 220

eave the city without passing through restful greenery. The two halves are connected by King William Street, at 42 metres (138 ft) wide, the broadest main
street of any Australian capital city – one reason for the lack of traffic jams.

The main intersection in Adelaide is where North Terrace crosses King
William Street. Every major attraction is within a few minutes' walk of this intersection.

Adelaide Festival Centre Ⓐ has better acoustics than the Sydney Opera
House (oddly, it looks like the Opera House with the sails chopped square). With
its concert hall, playhouse, space theatre, outdoor amphitheatre, bistro and restaurant, it hosts the nation's premier arts event *(see page 222)*. The centre overlooks **Elder Park**, by the River Torrens – once a rather unimpressive trickle,
but dammed to form a virtual lake. Visitors can choose to take a two-person
pedal boat out on the river or ride in the launch *Popeye* with a guide providing
a running commentary; a 40-km (25-mile) cycle track also runs along the river.

Back on North Terrace is the **Old Parliament House**, which now houses the
Constitutional Museum (Mon–Fri 10am–5pm; Sat, Sun noon–5pm), and next
to it the monumental "new" **Parliament House** Ⓑ, completed in 1939, which is
open to visitors (guided tours 10am–2pm; from Mar–Dec, when parliament is
sitting, you can watch proceedings). Just across the road is **Government House**,
the official residence of the Governor of South Australia.

Just behind the **State Library** is the **Migration and Settlement Museum** Ⓒ
(Mon–Fri 10am–5pm, Sat, Sun 1pm–5pm; entrance fee), housed in a former
poorhouse and tracing the history of immigration to South Australia.

The eastern wing of **North Terrace** is easily the most impressive walk in the
city centre. The **University of Adelaide** could have been transplanted from

*Adelaide's imposing
Parliament House
was first planned in
1889, but it was not
completed for 50
years because of a
dispute over a dome,
and did not open
until 1939. It still has
no dome and only
half a coat of arms.*

BELOW: Adelaide's
Festival Centre
in Elder Park.

Festival frenzy

Sydney, Melbourne and Perth all have their arts festivals, but none compares in size, prestige or sheer excitement to Adelaide's. Held in March on even-numbered years, the festival trades on the city's natural advantages. Few places in the world have such an extraordinary range of performance spaces, from the gleaming white Festival Centre to the outdoor amphitheatres and intimate lofts. The weather is nigh-perfect, with dry, hot days and clear, star-studded nights – and you can walk to every venue within about 15 minutes.

The festival actually operates on several levels. The "official" festival lures the high-profile international acts, and kicks off with free weekend concerts in Rundle Park, followed by firework displays. Tickets to the official shows are very reasonable compared with the prices charged in Sydney and Melbourne, and there is usually a string of free events, such as those in the Red Square, an amphi-

theatre made of giant containers from transport ships, where the best acts put on 20-minute "samples".

At the same time, the "Fringe Festival" is for lesser-known performers and artists. It is second in size only to Edinburgh's annual shindig: literally thousands of acts arrive from all over Australia, Europe and North America. The chaotic, organic nature of the Fringe is what gives Adelaide its buzz. The focus tends to be around the bars and restaurants of Rundle Street East, where the festivities continue until dawn at the Fringe Club, but buskers and performers spread throughout the city. Every spare corner of indoor space is devoted to some art exhibition, and every stretch outdoors to a site-specific installation. By any standards, it's a remarkable happening.

The Lion Arts Centre, on Morphett Street and North Terrace, houses the Fringe's administration. It also has year-round stages, galleries, craft workshops and studios. At the same time as the Fringe Festival, Adelaide hosts Writers' Week, an event that lures the literary heavies from around the globe. It is entirely free, with readings by famous authors and book launchings held in two marquees.

Although nothing quite matches the festival for action, things are not too quiet in South Australia for the rest of the time. In odd-numbered years, also in March, Adelaide hosts an enormous World Music Festival, known as WOMAD, in Botanical Park.

The Barossa hosts its own Music Festival every October. Most of its recitals are classical in nature and held in Lutheran churches – although the accompanying indulgent meals and fine wines might well have appalled the region's dour founding fathers.

Then, in early April in odd-numbered years, the Barossa Vintage Festival is a thanksgiving celebration for the region's grape harvest. The seven-day event, based in Tandura, includes lavish tastings, grape picking and treading contests and a vintage fair.

Between May and October most wine-producing areas hold food, wine and music festivals, the most notable being the Clare Valley Gourmet Weekend in May. McLaren Vale holds several, including a "Continuous Picnic" in October.   ❑

LEFT: dancers perform at multicultural festival.

xford, ivy-covered walls, dreaming spires and all. The **South Australian Museum D** (daily 10am–5pm) houses the world's largest collection of Aboginal artefacts, as well as an extensive Melanesian exhibit and a broad survey f regional natural history (the building can be identified by the huge whale keletons displayed behind glass walls). Next door, the **Art Gallery of South ustralia** (daily 10am–5pm) has a renowned collection of 20,000 prints and awings. Reopened after a $20-million make-over in 1996, it now displays the ountry's largest collection of Australian art.

East along North Terrace is **Ayers House E**. The home of Sir Henry Ayers, ho contrived to be premier of South Australia seven times – an Australian cord – and after whom Ayers Rock (Uluru) was named, it is now a restaurant d living museum protected by the National Trust (Tues–Fri 10am–4pm, Sat, un 1pm–4pm; entrance fee). The elegant bluestone mansion contains 40 rooms ating from 1846 to the 1870s, and the hand-painted ceilings and ornate chaneliers of the dining room and ballroom are particularly remarkable.

To the north of Ayers House lie the **Botanic Gardens F**, 40 hectares (100 cres) of lawns, trees, shrubs and lakes, with some exceptional botanical buildings s well, from the old Palm House brought from Germany in 1871 to the extrardinary Bicentennial Conservatory of 1988.

South of Ayers House, in Grenfell Street, is **Tandanya Aboriginal Cultural ıstitute G** (daily 10am–5pm; entrance fee), the venue for theatre, dance, talks, emonstrations and constantly changing exhibitions of arts and crafts, reprenting all aspects of contemporary Aboriginal culture. The Institute has a shop lling native arts and crafts, and a café where visitors can try "bush tucker".

The lively, busker-filled **Rundle Mall H** was the country's first traffic-free

Map, page 220

Henry Ayers, seven times premier of South Australia, used his grand home, Ayers House, for state functions. Its ballroom, the hub of the Adelaide social scene, was washed down with milk to make the floor fast and smooth.

BELOW: thousands flock to the biennial festival.

**Map,
page 220**

shopping mall, an idea of former state premier Don Dunstan, who in the 1960
turned Adelaide from a musty provincial centre into "the Athens of the South'
He also originated the Festival Centre and introduced some of the most progres
sive state laws in Australia – laws to protect consumers, decriminalise homo
sexuality, guarantee equal opportunity and give freedom of information. Dunsta
shocked staid old Adelaide, and much of Australia besides (on one occasion, h
wore pink hot-pants at a press conference, to the consternation of all).

In the centre of the city's square mile, King William Street opens out int
Victoria Square ❶, with beautifully laid-out gardens, a charming fountain an
a statue of Queen Victoria. Just to the west is Adelaide's **Central Market** ❷
(Tues 7am–5.30pm, Thur 9am–5.30pm, Fri 7am–9pm, Sat 7am–3pm) – easil
one of the most colourful in Australia. A giant covered area packed with stall
it sells cheap fruit, vegetables, cheeses, meats, spices and a variety of esoteri
imported foods. The market butchers are entertainers in their own right: eac
shop has a man out front, often in a blue-and-white-striped apron and with
voice like a cannon, auctioning off meat, cutting prices, offering deals on side
of lamb and meat trays piled with roasts and chops. There are also stalls sellin
books, crafts, jewellery and clothing, and cafés and cheap eateries.

The market encompasses Adelaide's **Chinatown**, which spills out into Gouge
Street, one of the city's four main restaurant strips. The others are O'Conne
Street (North Adelaide), Rundle Street (East End) and Hindley Street (Wes
End). Between them, they provide Chinese, Indian, Turkish, Italian, Malaysia
Japanese, Greek, African, Vietnamese, Russian, Lebanese, Thai and eve
Australian eateries. It will come as no surprise to learn that Adelaide has mor
restaurants per capita than any other Australian city.

BELOW: the fruit and
produce market
East Terrace.

ills and beaches

osmopolitan as it can be, Adelaide never loses that country-town feeling. You
an drive across the city in half an hour, and you can be in beautiful country-
de within a few minutes from any point. Take any one of a dozen roads up into
e **Adelaide Hills** and you can easily get lost in leafy, winding laneways. The
ills are littered with small commuter suburbs like **Blackwood**, **Aldgate** and
rafers, some of them strikingly pretty. There are pubs with hilltop views and
staurants like Windy Point where you can see the entire city laid out at night
ke a page from a fairy tale.

The pubs and restaurants of the Hills make Adelaide just as pleasant to visit in
e winter as in the summer. In winter the Hills are lush and green, and there are
lenty of conservation trails to walk with hotels at the end, where a roaring open
re and a soothing glass of port await you.

Another Adelaide ritual is to take the Glenelg tram from the city centre to the
each. The ride takes about 20 minutes and, while **Glenelg** has seen better times,
e beach is wide, white and wonderful. If it's too crowded for your liking, all
ou have to do is stroll down a little further; it goes on for miles. On your return,
uy a treat of fish and chips to eat on the tram and wash the meal down with a
ottle of local sparkling wine. For a couple, the whole proletarian picnic will
ost around $30: fares, fish and chips, bubbly and all.

Adelaide's coastal border is fringed by endless ribbons of white sandy beaches.
f you're the sensual type, drive down Main South Road for 20 km (12 miles)
ntil you see the turn-off on the right to **Maslin's Beach**. It's an official nude
each, one of the state's best. It's friendly and family-oriented, but be warned:
he gulf waters are fed by the Southern Ocean and the water can be brisk.

**Map,
page 226**

*A fish restaurant
with a difference is
found on board* HMS
Buffalo *at Glenelg, a
replica of the ship
that brought the first
settlers to South
Australia. You eat in
the main cabin, using
19th-century pewter
tankards and
tableware.*

BELOW: the Barossa
Valley is Australia's
oldest wine-
growing area.

South Australia

Valleys of vines

Adelaide sits amid the country's greatest wine regions, of which the **Barossa Valley ❶** is easily the most famous. It's debatable whether the dour German Lutherans who settled the place over a century ago would have approved of the goings-on there today, but no wine lover finds much to complain about in the district that lies only 50 km (30 miles) northeast of Adelaide.

It takes about an hour to drive to the valley, which is a 30-km (19-mile) hollow in the rolling wheatfields. Thousands of hectares and row after row of vines, comprising nearly 40 vineyards, keep the Barossa's name at the top of sophisticated wine lists worldwide. The German heritage shines in the proliferation of Lutheran churches, vineyard names such as Kaiser Stuhl and Bernkastel, and the calorie-laden wares in the delicatessen windows. Nearly all the wineries have tasting and sales rooms, and many have barbecue and picnic areas as well as restaurants and pubs. Like a well-stocked cellar built up over many years, the wineries are spread the length of the Barossa Valley Highway.

First stop is the major agricultural centre of **Gawler**. Like Adelaide, Gawler was designed by Colonel William Light. In the old centre of Church Hill are most of the fine churches and beautifully designed residences that gave Gawler its reputation for elegance. The beauty of the old town is enhanced by its proximity to the junction of the North and South Para rivers. South Australians make some fine beers, and Gawler's old pubs are an ideal place to sample them. The Railway Hotel, Old Bushman and Kingsford are all more than 120 years old.

The road continues through **Lyndoch** in its forest setting and **Tanunda**, the most distinctly traditional German town, to the commercial centre of **Nuriootpa**, which is situated on the **Para River**. The old Lutheran churches are of abiding

Map, page 226

Unlike many of the other Australian states, South Australia was colonised by free settlers, without any help or hindrance from convicts.

BELOW: tasting alfresco at a Barossa Valley shindig.

At the Clare Valley Gourmet Weekend in May, instead of a ticket you buy a glass that you can take to as many wineries as you like, sampling their vintages and eating food chosen to match the wines.

BELOW: leisurely pursuits at Port Augusta.

beauty, with spires rising above quaint bluestone villages. Foremost among them are **Langmeil** at Tanunda, famed for its tree-lined Long Walk and where Pastor Kavel, founder of the church in Australia, is buried; the nearby **St John's** dedicated in 1868 by dissidents from Langmeil; and **Herbige Christe** at Bethany where the Germans settled in 1842.

Many Barossa wineries have not only excellent produce but also magnificent grounds and buildings, like the palm groves at **Seppeltsfield** (which date from 1852), the battlements of **Chateau Yaldara**, and the two-storey blue-marble buildings at **Yalumba**. A number of restaurants have German-style cooking; the best-known are Die Galerie, a combined bistro and art gallery at Tanunda, and the Weinstube, on the main road between Tanunda and Nooriootpa.

Although the Barossa is the best-known wine-producing area in Australia, it is only one of five major wine regions within easy driving distance of Adelaide. **Clare ❷** is the centre of the wine area of the Clare Valley/Watervale region about 130 km (80 miles) north of Adelaide. Fifteen wineries in a 25-km (15-mile) strip are open to the public for sales. Among those that hold inspections are Quelltaler, established in 1870 and still retaining its original stone architecture; Sevenhill Cellars, established in 1851 by German Jesuit priests; and the well-known names of Taylor's Chateau Clare, Robertson's Clare Vineyards and the Stanley Wine Company.

For the 40 vineyards of the **Southern Vales**, follow the signs to **McLaren Vale ❸**, 42 km (26 miles) south of Adelaide. Cartographers battle to fit all the 40 vineyards on the map; they read like a wine lover's roll of honour: Seaview, Hardy's Tintara, Wirra Wirra and Reynella. This is mainly a red-wine region.

In the southeast of the state, the vineyards of the **Coonawarra ❹** area are

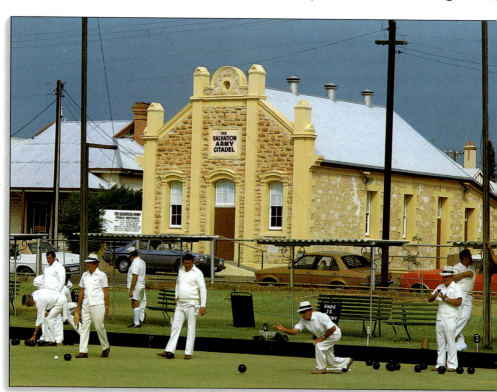

ustly famed for their reds. Vineyards at **Keppock** and **Padthaway** are becoming equally well-known. Padthaway Estate Homestead, now an exclusive hotel, is an imposing stone mansion in an oasis of green English-style gardens. The property was taken up as a sheep run in 1847, and the homestead was built in 1882. Today a number of vineyards spread over the acres where sheep once grazed.

Renmark, on the Murray River, is the start of South Australia's riverland. The area's orchards produce 2 million tonnes of fruit a year, and it also has 16 vineries, including names such as Angoves and Renmano at Renmark, Berri Estates at Glossop, and Penfolds at **Waikerie**. The specialities of the region are brandies and fortified dessert wines.

North from Adelaide

The **Flinders Ranges** extend from near Port Pirie, where Mount Remarkable 975 metres/3,150 ft) is the first major peak, to past Mount Painter in the desert and salt lakes to the north. At the top of the **Spencer Gulf**, the road turns away from the ocean and heads into the arid heart of the continent. Here lies **Port Augusta** which, with Port Pirie and Whyalla, forms the basis of South Australia's industrial heart, known as the Iron Triangle. From Port Augusta, the road runs northeast through **Quorn**, then on to **Hawker**, the nearest township to the northern Flinders Ranges.

By a fortunate coincidence, the most spectacular feature of the Flinders Ranges is also the most accessible. **Wilpena Pound** at the southern end of the Flinders Ranges National Park ❺ is a raised valley surrounded by quartzite hills. St Mary's Peak is the highest point in the ranges at 1,165 metres (3,758 ft).

The only way into the Pound is on foot: hike past an old homestead to a low

Like many geological features, the walls of Wilpena Pound are held by Aboriginal legend to be the petrified forms of animal ancestors – in this case, two giant serpents coiled in a circle.

BELOW: spectacular Wilpena Pound in the Flinders Ranges.

TIP

You should not attempt the Strzelecki Track or the Birdsville Track without extensive Outback driving experience, a four-wheel-drive vehicle and a lot of preparation. The Strzelecki Track has no petrol, water or supply station for 500km (300 miles) between Lyndhurst and Innamincka.

BELOW: down the lonely Strzelecki Track.

point on the lip, which provides a good view down into the pound itself. By comparison with the thin, rocky soil and arid landscape outside, the pound floor is richly vegetated. In fact, Wilpena Pound attracts considerably more rainfall than neighbouring regions. Although the exterior walls of the pound are steep, the inside slopes are relatively gentle, and even St Mary's Peak requires no more than a strenuous lengthy bushwalk. Although Wilpena Pound looks like a crater, it is the result of folding rocks, not the impact of a celestial object.

If Wilpena is your only destination in the Flinders, it is worth your while to take the time to detour north past the natural feature known as the Great Wall of China, then through **Parachilna Pass** to join the main Leigh Creek Road before heading south. Coming out of the pass, you emerge onto plains that typify central Australia; from here, as you look back, the open lip of Wilpena Pound clearly shows its strikingly symmetrical form.

The northern end of the Flinders Ranges more closely resembles the other mountains of central Australia. The base for exploring the **Gammon Ranges National Park** ❻ is **Arkaroola**, a small settlement geared to the needs of tourists. Gorges and valleys filled with wild flowers and endless variations on the recurrent themes of rock, eucalyptus and folded hills prevail. Only a short drive north of Arkaroola is the tiny oasis of **Paralana Springs**. The radioactive water that bubbles up here (and was once promoted as a primitive health spa) is the last reminder of volcanic activity in Australia. Not far north is a good vantage point to see the outline of the northern Flinders Ranges. From a high point to the south, they decline like a wedge to a series of small bumps which are, in turn, consumed by the vastness of the outback.

The roads north – the **Birdsville Track** ❼ or the **Strzelecki Track** ❽ – are

Map, page 226

rough adventures, both aiming towards the distant Queensland border. Not everyone likes the desert, but those who do will find the continual but almost imperceptible changes in scenery endlessly fascinating.

Along the Strzelecki Track, the last stop in South Australia is **Innamincka** ➒, a settlement with a population of fewer than 200 people where the only two buildings of note are the general store and the pub. Camping by **Coopers Creek** after a few beers at the pub is the embodiment of the Outback.

The Birdsville Track lies deep in the Australian psyche. It was developed as a route for driving cattle from western Queensland to Marree, SA, where they could be loaded onto rail cars heading south. **Marree** ➓ itself was a trading depot for the Afghan camel drivers who opened much of central Australia. These days, the track has no commercial purpose, but it remains an icon and a testing ground for those reliving the pioneering spirit.

On the sealed Stuart Highway, which stretches 1,370 km (850 miles) from Port Augusta to Alice Springs, the tiny settlement of **Pimba** marks the turn-off to **Woomera** ⓫, the rocket and research base that was opened to the public in 1982 with displays detailing the early days of rocketry. The base was set up soon after World War II by the Australian and British governments.

Coober Pedy ⓬, halfway to Northern Territory on the Stuart Highway, is the best-known town in outback South Australia. This is the world's largest opal field (for white opals), where the relentlessly hot climate (sometimes soaring to 50°C/122°F or more) has forced the inhabitants to live underground.

At first glance, the town looks like a hard-hit battlefield. The almost treeless terrain consists of hundreds of mounds of upturned earth and abandoned mines where fossickers have rummaged through the landscape in search of precious

BELOW: Crocodile Harry's dugout home at Coober Pedy.

gems. If you should arrive during one of the regular duststorms that sweep across the area, you could be excused for believing the apocalypse was nigh. But beneath the surface there are homes, shops, restaurants and even churches. There is an underground hotel, too, suitable only for non-claustrophobics. Visitors should note the beautiful natural patterns in the bare clay walls (and the lack of windows, compensated for by good air conditioning).

Unfortunately, the rapid increase in traffic aiming for the centre has changed Coober Pedy into a near caricature of its early self. For a more genuine experience of an outback opal town, venture off the beaten track to **Andamooka** ⓭, due north from Woomera, where fewer than 500 people dwell, but be aware that any rainfall can quickly leave you stranded.

Coorong and beyond

To the southeast of Adelaide, around the mouth of the **Murray River**, lies an indefinable maze of sandbanks and estuaries. This is the **Coorong National Park** ⓮, a haven for many waterfowl. The main features are the sand dunes of the **Younghusband Peninsula** that separate the shallow waters of the Coorong from the Southern Ocean, and the **Coorong** itself (*karangh* or "narrow neck" to the Aborigines), a long, thin neck of water stretching 135 km (84 miles) from Lake Alexandrina and Lake Albert at the mouth of the Murray River to the salt-pans and marshy ponds at the southern end.

If you lack a four-wheel-drive vehicle, it's a half-hour walk across the dunes to the ocean beach, an endless area of golden sand left mostly to the seagulls, oystercatchers, pelicans and occasional fishermen. A great number and variety of waterfowl feed on the waterplants in the lagoons and drink at the fresh-water

The name Coober Pedy comes from the Aboriginal words kupa peti, which loosely translate as "white fellow's underground burrow". The subterranean household in "Mad Max III: Beyond Thunderdrome" was located here.

BELOW: a paddle-steamer on the Murray River.

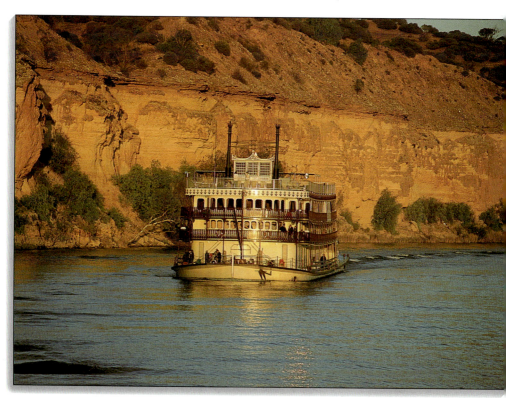

oaks. For thousands of years the Aborigines lived here, netting fish in the lagoons, collecting cockles on the beach and fashioning reeds for rafts and baskets. For a closer look you can still travel part of the old bullock-cart track that winds along the water's edge, and camp anywhere in the national park. But to explore the Coorong fully, you need time, preferably a boat and, in the heat of summer near the drying salt-flats, a strong nose! The spirit of the Coorong was well captured in the 1976 film *Storm Boy*.

South of the Coorong is a series of seaside holiday resorts, with this part of the coast renowned for its shellfish. At **Kingston** you can buy delicious fresh lobster at the jetty. In **Robe**, once an important port and retaining much of its early character, the Caledonian Inn, licensed in 1858, still caters to weary travellers. A stone near the harbour commemorates the thousands of Chinese who disembarked here in the 1850s and tramped hundreds of kilometres through the bush to the Victorian gold-diggings, to avoid the £10 arrival tax imposed at Victorian ports. Robe tends to be full in school holidays and overflows at Christmas and on New Year's Eve, but is a lovely, peaceful spot for the rest of the year.

Mount Gambier ⑮ is the centre of a large softwood industry where mills turn pine plantations into planks. The city nestles on the side of Mount Gambier, a 5,000-year-old extinct volcano. Within its rim lie three craters, four lakes, and the mystery of why the largest, **Blue Lake**, turns from winter grey to brilliant azure each November. Outside the city are the Tantanoola limestone caves.

Further north, the **Naracoorte Caves** contain not only beautiful limestone formations but also a fossil cave where the traces of many extinct animals are being unearthed. They include giant kangaroos, a wombat the size of a hippopotamus and a marsupial "lion".

The riverland

Renmark ⑯, northeast of Adelaide near the Victorian border, was the birthplace of the Murray River irrigation area in 1887. The riverland today shows the viability of the project as you drive along the **Sturt Highway**, roughly following the river, through extensive orchards and vineyards supported by the Murray's waters. River transport is prominent here, too, with the paddleboat days remembered in the old steamer moored as a floating museum. There are several paddlewheel vessels (the *Proud Mary*, *Murray Princess* and *Murray River Queen*) running five- and six-day cruises along the river. Houseboats can be hired at Renmark, Loxton, Berri and Waikerie.

Barmera and nearby Lake Bonney are the recreational heart of the riverland. **Lake Bonney** attracts a wide variety of watercraft: mainly windsurfers and sailing boats. In 1964, the pace increased considerably when Sir Donald Campbell used the lake for an attempt on the world water-speed record.

The air currents from the plains around **Waikerie** have made it one of the world's leading soaring centres. In summer, when sun-heated air rises in powerful thermals, gliders can be seen throughout the region. For flights, check with the Soaring Centre. Waikerie's apt Aboriginal name, which means "anything that flies", refers to the abundant birdlife in the nearby **Hart Lagoon**.

Map, page 226

Tantanoola, near Mount Gambier, became famous in the 1890s for the legendary "tiger" which terrorised the district. When shot, it proved to be an Assyrian wolf. The stuffed carcass now gazes glassily at drinkers in the bar of the local hotel.

BELOW: seals on Kangaroo Island.

Peninsulas and islands

The deeply indented coastline of South Australia has made a set of natural divisions, each with its own appeal. The **Fleurieu Peninsula**, south of Adelaide beyond McLaren Vale, is a popular holiday area for South Australians. **Victor Harbour** is the main resort – its hotels, motels and guest houses are often full during school holidays. Among Victor's attractions are the fairy penguin colony on Granite Island (connected to the mainland by a causeway with a horse-drawn tram), an adventure park and winter whale watching.

Cape Jervis at the end of peninsula is the stepping-off point for **Kangaroo Island ⓱**. Until the end of the last Ice Age, 8,000 years ago, the island (Australia's third largest, after Tasmania and Melville) wasn't separated from the mainland. Even now, the finger of the Dudley Peninsula on the island appears to be reaching towards Cape Jervis. The island's main towns are **Kingscote**, **American River** and **Penneshaw**. Fishing, exploring the scenery and observing wildlife are the main activities for visitors. Seals, sea lions, penguins, echidnas, kangaroos, emus and koalas all live here, along with many seabirds. At the large **Flinders Chase National Park**, the only enclosures are to keep the persistent wildlife away from picnickers.

From the gentle sandy beaches of the **Dudley Peninsula** to the pounding surf on the headland of **Cape du Couedic**, Kangaroo Island has a wide range of terrains. The lighthouse at the cape was built in 1906 as an essential navigation aid for coastal shipping. Near it lie two unusual features: **Remarkable Rocks**, a collection of granite boulders worn by the sea into fantastic shapes, some resembling animals and birds, others like Henry Moore sculptures; and **Admirals Arch**, a 20-metre (64-ft) maw rimmed with blackened stalactites as fangs, fram-

The first European to see Kangaroo Island – and name it – was Matthew Flinders, whose crew killed several kangaroos here in 1802. The island became the site of South Australia's first colony, settled by a motley crew of sealers and escaped convicts in 1806.

BELOW: the aptly named Remarkable Rocks on Kangaroo Island.

ng a maelstrom of surging waves. These are primeval sites at odds with the placid nature of other parts of the island.

A loop of picturesque **Yorke Peninsula** ⑱ takes in the east-coast port of Ardrossan with its attractive water access and, down the coast, **Edithburg** with its splendid clifftop views and its famous old pub, the Troubridge Hotel. The town's cemetery includes the graves of the 34 victims of the 1909 wreck of the *Clan Ranald.* The scenic route south to **Yorketown** is a magical drive offering great coastal views of offshore reefs popular with local scuba divers. Yorketown is a small farming town surrounded by a series of salt lakes.

Towards the southwestern extremity of the peninsula is the great horseshoe-shaped sweep of **Pondalowie Bay**. Located in a national park, the bay is a fishing, diving and surfing paradise made even more appealing by its remoteness. A full seven hours' drive from Adelaide, it is a great place to camp and enjoy the beauty of the Southern Ocean coastline.

The ports of the Yorke Peninsula's west coast indicate its importance as a barley-growing area. It was from places such as **Port Victoria** that the early sailing ships left to race back to Britain and Europe with their cargoes of grain. Barley and fishing still play important parts in the peninsula's modest economy, but mineral wealth contributed a colourful chapter to the area's history. The discovery of copper at **Kadina** and **Moonta** led to the mass migration of Cornish miners and their families from southwest England. Along with the port town of **Wallaroo**, the two hamlets grew as solid Cornish communities with strong Methodist influences, catering to 30,000 people. The boom period has long passed but the contribution of the Cornish Cousin Jacks and Cousin Jills, as they were known, remains an indelible part of the peninsula's heritage.

Map, page 226

BELOW: a road train heads west on the Eyre Highway.

Map, page 226

There is plenty of water beneath the arid sands of the Nullarbor Plain, where underground streams have carved out huge caverns. World cave-diving records have been set here, and one adventure travel company even offers subterranean rafting trips.

BELOW: flowers bloom after rain in the Strzelecki Desert. **RIGHT:** an Aboriginal cowhand.

The long road west

Of all the great Australian highway routes, the 2,000-km-plus (1,240-mile-plus) stretch from Adelaide to Perth is the one most frequently flaunted, with "We crossed the Nullarbor" stickers displayed on car and van windows. However, the road itself is no longer the challenge – rather it's the cost of fuel to propel a vehicle across several thousand kilometres of nothingness.

On the drive west towards Perth, the **Eyre Peninsula** ⑲ and the attractive township of Port Lincoln exert strong pressure to detour. Explorer John Eyre ploughed through the area in 1841 and, although burnt almost to a frazzle by the harshness of the hinterland, he was impressed by the spectacular coastline. The peninsula has its own historical charm and romance in places like **Coffin Bay** and **Anxious Bay**. **Port Lincoln** itself has a large fishing fleet, cruises, exclusive islands for hire – even a museum of barbed wire. At **Point Labatt**, on the Flinders Highway, you'll find the only seal colony on mainland Australia.

Ceduna ⑳ (pop. 2,700) is the centre of a large pastoral industry, but surfers from both east and west coasts know it as a favoured stopping-off place in their pursuit of waves. It's blessed with golden beaches; Cactus is the break surfers speak of with the greatest reverence. The navigator Matthew Flinders gave nearby **Denial Bay** its name when he realised it was not the access to the elusive "Inland Sea" that the early white explorers were certain existed.

Inland from Ceduna is the 106,000-hectare (262,000-acre) tract of **Yumbarra Conservation Park**. Its sandy ridges and granite outcrops appear inhospitable but the local wildlife, particularly emus and kangaroos, find it ideal. In winter the top of the bight is also a favourite spot for whale watching.

Ceduna is South Australia's most westerly town. From here to Norseman in Western Australia it's 1,232 km (765 miles), and any other point shown on a map along the way is nothing more than a water storage base or a fuel station. That's what makes crossing the Nullarbor Plain such an intimidating prospect. There are no trees on the plain (nullarbor is Latin for "no tree"), as the limestone is unable to hold rainwater.

The **Eyre Highway** hugs the coastline on its long route to Western Australia, passing through the **Nullarbor National Park** ㉑ during the last stretch of South Australia. For the earlier pioneers, the coastal route was much harsher than the alternative of the interior. While vast stretches of the coastline are devoid of fresh water, limestone sinkholes in the plain might have provided ready supplies. The Aborigines had been aware of this for centuries, but the early white explorers learned the hard way.

The desert is also traversed by the Trans-Australian railway, one of the world's great rail journeys, with one straight section that stretches 479 km (298 miles), making it the world's longest.

The first impression of the coastline of the **Great Australian Bight** is of the kilometres of sand dunes stretching along the great expanses of beach. These dunes suddenly give way to the sheer cliff formations that make the coastal strip near the Western Australian border one of the most spectacular along the continent's great shoreline. ❑

Queensland

0   200 km

0   200 miles

Badu I.   Moa I.

Thursday I.   21   Horn I.   *Torres Strait*

Prince of Wales I.   Cape York

Bamaga   20

Jardine River N.P.

Cape Grenville

Weipa   Iron Range N.P.

Gulf of Carpentaria

Cape **York**

Coen   *Princess Charlotte Bay*

Cape Melville

Kowanyama   **Peninsula**   19   Lakefield National Park

Mornington I.   18   17   Cooktown

Wellesley Is.   Laura   Helenvale

Bentinck I.   Lakeland Downs   Cape Tribulation N.P.

Burketown   Mossman

Karumba   Mungana   16   Port Douglas

Riversleigh   Mareeba   14   Cairns

Normanton   **Atherton Tableland**   15   Atherton

Croydon   Ravenshoe   Innisfail

Mt. Surprise   Tully

Camooweal   Greenvale   Hinchinbrook I.

Ingham

Mt. Spec N.P.

Charters Towers   22   13   Townsville

Lake Moondarra   Magnetic I.

Mount Isa   23   Cloncurry   Ayr

24   Flinders Hwy.   Porcupine Gorge N.P.   Bowen

Julia Creek   Whitsunday Group

Dajarra   Hughenden   Proserpine

Kynuna   12   Mackay

Middleton   Sarina

Boulia   Winton   Muttaburra   *Broad Sound*

Tropic of Capricorn   Clermont   Yeppoon

Longreach   11   Emerald   Rock-   10   Great Keppel I.

Bedourie   25   Barcaldine   hampton   Heron I.

Dingo   Gladstone

Birdsville   Blackall   Biloela

26   Windorah   **Carnarvon National Park**   Bundaberg

Yaraka   9   **Carnarvon Gorge**   Hervey   Great Sandy National P

Queensland   Taroom   Childers   Bay   Fraser Isl

Clifton Hills   Augathella   7   Maryborough

South   Quilpie   Charleville   Mitchell   Gympie   6

Innamincka   Roma   Murgon   Noosa

Australia   **Sturt**   Miles   Nanango   Maroochydo

Desert   **Darling Downs**   5   Sunshine Coa

Marree   Thargomindah   Dalby   Caboolture

Lyndhurst   **Gammon Ranges N.P.**   Cunnamulla   Moonie   Moreton I.

Hungerford   Toowoomba   3   **Brisbane**

Leigh Creek   Sturt N.P.   Wompah   Bollon   St. George   Warwick   Ipswich   Surfers Parac

Lake Torrens   Milparinka   2   44   Gold Coa

Packsaddle   Barringun   Goodooga   Stanthorpe   4   Lamington N.P.

Hawker   **New South**   Wanaaring   Goodooga   Murwillumb

Euriowie   **Wales**   Bourke   *Gwydir Hwy.*   Moree   Tenterfield   Lismore

Flinders Ranges N.P.   Brewarrina   Collarenebri   Ballina

Mootwingee N.P.   Walgett   Glen Innes

Broken Hill   Wilcannia   Coolabah   Narrabri   Grafton

Cockburn   Menindee   Cobar   Coonamble   Tamworth   Coffs Harbour

Nyngan   Gilgandra   Port Macquarie

Coral Sea

Great

Barrier

Reef

P A C I F I C

O C E A N

GREGORY RANGE

GREAT

DIVIDING

RANGE

GREY RANGE

FLINDERS RANGES

NEW ENGLAND RANGE

QUEENSLAND

This is Australia's holiday state, the most visited destination after Sydney. Its major attractions include magnificent beaches, the Great Barrier Reef and unique rainforest areas

Maps, pages 240 & 242

Queensland, the Sunshine State, is where the rest of Australia wants to be when winter arrives. Its vast coastline has endless golden beaches, offshore archipelagos, and crystal-clear waters. Staggering stretches of nd remain entirely unspoilt; other stretches are dotted with small resorts, and ll others given over to pockets of Miami-style development. But Queensnd is not to be missed. Apart from all its other attractions, it contains the ird point on the triangle which every overseas visitor wants to see – Sydy, Ayers Rock and the **Great Barrier Reef**.

Despite Queensland's former image as a political, cultural and social backater, it has been increasing its population by around 1,000 a week for some years, through the internal migration of what Queenslanders fondly call Mexicans" (people from south of the border). In 1991 the state's population is 2,996,000; by 2003 it was 3,797,700. These new arrivals, who claim they n be identified by the relative ease with which they can spell their own imes, soon adopt the Queensland style of remaining aloof from the southern ates and Canberra, soaking up the sun while idly dreaming of secession from e Commonwealth. They're considered to be true Queenslanders when they gin enunciating a flat "eh" (to rhyme with "day") at the end of every other ntence. ("Hot. Eh!" Means "It's a hot day, isn't it?")

From a visitor's point of view, there is much more the state than the Reef (which admittedly extends ong most of the coast, from south of Rockhampton beyond the tip of Cape York). Queensland fulfils at often overstated promise of tourism in having mething for everyone – as well as a climate that lows you to enjoy its attractions to the full.

PRECEDING PAGES: cruising the Great Barrier Reef.
BELOW: homespun entertainment in Cooktown.

new spirit

ecause of its enormous size, Queensland has sev- al important regional centres, but its major interna- onal gateways are **Brisbane**, its capital and prime ateway in the south, and **Cairns** in the tropical north. Australia's third-largest city, "Brissie", as it is known the locals, scatters its 1.55 million inhabitants so fectively over a series of low hills that sometimes it easy to forget that it's situated on a river. Although early half of Queensland's 3.8 million population ves here, and the metropolitan area is gargantuan ,220 sq. km/470 sq. miles), Brisbane remained until cently "the world's biggest country town".

Although now a wealthy and cosmopolitan urban ntre, it still retains something of a country heart and ountry morality, and is still wary of "meddling south- rners" – especially those from Canberra. The other de of the "country" coin is that Brisbane is as hos- itable a place as you are likely to find.

Like Sydney and Hobart, this easy-going city emerged from nightmarish beginnings. A convict settlement was established at nearby Moreton Bay in September 1824, when the first party of prisoners – the "hardest cases", convicted of further crimes since arriving in Australia – arrived from Sydney. Many of the convicts died, victims of the tyrannies of the guards, hunger, tropical disease and an indifference towards prolonging their own wretched lives.

The first convict establishment was at Redcliffe, but due to a shortage of water the penal settlement moved up the river to the site of today's Brisbane city centre. The colony was named after Sir Thomas Brisbane (then Governor of New South Wales); the present government and city shopping precinct overlie the original convict settlement. After the transportation of convicts to the colony ended, the area was opened up for free settlement in 1842.

Modern Brisbane displays few reminders of those days, but the 1828 **Old Windmill** in Wickham Terrace (Brisbane's oldest building) is one. Because of a fundamental design flaw it never worked as a windmill, and to grind corn and maize for the settlement convicts were put to work turning a tread-mill, which became known as the "tower of torture".

A less barbarous phase of 19th-century history is revealed on the city's **Heritage Trail** (maps available from City Hall, Queen Street). Although many fine buildings went under the wrecking ball during successive surges of development, Brisbane still has many old "Queenslanders" – shady wooden homes built on stilts to maximise the circulation of cooling air.

The old residential area of **Spring Hill** most clearly defies Queensland's development-mindedness with its maze of early houses. Since it was raised in 1889, the spire of nearby **St Paul's Presbyterian Church** has been a Bris

The man-powered "windmill" was generally worked by 25 convicts at a time, but when it was used for special punishment, 16 were kept on it for 14 consecutive hours.

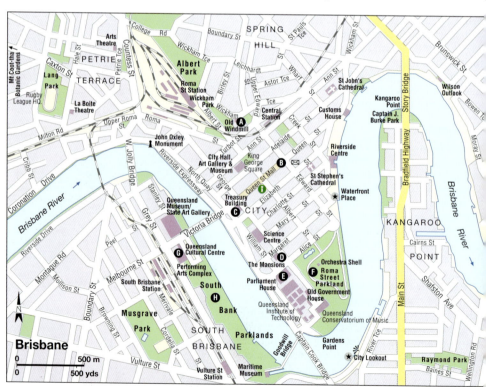

ane landmark. Sites such as **King George Square** (adjacent to the imposing andstone **City Hall**) provide restful spots for city workers at lunchtime.

One block to the south is **Queen Street Mall **, a pedestrian area conaining boutiques, department stores and cafés, some of them in fine late-9th-century buildings. Glittering glass office blocks now dominate the city kyline, but lovers of architectural history acclaim the **Treasury Building** as the finest example of Italian renaissance style in the southern hemiphere. Walk south along George Street to **The Mansions** , a group of 890 terraced houses with handsome red-brick facades and pale sandstone rcading, now occupied by classy shops and restaurants.

Further down George Street is Queensland's **Parliament House** , begun 1865. To the frustration of the architect, Charles Tiffin, who had won a ationwide contest with his design based on French Renaissance lines, it took 4 years of sporadic building to see the work completed. There are five conucted tours daily, from Monday to Friday, when Parliament is not sitting. When Parliament is in session (usually May–Oct) a gallery pass enables you to sit in on parliamentary debates which, given the spirited nature of the tate's politics, can be unusually entertaining.

ubtropical strolls

risbane's subtropical setting cannot be ignored, as it dictates so much bout the pace, taste and lifestyle of the city's dwellers. From business xecutives seen strolling out to lunch attired in their summer garb of short-leeved shirt, without the neck ties that tend to identify southerners, to a arty of revellers out for a moonlight river cruise on a warm summer's

Map, page 242

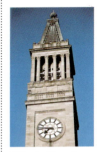

Take the lift to the top of City Hall's clock tower (closed Sun) for the best view of Brisbane city centre.

BELOW: a typical "Queenslander".

*Seafood is excellent
everywhere in
Queensland,
including Brisbane,
and don't be deterred
by odd names:
"banana prawns"
are just large
shrimps, while
"Moreton Bay bugs"
are small crayfish.*

BELOW: the artificial
beach at South
Bank Parklands.

night, Brisbane is a city delightfully in the grip of its balmy climate. In spring, the air in the city's 105 sq. km (40 sq. miles) of parks and gardens is fragrant with the scent of subtropical flora.

The newest addition to Brisbane's parks is perhaps the most beautiful. Right beside the CBD, the ugly, noisy Roma Street railway shunting yards have been converted into the **Roma Street Parkland** ❻, a splendidly diverse area of waterfalls, lakes, misty crannies of tropical vegetation, and cultivated floral displays that attract their own eco-system of insects and birds.

Cross the river by **Victoria Bridge** to reach Brisbane's most impressive complex, the **Queensland Cultural Centre** ❼. It includes a fine **Performing Arts Complex**, the **Queensland Art Gallery** (daily 10am–5pm) and the **Queensland Museum** (daily 9.30am–5pm, free guided tours Mon–Fri 11am, 1pm and 2pm, Sat–Sun 11am, 2pm and 3pm). Nearby is the Convention and Exhibition Centre.

The site of the 1988 World Expo, **South Bank Parklands** ❽, has put many of the former Expo pavilions to innovative use. Its attractions include a swimming pool with sandy beaches in the 16 hectares (40 acres) of riverside parkland, and a diverse array of restaurants that take maximum advantage of the city's weather. This is the place to head on a sunny day for an outdoor meal. Brisbane, once a culinary desert, now enjoys a reputation for chefs who take advantage of their state's natural resources: giant mud crabs, ripe avocados, macadamia nuts, mangoes, barramundi, coral trout, oysters, as well as exotic tropical delights. You may wish to bring your swimsuit: South Bank even has a large swimming lagoon at **Kodak Beach**, complete with imported sand, which is much more pleasant than it sounds.

In Brisbane, there is no sense of urban entrapment. Just 8 km (5 miles) west of the city centre, in the suburb of Toowong, is the **Mount Coot-tha Botanic Gardens**. Spread over 57 hectares (141 acres), it is a haven of ponds and parkland, where thousands of plant species thrive. There is also a **planetarium** in the grounds. Further west, rainforest-cloaked mountains shelter the city and offer a generous choice of picnic spots, bush walks and wilderness areas; all within half an hour's drive of the city centre.

To the east, downstream along the Brisbane River, you can reach the various beaches of **Moreton Bay** and the islands (some unpopulated) that make this a vast fishing and sailing paradise. Moreton Island features **Mount Tempest**, at 285 metres (935 ft), the world's highest stabilised coastal dune.

The Gold Coast

South of Brisbane, the 32-km (20-mile) stretch of coast from Coolangatta to Surfers Paradise – bushland just two generations ago – is the fastest-growing tourist and residential area in Australia. And, despite recessions, real-estate millionaires are as common as cases of sunburn. The **Gold Coast** ❶ is hideous in parts, beautiful in others, but never dull. The beaches, particularly **Burleigh Heads**, set in a national parkland, are strikingly gorgeous, while the high-rise skyline of **Surfers Paradise**, holiday headquarters for Australia's rich and tasteless, must now rank with Ipanema, Miami and Cannes for architectural overkill: famously, the skyscrapers at Surfers cast shadows over the beach every afternoon. But that no longer matters by night, when the party-goers take over the streets, casinos and restaurants.

The Gold Coast has no shortage of family-oriented theme parks. Surfers has performing dolphins at **Sea World**; **Dreamworld**, a large amusement park with a reassuringly Australian atmosphere, was the location of the Big Brother reality TV programme; the **Currumbin Wildlife Sanctuary** is overwhelmed by flocks of lorikeets at feeding time and **Wet and Wild** is the largest aquatic park in the southern hemisphere. And if the heat gets to you at the beach, incredibly at **Snow World** you can spend a maximum of 20 minutes enjoying unique ice carvings, ice slides and snow fights. But looming over all as the tourism drawcard is **Movie World**, the only Hollywood theme park in the southern hemisphere. To fill in the nights, and empty your pockets, there is always **Jupiters Casino** in the Conrad International Hotel complex in Surfers.

Inland from Brisbane, the countryside is almost entirely ignored by tourists. Here, the tablelands give way to the **Darling Downs**, a vast area of beautiful, rolling plains and rich soil. The city of **Warwick** ❷ serves as a base for the dairy, beef and horse-stud industries. On the banks of the Condamine River, the second-oldest town in Queensland retains a good deal of historical character. As with so many Australian towns, Warwick's salad days coincided with the discovery of gold nearby. There are some beautiful buildings remaining but its most famous feature is its annual month-long Rose and Rodeo Festival, which attracts the best Australian cowboys in October.

Maps, pages 240 & 242

The elevated town of Stanthorpe, near Warwick, invariably makes the evening TV weather report with the coldest temperatures recorded in Queensland. The lowest ever was –14.6°C (5.7°F).

BELOW: Surfers Paradise.

The Glasshouse Mountains were named by Captain Cook, but it is not clear why. Either he saw reflections in their smooth sides, or they reminded him of glass furnaces in his native Yorkshire.

BELOW: Sunshine Coast companions.
BELOW RIGHT: Nambour's Big Pineapple.

Hilly **Toowoomba** ❸ is not just Queensland's largest inland city (with a population of 90,500) but also a garden city of some note. Situated on the rim of the Great Dividing Range, with the Darling Downs laid out before it, Toowoomba is colourful all year but sensational when spring flowers bloom.

Lamington National Park ❹ lies in the McPherson Ranges directly behind the Gold Coast. This vast and dramatic rainforest park offers some of Australia's best bushwalking, with several appealing mountain lodges. Occupying part of the rim of an ancient volcano, Lamington has walks through a dense canopy of forest with a wide range of ferns and hundreds of species of orchid.

"Crikey Country"

On the **Sunshine Coast** ❺, an hour north of Brisbane, tourism takes on a kitschy grandeur. First is a cartoon Aussie boozer, the Big Ettamogah Pub, and just off the Bruce Highway, 6 km (4 miles) south of **Nambour**, is an enormous fibreglass pineapple, accessible from an off-highway **Nambour Tourist Drive**, offering local fruit products, a tour of the pineapple farm, and a potted review of the pineapple industry in a theatrette inside the pineapple.

All this can distract visitors from what is, after all, one of the most gorgeous stretches of Queensland's coastline also, on the highway north of Brisbane keep an eye out for the dramatic forms of the **Glasshouse Mountains** to the west, which rise sheer from the grassy plains). Beaches such as **Maroochydore** and **Coolum** are gems. Along the Glasshouse Mountains tourist road at Beerwah, you'll find the popular **Australia Zoo**, home of Steve Irwin, the showman crocodile hunter, whose entertainment includes a daily demonstration of how to manage the reptiles while avoiding saurian ingestion.

The new **Sunshine Highway** takes you straight to **Noosa** , bypassing
e sleepy hollow of Yandina, where it's worth a detour into the Ginger Fac-
ry, if only for a ginger-flavoured ice cream. Noosa has been called the Cannes
Australia, a heady blend of beauty, sophistication and high finance.
estling beside the usually tranquil waters of Laguna Bay, Noosa for many
ople comes close to distilling the essence of the Australian Dream.
Today it is a collection of townships strung along the coast. The perfectly
lindrical waves that wrap around the points of Noosa's national park rank
nong the world's finest, and soon surfers made the resort their Mecca.
ames of local beaches – **Ti-tree Bay**, **Granite Beach**, **Fairy Pool**, **Devil's
itchen** – captured, for them, the enchantment of Noosa.
Publicity soon lured a different clique – the wealthy early retirees of Sydney,
elbourne and Adelaide. From the moment they saw Noosa Heads, these
fugees from colder climes began buying up large tracts of the best land. Today,
e village of Noosa and Noosaville (pop. 11,500) is lined with glitzy restaurants
d boutiques, although it can't seem to shake off the raffish charm of old.
nly a few metres from Hastings Street Noosa's main business thoroughfare
vimmers still float lazily in a sea so clear you can see whiting and flathead scud
ross the bottom. Sheltering Noosa from the prevailing southeasterly winds is
e headland, gateway to the 334-hectare (825-acre) **Noosa National Park**, an
ea of woodland and marshes on the south bank of the Noosa River.

ravelling north

here is strong appeal in flying directly towards the sunshine of the Far North
ther than driving up. **Highway One**, the main coastal route from Brisbane

Map,
page 240

*Plan your
Queensland trip
according to the
season: from
Dec–Apr the far
North experiences a
tropical monsoon
season known as
"The Wet". From
May–Oct the north
enjoys a near-perfect
climate, while the
south is a little cool
for swimming.*

BELOW: befriending
the wildlife by
Noosa River.

Fraser Island

Fraser is the world's largest sand island, although its ecology is unlike that of any other – a fact that put it on the UN's World Heritage list in 1992. Instead of barren desert, the entire interior is covered with a rich patchwork of forests whose muscular vegetation manages to survive on the nutrients in only the top 15 cm (6 inches) of soil.

The island's landscape changes every few hundred metres, from classic Aussie scrub and reed-filled swamps surrounded by 60-metre (200-ft) satinay trees, to vast expanses of lush rainforest, with plants so dense that they almost block out the sunlight. Amid the forests are some 40 freshwater lakes, including both "perched" (above sea level) and "window" lakes (at or below sea level). Some of them have water the colour of tea, while others are perfect blue with blinding white sands – **Lake Mackenzie**, for example, looks like a Caribbean scene.

This magnificent island has been reshaping itself again and again over thousands of years. Enormous sand dunes creep like silent yellow glaciers, consuming entire forests then leaving them behind, petrified and ghostly. But plant life always revives in their wake; there are more independent dune systems on Fraser, showing sand and vegetation in different stages of interaction, than anywhere else on earth.

The island won a permanent place in the white Australian psyche in the 1830s, when some shipwrecked British sailors were probably killed here by local Aborigines; the lone survivor, Eliza Fraser, spent many months living with local people before being "rescued" by an escaped convict. British settlers then used the island as a sort of natural prison camp for Aborigines. When fine wood was discovered soon after, the British herded the Aborigines off, killing many, it is said, by driving them into the sea.

For the past 20 years, Fraser Island has been at the centre of Australia's most vicious conservation disputes. In the 1970s came the battle to stop mining (the sands are rich in rutile and zircon); in the 1980s came the long-running, and finally successful, campaign to ban logging on the island.

There are still arguments about how to manage the booming number of annual visitors – from 10,000 in the early 1970s to 350,000 today. There can be no other World Heritage site so available to the public, and the island's four ranger stations are kept busy trying to manage the resource so that visitor pressures don't do more damage than logging did.

For a small fee, anyone can bring a four-wheel drive vehicle over from the mainland, bounce along the island's trails, rip up and down **Seventy-Five Mile Beach** on the east coast and camp in designated areas. (Note that a four-wheel drive is essential; tyre pressure should be reduced for beach travel, which should be attempted only at low tide.)

There's plenty of variety. Fishermen head for **Waddy Point**, while nature-lovers seek out the soft sands of the deserted beaches (swimwear optional). The **Great Sandy National Park**, covering 840 sq. km (325 sq. miles), is a jigsaw of lakes, dunes, forest and beach, unlike anything else in the world. ❑

LEFT: the white sands of Lake Mackenzie.

to Cairns, stretches for 1,703 km (1,058 miles) and, although it is being continually improved, it's still a poor road in places, requiring careful driving. But there are many attractions along the way, albeit widely spaced, so the temptation of the drive lures thousands every year. Be prepared for suicidal wildlife conspiring to line the pockets of mechanics, panel-beaters and windscreen replacement services. Don't think of it as a "highway" in the American or European sense; much of it is just a good-quality undivided two-lane road. A sturdy hire car (with air conditioning) offers the most peace of mind.

Distances between coastal centres can be vast and, by comparison with more populated areas in the south of Australia, rural Queensland remains something of a frontier. Still, small diversions from the route north from Brisbane offer dozens of points of access to magnificent uncrowded beaches, pristine rainforests, tropical islands (anything from uninhabited to overpriced resorts), authentic country pubs, splendid fishing and diving, mouth-watering local tucker and encounters with people both unconventional and downright bizarre. However, you'll often have to deviate from the highway to find the attractions – or even to glimpse the ocean.

Highway One takes you through **Gympie** (pop. 12,000), a one-time gold-mining town which hosts a week-long Gold Rush Festival every October, then to **Maryborough** ❼ (pop. 26,000), which has a railway museum and some fine old Victorian buildings. From nearby **Hervey Bay**, a barge will carry you and your vehicle over to **Fraser Island** ❽ *(see page 248)*. A four-wheel-drive vehicle is needed to explore the island; these can be hired locally.

The next major town north of Maryborough is **Bundaberg** on the coast, 45 minutes from Highway One. The town (pop. 59,000) is universally recog-

Map, page 240

TIP

Queensland's burning sugar-cane plantations are spectacular, but, if you stop to take roadside photographs, beware of angry snakes evicted by fire from their homes.

BELOW: the sugar-cane fields are ignited in winter to rid them of debris and insects.

TIP

From August–October humpback whales in great numbers pass through the strait between the mainland and Fraser Island, on their way back to the Antarctic. Arrange a whale-watching boat trip in Hervey Bay.

BELOW: Aboriginal art at Carnavon Gorge.

nised by Australians because of its most famous product, Bundaberg rum, and an inexpensive tour of the distillery (daily 10am–3pm) also buys you a museum visit and a taste of the product. This is the heart of sugar country, and the invigorating dark rum, affectionately known as "Bundy", is ritually drunk with Coca-Cola ("Bundy 'n' Coke"). From Bundaberg, flights operate to **Lady Elliot Island**, 85 km (53 miles) away, and the southernmost resort of the Great Barrier Reef *(see page 265)*.

Childers, on the highway to the north, is a National Trust-listed town surrounded by rolling hills covered in the sugar cane which thrives on the rich red soil. The town, remembered unfortunately for a fire in a backpacker hostel in which many British and Australian backpackers died, encapsulates the early architecture of the cane-growing regions. Turn off to **Woodgate Beach** and **Woodgate National Park**, about 40 km (25 miles) down the side road.

Pass up the next detour, to the surprisingly attractive industrial centre of **Gladstone**, unless you happen to be interested in the world's largest aluminium plant ($355 million to construct) or you are one of the fortunate heading out by ferry or helicopter to **Heron Island**, perhaps the Reef's most eulogised resort, noted for its diving facilities *(see page 265)*.

The Dawson Highway, heading west from Gladstone, is the route to one of Queensland's best national parks at **Carnarvon Gorge ❾**. This 30-km (16-mile) sandstone gorge has a profusion of palm trees, cycads, ferns and mosses. There are also fine examples of Aboriginal rock paintings.

Back on Highway One, sprawling only a few kilometres north of the Tropic of Capricorn (which is marked by a roadside spire), **Rockhampton ❿** is the commercial heart of central Queensland and the centre of the state's beef

Map,
page 240

ndustry. A colourful local personality and former mayor of "Rocky", Rex Pilbeam, had a baggy-necked Brahman bull cast in concrete and erected at the northern entrance to the city (the Brahman is the breed favoured by cattlemen to the north), and a similar sculpture of a Hereford (the British breed favoured by farmers in the south) at the southern end. When the beasts were made, Pilbeam – anticipating playfulness by local lads – had several spare sets of testicles of each animal placed in storage. Souvenir-hunters struck the Brahman almost immediately. They were dumbfounded when the mayor ordered his workmen to bolt on a replacement appendage the very same day.

Rockhampton, a sprawling city with a population of about 65,000, with modern pubs and office blocks interspersed among older buildings, is a commercial centre for thousands of square kilometres of rich grazing country to its west, where heat, drought, floods and fires have shaped a hardy breed of remote survivors on the large, scattered cattle stations of the Dawson and Fitzroy river valleys. Their isolation generates fiercely parochial attitudes – a point worth bearing in mind if you should catch yourself discussing Sydney or Melbourne (or even Brisbane) in terms too complimentary for local tastes.

"Rocky" itself can be insufferably hot, but don't let this bother you. Just slip quietly away on a 40-km (25-mile) detour to **Yeppoon** on the coast for a dip, some excellent local seafood and a look at the once-controversial **Capricorn International Resort**. Just north of Yeppoon, this Japanese development adjoins an uninspiring tidal beach, and its construction was the subject of more than a decade of outlandish rumour, prejudice and even a bomb attack.

From Rockhampton, an adventurous traveller might consider a three-hour detour on the sealed road running west to the **Emerald ⓫** irrigation area, fed by the huge Fairbairn Dam, a centre for the farming of cotton, citrus fruits, grapes and fodder crops. It is also a gateway to the famous central Queensland **gem fields**, where scores of latter-day pioneers fossick for precious stones. There's nothing fancy about the gem fields; in tents, caravans and tumbledown tin shacks the miners have traded traditional comforts for the freedom and excitement of their own frontier, their rewards being sapphire, topaz, amethyst and jasper. These are the largest sapphire-producing fields in the world, and some fossickers have struck it rich in their first week ("Come stub your toe on a fortune!" urge the tourist pamphlets).

Although it is very much the long way round, you can continue from Emerald to rejoin Highway One near **Mackay ⓬** (pop. 75,000). A large tourist information centre now operates in a replica of the Richmond Sugar Mill, the first in the area. Fanned by tropical breezes and surrounded by a gentle rustling sea of sugar cane, Mackay is a pleasant city of wide streets and elegant old hotels.

Inbound airline passengers for the beautiful Whitsunday Passage arrive at **Hamilton Island**. From there, it takes only about 40 minutes to reach **Shute Harbour** or **Airlie Beach**, the other jumping-off point. From Abel Point, boats take passengers on idyllic cruises around the Great Barrier Reef or deliver guests to islands such as **Hamilton, Hayman, Hook, Linde-**

Queensland's famous cane toad was first introduced from Hawaii in 1935 to combat beetles that attacked the sugar cane. But the toads reproduced prolifically and have become a nuisance in their own right.

BELOW: deep-sea fishing off Beaver Cay on the Reef.

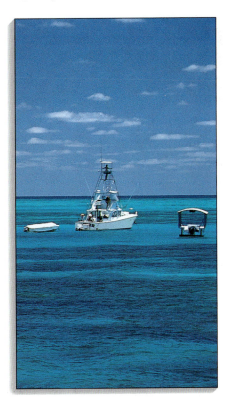

If you don't have the time or inclination to visit the Reef itself, the Great Barrier Reef Wonderland in Townsville (daily 9am–5pm) is the world's largest coral-reef aquarium. Get close to the coral and fish (including sharks) from the safety of an under-water glass tunnel.

BELOW: local boats offer idyllic cruises.

man and **South Molle** *(see pages 267–8)*. Ideal for a day visit, Airlie Beach and Shute Harbour both offer fine restaurants and a variety of accommodation from backpacker to four-star.

Townsville ⓭ (pop. 110,000) is a relaxed and graceful place. It's built around a busy but unattractive harbour at the base of the rather ugly Castle Hill, while Flinders Street, its main thoroughfare, is notable for its fine late-19th-century architecture. The city is the commercial hub for the area's rich copper, beef and refining industries, and for the visitor, its centrepiece is the city's newly developed beachside playground along the 5-km (3-mile) **Strand**, adjoining the Sheraton Breakwater Casino, the Great Barrier Reef Wonderland, and a water park playground. Townsville's residents congregate here to sun-bake, barbecue, browse and bird watch. On top of nearby **Castle Hill** is a tourist lookout. In a typical display of civic pride, an early resident deduced that if Castle Hill were just a few metres higher, it could officially be called a mountain. He began carting soil up the hill and dumping it on top. The town never got its mountain, but the project was in itself a kind of monument to obscure endeavour everywhere.

Townsville's relatively green hinterland strip is bordered by rocky mountain ranges that eventually give way to the inland savannah. About 10 km (6 miles) north of Ingham, as you reach the top of a steep hill, you are suddenly treated to one of the most breathtaking sights of the whole coastal trip. Be ready to stop and admire the Bali Hai beauty of **Hinchinbrook Island** across the narrow mangrove-lined channel. Accessible from Cardwell by boat, the jagged peaks, golden beaches and luxuriant rainforests of **Hinchinbrook National Park** can be fully explored by experienced hikers, and at least sampled by the less adventurous.

From Cardwell northwards the highway sticks pretty close to the coast, offering plenty of diversions to peaceful little spots for picnics, fishing and water sports. Most maps of the north carry a warning to beware of box jellyfish in summer months. Despite attempts by some vested tourist interests to play down the danger of stingers, it's best to take these warnings very seriously. Box jellyfish stings can be fatal, but all popular beaches have stinger net enclosures that are safe for swimmers, along with vinegar for medication in case a tentacle manages to get through.

Gateway to paradise

And so on to **Cairns** ⓮ (capital of Tropical North Queensland). Until the 1980s, this was a sleepy provincial backwater wallowing in a tropical swamp. Not terribly much had changed since it was founded just over a century before, on some not very picturesque mangrove flats, to service the gold and tin fields further inland. Then the tourism boom hit. There's still a core of old-style tropical charm in the languid pubs and distinctively Queensland-style porches. But today Cairns, with a population of 120,000, has a modern international airport, bustling shopping malls, and restaurants with cuisine from every corner of the globe with menus posted in English, German and Japanese. Almost any sporting activity – diving trips to the Reef, bungy jumping, whitewater rafting, tandem parachuting, hiking the

Atherton Tableland – can be arranged from its hotels and travel agencies.

The focus of Cairns remains the **Esplanade**, a great place for people-watching. The waterfront is lined by high-rise hotels and backpacker accommodation, and there's always an array of picnicking locals beneath the Moreton Bay figs and palms. Its centrepiece is a huge landscaped swimming lagoon, its lawns carpeted with minimally clad sunbathers, and with a full-time picnic atmosphere. A seven-day leisure retail shopping centre, the **Pier Marketplace**, with weekend markets, and a marina for the region's marlin fishing fleet and pleasure boats dominate the waterfront. The **Cairns Museum** (corner of Lake and Shields streets) has exhibits on the more rough-and-ready past of the area, while the elegant **Regional Art Gallery** (corner of Abbot and Shields streets) has local artists' work on display and often gets exhibits from "down south" (it's a slightly surreal experience to wander in from the tropical scene and come face to face with an Old Master on the walls).

But the real attractions of Cairns lie beyond the town limits. Directly inland rises the lush, cool plateau of the **Atherton Tableland ⑮**. Like the rest of the region, it was opened up by prospectors in the 1870s. It is now a major dairy farm area, with a range of B&Bs and farm-stay accommodation with names like Gumtree Getaway and the Honeyflow Homestead. Further west are the **Undara lava tubes**, one of the best examples of lava-tube formation anywhere on the planet. Some of the tubes are 15–20 metres (50–65 ft) wide and high. Full resort accommodation is offered in beautifully restored vintage rail carriages relocated there for the purpose. It's also a Savannah Guide Station.

These days, most tourists divide the pleasant 64-km (44-mile) return trip from Cairns to **Kuranda** (pop. 600) into two experiences. The train, with vin-

Map,
page 240

BELOW:
Cairns Museum.

tage coaches, takes you in one direction, climbing tortuously through spectacular scenery, through tunnels and past impressive waterfalls; the other half of the journey is by Skyrail, the aerial tramway that almost brushes the rainforest treetops. Kuranda's craft market (Wed, Thur, Fri and Sun) is just one attraction. Kuranda's station is charming and there's a butterfly sanctuary and two aviaries. Unconcerned about perceptions of hyper-individuality, a local business built an ugly ark in the main street, modelled on the Biblical original, to house restaurants, shops and artisan stalls, but which is largely empty.

North of Cairns, the **Cook Highway** runs through one of the most classically gorgeous parts of Australia. Strings of uncrowded, palm-fringed beaches (including those of the beachside suburbs of **Trinity**, **Kewarra** and **Palm Cove**) look as Hawaii must have done before developers arrived. The Great Barrier Reef comes within 15 km (9 miles) of the shoreline, and from various ports diving boats head out to the sand cays and coral reefs.

Some 80 km (50 miles) from Cairns lies **Port Douglas** ⓰ (pop. 3,700), which has become a popular alternative jumping-off point for the northern Barrier Reef. Like most of the coastal settlements, it was founded after a gold rush in the 1870s, when the Gugu-Yalangi Aborigine were forced from their land; for a time it was more important than Cairns, but it died when the gold ran out. For the next century, Port Douglas boasted little more than two pubs and a meat-pie shop. Today, the pubs and pie shop are still there, but they've been surrounded by glitzy new resorts like the Sheraton Mirage, which has hosted former US President Bill Clinton and Germany's former Chancellor Helmut Kohl. Still, "Port" has held on to its laid-back atmosphere, with a lavish touch of eccentricity, and is often compared to Key West in the 1950s.

A new rival to the Cairns-Kuranda railway is the Skyrail from Smithfield to Kuranda, the world's longest cableway. You can travel one way on the train and the other dangling in a gondola over the rainforest and across Barron Gorge.

BELOW: on the train from Cairns to Kuranda.

Along the narrow main street are open-air cafés and restaurants, some of which conduct cane-toad races at night. The Four Mile Beach is among the region's most beautiful, and every morning dozens of boats head out for day trips on the Reef: just offshore are the immensely popular **Low Isles**, while a string of excellent snorkelling spots is only an hour away *(see page 269)*. Operators range from the tiny sailships catering for only a dozen passengers to the sleek modern motorboats taking around 20, and the massive Quicksilver catamarans that can shuttle several hundred people at a time.

Just north of the Port Douglas turn-off is **Mossman Gorge**, perhaps the easiest way to get into the **Wet Tropics World Heritage Rainforest** *(see page 256)*. A 3-km (2-mile) walking circuit runs past mountain streams and lush, dripping foliage. Slightly further north, past rich sugar-cane country, the village of **Daintree** is the jumping-off point for river trips. Just after dawn, the birdlife is extraordinary (parrots, ospreys, great white herons). Later in the day, you'll see saltwater crocodiles lounging in prehistoric bliss.

Cross the Daintree River by ferry (6am–midnight) and drive for 36 km (23 miles), on sealed road for all but about 5 km (3 miles), to **Cape Tribulation**. It's an incongruous name for one of Australia's most serene corners, but then Captain Cook was in a poor mood after his ship, the *Endeavour*, ran onto an offshore reef in 1770. "This was where our troubles began," he noted in his log, and his choices for Mount Misery, Cape Sorrow and the like confirm that he wasn't having a relaxing voyage.

Troubles returned in the early 1980s, when the Queensland government decided to push a road through the rainforest to improve access for tourists and remote Aboriginal communities. Hundreds of "greenies" descended on Cape

Map, page 240

BELOW: the Low Isles are a popular day-trip destination.

The world's oldest rainforest

Stretching from Mossman through to Cairns, Cape Tribulation and Cooktown is tropical rainforest that's at least 100 million years old (compared with the Amazon's paltry 10 million).

All the earth's rainforests are thought to have begun around present-day Melbourne some 120 million years ago, when Australia was a part of the great continent of Gondwanaland. When Oceania broke away, 50 million years ago, the drier land began to replace tropical conditions. The rainforests that once covered Australia retreated to less than 1 percent of the continent; logging since European settlement has reduced that to 0.3 percent.

North Queensland's rainforest – now protected as part of the Wet Tropics World Heritage area and a patchwork of national parks – has the highest diversity of local endemic species in the world. Fully one-fifth of Australia's bird species, a quarter of its reptiles, a third of its marsupials, a third of its frogs and two-fifths of its plants are here in a mere thousandth of the Australian landmass.

Conservationists waged battles throughout the 1980s with the timber industry and the Queensland government. Overall, the "greenies" triumphed over the bulldozers and today most North Queenslanders accept the importance of the wet zones.

As for the seething tangle of vines and ferns itself, it has always deployed a wide array of defences against intruders. First off, there's the taipan snake, whose bite is 300 times more toxic than a cobra's. Some other native snakes are nearly as dangerous. However, deaths by snakebite are rarer than deaths by lightning strike.

The local (non-venomous) python is hardly worth a mention, although the largest recorded scrub python, found in the Tully area, measured 8.5 metres (28 ft) long. The saltwater crocodiles that lurk in the remoter rivers here only grow up to about 6 metres (20 ft) – but that's still enough to grab the unwary by the legs and spoil their day with the "death-roll" they use to disable and eventually kill their victims.

If you see a tree goanna – a giant speckled lizard with enormous claws – don't startle it: it may confuse you with a tree, climb up your leg and disembowel you. A kick from a frightened cassowary – a 2-metre (6-ft) high flightless bird with a bony crown – can tear open your rib cage. If you meet one in the bush, don't feed it and give it plenty of room.

The barking or bird-eating spider, with a leg-span up to 15 cm (6 ins), may be found in areas bordering on rainforest and can deal you a nasty bite.

Even some plants are armed and dangerous. The heart-shaped Gympie vine, for example, injects silica spines into any skin unlucky enough to brush it – described as "like a blow-torch being applied to your flesh." Another plant, much more common, is the Lawyer Cane, a slender, vigorous climbing palm, with numerous barbed hooks that grab at your clothing and skin and stop you in your tracks – which is why it's called "wait-a-while". The barbs, however, are not poisonous. ❑

LEFT: ancient ferns at Cape Tribulation.

Map, page 240

Trib to throw themselves in front of the bulldozers. Ironically, this focused so much attention on the area that Cape Trib became a household name in Australia, and is now firmly on the tourism map. The road was eventually completed, but meanwhile the outcry prompted a United Nations World Heritage listing for the Daintree area, which is now part of a national park – so everybody wins.

Today, the isolated, other-worldly atmosphere of Cape Trib has barely changed on the surface. There is a scattered community with a few grocery stores; except for a couple of hours in the middle of the day, when tour buses arrive from Cairns, there are usually fewer than a dozen people on the beaches. Nestled in rainforest-covered hills are a cluster of new high-quality "eco-lodges". Although far fewer people come here than go to Port Douglas, there are coral reefs close to the shore, a very unusual phenomenon. One catamaran runs daily to **Mackay Cay**, one of the better dive sites on the Reef.

The coastal road to Cooktown, so strenuously opposed by the greenies, is now a reality – although barely. You need a four-wheel drive vehicle to bounce through tunnels of virgin forest, plough across shallow rivers and steep 45-degree inclines. Although you glimpse the sea rarely, the views and sense of isolation are well worth it. The road is open all year with extreme caution – but watch the tide at Bloomfield River unless you'd like to contribute to the crocodiles' diet while you swim downstream after your retreating vehicle. Otherwise, in a conventional vehicle, you can make the journey from Cairns on the inland **Cape York Development Road**, which still has a small unsealed section beyond Lakeland Downs, the remainder having an all-weather surface; the road was due to be fully sealed in 2005. Call in at the Lion's Den pub, just off the highway at **Helenvale** – it's one of the oldest in north Queensland, with

If you take a cruise on the Daintree River, don't trail your hand in the water. The saltwater crocodiles ("salties") that live here are opportunist carnivores.

BELOW: a deserted beach at Cape Trib.

*Cooktown celebrates
Captain Cook's
enforced stay with
a statue and a
Discovery Festival
every June,
re-enacting his
arrival in 1770.*

BELOW: Captain
Cook's landing
re-enacted.

the original wooden bar, piano and a vast array of pickled snakes.

At the end of the line is **Cooktown** ⑰ for the beautiful Whitsunday Passage (pop. about 2,000), a place that has always had a Wild West reputation as an isolated tropical refuge which you could escape to when nowhere else would have you. It is located on the mangrove estuary where Captain Cook spent seven weeks repairing the *Endeavour*. The local Gugu-Yalangi people were friendly, and it was the most significant contact between Aborigines and Europeans to that date, allowing Sir Joseph Banks to make more detailed studies of local wildlife than he had been allowed at Botany Bay. (Banks was introduced to a creature they called the *kangaru*, although it was actually a wallaby, a smaller marsupial.)

When an Irish prospector struck gold at the Palmer River in 1873, Cooktown became one of Australia's busiest ports, with 94 pubs (many little more than shacks) and 35,000 miners working on the goldfields. There's a mural in the Middle Pub depicting those days; miners blew thousands of pounds' worth of gold dust in a single night, chasing women like the legendary Palmer Kate, passing out on drugged whisky and waking up penniless in the swamps.

Cooktown still thrives on the memories, and it has maintained a languid charm. Poking between palm trees on the wide main street are many late-19th-century buildings, including the three surviving watering holes (to avoid confusion, known as the Top, Middle and Bottom pubs). The **James Cook Historical Museum** (daily 9.30am–4.00pm), on the corner of Helen and Furneaux Street, is one of the best in Australia and is located in the former convent of St. Mary; exhibits include the original anchor of the *Endeavour*, retrieved from the Reef. The Cooktown cemetery, just north of town, is full of its own stories of the old pioneers.

The last frontier

Beyond Cooktown sprawls the **Cape York Peninsula**, a popular destination for four-wheel drive expeditions in the dry season. The red-dust road runs from one lonely bush pub to the next, past anthills, forests full of screaming cockatoos and vast sandstone bluffs rich in Aboriginal rock art. Most accessible is the **Quinkan Reserve**, set up by the Australian artist and writer Percy Trezise; there is a bush camp to stay overnight at **Jowalbinna**.

The tiny township of **Laura** ⓲ (pop. 100) lies at the southern tip of the **Lake-field National Park** ⓳, an expanse of marshland, lagoons, mangrove swamps and rainforest that is rich in flora and fauna. You need to be an experienced four-wheel-driver to explore the park; take advice from the ranger stations.

From Cooktown, it takes three or four days, even in the dry season, to reach Australia's northernmost point, the tip of **Cape York** ⓴. The journey passes the bauxite-mining town of **Weipa** and the Jardine River Crossing (which has a ferry). At the end of the line, at the Torres Strait, are campgrounds and at **Punsand Bay**, the closest population to the continent's northernmost tip, only 6 km (4 miles) to the northeast.

Boats run from **Red Island Point** (Bamaga) to **Thursday Island** ㉑, administrative centre of the Torres Strait Islands, many of which were named by Captain Bligh when he passed through on an open longboat after the *Bounty* mutiny. From June to September, the ferry also operates from Punsand Bay. Thursday Island (pop. 3,500) was once one of the world's great pearling stations. Although there are no specialised tourist traps and no beaches of note, "T.I." is a pleasant enough place to lay up after the rigours of the road, with a surprisingly cosmopolitan mix of inhabitants – a carefree and friendly

Map, page 240

TIP

Some car rental firms now allow you to take their vehicles as far as Cooktown, with a stipulation that you don't wander off the main road. To help you explore the Cape York Peninsula further, travel agents can organise a tour with an experienced driver.

BELOW: five percent of the population of Laura.

The Flying Doctor Service was started in Cloncurry in 1928 by the Rev. John Flynn to provide "a mantle of safety" over the Outback. Its first plane was supplied by the Queensland and Northern Territory Aerial Services (QANTAS).

crowd who like to party. There are four old pubs, the much more modern Jardine Motel, and a Japanese cemetery from pearling days.

A little-known but special way to take a close look at the Far North Queensland coastline and the Torres Straits, is a five-day return voyage from Cairns on the MV *Trinity Bay*, a working cargo ship supplying the remote Cape York communities all the way up to Thursday Island. It's air conditioned and comfortable, and dress and conversation are informal.

The Queensland Outback

As you head inland from Townsville along the Flinders Highway, the countryside rapidly turns from lush tropical green to the parched semi-arid Savannah of Australian myth. **Charters Towers ㉒**, 135 km (84 miles) en route, owes its era of prosperity to Jupiter, an Aboriginal boy who in 1872, while on an expedition with prospector Hugh Mossman, found gold in the area. The good times transformed a tiny town into a truly commercial showplace with splendid architecture. The carefully restored **Stock Exchange** in the historic Royal Arcade is one of the city's fine 19th-century landmarks. This is Queensland's largest gold-producing region, and half a dozen companies are now re-working old sites in the area.

The highway forges west through **Hughenden**, centre of the large Flinders River pastoral district. Nearby, in a 3,000-hectare (7,410-acre) national park, is the majestic **Porcupine Gorge** with its sheer 120-metre (400-ft) high walls. **Julia Creek** is known for its vast shale-oil deposits and its impressive cattle sale yards. If you happen to be there during a sale, the auctioneers are well worth watching and listening to. A cluster of buildings at McKinlay were used as "Walkabout Creek" in the first *Crocodile Dundee* film.

Cloncurry ㉓ (pop. 2,300) was the first base of the Royal Flying Doctor Service in 1928. In 1988, John Flynn Place was opened by Prince Andrew as a memorial to its founder.

Mount Isa ㉔ (pop. 24,000) is a mining city truly in the middle of nowhere. A rich lode of lead, silver, copper and zinc was discovered here in 1923, and a tiny tent settlement rapidly developed into Australia's largest company town. In fact, the municipal boundaries of "The Isa" extend for 41,000 sq. km (15,830 sq. miles) – an area the size of Switzerland. There are organised underground tours to visit the mine every weekday. Away from the mines, the people of Mount Isa relax at the artificial **Lake Moondarra** or socialise in any of the numerous licensed clubs, which welcome visitors. This is also rodeo country: in August, Mount Isa hosts a three-day event, the richest in Australia and the largest in the southern hemisphere.

The **School of Distance Education** (formerly the School of the Air), first established in Cloncurry, now operates from here, providing children on remote properties with direct radio and internet contact with a teacher. Its premises adjoin the Kalkadoon High School on Abel Smith Parade and can be toured.

The **Riversleigh fossil field**, northwest of Mount Isa, has recently gained attention for its fossil-rich sites, which were put on the World Heritage list in

BELOW: finding the way at Mount Isa.

994. At 15–30 million years old, they are a mine of information about Australia's prehistoric fauna. Information regarding access to the sites is available at the Riversleigh Fossil Display & Interpretive Centre in Mount Isa.

Further south in Queensland's Outback, **Longreach** ㉕ is home to two major Outback heritage attractions. First, a local manufacturer helped develop the **Australian Stockman's Hall of Fame** as a fascinating tribute to the cattle drovers, shearers, jackaroos and entrepreneurs who opened up Australia to European settlement. Longreach was also where Qantas set up its first operational base in 1922, and its original hangar, with the old sign still on it, has become part of the multi-million dollar **Qantas Founders' Museum**, which also displays a retired Qantas Boeing 747 jumbo jet (still in flying condition), replicas of its early fleet of biplanes, and a comprehensive historical and pictorial record of the national airline's growth, which spans over 82 years.

Southeast of Longreach, **Blackall** was where Jackie Howe monumentally sheared (the Australian version is "shore") 321 sheep in a single day in 1892, using blades. Even after the introduction of machine shears, his record wasn't broken until 1950.

In the far west of Queensland, **Birdsville** ㉖ only has a population of 100, but each September that grows by five or six thousand for the Birdsville Picnic Races, when about 300 light aircraft cram the airport, with their pilots and passengers camped under the wings. The 1884 Birdsville Hotel is one of Australia's legendary watering holes. West of here are only the dry sand dunes of the **Simpson Desert**, an endless wasteland reaching towards Alice Springs. A huge sandhill called **Big Red**, 36 km (22 miles) to the west, marks the beginning of the famous Birdsville Track and is a popular spot for sunset parties. ❏

Map, page 240

Birdsville's water, from a 1,200-metre (4,000-ft) well, is drawn at near boiling point. It sits in cooling ponds until it has reached normal temperatures.

BELOW: a couple of Birdsville locals.

THE GREAT BARRIER REEF

The Reef is not only Queensland's major tourist attraction, it is one of the natural wonders of the world. It's the largest coral reef on earth – and also one of the most accessible

Map, page 266

AUSTRALIA
Perth
Sydney

The world's largest coral reef in fact consists of over 2,500 separate, inter-connected reefs stretching over 2,300 km (1,430 miles) from the northern tip of Australia's continental shelf to just north of Bundaberg in the south. The reef comprises layer upon layer of "stony coral" that use the sun's rays to produce food, and in turn energy, to form their calcium carbonate skeletons. It is these skeletons which over millions of years have formed coral reefs.

The Great Barrier Reef Marine Park was established in the 1970s to help protect this magnificent natural resource. The Reef was placed on the World Heritage list in 1981, fulfilling every criterion of the convention. The Great Barrier Reef Marine Park Authority manages the Marine Park and the activities that may occur within it such as tourism, fishing and research.

There are a number of real threats to the Great Barrier Reef's fragile ecosystem. In the past 70 years, the Reef has suffered from increasing impacts from human activities. For example, anchoring sometimes causes significant damage to coral, and snorkellers or divers may brush against polyps killing or damaging them. The Reef is also under pressure from the effects of poor water quality, which is often caused by human land uses such as agriculture activities and coastal development.

The 20 or so resort islands inside the Great Barrier Reef Marine Park offer many attractions: lodging varies from five-star resorts to backpacker hostels and campgrounds; some are dry, barren and windy; others are lush and covered with rainforest. Many islands can be reached by seaplane, light plane or helicopter. The major islands for visitors, from south to north, are:

PRECEDING PAGES: a Heron Island beach.
LEFT: beneath the waves.
BELOW: Brampton Island.

The Southern End

Lady Elliot Island ❶ A quiet and beautiful 42-hectare (103-acre) coral cay at the bottom of the Reef, with bungalow accommodation and some permanent tents. Reached by air – 80 km (50 miles) from Bundaberg – Lady Elliot's resort is slightly less expensive than many others, with the bonus of being on a coral cay, which provides easy access to good diving and snorkelling.

Lady Musgrave Island ❷ A tiny cay available only for day trippers or campers by boat from Bundaberg. It offers good diving and snorkelling within a brilliant blue lagoon; camping is allowed with a National Parks permit.

Heron Island ❸ Only 1 km (⅔ mile) long, this is the Reef's most famous coral cay and, according to aficionados, number one for diving (along with Lizard at the northern fringe of the Reef). The Reef is certainly at its most accessible: literally, where the beach ends, the coral begins. Visitors must stay at the Heron Island Resort. There is abundant marine life, all kinds of coral, and easy access from Gladstone by plane or by fast catamaran.

Great Keppel Island ❹ The resort used to sell itself on

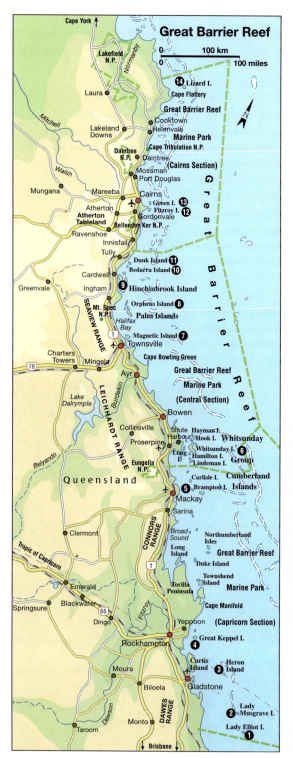

Great Barrier Reef

the slogan "Get wrecked on Great Keppel", aimed at younger holidaymakers. It was re-branded to a "family" image but has since been reclaimed by the 18–35 age group although anyone can enjoy it. There are excellent white sandy beaches, long hiking trails, views of the mainland, and plenty of social activities. Great Keppel is not directly on the Reef (although there is coral in most of the bays), so short cruises run out for divers. Access is by air from Rockhampton or by sea from Rosslyn Bay (it lies only 13 km/8 miles offshore).

Brampton Island ❺ A mountainous island, one of the Cumberlands, 32 km (20 miles) offshore from Mackay. The resort is set in a tropical garden surrounded by coral and calm seas. There is sailing and water skiing in the bay, good beaches and rainforest walks; at low tide you can walk across a sand spit to neighbouring Carlisle Island. Access is from Mackay and Shute Harbour. Because of the distance there is no day-tripper access.

The Whitsundays ❻

Lindeman Island At the southern end of the archipelago, Lindeman's resort is Australia's first Club Med, and beyond the buildings it has retained the beauty of its natural setting. There is tennis, swimming and fishing, and 20 km (12 miles) of bushwalking trails through 500 hectares (1,230 acres) of national park. There are good views over to other islands of the Whitsunday group. The access is from Mackay, Hamilton Island and Proserpine.

Long Island Has three very different resorts, both only a short boat trip from Shute Harbour. Club Crocodile is a resort for all ages, and particularly popular with the young. Peppers Palm Bay Resort is ideal for a back-to-nature holiday. It has lovely beaches, clear water and coral, and offers solitude. Bring a good book. The self-catering Whitsunday Wilderness Lodge provides camping cabins.

Hamilton Island The group's largest, most aggressively marketed resort. Complete with a high-rise hotel, it has a floating marina, a jet airstrip with direct flights to major cities (and also the surrounding islands) and a full sports complex. With a pseudo-South Seas main street once described as "Daiquiri Disneyland", Hamilton Island is a "scene" – not the place for a quiet island sojourn.

Whitsunday Island The largest of the Whitsunday group, covering 109 sq. km (42 sq. miles), with no resort, but the fabulous Whitehaven Beach; a great option for campers (permit required).

South Molle Island Self-contained resort on a large, hilly island. Popular with families; diving, swimming, sailing, golf, fishing and shops are all offered. Children are well catered for. Access from Shute Harbour or Hamilton Island.

Daydream Island A popular family resort with all the necessities for a good time at a reasonable all-inclusive tariff. Great beaches and a wide range of activities.

Map, page 266

Not all of the Reef's islands are made of coral. In fact, nearly all of the popular resort islands are continental in nature – the tips of offshore mountain ranges. The true coral cays of the real Reef are more numerous, but tend to be smaller and more fragile.

BELOW LEFT: snorkelling round the coral.
BELOW: a Marine Park ranger.

Map, page 266

TIP

The best time of year to visit the Reef is May–October. In mid-October, the first signs of the approaching "Wet" appear: variable winds, increasing cloud and showers. By January, it rains at least once most days.

BELOW: Quicksilver catamaran moored to a pontoon.

Just 15 minutes by launch from Shute Harbour; access also from Hamilton Island

Hook Island This is the second-largest island in the Whitsundays and provides budget camping and cabin accommodation as well as services for visiting yachts. There is an excellent underwater observatory here.

Hayman Island An exclusive five-star resort set in a coral-trimmed lagoon close to the outer Reef and a big favourite with Australian honeymooners. Fine beaches and fishing are complemented by the resort facilities, where no expense has been spared. Dining on Hayman is gourmet and silver service. This is certainly not a resort for the thong and T-shirt set. Access from Hamilton Island, Proserpine, Shute Harbour and Townsville.

The Centre to the North

Magnetic Island ❼ A large (5,000-hectare/12,400-acre) island and a national park, this pleasant populated (2,300) haven, almost an outer suburb of Townsville, has a wide range of accommodation and facilities for day trippers – you can even bring your car on the ferry. Plenty of walks in the rainforest, or up to the 500-metre (1,640-ft) Mount Cook; there is a koala and wildlife park at Horseshoe Bay. Mountain bikes, scooters and mini-mokes can be rented.

Orpheus Island ❽ In the Palm group northeast of Townsville and very close to the outer Reef. Wonderful sea shells to be found on the beaches. An exclusive resort hidden among the trees offering good accommodation and entertainment. Seaplane access from Townsville.

Hinchinbrook Island ❾ A large and spectacular island, dominated by mountains dropping sheer to the waterline. Almost the whole island is devoted to national parkland, featuring rainforests, mangrove swamps and superb beaches. The small Hinchinbrook Island Wilderness Lodge is ideal for the serious bushwalker or naturalist. The 3–5 day Throsborne Trail trek is one of the best in the world. Access is from Cardwell.

Bedarra Island ❿ A small fragment of the Family Islands, with an extremely exclusive resort set in rich rainforest. (For a fabulous fee, guests stay in bungalows so far separated from one another that they feel as if they are alone on the island.) Lovely white beaches and tranquil coves. Access is via Dunk Island.

Dunk Island ⓫ This was where the recluse E.J. Banfield lived for 26 years at the turn of the 20th century, writing his classic *Confessions of a Beachcomber*. A rich rainforested, national park with a large resort nestled in one corner and a camping ground alongside it. Fine resort facilities and entertainment. Access is from Townsville, Cairns and Mission Beach.

Fitzroy Island ⓬ Totally surrounded by coral reef, a great place for diving and fishing. The resort was recently extended. Access is from Cairns (6 km/4 miles offshore).

Green Island ⓭ A tiny coral cay just off Cairns with a good underwater observatory. Mostly for day trippers.

Lizard Island ⓮ The most northerly of the resorts and home, during the season, to the marlin boats. Lizard allows access directly from the beach to the Reef and is the step-off point for the world-famous Cod Hole dive site, too. A small resort caters to the taste of wealthy sports fishermen and divers from all over the world. ☐

Visiting the Reef

Regardless of your reason for visiting the Great Barrier Reef, weather will play an important part in your enjoyment of its scenic attractions. From late April through to October it's at its best, the clear skies and moderate breezes offering perfect conditions for coral viewing, diving, swimming, fishing and sunning. In November the first signs of the approaching "Wet" appear: variable winds, increasing cloud and showers. By January it rains at least once most days.

The easiest way to visit the Reef is not to stay on an offshore island but to take a day-trip from **Cairns** or **Port Douglas**. Every morning dozens of fully equipped diveboats and catamarans head out from the two centres to various pre-selected sites. You can also take Reef trips from **Cape Tribulation**.

About an hour later, wherever you leave from, you'll be moored by the coral. Because the water is so shallow, snorkelling is perfectly satisfactory for seeing the marine life (in fact, many people prefer it to scuba diving; even so, most boats offer tanks for experienced divers and "resort dives" for people who have never dived before).

Above the waves, the turquoise void might be broken only by a sand cay crowded with sea birds, but as soon as you poke your mask underwater, the world erupts. It's almost sensory overload: there are vast forests of staghorn coral, whose tips glow purple like electric Christmas-tree lights; brilliant blue clumps of mushroom coral; layers of pink plate coral; bulbous green brain coral.

Tropical fish with exotic names slip about as if showing off their fluorescent patterns: painted flutemouth, long-finned batfish, crimson squirrel fish, hump-headed Maori wrasse, cornflower sergeant-major.

Thrown into the mix are scarlet starfish and black sea cucumbers (phallic objects that you could pick up and squeeze, squirting water out of their ends). You definitely don't pick up the sleek conus textile shells – they shoot darts into anything that touches them, each with enough venom to kill 300 people. There are 21 darts in each shell, as one captain notes,

"so if they don't get you the first time, they'll get another try."

Almost all Reef trips follow a more or less similar format. There's a morning dive, followed by a buffet lunch; then, assuming you haven't eaten too much or partaken excessively of free beer, an afternoon dive. There should be a marine biologist on board, who will explain the Reef's ecology. Before you book, ask about the number of passengers the boat takes: they vary from several hundred on the famous Quicksilver fleet of catamarans to fewer than a dozen on smaller craft.

As a general rule, the further out the boat heads, the more pristine the diving (the Low Isles, for example, near Port Douglas, have suffered). But don't be conned by hype about the "Outer Reef" – as the edge of the continental shelf it may be the "real" Reef, but it looks exactly the same as other parts.

Even in the winter months, the water here is never cold, but it is worth paying a couple of dollars extra to hire a wet suit anyway; most people find it hard not to go on snorkelling for hours in this extraordinary environment. ❏

RIGHT: hire a wet suit and stay down longer.

THE WORLD'S LARGEST LIVING THING

The Great Barrier Reef is not just the largest mass of living organisms on earth but is also an incredibly complex and diverse ecosystem

When the Reef was put forward for World Heritage listing, the nomination said: "Biologically, the Great Barrier Reef supports the most diverse ecosystem known to man. Its enormous diversity is thought to reflect the maturity of an ecosystem which has evolved over millions of years…"

At the heart of that ecosystem is the humble polyp, a tiny animal consisting of not much more than a mouth and surrounding tentacles to feed it – plus of course a limestone skeleton into which it withdraws during the day. It is the remains of these skeletons that form the basis of the reef. Individual polyps are linked by body tissue (to share the colony's food) but the main source of a photosynthetic coral's food is algae cells within its tissue called Zooxanthellae, which convert the sun's energy into nutrients for the coral. This massive accumulation of plant and animal life can truly be said to be the largest living thing in the world.

OTHER INHABITANTS

The Reef is home to a fantastic variety of marine life, including more than 1,000 species of fish, from the relatively plain to the ornately bizarre. They include sharks (such as the white-tipped reef shark, *above*), the huge but strictly vegetarian manta ray, and some of the largest black marlin in the world. There are thousands of different crustacea (crabs, lobsters and shrimps), starfish with feathery arms or brittle, spiny fingers, sea urchins and sea slugs, and a seemingly infinite variety of shellfish. Dugongs feed here, and it is a breeding area for the humpback whale and green and loggerhead turtles.

△ **LURKING KILLER**
For a moray eel, a coral cave is a convenient hiding place from which to ambush prey. The moray grows to 2 metres (6½ ft) in length and is a ferocious predator, with sharp teeth and a savage bite.

◁ **ARMOURED DIGGER**
The shovel-nosed lobster (also called the slipper lobster) is one of the thousands of species of crustacea that inhabit the Reef. It uses its "shovel" to plough up the sea-bed in search of food.

KING-SIZE COD
The Cod Hole is a spot on the outer reef 40 minutes by boat from Lizard Island. It is noted for its concentration of very large fish, such as this giant potato cod, which probably weighs 60 kg (130 lb).

◁ BLOOMING FLOWER
Not all corals use the sun's rays to provide their food. Some, such as this Tubastrea, or sun coral, live in the shade in strong currents, and feed by filtering food from the water.

△ SUBMARINE STAGHORN
There are some 300 species of stony (hard) coral, of which Acropora or staghorn corals are the most common. They appear in many forms and many colours, including the beautiful lilac version above.

◁ SEND IN THE CLOWNS
A family of pink clown fish live symbiotically with a sea anemone. The anemone is not a plant but an animal, closely related to coral, but consisting of one large polyp. Anemones feed on particles that drift by, helped in this case by the feeding activities of the clown fish.

△ FAN WORSHIP
The sea fan belongs to a group known as Gorgonians (other members include sea whips and sea feathers). They all have a flexible spine of horn-like material, with the polyps living on the outside. The intricate colony that makes up a sea fan can grow to 3 metres (10 ft) in diameter.

THE REEF'S GREATEST ENEMY?

For years, the most famous threat to the Reef was thought to be the crown-of-thorns starfish *(above)* ugly creature that clamps on to coral and effectively spits its stomach out. Its digestive juices dissolve the polyps and leave great expanses of coral bleached and dead. The crown-of-thorns is poisonous to other fish and almost indestructible: it can regenerate to full size from a single leg and a small piece of intestine.

Altogether, it's an unpleasant creature but at least it was once relatively rare. With only a few around, it was easy to ignore its depredations on the Reef. But in the early 1960s the pattern changed. Instead of a few crown-of-thorns starfish, suddenly there were millions. Green Island was the first to see the plague, in 1962. From there it spread southwards, reaching the reefs around Bowen by 1988. Surveys between 1985 and 1988 established that about 31 percent of the reefs examined had been affected. Even after millions of dollars' worth of research, no one knows what caused the proliferation of the starfish. Furthermore, no economic way to get rid of the pest has presented itself.

Recently, however, marine biologists have decided to let the crown-of-thorns run its destructive course. The latest wisdom posits that it isn't a genuine threat at all but a natural, if poorly understood, part of the Reef's life-cycle.

NORTHERN TERRITORY

Less than one percent of Australia's population lives in the vast Northern Territory, an untamed region with a climate, a landscape and a history all its own

Map, page 274

The Northern Territory, or just "NT", is Australia in epic mode. Things here are larger than life – the sky, the distances, people's dreams and visions, the earth itself. An area of 1.35 million sq. km (521,000 sq. miles) – more than double the size of France, yet inhabited by just 200,000 people – gives you plenty of room to move. As you'd expect, the locals are a breed apart: tough, laconic, beholden to no one. Like the inhabitants of any inhospitable environment, they possess friendliness by the bucketful, a truly egalitarian spirit, and a wicked sense of humour. Many Australians visiting NT's Outback from their urban havens in the south and east feel as though they have entered foreign land, which can be disconcerting. They find a kind of detachment, a floating feeling of insubstantiality inspired by the uncomfortable knowledge that nothing human beings do here can ever touch the soul or the brute power of this ancient, beaten-down land.

Despite its size, NT fits neatly into a travel itinerary. There is the Red Centre – Alice Springs and the stunning hinterland in the Territory's south; various points along "The Track" (the Stuart Highway) heading north; and the "Top End", Darwin, Kakadu and surroundings. The distance between points of interest can be intimidating – roughly 1,600 km (1,000 miles) from Alice to Darwin – but only by driving through NT do you get a true sense of its grand and ancient terrain.

Apart from the Top End, which is swamped by a tropical monsoon each February–March, pretty much all of the Territory is an arid zone. Rainfall is minimal, averaging about 250mm (9.8 inches) a year. But, when rain does come, it comes Outback-style: no half measures.

The Red Centre

Australia's Red Centre is the heart of the country in more ways than one. For many visitors, Australia is primarily a nature trip, and it is here in Central Australia that the continent's greatest natural feature stands – **Uluru**, or **Ayers Rock**. But just as two-thirds of The Rock's awesome mass lies hidden beneath the ground, so Uluru and the other main tourist sights represent the mere tip of the great inselberg that is the Outback.

Incidentally, "Red Centre" isn't just a cute name. The sand and rock around here is red because of iron oxides found in the sandstone. The skins of the "white" inhabitants are more often a ruddy red. The sun is red when it drops, and red scars mark the flow of mineral-rich, ultra-healthy water. Even some of the kangaroos are red.

Alice Springs ❶ – or "The Alice" – is the natural base for exploring the Red Centre. It is a grid-pattern, sun-scorched town of squat, mostly modern buildings, which crouches in one of many gaps (or Outback oases) in the rugged **MacDonnell Ranges**. These hills – which turn an intense blue at sunset, as if lit internally – act like a wagon train, a protective ring that might just keep

LEFT: Lake Amadeus, near Ayers Rock.
BELOW: driving through the Red Centre.

Map,
page 274

he expanse of the Outback at bay. Alice has enjoyed a recent, tourism-inspired boom, based on Uluru and Aboriginal art and culture. Its present population of 27,500, one-tenth of which is Aboriginal, represents the greatest demographic concentration for 1,500 km (900 miles) in any direction. By no means a picture-postcard town, Alice none the less has strange powers of attraction: visitors find themselves drawn again and again to this incongruous outpost, and many who come here for short-term work wake up 10 years later and wonder what happened. It's not always easy to meet someone who was actually born in Alice.

White settlement began here in 1871 in the form of a repeater station on the Overland Telegraph Line, constructed beside the permanent freshwater springs. Lying 4 km (2½ miles) north of the present township, the **Telegraph Station** (tours daily from 8am) and **Springs** form a popular tourist site. Then, as now, water dictated all human movement and settlement, and the line, running from Adelaide through Alice and up to Darwin, followed virtually the same route as the track does now. The line linked the cities of Australia's south and southeast with the rest of the world, as it continued from Darwin through Indonesia to Singapore, Burma, British India and across Asia and Europe to colonial headquarters in London. Keeping the line open was a full-time job, and it is still possible to see some of the original telegraph posts, now disused, rising from the hard earth.

Alice developed slowly; in 1925, it had just 200 residents. Four years later, the coming of "The Ghan" – which at that time ran from Adelaide via Oodnadatta to Alice, named after Afghan camel drivers who pioneered transport in these parts – saw things pick up, but the trip was fraught with hazards. In the mistaken belief that the Outback never flooded, the track was routed across low-lying terrain; consequently, the train was often stranded in nowheresville, with

The Todd River was named after Charles Todd, the postmaster-general of South Australia, who began the telegraph line from Adelaide to Darwin in 1870. The springs discovered in the dry river bed were named after his wife, Alice Todd.

BELOW: the old telegraph station at Alice Springs.

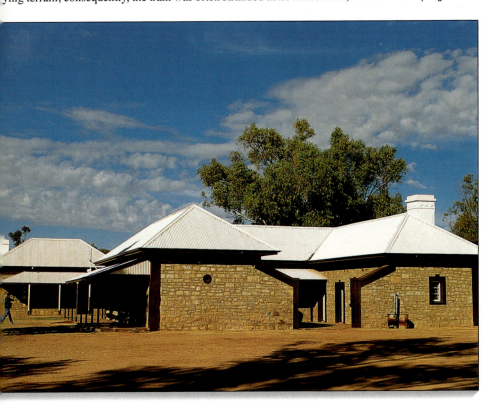

For a taste of what the Afghan camel drivers experienced, visit the Frontier Camel Farm, 4 km (2½ miles) along the Ross Highway (open daily 9am–5pm). You can take a one-hour camel ride, or ride a camel to breakfast or dinner.

BELOW: "The Ghan": 48 hours from Adelaide to Darwin.

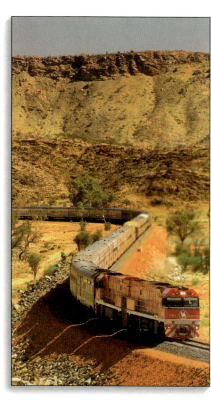

additional supplies having to be parachuted in to the hapless passengers. A new flood-proof route was completed in 1980, and the Ghan remains one of Australia's great rail journeys. In February 2004 Alice Springs ceased to be the end of the line, when the Alice–Darwin 1,420-km (880-mile) extension was completed. The event fulfilled a century-old promise of a key economic and tourism link.

In Alice, spend your first sunset on **Anzac Hill** to get the lie of the land. One of the town's most popular attractions is the **Royal Flying Doctor Service Visitors' Centre** (tours Mon–Sat 9am–4pm, Sun 1–4pm). The service, established in 1928 by the Rev. John Flynn – who now graces the $20 bill – provides essential medical treatment to many isolated communities and cattle stations the length and breadth of the Outback. Flynn's grave is 7 km (4 miles) west of Alice on Larapinta Drive – he is pinned down in perpetuity by one of the Devil's Marbles, poor chap.

Another popular spot is the **Alice Springs School of the Air** on Head Street, which services the educational needs of far-flung children. The school, unique in the world, conducts primary-level classes via radio, and the most notable of its 26 bases across the Outback is in Alice, covering an area of 1.3 million sq. km (500,000 sq. miles). It is the world's biggest classroom, and visitors can listen to lessons being taught there.

The **Alice Springs Desert Park**, just outside Alice at the base of the MacDonnell Ranges, is a must-see primer for anyone about to explore the desert. Its 35 hectares (86 acres) contain 320 arid-zone plant species and more than 400 desert-dwelling animals. The birds of prey nature theatre, where wild birds interact with park rangers in an astonishing way, is unforgettable.

The **Alice Springs Cultural Precinct** (10am–5pm; entrance fee) on Larapinta Drive contains the Strehlow Research Centre, the Namatjira Gallery, the Museum of Central Australia, the Memorial Cemetery, the Aviation Museum and the Araluen Centre, with four galleries.

The **Strehlow Centre** chronicles the life and work of Ted Strehlow, who was born at Hermannsburg, the Lutheran mission established in 1877. He became a patrol officer and researcher among the Arrernte people, winning their trust, and artefacts from his comprehensively documented collection that are not culturally sensitive are on display at the centre.

For non-aviators, the **Aviation Museum** is uninspiring; the cemetery is more interesting because the famous Aboriginal landscape painter, Albert Namatjira, and the legendary gold seeker Harold Lasseter (whose lives form a pretty comprehensive recent history of the region) are buried there, as are a number of Afghans, in a separate section at the back, facing Mecca.

If you find yourself in Alice in September, don't miss the **Henley-on-Todd Regatta**. This grandly named event is a boat race unlike any other. The "boats" are bottomless wraparounds, and teams of about eight runners inside each one race along the dry bed of the Todd River. Much merriment is had by all, and it is the only time in the year that the white population takes over the bed of the Todd, usually inhabited by groups of Aborigines camping under the gums.

Alice's immediate surroundings offer numerous

ttractions. To the east, in the **Eastern MacDonnell Ranges** , Emily Gap, esse Gap, **Trephina Gorge**, **Ross River Homestead**, **N'dhala Gorge** and the d gold town of **Arltunga** are interesting excursions.

Stretching west from Alice is the **West MacDonnells National Park** ❸, incorporating many of the gaps in the ranges. These include **Simpson's Gap**, ccessible via an excellent cycle path from Alice; **Standley Chasm**, with walls narrow that you'll have to sidle your way through; **Serpentine Gorge**; the **Ochre Pits**, used by Aborigines for centuries; **Ormiston Gorge and Pound**, with some fine walking trails; **Glen Helen Gorge**, with a comfortable lodge earby; and **Redbank Gorge**. A 223-km (138-mile) walking track, the **Larapinta Trail**, constructed by local prisoners, connects many of the attractions of the MacDonnells. Guided treks along the whole track can be arranged in Alice.

To the south is **Finke Gorge National Park** ❹, featuring the picturesque Palm Valley, with its distinctive Red Cabbage palms, and the Finke River, whose watercourse is the oldest in the world at 100 million years. This park is accessed via Hermannsburg, by 4WD only.

Due west of here is one of Central Australia's star attractions – spectacular **Kings Canyon** and **Watarrka National Park** ❺. The 350 million-year-old canyon shelters a permanent rockpool, aptly named the Garden of Eden and visited during the magnificent four-hour **Canyon Rim Walk**. A nearby Aboriginal-owned resort offers a good range of accommodation and facilities.

The new **Mereenie Loop Road** is a dirt road that connects Watarrka National Park with Namatjira Drive and attractions like Glen Helen Gorge. The track skirts the desert's eastern edge and should not be tackled by a conventional vehicle without local advice. Beware of crossing camels.

Map, page 274

Paradoxically, water in the Todd River is the last thing Alice's annual "regatta" needs. In the unlikely event of rain in September, the event is cancelled.

BELOW: the Henley-on-Todd Regatta.

TIP

The best time to visit
Rainbow Valley is
in the early morning
or late afternoon,
when the slanting
sun highlights the
many hues of the
rock formations.

From Alice to Uluru

South of Alice lies **Pine Gap**, off-limits to visitors but notable as the largest US communications and surveillance base in the Asia–Pacific region. Most of the 400-odd Americans employed here live in Alice; they hold weekend barbecues and baseball games in town parks, and blend with the local community.

The Aboriginal rock carvings at **Ewaninga**, of undetermined age, remain cryptic and alluring. Kaleidoscopic **Rainbow Valley** ❻ is a stunning rock formation (with primitive camping conditions), as is **Chambers Pillar** ❼, a solitary upstanding red ochre outcrop inscribed with the names and dates of early explorers, who used it as a convenient landmark.

The **Henbury Meteorite Craters** ❽, just off the Highway, consist of 12 indentations, about 5,000 years old, the biggest of which (180 metres/590 ft wide by 15 metres/49 ft deep) was caused by four meteors, each the size of a 200-litre (44-gallon) drum. The craters have become occasional pools, sprouting plants and attracting a variety of animal life.

En route to Uluru is **Curtin Springs**, a sprawling cattle station established in 1930 to breed horses for the British Indian Army. The roadside pub may look like a showroom for weird and wonderful tourist paraphernalia, but it's actually a hotbed of controversy. For years local Aborigines have been writing themselves off on the highways after drinking here, and recently an Aboriginal women's group has successfully lobbied government to restrict the drinking of blacks – a rare case of positive reverse discrimination.

Dominating the horizon is **Mount Conner**, a table-top monolith that many people initially mistake for Uluru. Conner, at 700 million years old, is 150 million years older than Uluru and Kata Tjuta and, amazingly, just 4 metres (13 ft

BELOW: the road to
Kata Tjuta.

Map,
page 274

ower than Uluru. The only ways to visit Mount Conner are by helicopter or with Discovery Ecotours, both based in Yulara.

From here, the road leads to Australia's great Outback icon, **Uluru ❾** (Ayers Rock; entrance fee for a 3-day pass), whose National Park was World Heritage-listed for its natural significance in 1987, and for its cultural significance in 1994. It was first sighted by a European in 1872 when explorer Ernest Giles noted a prominent hill in the distance. The following year, William Gosse discovered that the "hill" was in fact "one immense rock rising abruptly from the plain". After climbing it barefoot and soaking up its mystical aura, he enthused: "This rock appears more wonderful every time I look at it." The observation remains true.

Uluru means "meeting place", and many Aboriginal Dreaming tracks or "songlines" intersect here. Spirituality is often grounded in common sense and Uluru, with its permanent waterhole, abundant animal life, shelter and firewood, has been saving lives for millennia. The rock is sacred to the local Anangu people, who resumed ownership of the lands inside the National Park in 1985, in a historic "hand-back" ceremony. The Anangu have a controlling interest on the park's board of management; the chairperson is Anangu, and the meetings are bilingual (Pitjantjatjara and English). No park policy or development occurs without consultation. The Anangu receive over $2 million in revenue under the terms of the hand-back, but there is a caveat: tourists are allowed to climb over the rock on a defined path, while their sacred places are still out of bounds.

Climbing Uluru is a major attraction for many visitors, but is considered by resident park rangers and rescue teams to be a dangerous activity. More than a dozen climbers have been killed, and every few days someone has to be rescued. The Anangu would prefer that no-one climbed, but at the same time they respect tourists' urge to do so. In one local language, the word for the ubiquitous tiny black ant is *minga* – it is also the word for tourist. This cutting-edge ecotourism is about as happy as this sort of cross-cultural marriage of convenience gets. Recognising that the climb cannot be closed until more alternative activities are in place, the board of management took a step towards this with the opening of a new Cultural Centre in October 1995 to mark the 10th anniversary of hand-back. An alternative to climbing is the 9.4-km (5.8-mile) "base walk" around the rock, which is well marked. A self-guiding brochure is available from the Cultural Centre and numerous interpretive signs are displayed.

While more walks in the rock's vicinity are scheduled, **Kata Tjuta ❿** or **The Olgas** has a number of excellent trails, including the three-hour **Valley of the Winds** circuit. No climbing of Kata Tjuta (which means "many heads", referring to the 36 domes) is permitted and, just in case you get the urge to take home a souvenir rock or two, bear in mind that the park authorities receive, on average, two letters a week from visitors returning rocks they had taken, claiming that their luck has been bad ever since their stay in Uluru.

The 380,000-odd annual visitors to the national park are serviced by the award-winning **Yulara Resort**, which has been given a major refurbishment. There is

Uluru is the world's largest monolith. It stands 348 metres (1,142ft) tall and its circumference at the base is almost 9km (5½ miles).

BELOW: sunset over satellite transmitters.

The Yulara Resort has seven different tiers of accommodation, ranging from a camping ground to a luxury resort. Its water supply is drawn from underground rivers.

BELOW: a pair of Devil's Marbles.

a wide range of tours and activities available, and the sight of a sunset traffic jam has to be seen to be believed. Uluru, like the entire Red Centre, will humble you with its scale and overwhelm you with its beauty.

Up the track

Anyone seeking the old-style Outback experience of endless long, hot, dirt roads may like to leave the highway 21 km (13 miles) north of Alice Springs and head northwest along the **Tanami Track ⑪** to rejoin "civilisation" 1,050 km (660 miles) away at Halls Creek in the Kimberley. But, for most tastes, the 1,500-km (930-mile) route along a good paved road to Darwin will suffice.

Heading north from Alice, one passes through the tiny community of **Barrow Creek**, before reaching the **Devil's Marbles Conservation Reserve ⑫** (403 km/250 miles from Alice), a series of granite boulders that litter either side of the highway for several kilometres. Some of the larger ones stand precariously balanced on tiny bases. It's thought they were once part of one solid block, broken and gradually rounded by wind and water erosion. The local Aboriginal people believe them to be the eggs of the Rainbow Serpent.

Tennant Creek ⑬ (504 km/313 miles from Alice) is a gold town, although only one major mine is still in production. Gold was discovered in 1932 but the rush was short-lived and it seemed destined to become a ghost town, until the discovery of copper in the 1950s brought new prosperity. The town is 12 km (7 miles) from the creek; the story goes that a cart carrying timber to build the first pub for the miners became bogged here. It was too much trouble to continue, so the hotel was erected on the spot. With a tree-lined double highway and a population of over 3,500, the town bears few signs of such a haphazard beginning.

To explore the remote **Barkly Tableland**, take the Barkly Highway east for 185 km (115 miles), then turn north onto the Tablelands Highway and towards the remote township of **Borroloola** (pop. 600), just inland from the Gulf of Carpentaria and famous for its barramundi fishing. Like any journey that involves driving into the true Outback, this route requires ample preparation, including fuel, emergency rations and water. The last leg to Borroloola is on the Carpentaria Highway, an excellent sealed road.

North of Tennant Creek, the tiny township of **Renner Springs** marks a geographical and climatic end to the long, dry journey through the Red Centre: this is the southern extremity of the monsoon-affected plains of the "Top End". But the changes are slow and subtle. Termite mounds are fascinating features of this scrubby country. They are usually about 3 metres (11 ft) high and point north–south, a position that allows termites the maximum benefit of both heat and shade. This orientation inevitably led to them being called "magnetic anthills", and at first glance it does look as if they are built on compass bearings.

At **Elliott**, depending on your schedule, golfers may care to enjoy the far-out experience of playing nine holes on a desert course with well-kept greens.

Newcastle Waters is an historic stock-route junction town established as a telegraph station. In 1872 at **Frew's Ironside Ponds**, some 50 km (31 miles) north of Newcastle Waters, the respective ends of the telegraph wire were joined to establish the overland communication link.

The **Daly Waters Pub** ⓮ is worth a pause for a drink and rest. Built in the 1930s as a staging post for Qantas crew and passengers on multi-hop international flights, it is full of related memorabilia. **Mataranka** ⓯ is a small town that was really put on the map only when an earlier rail track from Darwin was

Map, page 274

The Aboriginal Land Act of 1976 returned about one-third of NT to Aboriginal ownership. You need a permit to enter many Aborigine-controlled areas, but not to drive through them on a public road.

BELOW: "magnetic" termite mounds always face east–west.

Jeannie Gunn, the author of the 1908 Outback novel We of the Never Never, *was the wife of the manager of Elsey Station, and the first white woman to set foot in this area. The saying goes that those who live in the region can "never never" leave.*

laid in 1928. Before that, it was part of the huge Elsey farming property (in 1916 Mataranka Station was established as an experimental sheep run, a project doomed to failure in this classic cattle country). Today, the surprise attraction is the **Mataranka Homestead Tourist Resort**, a 4-hectare (10-acre) section of tropical forest, including palms and paperbark trees adjoining the **Elsey National Park**. The nearby sparkling **Mataranka Thermal Pool**, with a water temperature of 34°C (93°F), is a real oasis amid the north's arid surrounds. Also adjacent to the tourist park is a replica of the Elsey Station homestead, made for the 1981 film *We of the Never Never*.

Katherine, 103 km (63 miles) to the north, is the Top End's second most important town after Darwin. It has a population of 10,500 and a well-developed infrastructure of shops, camping grounds, hotels and motels. Since colonial days, Katherine has been an important telegraph station and cattle centre.

To the east of the township, **Katherine Gorge** is one of the best-known features of the Territory. It's a massive stretch of sandstone cliffs rising to more than 100 metres (330 ft) above the Katherine River, with 13 main canyons. The gorge is best explored by water. Tour boats operate mostly on the lower two canyons, but the more inquisitive traveller can explore the other 11 gorges upstream – by either hiring a canoe or swimming – for a total of 12 km (7 miles) before the river widens out again. (The small crocodiles looking on are freshwater and don't attack humans, although they can be unnerving.) The gorge system is part of the 1,800-sq. km (695-sq. miles) **Nitmiluk National Park** ⓰ that deserves at least a couple of days. There are also several walking trails in the park that follow the top of the escarpment, looking down into the gorge. Katherine is also home to a Savannah Guide Station. These eco-accredited specialist

BELOW: the mighty sandstone cliffs of Katherine Gorge.

guides focus on heritage, culture, and preservation of the natural environment.

From Katherine the Victoria Highway strikes west towards the Kimberley region of Western Australia. Just before the WA border, there is a turn-off to **Keep River National Park**. Like the better-known formations across the border in the Bungle Bungle National Park, Keep River features a series of fascinating banded sandstone towers that shelter a wide range of vegetation and animal life.

The richness of Kakadu

One of the brightest jewels in the whole array of Australian wilderness lies to the north of Katherine, at **Kakadu National Park** ⓱ (entrance fee for a 7-day pass). The park's prime accommodation and commercial centre is Jabiru, 250 km (155m) southeast of Darwin. The richness of Kakadu defies description. Here, where the Arnhem Land Escarpment meets the coastal floodplains, scenic splendour, ancient Aboriginal culture and paintings and an incredible array of flora and fauna come together in a brilliant, coherent whole.

The statistics of Kakadu – which is now on the World Heritage list – give some indication of what this area has to offer. The park covers 19,804 sq. km (7,200 sq. miles), with further extension likely. It is home to a quarter of all Australian freshwater fish, over 1,000 plant species, 300 types of birds, 75 species of reptiles, many mammals and innumerable insects. Its world-famous galleries of Aboriginal art – particularly at Nourlangie and Ubirr rocks – give a significant insight into the dawn of man more than 20,000 years ago. In Kakadu the oldest evidence for the technology of edge-ground stone axes has been found.

Coming into Kakadu from the south, via the road from **Pine Creek**, one should detour into **Gunlom**, with its magical combination of waterfall and

Map, page 274

BELOW: Kakadu National Park is scenically splendid.

It is possible that the earliest paintings at Ubirr Rock are up to 23,000 years old – which would make them the oldest art works known anywhere on earth.

plunge pool. This oasis featured in the 1986 movie *Crocodile Dundee* and is even more beautiful than its celluloid image.

Most visitors approach Kakadu along the sealed **Arnhem Highway** from Darwin. This road actually terminates at **Jabiru**, a service town for the Ranger Uranium Mine; the mine operates in an enclave surrounded by the national park and near to **Arnhem Land**, a great expanse of Aboriginal land that is closed to tourists. The juxtaposition of national park and uranium mine has provided ongoing controversy in Australian politics for years.

A good introduction to Kakadu is a boat tour on **Yellow Waters**, which offers the finest natural wildlife viewing anywhere in Australia. You are likely to see saltwater crocodiles, Jabiru storks, brolga cranes and a host of water birds, resident and migratory – but only during the dry season (May–Sept). During The Wet, when water is plentiful, the animals disperse across the region, and successful viewing is more haphazard.

Other easily accessible sights within the park are the paintings of **Ubirr Rock** and the towering faces of **Nourlangie Rock**. The splendid **Bowali Visitor Centre** has a permanent display setting out the features of the park. The **Marrawuddi Gallery** features displays of Aboriginal art, books and gifts.

However, Kakadu's flatlands and the most famous tourist attractions aren't the most scenically splendid parts of the park. To see what makes Kakadu special, head out to one or more of the waterholes nestled at the base of the escarpment.

The most popular conjunction of swimming hole and waterfall is **Jim Jim Falls**. The deep, cool pool and the nearby sandy beach are remarkably attractive and have the distinct benefit of being easy to visit, at least when the access road is open (June–Nov). Effort is well rewarded for those who decide to walk into nearby **Twin**

BELOW: ancient Aboriginal art at Ubirr Rock.

Falls, where the two strands of water drop right onto the end of a palm-shaded beach. However don't swim there because large and possibly hungry crocodiles have been known to move in. Both Jim Jim and Twin Falls turn into seething maelstroms during wet season flooding, at which time they are inaccessible to anyone without a helicopter. In the dry season, they are tranquil places of exquisite beauty.

On the Arnhem Highway to Darwin you cross the **Adelaide River**, and at that point you'll find the *Adelaide River Queen*, (tel: 08-8988 8144) which can take you on a short (90-minute) river cruise to see the "jumping crocodiles" which leap almost clear of the water when offered a slice of steak, just as they do when catching birds and bats in mid-air.

The Top End lifestyle

Darwin , capital of the Northern Territory, is a city with two histories: pre-Tracy and post-Tracy. It was founded in 1869, after more than four decades of failed settlements in the North – abandoned one after another because of malaria outbreaks, cyclones, Aboriginal attacks and supply failure due to the sheer distance from the other white settlements. Named after the naturalist Charles Darwin, one of whose shipmates on the *Beagle* discovered the bay in 1839, it drifted on in a tropical stupor for decades, punctuated only by the discovery of gold at Pine Creek in 1870, a minor "revolution" in 1919. Some 243 people were killed and another 300 injured in the first savage surprise Japanese bombing attack in February 1942, and Darwin suffered repeated raids over the following 18 months.

Then, in four furious hours on Christmas Eve 1974, Cyclone Tracy swept in from the north and flattened the city. With gusts up to 280 km (175 miles) an hour, the hurricane destroyed more than 5,000 homes – 80 percent of the city.

Map, page 274

TIP

Darwin is usually unbearably hot in the middle of the day. If you plan to explore the city on foot, take your tour in the early morning or late afternoon.

BELOW: Darwin's Parliament House.

TIP

As an alternative to walking, explore Darwin on the Tour Tub, an open-topped minibus that allows you to get on and off anywhere on its circular route.

BELOW: Darwin's weekly Mindil Beach Market.

Fewer than 500 buildings were left intact. The dead and missing totalled 66 in one of the most dramatic natural disasters in Australian history. With massive government funding, the city was rebuilt in the knowledge that the character and ambience of the old Darwin had been blown away forever.

Historical buildings and most of the old-style Darwin were levelled, to be replaced by a modern, more commercialised city. But of the over 30,000 residents evacuated in the nation's fastest-ever mass population shift, the majority returned. The city's population, Australia's most multi-cultural, is now around 100,000. The place has a pace that might – almost – be described as brisk, at least by Northern Territory standards.

Once the neurotic front line of White Australia, Darwin's populace now reflects its proximity to Asia: the mix of some 50 cultures including Aborigines, Vietnamese, Filipinos, Malays, New Guineans, Pacific Islanders, Japanese and Indonesians – and Greeks and white Australians – provides a strong cosmopolitan flavour. That mix might have become more predominantly Asian had the Japanese advance in World War II not been stalled at New Guinea. When the Japanese bombed Darwin's port, there was mass panic, desertions, the evacuation of the civilian population, and looting of homes by some of the army marshals who remained. The desperate dash for safety in the south became known derisively as the "Adelaide River Stakes".

The focal point of the city's defence was the **Old Navy Headquarters**. This simple stone building, dating from 1884, was a police station and courthouse. It and other historical buildings such as **Fannie Bay Gaol** (1883) and **Brown's Mart** (built in 1885, and the oldest in the city centre) contrast with Darwin's new cyclone-proof architecture, represented by the city's new high-rise hotels, MGM **Grand Darwin Casino** and **Parliament House**.

Despite the changes, it is Darwin's natural charm and the relaxed "Top End" lifestyle that give the new city its appeal. The town is flanked by great expanses of golden sandy beaches and in the dry season – April to October – the vision of sand, clear blue skies and tropical flora (even waving palms) makes Darwin not far short of paradise.

For six months of the year **Darwin Harbour** becomes the playground of the area's boating populace. Many people swim here, even though huge saltwater crocodiles are regularly pulled from the water. It may be more relaxing to swim at nearby **Mindil Beach** or **Vestey's** (named after the cattle company that employed most Darwinians at the end of the 19th century). Mindil Beach is the scene of a sunset market every Thursday evening (Apr–Oct, 5–10pm), which has become one of Darwin's most popular events. The Asian food stalls alone are marvellous. Other markets are in **Parap** on Saturday morning (8am–2pm) and in **Rapid Creek** on Sunday (8am–1pm).

When the tides are right in early August at **Fannie Bay**, about 4 km (2½ miles) from the city centre, Darwin conducts its famous **Beer Can Regatta**. Thousands of beer cans are used to build a fleet of wildly imaginative, semi-seaworthy craft. The whole city turns out to watch them race or wallow in the bay. This event is in keeping with Darwin's reputation as the world's beer-drinking capital.

Thanks to post-Tracy funding, in 1981 the multi-million-dollar **Museum and Art Gallery of the**

Northern Territory (Mon–Fri 9am–5pm; Sat, Sun 10–5; free) was opened. Its five galleries include one of the world's best collections of Aboriginal art and cultural artefacts, and archaeological finds from the Pacific region. Don't miss the excellent collection of Aboriginal contemporary art, the Tiwi Pukumani burial poles and "Sweetheart", a stuffed saltwater crocodile 5 metres (17 ft) long. The **Fannie Bay Gaol Museum** (daily 10am–4.30pm; donation requested) displays old cells and gallows from the prison's grim past.

Darwin's tropical nature makes a visit to the 34-hectare (84-acre) **Botanical Gardens** worthwhile, and fish-feeding at the **Aquascene** in Doctor's Gully Road, near the corner of Daly Street and the Esplanade, is lots of fun, especially with children. Fish can be hand-fed at high tide every day, at times advertised in the local paper.

Finally, the **Wharf Precinct** has undergone a major renovation; on any balmy afternoon, head out to the end of the pier, where dozens of restaurants have set up outdoor tables. It's the perfect place to drink in the tropical air, watch the trawlers come and go, or drop a line to catch a passing Spanish mackerel.

Exploring the Top End

About 60 km (40 miles) south of Darwin on the Cox Peninsula Road, the **Territory Wildlife Park** provides a potted display of the Top End's varied bird, marine, and bush wildlife, and an aquarium representing an entire Top End river system, viewed from a shuttle train around the 400-hectare (988-acre) property.

A two-hour drive to the southwest of Darwin is **Litchfield National Park** ⓳, 1,153 sq. km (59 sq. miles) of sandstone plateau with pockets of rainforest. It is one of the best areas in the Top End for bushwalking, but is even more popular for its waterfalls and clear pools, which provide excellent swimming.

Map,
page 274

The citizens of Darwin drink more beer per head than anyone else in the world. The "Darwin Stubby" is reputedly the world's largest bottle of beer, containing 2¼ litres.

BELOW: a spin through the Top End mangroves.

Map, page 274

TIP

However tempting the sea might seem, it is unwise to swim off the coast of NT between October and May. Box jellyfish, whose sting can be fatal, are usually present in great numbers. Always observe the warning signs.

BELOW: the Top End's endless tidal flats.

Darwin is the ideal base for exploring the remote, mangrove-filled north. Easily reached by light plane is the **Cobourg Peninsula** ⓴. Because it's on Aboriginal land, permission is required before visiting, but that will be arranged by the tour operators. Cobourg was the site of one of the earliest attempts to establish a British base in northern Australia. Through a series of misadventures and bungles, Port Essington failed, but the bay in which it was built is a place of extravagant beauty in one of the most remote corners of the continent. **Seven Spirit Bay** here is perhaps the most out-of-the-way five-star resort in the world.

Splaying out to the north of Darwin like a giant ink-blot, the two Tiwi Aboriginal islands, **Bathurst** ㉑ and **Melville** ㉒, are among Australia's most isolated outposts. Although the mainland is only 80 km (50 miles) away, dugout canoes rarely survived the journey, so the Tiwi culture and language developed separately from that of other Aboriginal groups. Early Dutch explorers met with hostility, and when the British set up an outpost on Melville in 1824 it lasted less than five years, thanks to Tiwi sieges and tropical disease. As a result, the Tiwis largely escaped the scorched-earth period of Australia's colonisation. The first Catholic missionaries arrived here only in 1909. Control of their own affairs was returned to the Tiwis in the 1970s; most crucially, since they have never been moved, their land rights have never been disputed. This confident sense of possession may be why they are such an outgoing bunch; despite their once-fearsome reputation, they now bill their lands as the "Friendly Islands".

Visiting the islands is allowed only with a permit, organised by the Tiwi-owned tour company *(see facing page)*. It's worth the journey: this remote coastline alternates between croc-infested mangrove swamps and blinding white beaches where you can walk for mile after mile without seeing another person. ❑

An Aboriginal guided tour

Huge areas of NT are the property of different Aboriginal peoples, and outsiders can visit only with the local Land Council's permission. In recent years, responding to the upsurge of interest in their culture, many groups have started allowing carefully monitored visits. Aboriginal guides lead tours on their land from **Darwin**, **Alice Springs** and **Katherine**, lasting anywhere from a few hours to week-long hikes.

Typical of the new visits is the programme offered by the Tiwi people on **Bathurst** Island, about 80 km (50 miles) north of Darwin.

Bring swimming gear and a towel, because you're close to the equator and there are opportunities to cool off. Aboriginal-owned Tiwi Tours offer one-day visits and two-day camping tours, either of which begin with a 30-minute scenic flight from Darwin to Bathurst Island. Here your local guide takes you through the progressive, modern-day Aboriginal community of Nguiu (pronounced "new-you") and its museum with displays of traditional Aboriginal art and depictions of the Tiwi "Dreamtime" stories. The Early Mission Precinct has a Tiwi-style Catholic Church, where you'll hear about the colourful history of the early mission days, and how the Tiwi people have blended their culture with Christianity.

At the arts and crafts centres you'll see where the artists work and you can purchase Tiwi arts and crafts – and screen-printed fabric – at Island prices. At morning tea, spend time with some Tiwi women enjoying billy tea and damper (unrisen bread) while they work on their weaving and painting. Your guides and the women also demonstrate their totem dances, and perform a smoking ceremony to bless the visitors and explain the meanings behind them.

A scenic drive through the Bathurst Island wilderness takes you to a picturesque lookout, which is also the setting of a Tiwi burial site. You'll learn some of the complex rituals associated with the Pukamani Poles (burial poles), before lunch and a swim at a local waterhole. On your way back to catch your return flight to Darwin, you'll also hear about traditional "bush tuckers" (native foods), bush medicine, and natural fibres and dyes, used in traditional native clothing

If you've taken the two-day option, you'll head off to Moantu (the home of the Rainbow Serpent) and set up camp at a picturesque spot overlooking a large freshwater lake (no swimming here because of resident crocodiles). Take a walk over the sand dunes to admire the view and a Tiwi Island sunset before dinner around the campfire.

After breakfast you will be off to the westernmost point of Bathurst Island – Cape Fourcroy – to explore the rugged coastline. In season, a walk along this beautiful beach may reward you with the sight of tracks on the sand indicating a turtle nest.

The lakes attract a diverse range of native wildlife, so don't forget a camera (and a long lens if you have one). A visit to Tomorrupi Waterfall, where the swimming is safe, will cool you off in the refreshing water before a picnic lunch. This more relaxed visit is still packed with interest. ❏

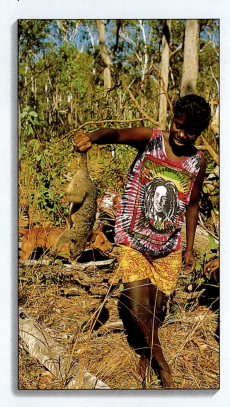

RIGHT: a guide shows how to hold a possum.

WESTERN AUSTRALIA

Maps,
pages
294 & 298

*Two-thirds of the population of "WA" live in its attractive capital,
Perth. The vast emptiness beyond includes barren desert,
lush forests, rugged canyons and far-flung gold-mining towns*

Western Australia is, quite simply, enormous. Covering more than 2½ million sq. km (960,000 sq. miles), it is much larger than Alaska and Texas combined. In fact, if "WA" was a separate country, it would be the ninth largest in the world – and the emptiest. India is about the same size, with a population of 700 million, whereas the whole vast, dry expanse of Western Australia is inhabited by just 1.9 million souls.

Being so far from the main Australian population centres on the east coast, WA conveys a feeling of utter isolation. **Perth** is the world's remotest state capital city, closer to Bali than it is to Sydney. Most of the state is parched and barren, but the north is lushly tropical and the southwest temperate. In springtime, between September and November, many visitors travel from the eastern states just to see the profusion of wildflowers that turn the south into a riot of colour. WA's vastness, small population and rugged scenery give this state a strong sense of being a new frontier, an impression heightened when only a few hours' drive from Perth takes you into pure Outback scenery.

When planning a trip in WA, it's a good idea to keep an eye on the map scale and distances. It's all too easy to outline a weekend tour through an apparently tiny proportion of the state – only to add up the distances and find this would mean driving 1,600 km (1,000 miles).

PRECEDING PAGES: a camel train on Cable Beach, near Broome.
LEFT: ancient boab trees.
BELOW: wildlife warning in WA.

The first arrivals

Western Australia was the arrival point for the first Australians. It is thought that, more than 50,000 years ago, the forebears of today's Australian Aborigines sailed across on bamboo rafts from what is now Indonesia, arriving in waves over many centuries. From the northwest, they gradually spread to occupy the whole continent.

The first recorded European view of the West Australian coast occurred in 1616, when a Dutch captain, Dirk Hartog, sailed to what is now Dirk Hartog Island near Carnarvon. The first English explorer known to have visited Australia was William Dampier, who was on the *Cygnet* in 1688 when it was repaired at what is now Cygnet Bay in the Kimberley. He was unimpressed with what he saw, finding the land useless and the Aborigines the "miserablest people in the world".

In 1827, amid fears that the French might seize the vast coastline, Captain James Stirling was despatched from Sydney to find a potential site for a western settlement. In 1829 the first colonists arrived to set up shop on a site he had spotted 16 km (10 miles) upstream on the Swan River. Surrounded by black swans, a village of some 300 residents was founded and named Perth.

Inducing other colonists to head west was no easy matter. An acute labour shortage led to convicts being imported in 1850, much to the disgust of many founding

TIP

The Perth Tram
Company operates the
City Explorer Tour,
which stops at main
attractions ($15). But
Perth also has a free
bus service in the city
centre, to encourage
people to use public
transport. Look out for
CAT (Central Area
Transit) buses.

fathers. By 1858, the population of Perth was still barely 3,000; far fewer white settlers ventured into the hinterland.

But gold changed all that. When news of the great finds of the 1890s at fields at Kalgoorlie to the east reached the outside world, Perth became the leaping-off point for one of the last great gold rushes. Still, many parts of the northeast were among the last to be settled in Australia, when some of the world's largest cattle stations were opened in the Kimberley. Throughout the 20th century, the discovery of mineral deposits throughout the state provided the main basis of its wealth – from uranium to gas and oil on the northwest shelf.

Perth, the Dallas of Australia

As in the gold-rush days, almost all visits to the wild west still start in Perth, whose population now stands at 1.4 million. Set on the west coast like a high-tech counterweight to the older, heavily populated eastern cities, the place has become a symbol of Australian confidence – many would say over-confidence.

Perth still lives in the shadow of the roaring 1980s, when it was the base of a wallet-full of multi-millionaires who worked so closely with the Labour politicians of the time that the state was referred to as "WA Inc." The whole extravagant facade collapsed after the 1987 Wall Street crash, and Australians looked on gleefully as one tycoon after another was implicated in corrupt dealings, charged and jailed. Today, Perth is a much-chastened city, but even its moderate new millennium style is well worth the long flight from the east.

The city has been planned to take full advantage of its natural setting. The dominant view is over **Perth Water** where the **Swan River** widens into a broad bay about 1 km (⅗ mile) across. The river continues to widen as it nears the

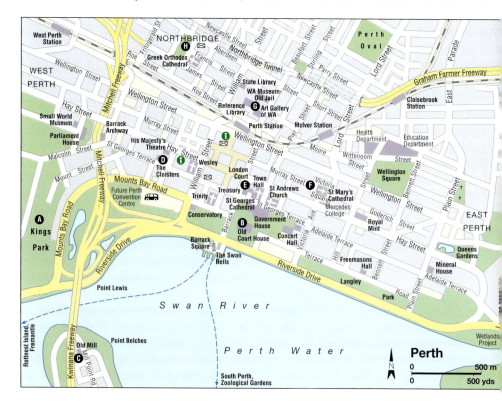

Map, page 294

ocean; many people have taken advantage of the aquatic blessing by building their houses on the shoreline. Fringing the river mouth are surfing beaches, while included in the city are over 1,000 sq. km (about 400 sq. miles) of parks, reserves and sports grounds. On the edge of the business district is **Kings Park Ⓐ**, a 400-hectare (988-acre) reserve of botanical gardens and bushland. Dominating the jetty on Riverside Drive is the spectacular **Swan Bells** (more popularly known as the Bell Tower) with its sail-shaped copper wings.

The mining booms since the 1970s have led many large multinational and West Australia-based companies to build huge office blocks in Perth. Their presence has dramatically changed the city skyline, causing older residents to complain that the city has lost its intimate country-town feel.

But the odd architectural gem can be found, even in the city centre. In the **Stirling Gardens** the **Old Court House Ⓑ** (1837) has a modest facade of Doric columns. Across the river is the **Old Mill Ⓒ**, now converted to a folk museum, where the first settlers ground their grain from the 1830s on. On the whole, however, buildings pre-dating the state's 1890s gold rush are rare. The Elizabethan-style **Cloisters** building Ⓓ was established in 1858 as the first public boys' school. Next to it stands a century-old fig tree that once shaded the school grounds. Today the Cloisters is incongruously shaded by modern office towers.

Government House (further along St George's Terrace, and only rarely open to the public) stands as a true reflection of the beginning of the state. Constructed in the 1860s by convict labour, it placed a regal stamp of authority on the new settlement. The emerging Australian "larrikin" characteristic shows through in the upstairs windows, cunningly fashioned in the shape of a broad arrow – the motif on the uniforms of the convict builders.

BELOW: the Perth skyline from across the Swan River.

The old **Town Hall** (Hay Street Mall) was the last building in Perth to be built by convict labour (commenced in 1867). It has been the site of various entertainments, from operetta to vaudeville, formal civic ceremonies and political meetings. It was notably a rallying-point for conscription in both World Wars.

The city architecture of the 1890s gold rush includes **His Majesty's Theatre** ("The Maj") at the west end of Hay Street. The surrounding precinct has been given a new lease of life, with top restaurants and cafés and designer-label shopping. Other buildings of the gold rush include the 1899 **Perth Mint** (corner of Hay and Hill streets, open Mon–Fri 9am–4pm, Sat–Sun 9am–1pm), among the world's oldest operating mints. Try picking up a block of gold worth A$250,000, minting your own medallion, or watch gold being smelted.

Two sections of town with contrasting histories are **London Court** 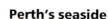 and **East Murray Street Precinct** . London Court dates back to 1937, a monument to mock Tudor kitsch whose curiosities include a clock tower at each end: one a replica of Big Ben at Westminster in London, the other of the Gros Horloge in Rouen, France. East Murray Street, by contrast, is the genuine colonial item. It appears on the original town plans of 1838 and now stands lined by early 20th-century buildings and old public offices. A huge fig tree shades pedestrians, offering a touch of gracious protection to an enclave just a few blocks from the busy city centre.

Beyond the railway station lies the **Perth Cultural Centre** , home to the **Art Gallery of Western Australia** (daily 10am–5pm; free) and the **Western Australian Museum** (daily 9.30am–5pm; free). The museum incorporates the lovingly preserved **Old Jail** (1856) with its fine stone doorway.

The Cultural Centre stands on the doorstep of **Northbridge** , where Perth's ethnic diversity is displayed on a plate, as it were. You can walk past tanks of live mud crabs and crayfish, smell the sharp tang of lemongrass, chew on chickens' feet or dim sum at eight in the morning, sip cappuccino with old men in the Italian cafés or have a beer on the balcony of an old pub, watching all the action on the streets below. As well as restaurants serving anything from tapas to takeaways, Northbridge has nightclubs and discos as lively as any in Sydney.

Perth's seaside

Fremantle , lying 19 km (12 miles) from the city centre, was brushed up for the America's Cup race in 1987 and has since become one of Western Australia's most popular attractions. Unlike glittering Perth, the old port's colonial charms remain intact, including the **Round House** (which actually has 12 sides), and the 1888 **Samson House**. On Finnerty Street, **Fremantle Museum** houses the Arts Centre and the History Museum, which recounts WA's convoluted past. A stunningly designed **Western Australian Maritime Museum** dominates the waterfront from Victoria Quay, while the **Shipwreck Gallery** on Cliff Street has many relics from the Dutch ships wrecked on the coast (including the most famous, *Batavia: see page 303*). **Fremantle Prison**, a maximum security jail until 1991, offers daylight and candlelight tours. Ghost sightings are not guaranteed but the tour incudes the gallows yard and hellish cell blocks built by convict labour in 1855.

TIP

You can visit Fremantle and Rottnest Island from Perth by ferry, leaving from the Barrack Street Jetty. There are regular flights to Rottnest. In addition, Boats head upstream to the Swan Valley's wine-growing area

BELOW: Western Australian Maritime Museum.

Map,
page 298

Fremantle is particularly lively at weekends; it has no shortage of trendy coffee shops and restaurants, while the bustling 1892 market is full of good souvenirs (Fri 9am–9pm, Sat 9am–5pm, Sun 10am–5pm).

While you're by the water, catch the ferry to little **Rottnest Island ❷**, 19 km (13 miles) off the coast, which was first settled as a natural prison for West Australian Aborigines. Today, "Rotto" is the traditional holiday spot for Perth families. Because private motor vehicles aren't allowed on the island, visitors tend to wobble along on bicycles, re-discovering long lost skills.

The pub, the Quokka Arms, originally served as the official residence of the Australian State Governor, and now has live music on summer evenings. Visitors to the island can spend their time boating, golfing, playing tennis or just lazing on a quiet beach. There are regular educational tours and a good museum. In summer, divers come here to explore the world's southernmost coral reef.

Rottnest ("Rats' Nest") Island was named by the Dutch explorer Willem de Vlamingh, who mistook its hordes of quokkas (small marsupials) for rats.

The Southwest of WA

South of Fremantle lies a series of beaches and bays known as Perth's resort coast. For fishing, boating and surfing, head for the sleepy resort town of **Rockingham**, or **Mandurah** on the Peel Estuary. In high season the towns and campsites are busy with holidaymakers, but for the rest of the year they can be enjoyed in relative peace. Down the coast is the green dairy town of **Harvey**, dating back to 1890. The nearby **Yalgorup National Park** can be reached by the old coast road for a solitary roam among the sand dunes or a spot of birdwatching around Lakes Clifton and Preston.

The city of **Bunbury** (pop. 50,000) is a busy port that owes its existence to Lt Henry St Pierre Bunbury, who travelled overland to the coast from Pinjarra in

BELOW: colonial architecture in Fremantle.

Western Australia

0 ——————— 400 km
0 ——————— 400 miles

N

Timor Sea

INDIAN

OCEAN

Admiralty Gulf

Cape Londonderry

Kalumburu

Wadaye

Joseph Bonaparte Gulf

Bonaparte Archipelago

Drysdale River N.P.

Kimberley Plateau

Mt. Hann 779

Wyndham

Kununurra

Lake Argyle

Buccaneer Archipelago

Cape Leveque
Lombadina
Beagle Bay

② ④

KING

Gibb River Road

Gibb River

LEOPOLD

Mt. Bedford 914

Purnululu National Park (Bungle Bungle)

②⑨

Nicholson

Windjana Gorge N.P.

Tunnel Creek N.P.

RANGES

Geikie Gorge N.P.

Halls Creek

② ②

Broome

Derby

② ③

② ⑤

② ⑥

② ⑦

Fitzroy Crossing

Lagrange

Fitzroy

Great Northern Hwy.

② ⑧ Wolfe Creek Meteorite Crater

Lajamanu Track

Montebello Is.

Dampier Archipelago

Port Hedland

② ①

Goldsworthy

Great Sandy

Desert

Barrow I.

Karratha

Cossack

Roebourne

Marble Bar

Lake MacKay

Dampier

North West Cape

Onslow

Millstream Chichester N.P.

Nullagine

Cape Range N.P.

Exmouth

① ⑨

HAMERSLEY

Wittenoom

Roy Hill

Fortescue

Rudall River N.P.

Western

Ningaloo Marine Park

Tom Price

Mt. Bruce 1235

RANGE

Tropic of Capricorn

Hamersley Range N.P.

② ⓪

Newman

Australia

Coral Bay

Paraburdoo

Little Sandy Desert

Lake Disappointment

Gibson Desert

Ashburton

Lake MacLeod

Collier Range N.P.

Canning Stock Route

Carnegie

Gunbarrel Highway

Bernier I.

1105 Mt. Augustus

ROBINSON RANGES

Great Northern Hwy.

① ⑧ Carnarvon

95

Lake Carnegie

Warburton

Dorre I.

Dairy Creek

Monkey Mia

Shark Bay

Wiluna

Warburton Road

① ⑦

Denham

Meekatharra

Mt. Maiden 590

Dirk Hartog I.

Murchison

Lake Austin

Agnew

Leinster

Laverton

Great Victoria

Kalbarri

① ⑥

Northampton

Sandstone

Mt. Magnet

Leonora

Desert

Anne Beadell Hwy

Kalbarri N.P.

Mullewa

Yalgoo

Lake Carey

Houtman Abrolhos Islands

① ⑤ Geraldton

Morawa

Lake Barlee

Port Denison

Three Springs

Mongers Lake

Paynes Find

Menzies

Eneabba

Forrest

Jurien

Moora

Wubin

Kanowna

Indian Pacific Railroad

Nambung N.P.

① ④

New Norcia

Kalgoorlie

① ①

Boulder

Nullarbor Plain

Madura

Eucla

Lancelin

Coolgardie

Kambalda

Cocklebiddy

Yanchep N.P.

Northam

Southern Cross

① ⓪

Eyre

Rottnest I.

②

13

94

Merredin

Lake Cowan

Eyre Hwy.

Fremantle

①

York

Kellerberrin

Johnston Lake

Norseman

Lake Dundas

Balladonia

Great Australian

Rockingham

Perth

Brookton

① ②

Wave Rock

Hyden

Bight

Mandurah

Narrogin

Lake King

Cape Le Grand N.P.

Cape Arid N.P.

Israelite Bay

INDIAN

Yalgorup N.P.

30

Wagin

Ravensthorpe

⑦

⑧

⑨

Bunbury

Donnybrook

Jerramungup

Esperance

Busselton

Nannup

⑥

Hopetoun

Archipelago of the Recherche

OCEAN

Cape Naturaliste

③ Margaret River

Manjimup

④

Fitzgerald River National Park

Cape Leeuwin

Pemberton

Mt. Barker

Stirling Range N.P.

D'Entrecasteaux N.P.

Walpole

Denmark

⑤ Albany

Maps, pages 294 & 298

36. Logging of the nearby forests brought the region prosperity; the jarrah and ckbutt hardwoods abound in the area, and can be seen in much of the early chitecture. Bunbury sits at the northern end of **Geographe Bay**, a large shel-ed waterway that has **Cape Naturaliste** as its northern spur. At Koombana ach, dolphins turn up most mornings to cast an eye over visitors.

On the southern coast of the bay, the resort town of **Busselton** (pop. 24,750) s a fine setting on the Vasse River. The 2-km (1¼-mile) jetty has an interpretive ntre and a $3.5-million underwater observatory.

Margaret River ❸, 280 km (173 miles) from Perth, is internationally famous r superb estate-grown and bottled wines. Names like Leeuwin, Xanadu, Moss ood, Devil's Lair and dozens more rival the world's best. This is crafted wine d a far cry from the mass-production of Australia's eastern states. Margaret ver's success sparked a Western Australian wine revolution that has encour-ed quality production from Swan Valley down to the Great Southern region. Surfing the big waves, visiting spectacular caves such as **Mammoth**, **Lake** and wel, and browsing local arts and crafts are alternatives to wine- (and beer-) sam-ing in an area that makes ample provision for holidaymakers.

Cape Leeuwin, to the south, is the southwest extremity of Australia and the action of the Indian and Southern oceans. This point is written into the marine re of many navies and marked the start of Matthew Flinders' odyssey when he t out to circumnavigate and chart the entire Australian coastline in 1790.

Inland lies the **Pemberton National Park**, a region of giant karri and jarrah es. Some are over 100 metres (160 ft) tall – the world's tallest hardwoods. The venturous can climb the giant **Gloucester Tree** to the fire tower, 60 metres (190 above the ground.

Travelling east along the coast road towards Denmark, d Albany, stop at Walpole to view the ancient Tingle For-t from a lofty steel-truss ramp 60 metres (200 ft) above e Valley of the Giants. The entire Treetop Walk is a 600-etre (2,000-ft) loop. Further east is the **Stirling Range ational Park ❹**, its conical hills and jagged peaks ris-g to 1,000 metres (3,300 ft) presenting challenging lks. A seasonal centre for wildflowers and native chids, it sees Western Australia's only snowfalls.

To the south, **Albany ❺** is the site where white settle-ent was first established in the western half of Australia – year before Perth. It was on Christmas Day 1826 that ajor Lockyer arrived from Sydney in the brig *Amity*. He as attracted by the splendid expanses of **King George und**, an enclosed waterway twice as large as Sydney arbour. Today tourists flock here from July to November spot whales in the Sound – an ironic attraction for a wn that was once the last operating whaling station in e southern hemisphere (until 1978). A museum, haleworld, tells the story.

Albany is also one of Australia's most picturesque towns, ith a wonderful bayside location and well-preserved 19th-ntury streetscapes. At nearby **Strawberry Hill** stands the ate's oldest house, built in 1836 for the first Government sident, Sir Richard Spencer. If you are prepared to do me climbing, there is plenty of exploring to be done. The st office with its shingled tower, is the oldest in Western ustralia, and the **Church of St John the Evangelist**, built

TIP

If you go bushwalking around Margaret River, be careful to avoid collapsed caves, which have left holes in the ground more than 100 metres (330 ft) deep.

BELOW: the peaks of the Stirling Ranges.

There are many French-derived place names in Australia. Esperance ("Hope") takes its name from a French frigate which moored in the bay while on a survey mission in 1792.

in 1848, is the earliest house of worship in the state. Overlooking King George Sound is a memorial to the **Australian Light Horse** who served in Egypt and Gallipoli in World War I. It was moved here from Port Said, Egypt after the 1956 Suez War. Nearby Mt Adelaide, a military history precinct, looks down on the waters where the ANZAC Dardanelles invasion fleet assembled in 1914.

Perhaps the most spectacular park in the region is **Fitzgerald River National Park 6**, 185 km (115 miles) northeast of Albany. It includes an impressive stretch of coastal landscape and also contains a group of mountains known as the **Barren Range**, with dramatic views of the Southern Ocean.

The easternmost town of **Esperance 7** (pop. 13,500), is 750 km (465 miles) from Perth. Local attractions include the salt-rich **Pink Lake** and the grave of Tommy Windich, an Aboriginal guide who accompanied explorer John Forrest on his two overland treks to Adelaide in 1870 and 1874.

Cape Le Grand 8 and **Cape Arid 9** national parks offer untainted coastal strips, an abundance of birdlife and some terrific campsites. Offshore lies the beautiful maze of islands called the **Recherche Archipelago**. On the road from Albany to the capes, the opportunity for idyllic camping, fishing and surfing presents itself at almost every turn.

Kalgoorlie and the goldfields

BELOW: gold town Kalgoorlie once had 90 hotels.

After you have crossed the vastness of the Nullarbor Plain from the east, **Norseman**, a gold town 725 km (450 miles) from the South Australian border, marks the end of the Eyre Highway. Here the traveller has the option of heading either south towards the coast at Esperance or north to the heartland of Western Australia's mineral wealth.

The birthplace of the West Australian goldfields was **Coolgardie** . In September 1892, it was the site of Australia's richest strike – producing 85 kg (200 lb) of gold in a single month. By 1900, Coolgardie was a town of 15,000 people with a score of hotels, half a dozen banks, three breweries, two stock exchanges and seven newspapers, but by 1905 the lode was running out. Today Coolgardie (pop. 4,241) is an attractive, historic township with elegant buildings.

Kalgoorlie ⓫ started off as Coolgardie's twin city, but it has survived as a thriving mining town of 29,000, the hub of a region of boom and bust. When an Irishman, Paddy Hannan, discovered gold here in 1893, it was soon realised that the wealth of the Kalgoorlie find far exceeded anything else ever found in Australia. Kalgoorlie's "Golden Mile" became the richest piece of real estate in the world. The countryside was denuded of its few trees for miles around. Water was in short supply, so a pipeline was built from a reservoir near Perth, more than 500 km (300 miles) away. Today, the area continues to yield 241 million grams (850,000 ounces) of gold a year.

Kalgoorlie's architecture retains much of its early charm, with the **Palace Hotel** being a fabulous example of Edwardian excess. The business district of Kalgoorlie is a leafy refuge from the moonscape of the diggings; the continuing trade in beer, prostitution and minerals still reflects much of the town's earlier freebooting ways. For miners who gamble on the earth's riches every day, other less legitimate forms of gambling thrive – especially "two-up", a uniquely Australian game based on the toss of two pennies. When the Burswood Casino was about to open in faraway Perth, the manager visited Kalgoorlie to see how Australia's most famous two-up school operated.

Many other towns haven't fared as well as Kalgoorlie. Ghost towns like

Map, page 298

Kalgoorlie's first mine is now the Australian Prospectors' and Miners' Hall of Fame, where you can tour a real gold mine, venture into Kalgoorlie's first mine shaft, pan for gold, and watch a gold-pouring demonstration.

BELOW: a modern gold-town bar.

Gwalia and **Kanowna** dot the area, while many outposts have seen their populations dwindle so much that they, too, will soon be deserted. In many of these centres stand the imposing relics of more prosperous days. Visitors can explore the stately hotels and offices and fantasise about Australia's Wild West era.

The most famous inland attraction of the southwest is **Wave Rock** ⑫, a natural feature that appears on almost every tourist brochure of Western Australia. The rock, near the town of **Hyden**, is both exciting and disappointing to visit. From below, this 15-metre (50-ft) high lip of solid granite looks set to curl over and crush bystanders. But, taking a wider perspective, one sees that the wave is just one wall of a huge granite dome, underscoured by erosion; and a walk along the top rather shatters the illusion.

Due west of the goldfields, farmers harvest the state's other golden bounty: wheat. **Merredin** ⑬ is a busy town at the heart of one of the world's great grain belts. It was founded in 1891 around a waterhole on the way to the goldfields, and has since become a research centre for improving the yield of the vast wheat properties found in the surrounding area. As a result, Merredin's annual agricultural show is one of the most prestigious in the state. The town's tree-lined main street is best during November when the jacarandas are in bloom.

Situated on the Avon River, **Northam** (pop. 3,600) is the central hub of the western wheatfields, and also the scene of a hell-for-leather river race each August, when hundreds of canoeists and power-boaters dash madly downstream in the Avon River Descent.

It wasn't until Robert Dale led an expedition over the Darling Range and into this 150-km (90-mile) stretch of fertile valley that the early settlers could be certain that the west held land capable of sustaining livestock and crops. The

BELOW: Wave Rock.

alley's towns were settled soon after the establishment of Perth. For an insight nto the pioneering history, **York**, with its extravagantly designed town hall, 'oodyay and **Mahogany Creek** are well worth exploring.

Jorth of Perth

'he Perth to Darwin route is Australia's longest capital-to-capital haul, and its nost desolate. At 4,027 km (2,502 miles), it is even longer than the Melbourne > Darwin trek.

A major attraction of taking the Great Northern Highway inland route rather han the coastal Brand Highway is **New Norcia**, 130 km (80 miles) from Perth. 'he settlement was established by Benedictine monks in 1846 as an Aboriginal nission. The monastery is still operating and many of the town's more impressive uildings aren't open to the public. However, the strong Spanish architectural nfluence, the museum and art gallery make the settlement well worth a visit.

Heading up the coastal Brand Highway, the tiny town of **Gingin** – 82 km (51 niles) north of Perth – is a good first stop. There are excellent fishing grounds ff the coast, 48 km (30 miles) to the west: estuaries such as the mouth of the /loore River at **Guilderton** are ideal for casting a line. Just to the south of 5uilderton is the **Yanchep National Park**. **Sun City**, one of WA's newer golf ourses, is nearby.

Although the Brand Highway is the "coastal route", it is actually quite a dis- ance inland: you must turn off to actually see the ocean. **Nambung National ʾark ⑭**, 29 km (18 miles) south of the coastal town of Cervantes, shouldn't be nissed. The **Pinnacles Desert** within the park is a bizarre sight: a world of lime- tone spires – varying from the size of a truck to smaller than a finger – all ris- ng from smooth sand dunes. When Dutch explorers irst saw the Pinnacles from their vessels, they thought hey had found the ruins of a long-deserted city. In fact, hey are entirely natural. Limestone formed around the oots of plants growing on stable dunes about 30,000 /ears ago. The plants died and the dunes moved on, eaving the calcified structures exposed.

A short distance up the coast is the tiny town of Jurien. This lobster-fishing centre is set on the shores of n attractive sheltered bay, framed by an arc of spectac- lar sand dunes. **Port Denison** (now referred to as)ongara-Denison), 170 km (105 miles) further up the oast, has Australia's biggest rock lobster grounds; over 00 fishing boats work the area.

Geraldton ⑮, 425 km (265 miles) north of Perth, upports a population of about 20,000 and is the admin- strative centre for West Australia's mid-coast region. t has a near-perfect climate, superb fishing conditions nd fine sandy beaches that stretch north and south of Champion Bay. This stretch of coast saw many ship- vrecks when early Dutch mariners heading for the East ndies were swept too far south.

The **Abrolhos Islands**, 64 km (40 miles) offshore, ave claimed many ships over the years. The most dra- natic wreck was of the Dutch East Indiaman *Batavia*, which ran aground in 1629. Survivors waited behind while the captain and a few crew headed off for Java in n open boat. While the survivors were awaiting rescue,

  Map, page 298

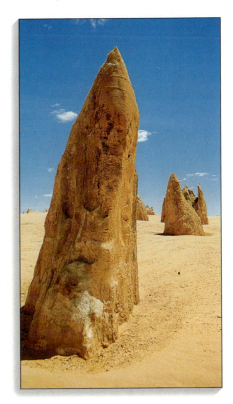

TIP

The best time to appreciate the Pinnacles is just before sunset, when the crowds have gone and long shadows give the twisted shapes an extra dimension.

BELOW: the odd limestone spires of the Pinnacles.

Wouter Loos and Jan Pelgrom, two Dutch mutineers from the Batavia *(see page 303), were dumped ashore at Kalbarri in 1629 – thus becoming Australia's first European residents.*

a mutiny broke out, driving loyal crewmen to a separate island. When the captain finally returned from his epic journey, many of the mutineers were hanged; two others were cast ashore to fend for themselves.

The Abrolhos sit on one of the finest reefs in the west of the country, and divers can still visit various wrecks. Many relics rescued from the deep are on view in the Western Australian Museum in Geraldton and at Fremantle's Shipwreck Gallery *(see page 296).*

For panoramic views of the area surrounding Geraldton, head for **Waverley Heights**. **Ellendale Bluffs** are notable for their sheer cliffs, at the base of which is a permanent waterhole. Locals will advise you to visit **Chapman Valley**, most spectacular in spring (Sept–Nov) when the wildflowers are in bloom.

A century ago, **Northampton**, 48 km (30 miles) north of Geraldton, was an important rural outpost. Recently it has been spruced up by residents to create an unusually pretty Outback town. Buildings such as **Chiverton House Museum** were built by convict labour; the cemetery in the grounds of Gwalia Church records the passing of the convicts and free settlers who first came to the area.

About 20 km (12 miles) away is **Horrock Beach**, with fine sand expanses and bays. When there is water in it, don't be surprised to see **Lake Hutt**, near Port Gregory, turn pink in the midday sun – a bizarre phenomenon caused by light refraction and naturally occurring beta carotene in the water.

Kalbarri National Park ⑯ features a combination of stunning river gorges and towering sea cliffs. The park's 190,000 hectares (469,000 acres) are set around the lower reaches of the Murchison River, which weaves its way to the Indian Ocean past the multi-hued sandstone formations of Red Bluff.

South of Carnarvon is the great system of peninsulas and inlets of **Hamelin**

BELOW: a gorge carved by the Murchison River in Kalbarri National Park.

Map, page 298

ool and **Denham Sound**. These two huge expanses of water are protected in the northeast by **Dirk Hartog Island**. A pewter plate, nailed in 1616 to a post on Cape Inscription by the Dutch explorer Hartog, marked the first known landing of Europeans on Australia's west coast. A replica of this plate is in the **Shark Bay Shire Office** (the original is back in Amsterdam).

Despite its name, **Shark Bay** is one place where every visitor ventures into the water. That's because this is the site of **Monkey Mia ⑰**, perhaps one of Australia's most delightful tourist attractions. In the small bay near Denham township, wild dolphins come to shore to be fed and mingle with visitors. This came about when local fishermen started tossing fish scraps overboard to following dolphins – by 1964, they were coming in to be hand fed. This unique interaction between humans and dolphins is still very delicate, so follow the rangers' instructions.

Monkey Mia is only the best-known corner of Shark Bay, which was declared a World Heritage area in 1991. Covering 2.3 million hectares (5.7 million acres), it comprises a series of cliff-lined peninsulas and islands with some 145 species of plants (28 endemic to the region, having developed in isolation). The extraordinary salinity of the southern parts of Shark Bay have allowed the growth of stromatolites at Hamelin Pool – giant masses of algae that are considered the oldest form of life on earth (they probably first formed 3 billion years ago). Somewhat more exciting to observe are the many dugongs, humpback whales and green and loggerhead turtles that roam the splendid arc bays.

On Shark Bay's slender land prongs, scientists are reintroducing furry marsupials with quaint names like burrowing bettongs and western barred bandicoots. These native species, almost eaten to extinction by introduced foxes and cats, now live behind predator-proof fences.

Carnarvon's main street, laid out over 100 years ago, is unusually wide because camel trains returning from the interior were required to turn in the space.

BELOW: WA has the world's least-populated coastline.

On the Ningaloo Reef you can swim with the world's largest fish – the whale shark. It's quite safe, because these monsters feed only on plankton.

Carnarvon  (pop. 6,700) is 1,000 km (600 miles) north of Perth on the beautiful **Gascoyne River**. Sitting just below the Tropic of Capricorn, Carnarvon has warm winters and tropical summers that encourage vibrant tropical wildlife, yield a huge banana crop and boatloads of succulent prawns. The town was established in 1883, though Dutch explorer Willem de Vlamingh first landed nearby in 1697. Game fishermen will relish the area; locals and tourists enjoy the swimming at picturesque **Pelican Point. Miaboolya Beach** is worth a look; so is the **Bibbawarra artesian bore** where water surface temperatures are at 70°C (158°F).

Moving north, the spectacular coastline, with blowholes, sheltered beaches and wild seascapes, also holds the land-locked **Lake MacLeod**, famous for its salt production. Inland, southwest of **Exmouth** is the **Cape Range National Park** ⑲, based along a rugged, dry limestone ridge. Boat trips through Yardie Creek Gorge are good, with predictable sightings of the delightful rock wallabies.

Offshore, **Ningaloo Reef** in its protected Marine Park stretches 260 km (160 miles) from Amherst Point around North West Cape into the Exmouth Gulf. Western Australia's largest coral reef, with 250 species of coral and more than 500 fish types, Ningaloo is an unspoilt delight for divers. Coral outcrops can be reached just 20 metres (65 ft) from the beach, though they extend 7 km (12 miles) into the ocean. Dolphins, dugongs, manta rays, giant cod and sharks abound. Whale sharks visit the reef from March to June, and Ningaloo is the only place in the world they are so accessible.

Coral Bay, 1,132 km (703 miles) from Perth, is the favourite holiday location for fishing and diving the Ningaloo Reef and new resorts are planned. Snorkelling tours go out from here or Exmouth.

BELOW: land and sea mammals meet in Monkey Mia.

The world's remotest mines

To the east of Exmouth lies the region called **The Pilbara**, focal point of the state's mineral wealth and one of the world's richest series of holes in the ground. Here, iron ore is king, and company towns seem to appear overnight amid the spinifex. Ore mined at such places as Tom Price and Mount Newman is freighted by rail systems to the coastline, where it is shipped off for national or overseas processing.

Map, page 298

The northwest was first explored by the English pirate and explorer William Dampier in 1688 and 1699, so names based on *Buccaneer, Cygnet* and *Roebuck* (his vessels) litter the coast. The **Dampier Archipelago** includes **Barrow Island**, the centre for the North West Shelf oil and gas fields. Far from being an environmentally threatened area, it is classified as a wildlife sanctuary and has some unusual animal, bird and plant life.

Roebourne is the oldest town in the northwest, but in recent years its importance has waned because of the clout of the newly established mining towns. The ghost town of **Cossack** is a reminder of the one-time might of the local pearling industry (before it moved north to Broome and beyond), while a jaunt up the **Fortescue River** reveals the lush area surrounding the Millstream, a bountiful supply of fresh water for many Pilbara towns. The **Millstream-Chichester National Park** is a fine outing for naturalists or hikers.

Marble Bar, WA, is renowned as the hottest place in Australia. Daytime temperatures regularly soar past 38°C (100°F), even in winter.

The magnificent **Hamersley Range National Park ⑳**, with spectacular gorges and awesome bluffs, can be reached from **Wittenoom**. Karratha, 40 km (25 miles) from the port of Dampier, has been developed as the work base for the mighty Hamersley Iron concern.

For an indication of just how much ore might be coming out of the ground, take a look at the loading facilities at **Port Hedland ⑳**. This seaside town, which copes with more tonnage than any other port in Australia, is almost exclusively geared to handle the iron ore from the huge open-cut and strip mining centres of The Pilbara. Port Hedland is built on an island linked to the mainland by three long causeways. Visitors can view the loading from the wharves where some of the world's largest ore carriers dock. The Port Hedland Visitors Centre offers daily tours of the BHP-Billiton Nelson Point and Port Authority workings and half-day tours of Dampier Salt and BHP's Boodarie Iron.

BELOW: a Broome pearl in an elegant Spanish pendant.

Port Hedland (pop. 11,300) has no shortage of drawbacks. Its tropical setting makes it prone to cyclones; its seas are considered unsafe for swimming, thanks to sharks and stonefish; and its industrial and mineral landscape might not be to everyone's liking. But the local fishing is excellent, there are nearby Aboriginal carvings, birdlife is abundant, and you can cool off in the town swimming pool or at Pretty Pool.

For a sampling of a real Western Australian Outback town, detour 193 km (120 miles) southeast to **Marble Bar**. With a population of less than 400, it owes its existence to discoveries of gold in 1891 and again in 1931. The disused **Comet Gold Mine**, 10 km (6 miles) to the south, has a museum and visitors' centre.

Coming from the south, along the vast monotony of the road between Port Hedland and Broome, the

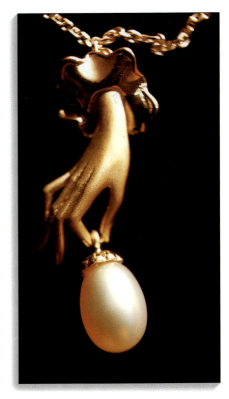

In March 1942 a squadron of Japanese fighters attacked the Allied flying boats moored off Mangrove Point, near Broome. Today, at very low tides, the remains of these planes can be seen in the bay.

highway describes a gentle arc along a stretch of coastline known aptly as the **Eighty Mile Reach**. During the 1920s, **Broome** ㉒ was the capital of the world pearling industry, with more than 300 luggers (pearling vessels) competing for finds off the northwest coast of Australia. For the mostly Japanese divers, the real wealth lay in the mother-of-pearl shell, which was used in jewellery and for buttons; a pearl was an unexpected bonus. But it was a dangerous job, as the Japanese Cemetery testifies. Broome went into the doldrums when plastic buttons flooded the market after World War II. The recent development of cultured pearls has revitalised the industry (although the farming now occurs in remote aquatic farms) and several Broome jewellery shops, including one owned by the dominant pearling operator, Paspaley Pearls, sell fine pearls in a variety of settings. A stroll through the timber dwellings of Chinatown, with its multilingual street signs, provides an insight into what the town was like in the pearling days.

With a large Asian population, Broome has retained enough character to be one of Australia's most fascinating communities. Aboriginal culture thrives here, with an Aboriginal radio and TV station (Goolari, known as "GTV"), which broadcasts partly in local dialect. And the town comes alive each August when fishermen, farmers, miners, drovers and tourists swell the population tenfold for the Shinju Matsuri – Festival of the Pearl.

Residents will point out such exotic attractions as the "Golden Staircase to the Moon", an optical illusion created when moonlight reflects on the ocean bed at low-water spring tides. At **Gantheaume Point**, when the tide is low, giant dinosaur tracks considered to be 130 million years old can be viewed.

The 22-km (14-mile) **Cable Beach** was so named when the underwater communication link between Broome and Java (and on to London) was established in the 19th century. Today it is the core of Broome's tourist industry, with an upmarket resort and crocodile farm complementing the glorious ocean beach itself. A ride on a camel train along the beach at sunset is a great experience.

Outback of the Outback

For Australians, the **Kimberley** region has a semi-mythical status as the country's final frontier. About half the size of Texas but with only 26,000 inhabitants, encompassing ½ million-hectare (million plus-acre) cattle ranches and enormous Aboriginal tribal lands, it was first explored in the 1890s but has opened to travellers only in the past 15 years.

The landscapes here are hallucinatory, even by Antipodean standards. The blood-red desert is sliced by lush, forest-filled gorges, where fresh-water crocodiles and prehistoric stingrays swim; the coastline is torn by tropical fjords with tidal waterfalls that "flow" horizontally. Everything is on a gargantuan scale: vast meteor craters, petrified coral reefs and desert rivers that swell from 100 metres (330 ft) wide in the dry season to 13 km (8 miles) wide in the wet.

Generations of isolation have left the Kimberley region the most Aboriginal part of Australia, with some immense tracts of tribal land and half the population black. Remote communities now have their own language newspapers and radio stations; Aboriginal guides work at the national parks and conduct

BELOW: honest advertising at a butcher's shop in the Kimberley.

ours of ancient cave paintings; there is also one of Australia's few Aboriginal-owned resorts (at Cape Leveque). This current independence was hard-
won. White ranchers arrived here in the 1890s after the world's longest – and
most gruelling – cattle drive across Central Australia. Soon the Kimberley was
the scene of a little-known Aboriginal uprising and of several massacres of
indigenous peoples by settlers. Aboriginal bushrangers roamed the Kimberley,
easily evading mounted police posses in the rugged terrain while newspaper
readers in faraway Sydney were both thrilled and horrified by their exploits.

Derby **㉓**, 216 km (134 miles) along the highway northeast from Broome, is
the administrative centre for the huge cattle-producing region of the West Kimberley. Unlike bustling Broome, with a population of 10,000, Derby is a sleepy
town where little seems to have changed over the decades. From here, sightseeing is mostly by light plane: taking a flight from Derby over **King Sound**
and the **Buccaneer Archipelago ㉔** beyond will unfold one of the world's most
spectacularly beautiful coastlines, a maze of islands, red cliffs and white beaches
– completely uninhabited except for the mining communities of **Cockatoo
Island** and **Koolan Islands**. Cruise vessels also operate along the coast.

From Derby, you can either follow the main, all-weather **Great Northern
Highway** or turn off onto the "Beef Road", the **Gibb River Road** which cuts
through the heart of the Kimberley. Seven km (4¼ miles) outside Derby is a huge
boab tree that is reputed to have been used as an overnight prison when trans-
porting prisoners in colonial times. The boab, (a close relation of the Southern
African baobab tree, is often known as the "bottle tree" and can have a circumference greater than its height – the girth frequently exceeds 10 metres (33 ft).

Windjana Gorge National Park ㉕ 145 km (90 miles) to the east, is worth a

Map,
page 298

TIP

The only sensible time
to visit the Kimberley is
April–September.
At other times it is
unbearably hot and
humid, with chances
of being isolated by
flash floods.

BELOW: beautiful
Manning Gorge in
the Kimberley.

Wolfe Creek Crater is 850 metres (930 yards) in diameter, with a rim 50 metres (165 ft) high.

visit for its eerie Wandjina figures in Aboriginal rock paintings, and its huge flocks of spooky, screeching white cockatoos. **Tunnel Creek National Park** ㉖, 35 km (22 miles) further on, allows you to walk through an underground stream course populated by bats. Only recently has this part of the Kimberley become accessible to people other than the toughest pioneers, cattlemen or prospectors. The roads are constantly being improved as the area opens up to tourism and development, but take heed of local warnings about road conditions.

East of Derby, on the Fitzroy River near the township of Fitzroy Crossing, is **Geikie Gorge** ㉗, 14 km (9 miles) long, with limestone cliffs up to 30 metres (100 ft) high. This is one of the most spectacular gorges in the northwest and a pleasant camping spot. There are conducted tours with Aboriginal rangers along the river, where freshwater crocodiles sunbake at the water's edge; down below, you can see sawfish and stingrays that have adapted to life in fresh water. On the eastern side lies **Fossil Downs**, a huge private cattle station (over 405,000 hectares/1 million acres), founded in 1886. It is the only Kimberley cattle station still owned by descendants of the original pioneers, the MacDonalds.

The Great Northern Highway cuts along the southern perimeter of the Kimberley before entering the new township of **Halls Creek** which, with its comfortable hotels and air-conditioned supermarkets, serves as a base for the regional pastoral industry. At "Old Halls Creek", remnants of the 1884 gold rush can be seen. The rush made a few prospectors rich, but the harsh environment and shortage of water ruined a good many more. South of Halls Creek, 130 km (80 miles) away, is the meteorite crater at **Wolfe Creek** ㉘, the second largest in the world – although it really comes into visual perspective only from the air.

The turn-off 110 km (68 miles) north of Halls Creek leads to a 4WD track to

BELOW: cruising Geikie Gorge.

ne of the most astonishing natural features in the world: the **Bungle Bungle Range**. The "Bungles" cover some 640 sq. km (247 sq. miles) of the Ord River Valley with a labyrinth of orange and black (caused by the black lichen and orange silica) horizontally tiger-striped, domed mountains. Within the canyons and gorges of the **Purnululu National Park** 🕙 are palm-filled grottoes, enormous caves and white-sand beaches. It's a wonderland with variations that no human mind would have envisaged. The rough track from the highway deters many, so a thriving industry has arisen in **Kununurra** to fly tourists over (and, more recently, into) the Bungle Bungles.

A true gem of the Kimberley lies to the north of Purnululu: **Argyle Diamond Mine** is the world's largest, extracting some 6 tonnes of diamonds each year. The Argyle Diamond Pipe was discovered in 1979 and remains the only source of deep-pink diamonds. Air tours to the mine are available from Kununurra.

Wyndham is the most northerly port in Western Australia, a small scattered community that has changed little since the days of the gold rush. You can see large crocodiles lying on the mudflats below the Wyndham wharf: cattle that miss their footing when being loaded onto ships provide an occasional meal.

The Ord River was dammed in 1971 to harness the monsoon run-off for irrigation; in recent years, this has opened up the east Kimberley to the cultivation of tropical crops. To the south, Lake Argyle in the **Carr Boyd Range** is the main reservoir, and boat tours are regularly conducted around it. The damming of the Ord River would have submerged **Argyle Downs Homestead**, home of one of the northwest's great pioneering families, the Duracks, so it was moved to a new location to escape the rising waters. It is now a museum to show how life was for the early settlers of the Kimberley. ❑

Map, page 298

The Kimberley is such an isolated region that the extraordinary "Bungles" were unknown to all but a few locals until 1983, when a photographer came upon them by chance.

BELOW: the Bungle Bungles glowing in the evening light.

TASMANIA

*Australia's smallest and remotest state is also the most temperate.
It has no arid Outback but plenty of cool forests, rugged mountains,
highland lakes, lush pasture and fruitful orchards*

Maps,
pages
316 & 324

he **Bass Strait** is only 200-km (120-miles) wide, but Tasmania remains a
world apart. Compared with the rest of Australia, the heart-shaped island is
compact and accessible. About the size of Ireland or Switzerland – 296 km
(184 miles) from north to south and 315 km (196 miles) east to west – "Tassie"
is ideal for a driving holiday. The countryside is strikingly green, with rolling
pastures framed by oaks, willows and poplars planted by homesick British settlers; tiny hamlets are full of convict-built mansions and "Devonshire" tea
houses; and the pace is calm and relaxed in an almost 19th-century fashion.

But Tasmania's greatest attraction lies in its empty spaces. Fewer than half a
million people live here, mostly clustered around the southern capital, Hobart,
and the northern city, Launceston. That leaves the island with the most lavish
swathes of protected wilderness in Australia: a higher percentage of bushland is
within national parks in Tasmania than anywhere else in the country.

Still, Tasmanians' attitudes to the environment are polarised. The island has a
zealous "greenie" lobby – the world's first Green political party began here –
but it is pitted against powerful logging and mining interests, as well as local
politicians with a passion for hydro-electric dams. The impressive park system
is the result of some bitter struggles, and today the island's environmentalists
continue the fight to save their unique ecosystems.

PRECEDING PAGES:
Lake Dove with
Cradle Mountain
beyond.
LEFT: there are
many well-signed
walks in Cradle
Mountain National
Park.
BELOW: punishment
irons at Port Arthur.

A bloody history

Along with its wilderness areas, another of Tasmania's
great lures is its huge wealth of historical sites. More
evidence of the colonial past has survived here than in
any other corner of Australia.

The island's European history can be traced back to
1642, when the Dutch navigator Abel Tasman stumbled
upon its shores and named it "Anthony van Diemen's
Land" in honour of the Governor-General of the Dutch
East Indies. A succession of other explorers arrived after
Tasman, including Cook (1777), Bligh (1788) and
Flinders (1798), who first circumnavigated Tasmania,
proving that it was an island. The French expedition of
Baudin (1802) propelled the British government into
settling the island – the second corner of Australia to fly
the Union Jack, after Sydney Cove.

Tasmania's isolation made it perfect as a penal colony
for repeat offenders: remote camps were set up at Macquarie Harbour and Maria Island in the 1820s before an
"escape-proof" prison was established at Port Arthur in
1832. Until 1856, when transportation to the colony was
abolished, this was one of the most dismal and dreaded
outposts in Australia.

At the same time, free settlers were coming into conflict with the Tasmanian Aborigines. When white farmers began throwing up fences for their stock and

claiming land, a frontier war began. In 1828, martial law was declared and soldiers were used to "clear" the land of natives. The few survivors were packed off to a mission station on Flinders Island in the Bass Strait, where they all promptly died of European diseases. This genocide of the Tasmanian Aborigines remains one of the bleakest chapters of Australia's grim colonial past.

Tasmania's last surviving full-blooded Aborigine, a woman named Truganini, died in 1876, and her bones were kept on display in Hobart until 1947.

Along the northwest coast

Many visitors arrive in Tasmania on the two super-fast *Spirit of Tasmania* day and night vehicle and people ferries between Melbourne and Devonport.

Situated astride the **Mersey River** and dominated by a glistening white lighthouse, **Devonport ❶** is home to 24,000 people and, like most other places in Tasmania, has a thriving crafts trade. The 133-km (82-mile) drive west to Stanley reveals one aspect of the classic Tasmanian landscape: lush cattle pastures and rolling hills on one side of the road, and beachside communities and resorts on the other. Take a detour into the tiny village of **Penguin**, where Australian municipal art reaches a surreal zenith: even the rubbish bins are penguin-shaped. Further on, the pulp mill at **Burnie** strikes a discordant note in the pastoral harmony, with visible pollution of land, sea and sky. The charming seaside town of **Wynyard** is dominated by a monolithic headland called **Table Cape**. A river meanders by its base; some of the best fish and chips in Australia can be had on the wharf at its confluence with the sea.

Stanley ❷ is a quaint fishing village that appears to have changed little in the past century; it nestles at the foot of The Nut, a table-top mountain at the end of a narrow isthmus. Founded in 1826, Stanley was the headquarters of the Van Diemen's Land Company, a pastoral group that had been signed into existence

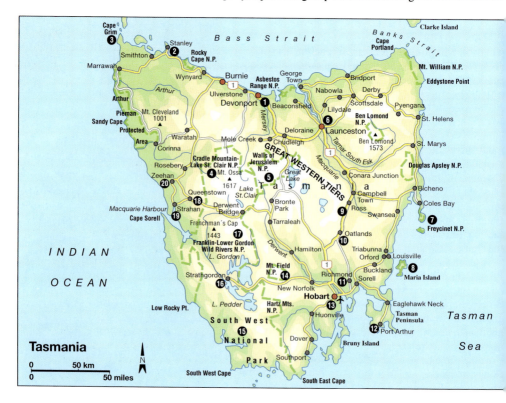

Tasmania

by a Royal Charter of George IV. The Company Store, built in 1844, can still be seen on the colonial waterfront. The company's dignitaries made their home in **Highfield House**, built in 1832 on a hilltop with a commanding view of the town and The Nut. A full restoration of Highfield is complete, and the house is open for inspection.

Map,
page 316

Further west lie **Smithton** and **Cape Grim** ❸, reputedly the windiest place in Australia, and a graveyard for 19th-century sailing ships. The Van Diemen's Land Company still operates farms in this wild and remote territory.

Dozens of small valleys lead up from the coast into Tasmania's central highland plateau, revealing picturesque farmlands. The most colourful diversion is found by taking the Castra road out of Ulverstone towards **Leven Canyon**: en route, this narrow winding road passes hectares of red opium poppy flowers (flowering in January), grown under strict government control for medical purposes. The canyon is a tremendously deep cutting, gouged out by the Leven River. There is a sensational look-out only 10 minutes' walk from the car park. More recently a walking track to the canyon floor has been opened, but it can be steep, slippery and tricky. The canyon floor is strictly for the serious hiker.

In spring (October in particular), a huge tulip farm on top of Table Cape provides one of the island's most spectacular colour shows.

This is one gateway to the **Cradle Mountain–Lake St Clair National Park** ❹, Tasmania's most famous wilderness area. Moraine lakes, expansive heathlands, mountain vistas, good trails and the chance to spot wildlife like wallabies, echidnas or wombats make this one of Australia's best walking areas. The six-day Overland Trek, through the length of the park, is considered the ultimate Aussie bush-walk, although only experienced and well-prepared hikers should attempt it. Several companies offer guided hikes along the track.

A popular alternative is to visit one or both ends of the giant park for easier,

BELOW LEFT: a backpacker enjoys the scenery of Cradle Mountain.

Tassie's Tiger

The Tasmanian tiger, or thylacine, was a wolf-like marsupial which grew to 1.3 metres (4 ft) in length. It was fearsome-looking, with a yellow body, and stripes on its back and jaws like a steel trap. Originally it preyed on wallabies and birds, but the sheep introduced by the settlers proved a palatable alternative. The "tigers" were energetically hunted by farmers eager to protect their flocks. The last four were caught in 1908 on Woolnorth Farm in the remote northwest of Tasmania, then sent to Hobart Zoo. Sadly, they could not survive in captivity and the last remaining "tiger" died in 1936 – within three months of being declared a protected species. Tasmanians have reported sightings of the creature ever since, but none has ever been confirmed.

TIP

December–May is the best time to visit Tasmania, when daytime temperatures peak at 20–30°C (70–85°F) and the east of the island is generally dry. Even the west is hospitable at this time of year – in winter and spring the rainfall there can be phenomenal.

BELOW: Cradle Mountain Lodge lies at the north of the National Park.

shorter walks. The northern end is the more accessible: one of the most spectacular views in Tasmania (of **Cradle Mountain**, with **Dove Lake**) can be had just from the car park. An easy two-hour hike runs around the lake; other trails of varying difficulty head up to the tea-coloured **Twisted Lakes**, the high moorland of the park and the peak itself. Even on short walks, at dawn or dusk there is the chance to see possums and wallabies, as well as quolls (native cats) and the plentiful Tasmanian Devils, which let out an astonishing shriek. For accommodation at the park's northern end, there's a campsite and the comfortable Cradle Mountain Lodge.

Cradle Mountain and the neighbouring **Walls of Jerusalem National Park** ❺ are part of a great highland plateau, rising from the western and southern coasts, sprawling across two-thirds of the island. Much of the land is elevated to about 900 metres (3,000 ft), with peaks rising to over 1,500 metres (5,000 ft); it embraces an area dotted with numerous lakes from tiny tarns to the expanse of the Great Lake, Australia's highest. Here rise the streams and rivers that run off in all directions, plunging through deep gorges on their way to the sea.

The gentle north

Heading east from Devonport on the Bass Highway, the historic town of **Deloraine** shelters in a valley of the Meander River backed by **Quamby Bluff** (1,226 metres/4,022 ft) and the Western Tiers. Settled in 1823 and containing many examples of early colonial architecture, the township has been protected by the National Trust of Australia. Certainly worth a visit, about 20 km (12 miles) from the town, is **Mole Creek** with its limestone caves and **Trowunna Wildlife Park**, where you can see all the animals that are so elusive in the bush.

Situated at the head of the idyllic **Tamar River**, surrounded by a rich agricultural area, **Launceston ❻** is Tasmania's second-largest city (pop. 63,000) and the commercial centre of almost half of the state. It's a pleasant, hilly city, graced with historical buildings, parks and gardens. A 10-minute walk from the town are two recreation areas, **Cataract Gorge** and **Cliff Gardens**, linked by a chairlift spanning the surging waters of the South Esk River. Another popular attraction is the **Penny Royal World** complex. These watermills from the early 19th century have been converted into two comfortable motels and an entertainment centre, connected by a vintage tramway. Launceston also has a number of active wool mills with a range of fine products for sale to the public.

One of the most popular attractions is driving along the **Wine Route**, visiting the vineyards that, since the 1970s, have produced some of Australia's finest vintages (experts say that the Chardonnay and Pinot Noir varietals are strongest in Tasmania). A round-trip of about 65 km (40 miles) skirts one side of the Tamar to reach the futuristic **Batman Bridge**, then returns on the other side through scenic orchards. Nearby **Nabowla**, 26 km (16 miles) northeast of Lilydale, has a large lavender farm – a vision of mauve in December and January.

From Launceston, the **Tasman Highway** heads east and then south down almost the entire length of the east coast to Hobart. The 434-km (270-mile) road has a good bitumen surface, is mainly two lanes wide and, although some sections traverse mountain passes, can be covered in just one day. Leaving Launceston on the 169-km (105-mile) leg to St Helens, the road heads northeast through lush farmlands and then winds through forest and fern-covered hills by a pass known as **The Sidling** to **Scottsdale**. Further on is **Derby**, on the Ringarooma River, an historic shanty town which was a prosperous tin-mining centre

Map, page 316

All of the vineyards around Launceston are open for public tastings, and many of them also have good restaurants.

BELOW: Tasmania has thousands of highland lakes.

TIP

If you take a driving
tour round Tassie,
don't be fooled by the
distances: many roads
wind through
mountainous terrain,
and routes are often
much longer than they
appear on a map.

between 1876 and 1929. The Tasman Highway then turns southeast and descends to **Pyengana**, where a side road runs for 10 km (6 miles) to the picturesque **St Columba Falls**. It's a further 20 km (12 miles) to **St Helens**, the largest of the east-coast towns with a population of 1,200. An old whaling town, it is now a fishing port and a popular family holiday spot for Tasmanians.

Heading south, the road follows magnificent surf beaches for 20 km (12 miles) to **Scamander**, then turns inland, climbs a mountain pass and descends again to the coast by the serpentine **Elephant Pass**, with regular glimpses of the ocean far below. (In recent years, the opening of the Chain of Lagoons link road has allowed an express option along the coast, but the Elephant Pass is worth the extra 15 minutes' driving for its stunning ocean views and patches of wet forest.) **Bicheno** (pop. 700) is a thriving holiday resort and a port for a small fleet of fishing vessels; when its European history began, in 1803, it was a grim whaling depot known as Waub's Harbour.

A turn-off 10 km (6 miles) south of Bicheno leads after 26 km (16 miles) to **Coles Bay**, gateway to the magnificent **Freycinet National Park 7**, which has excellent bushwalks. The fantastic **Hazards** – 300-metre (1,000-ft) hills of solid pink granite rising from the ocean – form a dramatic backdrop to the beaches, ocean pools and quiet bush paths where animals and birds are in abundance. A steep two-hour return walk across the peninsula brings you to the famous **Wineglass Bay**, with an exquisite, gently curving white-sand beach and crystal blue waters. The landscape here is dry and sandy, so carry plenty of water.

From **Swansea**, a sleepy holiday and fishing resort with some nice old buildings and a population of 550, the Tasman Highway follows the coast south to **Triabunna**, port for a commercial fishing fleet. The coast here is dominated by

BELOW: it's worth
the walk across the
Freycinet Peninsula
for this view of
Wineglass Bay.

Map, page 316

Maria Island **8**, 21 km (13 miles) offshore. The island was settled as a convict station in 1825, before the more notorious Port Arthur opened; it is now a wildlife sanctuary. At the nearby village of **Orford** are the ruins of the early settlement where convicts were loaded for passage; today, a ferry makes the crossing for campers and hikers wishing to explore the national park.

After crossing the **Prosser River** – which was named after an escaped convict caught on its banks – the Tasman Highway follows its stream through a rugged gorge to the old village of **Buckland**, with a fine 1846 church. The remaining 62 km (39 miles) of the highway cross a range of hills before descending to **Sorell**, named after the man who was Lieutenant-Governor in 1821.

As an alternative to the coastal route, the inland **Midland Highway** from Launceston passes through three of Tasmania's most famous colonial towns. **Ross 9**, settled in 1821, has a splendid sandstone bridge, considered the most beautiful in Australia, with 186 carvings cut by convict artist Daniel Herbert. Half an hour south lies the former convict way-station **Oatlands 10**, which has the largest collection of colonial buildings in the country: 136 have been dated to before 1837 – there are 87 of them on the main road alone – including (of course) an imposing courthouse and jail. Finally, **Richmond 11**, only 25 km (15 miles) from Hobart, is Tasmania's favourite historic town. Among its many attractions are Australia's oldest bridge, built of sandstone by convict labour between 1823 and 1825, and the oldest Catholic church in Australia, St John's (1837). It is one of the best-preserved colonial villages in the country, and is a thriving craft centre. Don't miss an inspection of the old jail, which once housed the likes of Ikey Solomons (believed to be the prototype for Fagin in Dickens' *Oliver Twist*) and bushranger Matthew Brady.

The corners of the main crossroads in Ross are locally called Temptation, Recreation, Salvation and Damnation. The buildings that occupy them, respectively, are the Man-O-War Hotel, the Town Hall, the Catholic church and the old jail (now a private house).

BELOW: an inhabitant of Wineglass Bay.

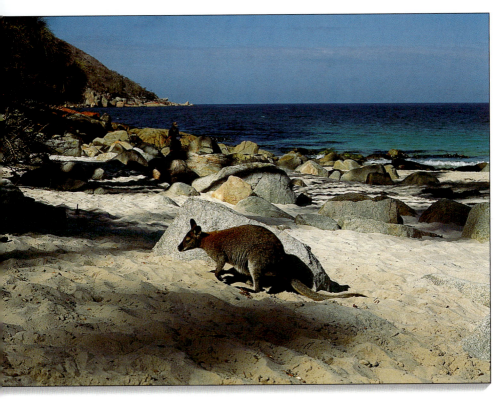

The Gulag Peninsula

Tasmania is riddled with historical sites, but the most popular with Australians remains the old penal settlement of Port Arthur on the Tasman Peninsula, 110 km (68 miles) from Hobart. From 1832 until well after the end of transportation in 1853, Port Arthur was the dumping ground for many of the colony's most dangerous convicts. It was set up on this remote site to be escape-proof: even if prisoners fled from the prison itself, they could never get past guards at the narrow isthmus of Eaglehawk Neck. Only 100 metres (328 ft) wide, it was lined with guard outposts and chained, savage dogs; the icy waters were held to be full of sharks.

A thriving village grew up around the prison, with farms, shops and Australia's first railway system (pulled by convicts instead of mules). Yet today the most striking thing about this once-degrading site is the sheer beauty of the

location: the extensive ruins are set amid rolling hills on the gorgeous Carnavon Bay.

The original prison was made of wood, and the ruins are mainly of buildings from the 1840s. Starting off from the information centre, head towards the long, squat sandstone **Penitentiary**. The best-known building in Port Arthur, this was a former flour mill converted to house prisoners. Two bushfires in the late 1890s gutted this and other edifices. Take a stroll up the path to the left to the **Commandant's House**, with an extraordinary view over the bay – it was one of the few wooden houses to survive the flames.

The path away from the bay runs past the eerie ruined hospital to the **Model Prison** – built in the 1850s on the radical concept of punishment being developed in Britain. Instead of physical pain, prisoners were subjected to total sensory deprivation: kept in tiny cells for 23 hours a day, they were not allowed to talk; for their one hour of exercise, they wore masks and were walked backwards and forwards in chains.

The worst offenders were put into total darkness for days on end. Not surprisingly, the treatment led to more derangement than rehabilitation – and indeed Port Arthur was used as a mental asylum after its prison function ended. Ironically, modern madness catapulted Port Arthur into the world's headlines in 1996 when a local gunman went berserk and massacred 35 people.

The **Museum** next door is worth visiting for its original convict garb, lashes, chains and cat-o-nine-tails. Finally, complete the circuit via the picturesque **Convict Church**, built in neo-Gothic style. Included in the price of admission is a harbour cruise, leaving from the information centre. Boats also run out twice a day to the Isle of the Dead, which became the cemetery for the prison colony. A lone convict lived on the island to dig the graves.

For the most evocative view of the ruins, Ghost Tours have become extremely popular: every night local guides lead the curious through the darkest crannies of the site, recounting the more gruesome side of Port Arthur's history. There has been no shortage of unearthly sightings in recent years to add spice to the stories.   ❑

LEFT: a model guard keeps watch at Port Arthur.

Both the coastal and inland routes meet at the detour to the Tasman Peninsula, site of Tasmania's biggest tourist draw, **Port Arthur** ⑫ *(see facing page)*. En route to Port Arthur, the village of **Nubeena**, once a convict farm, has become a popular holiday resort. At **Eaglehawk Neck**, the outermost, well-guarded gate of the prison, the rocky coastline displays several geological curiosities such as the **Tasman Arch** and the **Tessellated Pavement**, which seems tiled in a pattern too regular to have occurred naturally.

Tassie's friendly capital

With its manageable size, mountain backdrop, cool climate and low-rise buildings, **Hobart** ⑬ (pop. 180,000) resembles a compact European city. In fact, it is so much smaller than most of the mainland capitals that its inhabitants retain many of the hospitable traits often associated with country-town dwellers. Conservation rather than development has been the norm here and, despite modern attractions such as the **Wrest Point Casino** (Australia's first legal gambling house), the focal point of civic pride is Hobart's heritage.

The civil tranquillity of modern Hobart belies the fact that it and its neighbouring settlements were once the dumping grounds for some of the worst of Britain's criminals. When Governor Macquarie arrived in 1811, he was horrified at the disorderliness of Hobart and immediately drew up a plan to make the place more attractive by offering free land grants, loans and cheap convict help for free settlers. It was not long before Hobart's wharves were busy loading wool bales and cargoes of grain bound for Britain. The city's early days as a sailing port are remembered each 26 December when a fleet of racing yachts leaves another great port 1,000 km (600 miles) north for the Sydney–Hobart Blue Water Classic. Hobart

Map, page 316

Richmond has one of the best selections of Tasmanian wines at its wine centre in the middle of the village.

BELOW: the peaceful remains of Port Arthur's prison colony.

No. 40 Macquarie Street, now part of the Tasmanian Museum and Art Gallery, was built as a townhouse in 1808 and is probably the oldest continuously occupied building in all Australia.

BELOW: Battery Point is a complete colonial village.

becomes the party hub of Australia around Christmas–New Year, with the arrival of the yachts and a food and drink festival called "A Taste of Tasmania".

At other times of the year, the city's focus is still the water. In places, the Derwent River is 2 km (1⅓ miles) across; straddling the expanse is the graceful arc of the **Tasman Bridge**, showing few scars of the 1975 tragedy when it was struck by a freighter – this caused the roadway to collapse, killing 14 people.

Old Hobart is best tackled on foot. Abandon the car to explore such fine old haunts as **Battery Point**, still looking as it did a century or more ago. Historians say that this area is Australia's most complete colonial village. With its maze of old houses, uneven streets and quaint businesses, the district has the feel of a mythical old England, or a Maine maritime village. In a sloping park stands the gun battery that gave the area its name. Battery Point is dominated by **St George's Church**, with its colonial spire and 19th-century box pews.

The area includes the **Narryna Heritage Museum** (Tues–Fri 10am–5pm, Sat–Sun 2–5pm; entrance fee), in an 1834 colonial mansion furnished in period style, with vintage vehicles and tools in outbuildings. Nearby is the site of the old Maritime Museum, whose collection has been relocated to the main **Maritime Museum of Tasmania** (daily 9am–5pm; entrance fee), in Argyle Street, Hobart.

A row of old sandstone warehouses along the waterfront at **Salamanca Place** was once the business headquarters for Hobart's merchants. The whole area fell into disrepair until the late 1960s, when a group of artists turned one of the warehouses into a working space. A revival followed, and today Salamanca Place is the spiritual home of Hobart's small but vital creative community. It is now lined with galleries, cafés and restaurants, and the Salamanca craft market,

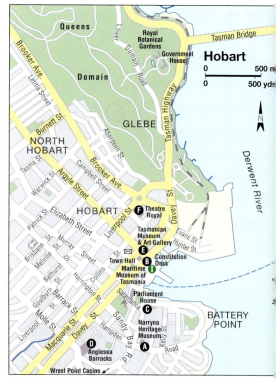

held every Saturday morning, is the biggest of its kind in Australia, a vibrant mix of the hip and the homespun.

Antarctic Adventure (tel: 03-6220 8220) in Salamanca Place highlights Tasmania's role in Antarctic exploration and maritime support. You can experience the Antarctic chill in a super-cold room; pilot a (simulated) icebreaker; imagine yourself pressing through an Antarctic blizzard, view exhibits of explorer Mawson's field camp; and marvel at the spectacular scenery in the cinema.

In all, Hobart has almost 80 buildings that rate National Trust "A" classification. One is **Anglesea Barracks** (Tues 9am–12.30pm), Australia's oldest military establishment, still in use by the defence forces and notable for its 18th-century naval guns and buildings which date back to 1814. The lake in the grounds of **Government House** was formed when convicts quarried on the site to remove sandstone used in building the Customs House, later to become Parliament House.

The **Tasmanian Museum and Art Gallery** (daily 10am–5pm, guided tours Wed–Sun 2.30pm; free) in Macquarie Street includes examples of Tasmania's fauna; Aborigine art and artefacts; and great examples of colonial art and furniture. To the north, in Campbell Street, is the **Theatre Royal** (guided tours Mon–Fri, except when rehearsals are in progress). It was built in 1834, making it Australia's oldest theatre, and restored to its original beauty after a fire in 1984. Sir Laurence Olivier described it as "the best little theatre in the world". Of course, it has a resident ghost.

Along the Lyell Highway

Heading west from Hobart, the 250-km (155-mile) Lyell Highway runs into Tasmania's wildest country. Some 14 km (9 miles) from Hobart lies the Cadbury's

Map, page 324

TIP

For a magnificent view of Hobart, take a drive up the narrow mountain road to the peak of 1,270-metre (4,165-ft) Mount Wellington, to the west of the city.

BELOW: the sun sets on the warehouses and market of Salamanca Place.

Mount Field is one of Tasmania's two ski fields – the other is Ben Lomond near Launceston. Both are at the mercy of unreliable snowfalls.

chocolate factory at **Claremont**; a half-hour further is **New Norfolk**, the centre of Australian hop farming, with a pristine collection of colonial buildings. Only 53 km (33 miles) out of Hobart is the turn-off to **Lake Pedder** and **Lake Gordon**. **Mount Field National Park** , about 20 km (12 miles) along the road, was Tasmania's first national park. Here the wide water curtain of **Russell Falls** descends 30 metres (100 ft) into a fern-filled gorge; the smaller, picturesque **Horseshoe Falls** is situated above them.

Lake Pedder and Lake Gordon are part of the vast **Southwest National Park**. Lake Pedder was the centre of great controversy in the early 1970s, when a dam was proposed to flood a unique inland white-sand beach. Conservationists lost this battle, and the beach disappeared. There was talk of "un-damming the dam", which holds 27 times the volume of water in Sydney Harbour, but this is now generally agreed to be impractical. The lake can be reached after a 2½-hour drive on a bitumen highway. The fishing is renowned and, skirting the shore of Lake Pedder, you can drive to the crest of the mighty curved Gordon Dam and try your luck.

Back on the Lyell Highway, the route runs into the highlands and through the "Land of 3,000 Lakes". Innumerable side roads lead to some of the world's finest trout-fishing waters. Catering mostly for fishermen, although very pleasant if you want to break your journey, is the chalet accommodation provided at Bronte Park.

A small cluster of buildings at **Derwent Bridge** heralds the turn-off to **Lake St Clair**. This entire segment of the highway was constructed only in the early 1930s; before that, access to the southern end of **Cradle Mountain–Lake St Clair National Park** *(see page 317)* was limited to a few intrepid bushmen. These days, there is an information centre, and there are many hikes, nature

BELOW: sunset on the Lyell Highway, from Queenstown to Hobart.

trails and picnic spots in the area. Several times a day, the ferry *Idaclair!* takes hikers to and from the furthest shores, where the Overland Track begins.

Heading west, the Lyell Highway climbs to cross King William Range before snaking down again through **Mount Arrowsmith Gorge**. The road suddenly descends from the open **Navarre Plain**, dramatically zigzagging down into a deep chasm with the road clinging to a precipitous slope. Away to the south, **Frenchman's Cap** (1,444 metres/4,737 ft) can be seen on a clear day. This is part of the **Franklin–Lower Gordon Wild Rivers National Park** ⑯, saved from damming by the massive "greenie" protests of the early 1980s. Where the highway crosses the Collingwood River, you may see rafters preparing to paddle down towards the **Franklin River** for the two-week journey to Macquarie Harbour. This is undoubtedly one of the world's great wilderness adventures, but it is notoriously dangerous and should be tackled only by the very experienced.

The road skirts the Raglan Range, and then descends via the **Victoria Pass**. The final stage, coming down Mount Owen to the mining centre of Queenstown, is probably the most ecologically distressing sight on any Australian highway: the mountains here were once covered with forest, but clouds of sulphur from the copper smelters used in the 1890s killed off any vegetation that hadn't already been cut down for firewood.

Queenstown ⑰ itself is perversely fascinating. It is full of buildings from the glory days in the early 1900s, including the Empire Hotel, whose wooden banister has been listed by the National Trust (trees were cut in Tasmania, sent to England for carving, then returned in pieces to be put together in Queenstown). Mining is still carried on here, and visits can be made to the pits; as well as copper, the area has produced vast amounts of gold, silver and tin.

Map, page 316

In 1864 trout and salmon eggs were packed in moss and ice and brought by sailing ship from England to Tasmania. Salmon never took to the Antipodes, but the brown trout thrived and provide wonderful fishing in Tasmania's lakes.

BELOW LEFT: the Tasmanian Devil is the rangers' icon. **BELOW:** Anzac war memorial in Queenstown

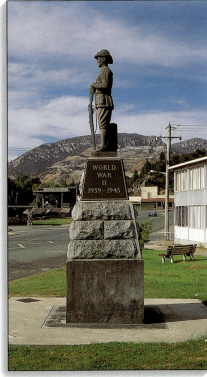

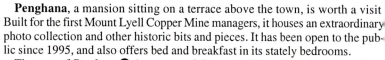

Map, page 316

The Huon pine, a conifer unique to Tasmania, grows extremely slowly – some trees are over 2,000 years old.

BELOW: paddling the Franklin River. **RIGHT:** Cape Raoul on the Tasman Peninsula.

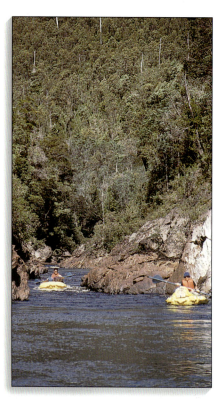

Penghana, a mansion sitting on a terrace above the town, is worth a visit. Built for the first Mount Lyell Copper Mine managers, it houses an extraordinary photo collection and other historic bits and pieces. It has been open to the public since 1995, and also offers bed and breakfast in its stately bedrooms.

The port of **Strahan** ⓰ (pronounced *Strawn*), 40 km (25 miles) away from Queenstown, has not been used by cargo ships since crossing the treacherous currents and shoals of Hell's Gates at the entrance to Macquarie Harbour became uneconomical. These days, tourism is the boom industry; the attractive buildings on the waterfront have been glossily restored, and the docks cater for a fleet of small cruisers heading for the World Heritage area. Strahan also offers seaplane flights over the Southwest National Park, horse-riding on the **Henty Sand Dunes** (part of the enormous **Ocean Beach**), boat-trips across Macquarie Harbour to view its fairy penguins, helicopter fishing trips and whitewater rafting.

Zeehan ⓱ (pop. 1,100) lies 47 km north of Strahan. In the late 1880s, this was a classic Wild West boom town, with more than 5,000 inhabitants, 40 hotels and its own stock exchange. Harry Houdini walked a tightrope across its main street; Caruso and Melba sang in its theatre. Zeehan's time at the top was short-lived – the mining boom was well over by 1908 – but many of the buildings from the days when it was the fourth largest town in Tasmania are still standing. The mineral collection in the **West Coast Pioneers' Memorial Museum** makes the 6-km (4-mile) detour into Zeehan well worthwhile.

From Zeehan, the Murchison Highway winds through spectacular mountain countryside northeast to **Burnie**. About 15 minutes from Zeehan is **Montezuma Falls**, the second-biggest waterfall in Tasmania and a sensational half-day walk, part of it along an old mining tramway. **Tullah**, the last west-coast town before the highway, makes a beeline for Burnie, and has a cute, historic steam railway, along which runs the "Wee Georgie Wood", the little train that serviced the town before the highway linked the west coast to the rest of the world in the 1940s.

An alternative route back north involves the recently completed Western Explorer. Dubbed the "Road to Nowhere" by Green protesters during a major confrontation over its construction, this mostly gravel link to **Waratah** and **Marrawah** is listed as a four-wheel-drive track. But if the weather has been dry for a while it is a rather pleasant, if slow, haul for a standard vehicle. However, it's advisable to check conditions locally if the weather is bad.

It passes through very isolated, wild, yet mostly featureless country, allowing a few glimpses of the **Tarkine Wilderness**, a huge stretch of temperate rainforest which the Greens were determined to protect from logging. They felt that the road was being pushed through only to prevent the protection of the rainforest. Many tourism operators argue that it allows travellers to do a real lap, taking in the gorgeous **Pieman River**, the healthy green dairy country and the dramatic coastline round **Arthur River** and Marrawah.

Anyway, the controversial road is there, so you may as well use it. From Zeehan to Marrawah is close to two hours' driving. You can be back in Stanley on the north coast in less than three hours. ◻

INSIGHT GUIDES

Travel Tips

✳ INSIGHT GUIDES Phonecard

One global card to keep travellers in touch. Easy. Convenient. Saves you time and money.

It's a global phonecard

Save up to 70%* on international calls from over 55 countries

Free 24 hour global customer service

Recharge your card at any time via customer service or online

It's a message service

Family and friends can send you voice messages for free.

Listen to these messages using the phone* or online

Free email service - you can even listen to your email over the phone*

It's a travel assistance service

24 hour emergency travel assistance – if and when you need it.

Store important travel documents online in your own secure vault

For more information, call rates, and all Access Numbers in over 55 countries, (check your destination is covered) go to **www.insightguides.ekit.com** or call Customer Service.

JOIN now and receive US$ 5 bonus when you join for US$ 20 or more.

Join today at

www.insightguides.ekit.com

When requested use ref code: **INSAD010**

OR SIMPLY FREE CALL 24 HOUR CUSTOMER SERVICE

UK	0800 376 1705
USA	1800 706 1333
Canada	1800 808 5773
Australia	1800 11 44 78
South Africa	0800 997 285

THEN PRESS **0**

For all other countries please go to "Access Numbers" at **www.insightguides.ekit.com**

* Retrieval rates apply for listening to messages. Savings based on using a hotel or payphone and calling to a landline. Corre at time of printing 01.03

(INS001)

powered by **ekit**

"The easiest way to make calls and receive messages around the world"

CONTENTS

Getting Acquainted

Area: 7,600,300 sq. km
(2,965,150 sq. miles)
Capital: Canberra
Highest point: Mount Kosciusko
(2,230 metres/7,300 feet)
Population: 20 million
Religion: Anglican (20 percent);
Roman Catholic (20 percent);
Uniting Church in Australia
(6 percent); Aboriginal and Jewish
minorities.
Time zones: EST, CST and WST
Currency: Australian dollar (A$ or
$AUD)
Weights and measures: metric
Electricity: 240 volts and 50 hertz,
three-pin plug
International dialling code: 61

Australia is the smallest continent,
the largest island, and is believed
to be the oldest landmass on the
planet. Roughly 4,000 km (2,500
miles) east to west and 3,200 km
(2,000 miles) north to south, its
coastline measures 36,738 km
(22,826 miles) and is washed by
three oceans and four seas. About
40 percent of Australia is tropical.
Separated from other landmasses,
Australia has evolved unique flora
and fauna.

Comparable in size to the US
(excluding Alaska), Australia is the
only continent occupied by just one
nation. The population is about 20
million, of whom approximately
410,003 people are indigenous.
Almost the entire population is
clustered in a narrow crescent
along the east coast and in the
south-west corner of the continent.

The Great Dividing Range,
stretching almost the whole length
of the eastern continent,
separates a narrow fertile strip on
the coast from the Outback. West
of the range the country becomes
increasingly flat and dry, and for
thousands of miles the horizon is
broken only by occasional
protuberances like Uluru, the
Olgas, and the stark Flinders
mountains and the Macdonnell
ranges.

In the far south of Western
Australia, a repeat of the mountain
range-coastal strip pattern heralds
the Indian Ocean.

Climate

The seasons in Australia are the
reverse of the Northern
Hemisphere's. September to
November is spring, December to
February summer, March to May
autumn, and June to August
winter. Since fine, mild weather
occurs during all seasons, any
time can be recommended for a
visit to Australia – although some
months are warmer and drier than
others.

About 40 percent of the country
lies in the tropical zone north of
the Tropic of Capricorn. In the Top
End around Darwin (the monsoon
belt) and near Cairns, there are
only two seasons: the Dry (April–
November) and the Wet
(December–March). In the Dry,
there are warm days, clear blue
skies and cool nights. The Wet,
however, is usually characterised
by heavy rain alternating with
sunny hot weather. On the Great
Barrier Reef most rain falls in
January and February.

In the southern temperate zone
seasons are more distinct. The
winter temperatures in Sydney are
usually a maximum of 12°C (50°F)
– chilly enough to require an
overcoat – while dry summer
temperatures can regularly hit
30°C (90°F) and higher. Snow falls
on the southern mountain ranges,
but not in the cities. Melbourne is
pleasant in spring, summer and
autumn, but winter can be grey
and miserable, especially in July
and August. Tasmania, the island
state off the southern tip of the
continent, is the coolest: summers
are by far the best time to visit
here, as winters can be damp and
depressing.

Western Australia has a
Mediterranean climate. There are
four distinctive seasons and
moderate temperatures in its
southern parts, while the north is
in the tropical zone, so Top End
conditions prevail.

In central Australia, summer
temperatures are generally too
high for comfort. In winter, the
nights may be cool, with clear
warm days.

Visitors should also bear in mind
the various Australian school
holidays; Christmas coincides with
the long summer school break,
which lasts throughout January.
Easter is another big break. If you
are travelling during these seasons,
book well in advance.

Government and Economy

Since 1901, the six former colonies
of Australia have been an
independent federal commonwealth
with a British-style parliamentary
system. Australia is a member of
the British Commonwealth.

There is a three-tiered system of
government: federal, state and
local. The Prime Minister heads the
Federal Government and is the
leader of the party holding the
greatest number of seats in the
lower house, known as the House
of Representatives. The upper
house is the Senate. The Head of
State is the Governor-General,
nominated by the federal
government and appointed by the
Queen.

Voting in Australia is
compulsory with a preferential
voting system. A premier leads
each state government.

To prevent the rival cities of
Sydney and Melbourne battling for
the honour of being the nation's
capital, the city of Canberra was
founded between the two in 1927.
The federal parliament is based
here. Like Washington DC in the
United States, Canberra lies in its

own administrative zone, the Australian Capital Territory.

There are two main political groups, the Australian Labor Party, and a more conservative coalition of the Liberal and National parties, which has been in power since 1995. Governors in each of the states, along with the Governor-General, represent the British Crown in Australia. This is generally a symbolic role. In a 1999 referendum Australians narrowly voted against becoming a republic. Australia has a deregulated free-market economy with a fairly extensive social welfare system.

There is a flat rate 10 percent goods and services tax (GST) on most products.

Time Zones

Australia has three time zones: Eastern Standard Time for the east coast states (Tasmania, Victoria, New South Wales, Queensland), 10 hours ahead of GMT; Central Standard Time (covering Northern Territory and South Australia) 30 minutes behind the east coast, 9½ hours ahead of GMT; and Western Standard Time (Western Australia), 2 hours behind the east coast, 8 hours ahead of GMT.

During the summer most states introduce Daylight Saving Time, moving the clock forward by 1 hour. New South Wales and Australian Capital Territory run daylight saving November–February; South Australia and Victoria November–March; and Tasmania October–March. Neither Queensland nor Western Australia use Daylight Saving Time.

Sun and Showers, Month by Month

Major Cities		Jan	Feb	Mar	Apr	May	June	July	Aug	Sep	Oct	Nov	Dec
Sydney	Maximum °C	26	25	25	22	19	17	16	17	20	22	24	25
	Minimum °C	18	18	17	15	11	9	8	9	11	13	15	17
	Rainfall mm	98	113	128	127	124	131	105	81	70	75	78	80
	Water Temp. °C	22	22	22	21	14	17	16	16	16	17	19	20
Melbourne	Maximum °C	26	26	24	20	17	14	13	15	17	20	22	24
	Minimum °C	14	14	13	11	9	7	6	6	8	9	11	13
	Rainfall mm	48	50	54	59	57	50	48	49	58	67	59	58
	Water Temp. °C	18	18	17	16	15	14	13	13	13	14	15	16
Brisbane	Maximum °C	29	29	28	26	23	21	20	22	24	26	28	29
	Minimum °C	27	20	19	16	13	11	9	10	13	16	18	17
	Rainfall mm	162	164	145	87	69	69	57	47	48	75	95	130
	Water Temp. °C	25	25	25	24	22	20	20	19	20	21	22	24
Adelaide	Maximum °C	30	29	27	23	19	16	15	16	19	22	25	28
	Minimum °C	16	17	15	13	10	8	7	8	9	11	13	15
	Rainfall mm	19	20	24	44	69	72	66	62	51	44	31	27
	Water Temp. °C	19	20	20	18	16	15	14	14	14	15	16	17
Perth	Maximum °C	30	30	28	24	21	18	17	18	19	21	25	27
	Minimum °C	18	18	17	14	12	10	9	9	10	11	14	16
	Rainfall mm	8	11	20	40	124	186	174	139	81	55	21	14
	Water Temp. °C	20	20	21	21	20	19	18	18	18	18	19	20
Darwin	Maximum °C	32	32	32	33	32	31	30	31	33	34	34	33
	Minimum °C	25	25	25	24	22	20	20	21	23	25	25	25
	Rainfall mm	391	330	260	103	14	3	1	2	13	50	126	243
	Water Temp. °C	29	29	29	28	28	26	26	24	27	27	29	29
Hobart	Maximum °C	22	22	20	17	14	12	11	13	15	17	19	20
	Minimum °C	12	12	11	9	7	5	4	5	6	8	9	11
	Rainfall mm	45	41	44	52	50	57	54	49	53	61	61	56
	Water Temp. °C	15	15	15	14	13	12	12	11	11	12	12	13
Canberra	Maximum °C	28	27	24	20	15	12	11	13	16	19	23	26
	Minimum °C	13	13	10	6	3	1	0	1	3	5	9	11
	Rainfall mm	59	57	52	47	52	38	37	45	48	69	64	58
Cairns	Maximum °C	32	31	30	29	27	26	25	27	28	29	31	31
	Minimum °C	24	24	22	22	20	18	17	18	19	21	22	23
	Rainfall mm	399	441	464	177	91	51	30	26	36	35	84	167
	Water Temp. °C	28	28	28	26	26	23	22	23	24	25	27	28

Planning the Trip

What to Bring

CLOTHING

Generally, Australians are informal dressers, especially when the weather is warm: comfort comes before tradition. However, for special occasions or dining in fine restaurants, formal attire or neat casual dress is required. While a jacket and tie are rarely required for men, the more elegant establishments would not welcome gym shoes or shorts. In other words, dress more or less as you would in other cosmopolitan cities.

If you visit Australia during summer, include at least one warm garment for the occasional cold snap. If travelling to the southeastern states during winter, include warm clothing, a raincoat and an umbrella – temperatures in Melbourne can get down to freezing at night. The weather in northern Queensland and the Top End of the NT (Northern Territory) is rarely chilly, even in August.

At any time of the year, solid, waterproof walking shoes are essential if you intend to go bushwalking. If exploring the Great Barrier Reef, bring along an old pair of plimsolls for reef walks. And always pack a hat.

Entry Regulations

CUSTOMS

There are no customs charges on personal belongings that are intended for use during your stay. You may import 250 cigarettes or 250 grams of tobacco, 1 litre of alcohol and dutiable goods to the value of A$400 in personal baggage. Strict laws prevent the entry of drugs, weapons, firearms and quarantine items.

Australian produce is of a very high standard because it is free from many insect pests and diseases common to other countries. This is due in part to the strict control on the importation of insects, animal and plant products, fruit, vegetables and seeds. Also note that, once inside Australia, there are a number of restrictions on taking fruit or vegetables between states.

Visas and Passports

All visitors require a passport and visa to enter Australia (the only exception to the visa rule is for New Zealanders, who require only a passport). Available from Australian consulates, online at www.eta.immi. gov.au, or travel agents, tourist visas allowing a stay of up to 3 months are free of charge and valid for a year from the date of issue. A fee is charged allowing for longer stays or for business visas.

Visitors must produce an onward or return ticket and sufficient funds to support themselves. Employment is not permitted for those on tourist visas. Under a reciprocal arrangement, British, Canadian, Irish, Dutch, Japanese and Korean visitors who are between 18 and 30 are eligible for a Working Holiday visa. This entitles them to a maximum stay of 12 months and some casual employment during that time. Such visas can only be applied for in the traveller's country of origin.

Regulations concerning entry requirements for Australia are continually updated. Information and applications for visas should be made to the nearest Australian Government representative in your home country. *(See Overseas Missions, page 338.)*

Laws strictly prohibit the export of protected Australian wildlife and products made from the skins, feathers, bones, shells, corals, or any part of protected species.

QUARANTINE

Australia is free of rabies, anthrax and foot-and-mouth disease, so all incoming animals are placed in quarantine. Dogs and cats are quarantined for up to 3 months.

Health

Australian doctors, dentists and hospitals all have modern equipment, high-level training and extensive facilities. They are also expensive.

New Zealand, Finland, Italy, Malta, the Netherlands, Sweden, the UK and Ireland have reciprocal health-care agreements with Australia, so visitors are entitled to free hospital treatment and Medicare (the Australian national health plan) benefits for GP treatment. Taking out a travel health and accident insurance policy before travelling to Australia is still recommended, however.

Vaccinations are not required if you are flying directly to Australia and have not passed through an epidemic zone or a yellow fever, cholera or typhoid-infected area in the 14 days prior to your arrival.

The sun in Australia has extremely strong ultraviolet rays, so extended exposure is not recommended, especially when the sun is at its fiercest between 11am and 4pm. A wide-brimmed hat and adequate-strength sunscreen are essential.

Money

Australia's currency is in dollars and cents. The coins come in 5, 10, 20 and 50-cent silver pieces and 1 and 2 dollar gold coins. Notes are A$5, 10, 20, 50 and 100. Amounts of over A$5,000 must be declared on entering and leaving Australia.

Travellers' cheques in any currency can be readily cashed at international airports and banks. Bureaux de change offices are open seven days a week and are located throughout major cities – but they usually charge a significant fee, so try to change money at banks when you can, despite the limited opening hours.

The larger hotels will usually exchange cash and well-known travellers' cheques. Major credit cards such as American Express, Visa, Diners Club, MasterCard and Bankcard are accepted nearly everywhere.

Australian currency cash withdrawals can be made from automatic banking machines that are linked to overseas banks.

Diary of Events

A list of some of the annual events held in Australia follows. Dates may vary, but the Australian Tourist Commission publishes a very comprehensive calendar booklet of current dates.

January
Australia-wide
Australia Day (26 Jan). There are parades and concerts around the country, including the Sydney Ferrython and Perth's Carnival on the Swan. Spectacular fireworks displays over most cities are held at the end of the day.
Melbourne
The *Australian Open* is a Grand Slam partner to the French Open, Wimbledon and the US Open. It annually attracts the world's best tennis players to Melbourne Park for two weeks.
Perth
Western Australian Cup (1 Jan). WA's premier horseracing event, held at Ascot Racecourse.
Tamworth (NSW)
Country Music Festival. Lively gathering of fans for continuous country music.

February
Adelaide
Adelaide Fringe Festival of the Arts (held every second year). New theatre, comedy, visual arts and

music. The cutting-edge bi-annual (even years) counterpart to the *Adelaide Festival of the Arts* when Adelaide comes to life for an exciting programme of international performing artists *(see box Adelaide Festival, page 370).*
Hobart
Hobart Cup Carnival. Tasmania's premier horseracing event held at Elwick Racecourse.
Melbourne
Heineken Classic. International golfing title at Huntingdale Golf Course.
Melbourne Fashion Festival. Designers and retailers in a stylish array of parades, special events and exhibitions.
Perth
Perth International Arts Festival. Three weeks of arts and multi-cultural activities.
Sydney
Sydney Gay and Lesbian Mardi Gras (throughout Feb). The parade on the last Saturday evening is the biggest and liveliest gay and lesbian mardi gras in the world.

March
Ballarat (VIC)
The Ballarat Begonia Festival. World-famous begonia display and ten days of festival activities attracts over 100,000 visitors.
Canberra
Royal Canberra Show. Typical agricultural show includes trade stalls, animals, crafts and horticulture produce, woodchopping, fireworks, etc.
Melbourne
Moomba Festival. Moomba means "having fun". Street processions, laser displays, waterskiing, fireworks.
Fosters Australian Grand Prix. The opening round of the FIA Formula 1 World Championship. The four-day event attracts the world's best drivers to the outstanding street circuit around Albert Park Lake.
Australian International Airshow. The biggest aviation and areospace event in the Southern Hemisphere. The biennial event (2005, 2007) is held at Avalon Airport.

Public Holidays

Public and school holidays affect availability of transport and hotel reservations, which often results in higher prices. The public holidays observed Australia-wide are as follows:

1 January	**New Year's Day**
26 January	**Australia Day**
late March/	**Good Friday,**
early April	**Easter Saturday and Monday**
25 April	**Anzac Day**
2nd Monday in June	**Queen's Birthday**
Early October	**Labour Day**
25 December	**Christmas Day**
26 December	**Boxing Day**

In addition, the states have their own public holidays, such as Victoria's Melbourne Cup Day (first Tuesday in November).

March/April
Melbourne
Melbourne Food and Wine Festival. Wine tastings and workshops, celebrity-chef demonstrations, live music and more.
Bendigo (VIC)
Awakening of the Dragon Festival (date is variable). The world's longest imperial dragon (100 metres/330 ft) parades through the streets every Easter Monday.

April
Barmera (SA)
Riverland Country Music Festival. Country music of all varieties in over 20 venues. Guest artists and presentation of State Awards.
Broome (WA)
Broome Arts and Music Festival. The remote pearling community comes alive with local artists markets, Aboriginal art exhibitions and poetry workshops.
Margaret River (WA)
Salomon Masters. Annual allcomers surfing event.
Melbourne
Melbourne International Comedy Festival. One of the world's top comedy festivals.

Melbourne International Flower and Garden Show. Australia's premier horticultural show.

Sydney
Royal Easter Show. Sydney's agricultural show and amusement park extravaganza, attracting one million visitors.

Tasmania
Targa Tasmania. Major car-racing event covering 2,000 km (1,240 miles) of Tasmania's scenic coastline and mountain passes.

May

Adelaide
Adelaide Cup Carnival. Morphettville Racecourse hosts races such as the Australasian Oaks, Derby Day, Oaks Day, Cup Day and Street Leger Stakes.

Alice Springs (NT)
Bangtail Muster. A day of Outback fun including a parade in honour of all cattlemen from Central Australia.
V8 Supercar Championships. At nearby Hidden Valley track.

Barossa Valley (SA)
Riverland Balloon Regatta. Beautiful visions of dawn and late-afternoon skies dotted with colourful balloons.

Clare Valley (SA)
Clare Gourmet Weekend. Wineries join with prominent restaurants to provide visitors with the complete gourmet experience as they tour the region.

Noosa (QLD)
Noosa Jazz Fest. Live jazz everywhere in this beach resort town, culminating in the famous "Woods" Picnic Concert.

June

Adelaide River (NT)
Adelaide River Show Rodeo, Campdraft and Gymkhana. Big money prizes and a packed programme of activities including a

Sydney Film Festival

Every June, art cinemas in Sydney showcase the best new films selected from recent film festivals around the world.

Festivals of Darwin

The August *Darwin Festival* celebrates the end of the tropical dry season with entertainment, arts and cultural events in parks and venues around Darwin. The festival strongly reflects the Asian-Pacific and Aboriginal communities of Darwin.

It overlaps with the *Darwin Fringe Festival*, which showcases local visual and performing arts.

bush dance and a country music talent quest.

Alice Springs
Beanie Festival. Typically quirky Northern Territory event with special classes to make "beanies" (close-fitting woollen caps) with accompanying feasting and drinking.
Finke Desert 200 km Race. Cars, bikes, buggies – anything that goes – race along the dry river bed from Alice to Finke, stop overnight and race back. Spectators camp along the river bank.

Alpine resorts
Opening weekend. The Queen's Birthday weekend is the signal for skiing enthusiasts to gather for the opening of the ski season – snow or no snow!

Barunga (NT)
Burunga Festival. Aboriginal people from all parts of the Northern Territory gather for four days of dancing, athletics, arts and crafts. Advisable to bring a tent.

Geelong (VIC)
National Celtic Folk Festival. Celebration of Scottish, Welsh, Irish and Cornish heritage with theatre, music, crafts, sports and food.

McLaren Vale (SA)
McLaren Vale Sea and Vines Festival. The McLaren Vale wineries present food and wine to visitors.

Mildura (VIC)
Mildura International Balloon Fiesta. Incorporating the Ballooning World Cup and National Championships; a visually spectacular event.

July

Alice Springs (NT)
Lions Camel Cup. Camels are brought from all over Australia to compete. A day of fun, with fireworks.

Darwin
Darwin Cup Festival. Cup Day is accompanied by a great carnival atmosphere and loads of live music. *Beer Can Regatta* (date is variable). Everyone in Darwin gathers on Mindil Beach to watch the traditional Darwin water race, where competing vessels must be constructed entirely of beer cans.

Melbourne
Melbourne International Film Festival. Melbourne's prestigious festival highlights new local films as well as foreign successes.

Stroud (NSW)
Stroud International Brick and Rolling Pin Throwing Contest. Four towns called Stroud (also in England, Canada and the USA) simultaneously hold this bizarre contest.

August

Broome (WA)
Shinju Matsuri Festival of the Pearl. A ten-day festival honouring Broome's Asian heritage. Pearl jewellery, Chinese feasts and more.

Geraldton (WA)
Sunshine Surfmaster. Big prizes at this event, which has been taking place for over 20 years.

Mt Buller (VIC)
World Aerials. The international aerial ski championships.

Mt Isa (QLD)
Mt Isa Rotary Rodeo. Australia's biggest rodeo, held every year since 1959.

Oenpelli (Arnhem Land; NT)
Garma Festival encourages the practice and preservation of traditional song, dance and ceremony, on Yolngu land in northeast Arnhem Land. Visitors need special passes.

Sydney
Sydney Marathon. The streets of Sydney are the course for this major marathon event.

Barossa Valley

Barossa Classic Gourmet Weekend (August). Wineries combine with restaurants to provide samples of gourmet fare.

Toowoomba (QLD)
Australian Heritage Festival. Jondaryan Woolshed hosts a week of historic rural Australian activities featuring bullock teams, steam engines and hand shearing.

August/September
Melbourne
Melbourne Writers Festival. Gathering of Australian and foreign writers for readings and discussion of their works, tel: 03-9645 9244.

September
Alice Springs (NT)
Henley on Todd Regatta. The world's first waterless regatta held on the dry bed of the Todd River. The final "Sea Battle" is fought with flour bombs and water canons between four-wheel drive "boats".
Bathurst (NSW)
Bathurst 1000 Touring Car Motor Race. Popular car-racing event is a six hour course on Mt Panorama.
Birdsville (QLD)
Birdsville Races. People from all over the country gather at this Outback town for horseraces to raise money for the Royal Flying Doctor Service.
Canberra
Floriade. Australia's largest spring floral festival.
Perth
Western Australia Wildflower Festival. Excellent opportunity to see a huge range of unique Australian wildflowers at their best at Kings Park.
Sydney
Festival of the Winds. The sky above Bondi Beach is filled with colourful kites of all shapes and sizes.

October
Alice Springs
Masters Championships. Veteran athletes of all ages compete in a wide range of sports.

Melbourne
Melbourne International Festival of the Arts & Melbourne Fringe Arts Festival. Seventeen days are set aside for the city's major arts festivals, tel: 03-9662 4242.
Phillip Island (VIC)
The Australian Motorcycle Grand Prix – the premier event on the international motorcycle calender.

November
Fremantle (WA)
Festival of Fremantle. Ten days of celebrations with exhibitions, concerts, and a huge parade and street carnival.

December
Eltham (VIC)
Montsalvat National Poets Spoken Word and Vision Festival. Poetry performed in beautiful grounds.
Sydney–Hobart
Sydney to Hobart Yacht Race. Famous blue-water yacht race has its dramatic Boxing Day start in Sydney Harbour.

Melbourne Cup

On the first Tuesday in November the whole of Australia stops for the running of this famous race at the Flemington Racecourse. It's accompanied by a huge carnival in Melbourne where the locals don their finest and most outrageous hats to attend.

Getting There

BY AIR

Almost all foreign visitors travel to Australia by air. Brisbane, Cairns, Melbourne and Sydney are the major international tourism gateways, with daily flights arriving from Asia, Europe and North America. Less frequent flights also arrive directly in Adelaide, Darwin, Perth and Hobart. More than 30 international airlines currently fly to and from Australia *(see Airlines, page 341).*

Getting to Australia can be expensive. Most travellers take advantage of excursion fares, with the price dependent on season. Fares vary widely, so it is important to seek the advice of a knowledgeable travel agent before purchasing a ticket.

Note that domestic flights are available to international travellers at much lower fares than to Australian residents. There are usually considerable price advantages in pre-booking your domestic travel along with your flight to Australia. Also, special pre-booked packages often incorporate inexpensive hotel and car rental rates.

Qantas usually offers good deals to Australia (it also operates Qantas Vacations, with package deals). Tickets can be booked directly by freephone: 1800-227 4500 (in the US); or 08457-747767 (in the UK).

Useful Addresses

TOURIST INFORMATION ABROAD

The Australian Tourist Commission supplies excellent information:
London:
Gemini House, 10–18 Putney Hill, London SW15 6AA
Tel: 020-8780 2229
Fax: 020-8780 1496
Los Angeles:
2049 Century Park East, Suite 1920, Los Angeles, CA 90067
Tel: 310-229 4870
Fax: 310-552 1215
Hong Kong:
Ste 1501, Central Plaza, 18 Harbour Road, Wanchai
Tel: 852-2802 7700
Fax: 852-2802 8211
Singapore:
101 Thompson Road, United Square 08-03, Singapore 307591
Tel: 65-6255 4559
Fax: 65-6253 8431
Local Office of the ATC:
Level 4, 80 William Street, East Sydney, NSW 2010
Tel: 1300-361 650 or 02-9360 1111
Fax: 612-9361 1388

Overseas Missions

Canada – Ottawa:
Australian High Commission, Suite 710, 50 O'Conner Street, Ottawa, Ontario, K1P 6L2
Tel: 1 613-236 0841
Toronto:
Australian Consulate-General, Suite 316, 175 Bloor Street East, Toronto, Ontario, M4W 3R8
Tel: 1 416-323 1155
Vancouver:
Australian Consulate, Suite 1225, 888 Dunsmuir Street, Vancouver, BC V6C 3K4
Tel: 1 604-684 1177
France:
Australian Embassy, 4 Rue Jean Rey, 75724 Paris Cedex 15
Tel: 33 140593300/2
Germany:
Australian Embassy, Wallstrasse 76–79, Berlin 10179
Tel: 49 30-880088-0
Hong Kong:
Australian Consulate-General, 23/F Harbour Centre, 25 Harbour Road, Wanchai
Tel: 852 2827 8881
Indonesia – Jakarta:
Australian Embassy, Jalan Hr Rasuna Said Kav C15–16, Jakarta Selatan 12940
Tel: 62 21-2550 5555
Ireland:
Australian Embassy, Fitzwilton House, Wilton Terrace, Dublin 2
Tel: 353 1-664 5300
Italy:
Australian Embassy, Via Alessandria 215, 00198 Rome
Tel: 39 06-852 721
Japan – Tokyo:
Australian Embassy, 2-1-14 Mita, Minato-Ku, Tokyo 018-8361
Tel: 81 35232 4111
Malaysia:
Australian High Commission, 6 Jalan Yap Kwan Seng, Kuala Lumpur 50450
Tel: 603 2146 5555
New Zealand – Wellington:
Australian High Commission, 72–78 Hobson Street, Thorndon, Wellington
Tel: 64 4473 6411
Auckland:
Australian Consulate-General, 7 PriceWaterHouseCoopers Tower, 194 Quay Street, Auckland
Tel: 64 93032 429
Philippines:
Australian Embassy, Level 23-Tower 2, RCBC Plaza, 6819 Ayala Avenue (Makati City), Manila
Tel: 63 2757 8100
Singapore:
Australian High Commission, 25 Napier Road, Singapore 258507
Tel: 65 6836 4100
Thailand:
Australian Embassy, 37 South Sathorn Road, Bangkok 10120
Tel: 662-287 2680
United Kingdom – London:
Australian High Commission, Australia House, The Strand, London WC2B 4LA
Tel: 44 20-7379 4334
Edinburgh:
Honorary Consul, 69 George Street, Edinburgh EH2 2JG
Tel: 44 131-624 3333
United States of America – Washington DC:
Australian Embassy, 1601 Massachusetts Avenue NW, Washington DC 20036-2273
Tel: 1 202-797 3000
New York:
Australian Consulate-General, 150 East 42nd Street, 34th floor, New York, NY 10017-5612
Tel: 1 212-351 6500
San Francisco:
Australian Consulate-General, 625 Market Street, Suite 200 (corner of Market/New Montgomery streets) San Francisco CA 94105-3304
Tel: 1 415-5361970
Atlanta:
Australian Consulate-General, Atlanta Financial Center, 3353 Peachtree Road NE, Suite 1140, Atlanta GA 30326
Tel: 1 404-7603408

On Departure

A departure tax of A$38, along with sundry other airport and government levies, is included in the cost of your international ticket, so it no longer has to be paid at the airport when you leave.

Disabled Travellers

Most new buildings, public transport and tourist attractions have wheelchair access and other facilities for the disabled. The major rental car companies have a small number of cars with hand controls (reserve at least 7 days in advance). Advance notice with relevant details of your disability will facilitate the best possible assistance from airlines, hotels or railway offices. Taxi fleets in state capitals all have cars that can carry wheelchairs. The Australian Tourist Commission can provide a fact sheet, *Travel In Australia For People With Disabilities*. Also, the National Information Communications Network (NICAN) provides a directory of accessible accommodation, recreation and other facilities. Contact NICAN at: PO Box 407, Curtin, ACT 2605, tel: 02-6285 3713; Freecall: 1800-806 769; www.nican.com.au.

The state automobile associations publish accommodation directories which include information on disabled access.

Practical Tips

Business Hours

General retail trading hours for stores are 9am–5pm, Mon–Fri, and 9am–4pm Saturday. Most shops open 10am–4pm on Sunday too. Late night shopping (until 9pm) takes place at least one night a week in the capital cities – usually a Thursday or Friday.

Restaurants and snack bars, bookshops and local corner stores are open until later in the evening and sometimes all weekend. Australians still enjoy the tradition of the weekend holiday and most offices are closed on Saturday and Sunday.

Banks open 9.30am–4pm Mon–Thurs and until 5pm on Friday. All banks, post offices, government and private offices, and most shops close on public holidays. *(see Public Holidays, page 335.)*

Tipping

Tipping is not the general custom in Australia – waiters are given a decent hourly wage. Most Australians round up the amount in restaurants, or leave the change. In the more formal places, it is becoming customary to give a little more than that – about 10 percent of the total.

Porters at luxury hotels once never received tips, but since many overseas visitors give them a dollar or two, there is an increasing look of expectancy. Porters at airports and taxi drivers do not expect to be tipped, but will hardly throw the money back if you do. "It's up to you" has become the common advice from Australians. In other words: nobody really expects a tip, but it's always appreciated.

Media

Each major city has one daily newspaper and in some cases two. *Sydney Morning Herald* (www.smh.com.au) and the *Melbourne Age* (www.theage.com.au) are the two most important capital-city dailies, and can be usually found around Australia. The only national daily newspapers are *The Australian* and *The Financial Review*. Numerous weekly magazines are sold alongside local editions of international publications, such as *Newsweek* (included in *The Bulletin*) and *Time*.

The largest-selling papers are the tabloids in Sydney (the *Daily Telegraph-Mirror*) and Melbourne (the *Herald-Sun*, online at: www.heraldsun.com). There are about 120 ethnic newspapers in either English or one of forty languages.

Australia has a high readership of magazines: in addition to 1,200 magazine titles, airmail copies of overseas newspapers and journals are readily available at specialist newsagents and numerous bookstores in major cities.

The number of television stations varies around the country. In some remote areas, the ABC (Australian Broadcasting Corporation) may be the only station. This is the national, advertisment-free, television and radio network – the equivalent of Britain's BBC. The capital cities also offer three commercial stations and the excellent SBS (Special Broadcasting Service) multi-cultural station, with shows in many languages with subtitles.

On radio, there is always ABC (FM and AM), plus a full spectrum of commercial and public broadcast stations, offering everything from rock to classical music.

Postal Services

Post offices open 9am–5pm, Mon–Fri. The service is reasonably efficient but not cheap.

Post offices provide fax services at urgent or ordinary rates, the cost depending on the rate selected and the destination.

Toll-free Phone Calls

Toll-free or freecall numbers are common in Australian business. Numbers beginning with 13 (ie. Qantas domestic 131 313) can be called from any phone in Australia at local-call rates; numbers starting with 800, 1300 or 1800 are freecall numbers (toll-free) when dialled from within Australia.

The front pages of the telephone directory give further information on all postal services, including telephone interpreter service, community service and recorded information service.

Post Restante: post offices will receive and hold mail for visitors. American Express offices will also hold mail for members.

Telecommunications

Emergency numbers: **police, ambulance, fire, tel: 000.**

Australia has several telecommunication operators including Telstra, Optus and AAPT. Rates vary between companies for long distance, but local calls on all networks are untimed.

INTERNET CAFES

Internet cafés are easily found all over Australia, particularly in the larger towns and cities – anybody from a concierge to a cop will happily point you in the right direction. We have not included any listings, as they change so frequently.

MAKING CALLS

Public telephones are located throughout cities and towns. Most public telephones take phonecards, which can be bought at newsagents and stores in various denominations. Dialling from hotel rooms is much more expensive than from a public or private phone.

Weights & Measures

Australia uses the metric system of weights and measures. Despite the change from the imperial to the metric system in the 1970s, a 183 cm person is still frequently referred to as being "6 feet tall" and many people still give their weight in stones (14 lb to the stone). The main conversions are as follows:

1 metre	3.28 feet
1 kilometre	0.62 mile
1 kilogramme	2.20 pounds
1 litre	2.1 pints (US)
1 litre	1.8 pints (UK)
0°C	32°F
(Centigrade)	(Fahrenheit)

Subscriber Trunk Dialling (STD) for calling long distance is available on all private and most public telephones. Dial the regional code (say 02 for NSW, 03 for Victoria, etc) followed by the local number. STD calls are cheapest after 7pm and before 8am.

International Calls

Direct-dialled international calls may be made from any ISD-connected private or public phone. International public phones may be found at city GPOs, rail termini and airports. There are off-peak rates to most countries which generally apply all day Saturday and 11pm–6am Sunday to Friday.

Tourist Offices in Australia

Tourist information within Australia is handled principally by state tourist offices:

ACT – Australian Capital Territory
Canberra and Region Visitors Centre, 330 Northbourne Avenue, Dickson, ACT 2602
Tel: 1300-554 114 or
02-6205 0532
Fax: 02-6205 0496
www.visitcanberra.com.au

New South Wales
Sydney Visitor Centre, 106 George Street, The Rocks, Sydney NSW 2000

Tel: 132-077 or 02-9240 8788
www.visitnsw.com.au

Northern Territory
Tourism Information Centre, 67 North Stuart Highway, Alice Springs, NT 8070
Tel: 134-383
Fax: 1800-808666
www.ntholidays.com

Queensland
Queensland Travel Centre, 30 Makerston Street, Brisbane 4000
Tel: 07-3535 4557
Fax: 07-3535 5044
www.tq.com.au

South Australia
South Australia Visitors Centre, 18 King William Street, Adelaide SA 5000
Tel: 1300-655 276
Fax: 08-8303 2249
www.southaustralia.com

Tasmania
Tasmanian Travel and Information Centre, 22 Elizabeth Street (corner of Davey/Elizabeth streets) Hobart, Tas 7000
Tel: 1300-655 145
www.discovertasmania.com.au

Victoria
Victoria Visitors Information Centre, Federation Square (corner of Flinders/Swanson streets), Melbourne
Tel: 03-9658 9658
www.visitvictoria.com

Western Australia
Western Australian Visitor Centre, Albert Facey House, Forrest Place (corner of Wellington Street)
Tel: 1300-361 351 or
08-9438 1160
Fax: 08-9481 0190
www.westernaustralia.net

These offices are generally open 9am–5pm weekdays plus Saturday mornings, and will provide brochures, maps, price lists and other information. They can often book accommodation, tours and transport for you. Most towns also have a local tourist information office.

Embassies and Consulates

If you need help with such matters as legal advice or a stolen passport while in Australia, most countries have diplomatic representations in Australia, with embassies in Canberra. There are also consular representatives in other major cities, the address and telephone numbers of which are easily found in the Yellow Pages under "Consulates and Legations".

Canada
Commonwealth Ave, Yarralumla, Canberra.
Tel: 02-6270 4000

Ireland
20 Arkana Street, Yarralumla, Canberra.
Tel: 02-6273 3022

Japan
112–114 Empire Circuit, Yarralumla, Canberra.
Tel: 02-6273 3244

Malaysia
7 Perth Ave, Yarralumla, Canberra.
Tel: 02-6273 1543

New Zealand
Commonwealth Ave, Yarralumla, Canberra.
Tel: 02-6270 4211

Papua New Guinea
Forster Crescent, Yarralumla, Canberra.
Tel: 02-6273 3322

Singapore
Forster Crescent, Yarralumla, Canberra.
Tel: 02-6273 3944

Thailand
131 Macquarie Street, Sydney.
Tel: 02-9241 2542
Fax: 02-9241 2543

United Kingdom
Commonwealth Avenue, Yarralumla, Canberra.
Tel: 02-6270 6666

United States of America
21 Moonah Place, Yarralumla, Canberra.
Tel: 02-6214 5600

Airlines

Aerolineas Argentinas
Sydney, tel: 02-9262 2844.
Air France
Sydney, tel: 02-9244 2100.
Air India
Sydney, tel: 02-9283 4020.
Air Nauru
Tel: 1300-369 044.

Air New Zealand
Tel: 132-476.
Air Niugini
Tel: 1300-361 380.
Air Pacific
Freecall: 1800-230 150
Alitalia
Sydney, tel: 02-9244 2400;
Melbourne, tel: 03-9920 3799;
Perth, tel: 08-9229 9212.
Alliance Airlines
Tel: 1300-130 092.
All Nippon Airlines
Tel: 1800-001 126.
British Airways
Tel: 1300-767 177.
Cathay Pacific Airways
Tel: 131-747.
Emirates Airlines
tel: 1300-303 777.
Garuda Indonesia
Tel: 1300-365 330.
Hawaiian Airlines
Sydney, tel: 02-9244 2377.
Japan Airlines
Sydney, tel: 02-9272 1111.
KLM Royal Dutch Airlines
Tel: 1300-303 747.
Korean Air
Sydney, tel: 02-9262 6000.
Lufthansa German Airlines
Tel: 1300-655 727.
Malaysia Airlines
Tel: 132-627.
Olympic Airways
Sydney, tel: 02-9251 2044.
Philippine Airlines
Sydney, tel: 02-9279 2020.
Polynesian Airlines
Sydney, tel: 02-9299 1733;
Melbourne, tel: 03-9611 0017.
Qantas
Tel: 131-313.
Regional Express
Tel: 131-713.
Singapore Airlines
Tel: 131-011.
Thai Airways International
Tel: 1300-651 960.
United Airlines
Tel: 131-777.
Virgin Blue
Tel: 136-789.

Getting Around

By Air

Australia's national domestic airline is Qantas. Its main competitor, Ansett Australia, unexpectedly folded in September 2001, but competition was restored on most routes by fast-growing Virgin Blue, tel: 136-789. Qantas operates regular scheduled flights between all capital cities and regional centres throughout Australia. It has its own terminals at domestic airports.
Qantas domestic and international
Tel: 131-313.
Qantas's subsidiary, **Australian Airlines**, operates from Cairns to a number of Asian destinations;
tel: 1300-799 798.

Special domestic fares are available for international visitors, so you're likely to get the best deal if you purchase your local flights when you buy your ticket to Australia.

Although many domestic flights are often fully booked, cheaper standby and advance-purchase seats are available on most routes, and you can save around 20 percent off the regular economy fare.

Flying Times

Sydney–Melbourne, 1 hr
Sydney–Perth, 4 hrs 50 mins
Melbourne–Adelaide,
1 hr 20 mins
Melbourne–Canberra, 1 hr
Brisbane–Sydney, 1 hr 25 mins
Brisbane–Melbourne,
2 hrs 20 mins
Adelaide–Alice Springs, 2 hrs
Perth–Adelaide, 3 hrs
Canberra–Sydney, 50 mins

Within Australia, discounts of up to 50 percent off the full fare are available when purchasing return economy fares in advance. You must book and pay for your ticket at least 10–14 days before departure and you cannot alter your booking within those times. Other, smaller, discounts apply if you are prepared to fly at off-peak times.

Excursion fares, discounts and packages are available from time to time. Some of the best deals include both air travel and accommodation outside the main holiday seasons – check with the airlines about what specials are on offer.

There are also regular price wars between airlines, which can result in some great deals. Check out the advertisements in the travel sections of newspapers.

Each state is serviced by a number of regional airlines such as the QantasLink group, Regional Express and Alliance, providing access to country towns and the more remote destinations.

By Bus

Lively competition between the major bus companies means many bargains are available when travelling by bus in Australia (the biggest company, with most services, is **McCafferty's Greyhound**, tel: 131-499 (Australia-wide).

The standard of coaches is high, with most having reclining seats, seats for the disabled, videos, washrooms and air-conditioning. All buses are strictly non-smoking. Bus terminals are well equipped with toilets, showers and shops and are generally very clean. However, you should be aware that distances are enormous in Australia, so think twice before hopping on the Brisbane–Cairns leg because it takes more than 24 hours.

McCafferty's Greyhound has an arrangement with Youth Hostels of Australia and Flag Motels, whereby the bus ticket is combined with accommodation vouchers; tel: 1800-800 260 for details.

There are many other bus

companies in Australia, offering a variety of transport/hotel packages ranging from 3–50 days and departing regularly from capital cities. Prices are per day inclusive of coach travel, accommodation and various day tours or driver "feature commentary". Some of the more adventurous routes are taken by deluxe four-wheel drive vehicles, incorporating camping out and accompanied by a cook.

Bargains by Bus

If you plan extensive bus travel in Australia, several discount plans offer unlimited travel within various time frames: from 7–90 days. There are also set-duration and set-distance fares.

By Train

A wide network of modern railways operates from coast to coast. The principal lines follow the east and south coasts, linking the cities of Cairns, Brisbane, Sydney, Melbourne, Adelaide and Alice Springs. The most comprehensive service is operated by **Countrylink**: reservations are required; tel: 132-232 (Australia-wide). In Sydney, tel: 02-8202 2000.

The line between Sydney and Perth is the famous **Indian–Pacific** run (so-called because it runs from the Indian Ocean to the Pacific Ocean). On its 3,955-km (2,457-mile) journey, taking 65 hours, the train crosses the Nullarbor Plain, with the longest stretch of straight track in the world. There's not much to see – nothing exists except scrub, blue sky and telegraph poles – but passengers are well catered for with comforts such as an observation lounge, bar and even a music room, complete with piano.

Other popular scenic rail journeys include the Overland, an overnight journey between Melbourne and Adelaide, and the **Ghan**, which runs from Adelaide to Darwin in the Northern Territory (see page 378).

TICKETS

The classes available are first, holiday and economy. First-class passengers have sleeping berths with showers in their cabin, a first-class restaurant and lounge. Other classes get aeroplane-style reclining seats and a buffet car.

An Ausrail Flexipass entitles you to unlimited travel on interstate and metropolitan trains and is valid for 7-day to 29-day periods.

The Great Southern Railway Backpackers pass is only available to foreign passport holders and is valid for up to six months.

For full information on all rail travel and passes, tel: 132-147.

By Sea

After arriving in Australia, a number of the international cruise lines continue around the coastline at a leisurely pace, stopping at Sydney, Brisbane and Cairns on the east coast, Melbourne, Hobart and Adelaide on the south coast, and at Fremantle in the west.

Day trips and cruises operate between mainland towns and the islands on the Great Barrier Reef. Six-day cruises run from Cairns to Cape York. The coral-fringed Whitsunday Islands are one of the best cruising and yachting locations in Australia (you can rent yachts from operators at Airlie Beach – the motto is, if you can drive a car, you can sail a yacht). River cruises and houseboat rentals are available on major rivers such as the Hawkesbury north of Sydney or the Mayall Lakes on the NSW north coast.

The only regular maritime services are the passenger and car ferries called *Spirit of Tasmania I* and *II*, operating between Melbourne and Devonport, Tasmania. The trip can be rough and takes about ten hours. Tel: 132-010.

Motorcycles and Bicycles

Both are available for hire throughout Australia. Thoughtfully designed systems of bicycle paths provide good views or access to tourist sites – a pleasant, healthy and evironmentally friendly alternative to the city bus tour.

By Car

CAR HIRE

By international standards, renting a car in Australia is expensive – even though there are three nationwide rental companies and numerous local ones in competition.

The big three rental companies are **Avis**, **Hertz** and **Budget**, whose rates are just about identical. The small outfits are usually much cheaper and offer special deals (such as weekend and standby rates), but they may not offer all the services and extras of the major companies – which can be extremely useful. These include substantial discounts for pre-booking overseas, and the ability to return the car at another city at no extra charge. Also be aware that many rental cars have manual, rather than automatic, gears (the latter are pricier).

The big three have offices in almost every town, as well as at airports and rail terminals. They offer unlimited kilometre rates in the city but when travelling in the Outback, rates are usually per kilometre. Compulsory third-party insurance is included in car rentals but collision damage waiver is an add-on. More comprehensive insurance plans are available for an additional fee, or your travel insurance may cover them. Most companies have 25 as their minimum driver age, or will charge a premium for drivers aged between 21 and 25.

Since driving a conventional vehicle off sealed roads may invalidate your insurance, four-wheel drive (4WD) cars are expensive but worth considering for safe Outback touring. Camper-vans are popular, especially in Tasmania; they aren't cheap, however, and it might work out more economical to rent a regular car and stay at budget hotels.

Basic Motoring Rules

- Australians drive on the left.
- The law requires you to keep your seat belt fastened at all times, whether as driver or passenger.
- Overseas licences are valid throughout Australia.

Motoring Advice

If you do opt to explore Australia by car, keep in mind that distances are often quite huge and towns may be few and far between. Many visitors on short-term trips opt to fly between major cities and rent cars for shorter excursions.

The major highways linking capital cities are all sealed and of a good standard, but you don't have to go far to find yourself on dirt roads. If you're heading into the Outback, great care should be taken. Make sure you have spare tyres, and enough fuel and water, and that somebody knows where you're going. In remote areas such as Cape York and the Kimberley, most 4WDs travel in pairs or teams, to assist one another when bogged.

The speed limit in a built-up area is 60 kph (37 mph) and sometimes 50 kph (31 mph) in suburban residential areas; in the country it is usually 100 kph (62 mph), unless otherwise signposted. There is random breath testing for alcohol in most states. If you exceed .05 percent blood-alcohol level (ie, more than three drinks), a hefty fine and loss of licence are automatic.

Fuel comes in super, unleaded and super-unleaded, and is sold by the litre, becoming more expensive in remote country areas.

For extended touring, visitors have been known to buy a new or used car and sell it at the end of their journey. Each state has an Automobile Association which will supply you with excellent maps and literature. For a small membership fee, they also provide a free, nationwide emergency breakdown service (highly recommended).

Automobile Associations

Sydney: National Roads and Motorists Association (NRMA), 388 George Street, Sydney, NSW 2000, tel: 02-8741 6000; Australia-wide: 132-132.

Melbourne: Royal Automobile Club of Victoria (RACV), 550 Princes Highway, Noble Park North, Victoria 3174, tel: 131-955.

Canberra: National Roads and Motorists Association (NRMA), 92 Northbourne Avenue, Canberra City, ACT 2601, tel: 131-122.

Perth: Royal Automobile Club of Western Australia Inc. (RACWA), 228 Adelaide Terrace, Perth, WA 6000, tel: 08-9421 4444 or 131-703.

Brisbane: Royal Automobile Club of Queensland (RACQ), Logan Road, Eight Mile Plains, Queensland 4113, tel: 131-111.

Adelaide: Royal Automobile Association of South Australia (RAA), 41 Hindmarsh Square, Adelaide, SA 5000, tel: 131-111.

Darwin: Automobile Association of the Northern Territory (AANT), 79–81 Smith Street, Darwin, NT 0800, tel: 08-8981 3837.

Hobart: Royal Automobile Club of Tasmania (RACT), corner of Patrick and Murray streets, Hobart, TAS 7000, tel: 131-111.

Hitchhiking

While Australia has a lower crime rate than most places, crimes against hitchhikers do occur. Hitchhiking is illegal in some states and discouraged by the police in others.

If you still choose to hitchhike, use common sense. Don't carry much luggage, look clean, and display a sign announcing your destination.

Drive Safely

In rural areas take regular breaks on long journeys. It is all too easy to be lulled by the monotonous landscape and fall asleep at the wheel.

Where to Stay

Accommodation

See *Where to Stay* in the state-by-state section for lists of recommended hotels.

Generally speaking, the standard of accommodation in Australia is high. In the capital cities and tourist areas you will find all the international hotel chains such as Hyatt and Sheraton as well as privately managed properties. There are many new developments following the Olympic Games building frenzy. Tourist areas in particular have undergone rapid growth.

While some destinations cater more to well-heeled international visitors (such as Port Douglas, QLD), other regions have recognised the income generated by the young backpacker market and can provide an excellent choice of budget accommodation (for example, Darwin, NT). Log onto www.yha.com.au for information on Australia's youth hostels.

Sydney's hotels are significantly more expensive than anywhere else in Australia. Seasonal fluctuations in price often apply in heavily touristic areas.

The hotels listed in this book have been broadly classified into four categories: International, Premier, Moderate and Budget:

International: properties of unquestioned five-star standard, whether they are hotels, resorts or historic manor houses.

Premier: four-star standard, offering a range of reliable services. Many of the hotel chains fall under this category.

Moderate signifies an emphasis on comfortable, well-kept properties, providing the amenities

Farms & Homes

For a holiday with a difference, you can stay as a paying guest with friendly Australian families in a private home or on a working farm.

B&Bs come and go, so the best source of current information is the **Australian Bed and Breakfast Council** (ABBC) at www.australianbedandbreakfast.com.au/

The ABBC is comprised of the state and territory B&B associations, with overall responsibility for more than 1,000 B&Bs, and its excellent website details them state by state.

Similarly, **Australian Farmhost Holidays** at www.australiafarmhost.com offer a huge number of farm-stay options state by state – everything from small dairy farms in the hills to vast grain farming and sheep- and cattle-grazing properties.

required by travellers, but without the added luxuries.

Budget accommodations are simple, clean and modest, catering to the needs of economy-minded travellers. Some backpacker hostels are also included in this category, offering dormitory and multiple-bed rooms, but in friendly and interesting environments.

Sites

Attractions

HISTORIC BUILDINGS

The National Trust in Australia owns many historic properties and is dedicated to preserving these buildings in all parts of Australia. All of them are open to the public and Trust members are entitled to free entry to any of them. If you intend to visit a number of Australia's historic buildings it may be worth joining. Annual membership costs A$56 for an individual and A$77 for families. Non-members can pay to see particular properties.

National Trust Offices

Australian Capital Territory
Australian Council of National Trusts, Unit 14, 71 Constitution Avenue, Campbell ACT 2612; PO Box 1002, Civic Square, Canberra, ACT 2608. Tel: 02-6247 6766; www.nationaltrust.org.au
New South Wales
National Trust of Australia, Observatory Hill, Sydney, NSW 2000. Tel: 02-9258 0123 www.nationaltrust.org.au
Queensland
95 William Street, Brisbane QLD 4000. Tel: 07-3229 1788;
South Australia
Level 2, 27 Leigh Street, Adelaide 5000. Tel: 08-8212 1133; www.nationaltrustsa.org.au
Tasmania
6 Brisbane Street, Hobart 7000. Tel: 03-6223 5200; www.tased.edu.au/tasonline/nattrust
Victoria
Tasma Terrace, 4 Parliament Place,

East Melbourne, VIC 3000. Tel: 03-9656 9800; www.nattrust.com.au
Western Australia
The Old Observatory, 4 Havelock Street, West Perth, WA 6005. Tel: 08-9321 6088; www.ntwa.com.au

NATIONAL PARKS

Information on Australia's national parks can be obtained from the offices managing each region:
ACT: National Parks and Wildlife Service
6 Rutledge Street, Queanbeyan ACT 2620
Tel: 02-6297 6144. www.act.gov.au
NSW: National Parks and Wildlife Service
102 George Street, The Rocks, Sydney, NSW 2000
Tel: 1300-361 967. www.nationalparks.nsw.gov.au
NT: Parks & Wildlife, Northern Territory
PO Box 496, Palmerston, NT 0831
Tel: 08-8999 4555. www.nt.gov.au\ipe\pwcnt
QLD: Parks & Wildlife Service
160 Ann Street, Brisbane, QLD 4000
Tel: 07-3227 8185. www.epa.qld.gov.au
SA: Environment & Heritage
91–97 Grenfell Street, Adelaide, SA 5000
Tel: 08-8204 9000. www.environment.sa.gov.au
TAS: Department of Parks, Heritage and the Arts
22 Elizabeth Street, Hobart 7000
Tel: 03-6233 5732. www.parks.tas.gov.au
VIC: Parks Victoria
Level 10, 535 Bourke Street, Melbourne, VIC 3000
Tel: 131-963. www.parkweb.vic.gov.au
WA: Conservation and Land Management (CALM)
Technology Park, Western Precinct, 17 Dick Perry Avenue, Kensington, WA 6151
Tel: 08-9334 0333. www.naturebase.net

New South Wales

Sydney

The heart of NSW (some would say of Australia) is Sydney, the state capital and the largest city on the continent, with a population of 3.8 million.

The first settlement in Australia was made in 1788 at Sydney Cove, now known as Circular Quay. Sydney today is a major port and a bustling centre of industry, business and manufacturing. It covers 1,736 sq. km (670 sq. miles), making it considerably larger than Rome or Los Angeles county.

Geographically, Sydney is divided by the harbour into north and south. The famous Sydney Harbour Bridge spans these two areas. Most of the places of interest, including the city centre, are to the south of the harbour. In a few minutes, you can walk from Circular Quay to the Opera House, the Harbour Bridge and the Centrepoint Tower, which is a good viewing point in the heart of the Central

Special Fares

If you planning to move about, purchasing a three-day *Sydney Pass* could be a worthwhile investment. It covers all bus and ferry transport, including Sydney Explorer buses, harbour cruises, the Tramway (shuttle between Central Railway Station and Darling Harbour) and a return on the Airport Express. The *Sydney Pass* is available for 3, 5 or 7 days. Travel passes offer cheaper weekly rates, and a *Travel 10* ticket gives a discount for 10 trips.

Business District. To reach the North Shore, catch a ferry from Circular Quay or go by train.

The Sydney Visitor Centre is at 106 George Street, tel: 02-9240 8788, freecall: 1800-067 676; fax: 02-9252 8738, open daily 9am–6pm. It has an enormous range of brochures, leaflets and accommodation details for Sydney, and contact details for other NSW travel centres. The Sydney Information Booth is located in nearby Martin Place, open 9am–5pm weekdays, closed weekends.

Getting Around

FROM THE AIRPORT

The green and yellow Airport Express buses depart every 20 minutes for the city, making key stops along the route. Trains run about every 15 minutes between the city and the domestic and international terminals.

The State Transit Authority operates all public transport in Sydney. For information on all STA trains, buses and ferries from 6am–10pm daily, tel: 131 500. The front of the White Pages phone book also has information on Sydney's transport system.

BY TRAIN

Electric trains are by far the quickest way to get around. The service is fairly frequent and covers a large area of Sydney, including the central "City Circle" stations. Some services end at midnight when a limited Nightrider bus service takes over.

BY BUS

Sydney's extensive bus services have their main terminuses at Circular Quay, Wynyard and Central Railway Station. The bus information kiosk is located behind Circular Quay on the corner of Alfred and Loftus streets. The red Sydney

Sydney Tower

For the best bird's-eye view of Sydney (and even the Blue Mountains), take a trip up Sydney Tower on top of the Centrepoint complex. Located on Market Street between Pitt and Castlereagh, the tower is 305 metres (1,000 ft) high and comprises a viewing gallery, sky-lounge café and revolving restaurant. Open 9am–10.30pm daily; until 11.30pm on Saturdays.

Explorer bus is an STA tourist service which operates a continuous loop around the city's tourist sights. From 8.40am–5.25pm daily, it leaves at 20-minute intervals from Circular Quay, and you can hop on and off whenever you like.

Covering the eastern suburbs coastal route all the way to Watsons Bay, the blue Bondi & Bay Explorer departs every 20 minutes from Circular Quay or Bondi Beach.

The Tramway, a bus that looks like a tram, shuttles between Central Railway Station and Darling Harbour/Pyrmont every 10 minutes.

The Monorail circles above the retail centre before crossing to Darling Harbour and provides good views.

FERRIES AND CRUISES

The ferries are by far the nicest way of getting around Sydney. They all depart from Circular Quay, where a State Transit Authority office issues timetables and brochures outlining cruise services free of charge (it's located opposite Wharf 4).

The longest ferry run in the harbour is the trip to Manly, covering 11 km (7 miles) in 30 minutes.

For efficiency, the alternative Jetcat does the trip in half the time and is slightly more expensive. The shortest ride goes to Kirribilli and offers a stunning panorama of the city skyline, the

Opera House and the Harbour Bridge within a 10-minute trip. Ferries can also be a quick way of getting to Taronga Zoo, Watsons Bay and a host of other attractions. The Rivercat, a high speed catamaran, cruises all the way up the Parramatta River.

There is a variety of harbour cruises leaving Wharf 4 at Circular Quay through the morning, afternoon and evening. Two-hour "coffee cruises" depart at 10am and 1pm daily; reasonably priced, they provide good overviews of Sydney, with interesting commentary, unlimited coffee and biscuits, and comfortable seating. There are many other privately run harbour cruises but, in general, those run by STA ferries are less expensive.

LIGHT RAIL

Sydney's light rail glides from central station to Wentworth Park. Extensions to Glebe and the inner west and a loop through the city to Circular Quay are proposed.

TAXIS

All Sydney taxis are metered, so do not ride unless the meter is on. There is an initial A$2.65 hiring charge (called "flag fall"), then A$1.45 per kilometre thereafter. Between 10pm and 6am, this rate increases by 20 percent. A phone booking costs A$1.25 extra. The main taxi companies serving the inner city are:

Premier Cabs: 131-017
Taxis Combined: 02-8332 8888
Legion Cabs: 131-451
RSL Cabs: 02-9581 1111

In addition, there are companies that operate water taxis on the harbour. These are quite expensive – the price depends on the distance and time of day.

Harbour Taxis: 9299-0199
Taxis Afloat: 9955-3222

Where to Stay

IN SYDNEY

International (A$300–1,100)
Hotel Inter-Continental
117 Macquarie Street
Tel: 02-9253 9000
Fax: 02-9240 1240
www.interconti.com
Grand historic Treasury building provides the introduction to a spectacular central skylit courtyard, with accommodation rising above. Many rooms with classic harbour views. Located in the Circular Quay area, within minutes walking distance of the Opera House and harbour.

The Observatory Hotel
89–113 Kent Street
Tel: 02-9256 2222
Fax: 02-9256 2233
www.observatoryhotel.com.au
Discreet and elegant alternative to large hotels, tucked away behind Observatory Hill in The Rocks. Sydney's most sumptuous suites with antique-style furnishings, deep baths and excellent service. Facilities include a stunning star-ceilinged indoor pool and health spa, as well as an excellent restaurant. Popular with small groups of well-heeled business folk and romantic Sydneysiders.

Park Hyatt Sydney
7 Hickson Road, The Rocks
Tel: 02-9241 1234
Fax: 02-9256 1555
www.sydney.park.hyatt.com
Rated as the most luxurious hotel in Sydney, where every attention is paid to personal service. Spacious, supremely comfortable rooms have privileged water-level views of the harbour and Opera House. Ideal location in The Rocks area.

Quay West Sydney
98 Gloucester Street, The Rocks
Tel: 02-9240 6000
Fax: 02-9240 6060
www.mirvac.com.au
Another of the modern towers that front Sydney Harbour, but this one has self-contained luxury apartments, as well as executive penthouses. There's also a

Standard Categories

- **International** Hotels, resorts or historic manor houses of unquestioned five-star standard
- **Premier** Four-star standard, including hotel chains, with a range of reliable services
- **Moderate** Comfortable, well-kept properties
- **Budget** Simple, clean and modest accommodation

Roman bath-style swimming pool.
Shangri-La Grand Hotel
176 Cumberland Street, The Rocks
Tel: 02-9250 6000
Fax: 02-9250 6250
www.anahotel.com.au
Quintessential harbour views can be had from every room of this award-winning, 573-room modern tower hotel, one of several in The Rocks/Circular Quay area. Four excellent restaurants in the hotel.

Sheraton on the Park
161 Elizabeth Street
Tel: 02-9286 6000
Fax: 02-9286 6686
www.sheraton.com
Huge rooms with dramatic city and park views.

Sir Stamford at Circular Quay
93 Macquarie Street
Tel: 02-9252 4600
Fax: 02-9252 4286
www.stamford.com.au
Classical French furnishings and beautiful paintings create a distinguished ambience. Located in the business district, this is a "clubby" place, popular with business people. The excellent restaurant is *the* place to close a deal.

Premier (A$120–300)
Harbourside Apartments
2A Henry Lawson Avenue, McMahons Point
Tel: 02-9963 4300
Fax: 02-9922 7998
Terrific harbour views of the Opera House underneath the Sydney Harbour Bridge. Compact but comfortable – and the city ferry is right on the doorstep.

Hyde Park Plaza
38 College Street, Sydney
Tel: 02-9331 6933
Fax: 02-9331 6022
www.mirvachotels.com.au
Overlooking Hyde Park in the centre
of the business district, large
apartment-style rooms including full
kitchen facilities. Functional design.

Kirketon Boutique Hotel
229 Darlinghurst Road,
Darlinghurst 2010
Tel: 02-9332 2011
Fax: 02-9332 2499
www.kirketon.com.au
In the epicentre of hip Darlinghurst,
ultra-modern, minimalist-style
accommodation with restaurants
and bars.

Medina-Executive
359 Crown Street,
Surry Hills
Tel: 02-8302 1000
Fax: 02-9361 5965
www.medinaapartments.com.au
Surry Hills is an attractive and
peaceful terrace-house suburb not
far from the city centre, with a
concentration of galleries, antique
shops and restaurants. These are
serviced apartments.

Simpsons of Potts Point
8 Challis Avenue, Potts Point
Tel: 02-9356 2199
Fax: 02-9356 4476
www.simpsonspottspoint.com.au
Beautifully restored historic house
with authentic period decoration
throughout. Potts Point is known for
fashionable restaurants and cafés;
easy access to the city by bus or
train.

Sir Stamford Double Bay
22 Knox Street, Double Bay
Tel: 02-9302 4100
Fax: 02-9302 4140
www.stamford.com.au
Fastidious interior decoration, with
valuable original artworks. Each room
has a carefully designed theme –
there's even a Manhattan loft-style
room. Double Bay is a wealthy
suburb close to the city, known
primarily for its fashionable shopping.

The Waldorf Apartment Hotel
57 Liverpool Street
Tel: 02-9261 5355
Fax: 02-9261 3753
www.warldorf.aust.com

Glitzy tower containing one- and two-
bedroom apartments with good
views over the city centre and
Darling Harbour. At the high end of
this price range.

Moderate (A$80–200)

Coogee Bay Hotel
Corner of Coogee Bay Road and
Arden Street, Coogee
Tel: 02-9665 0000
Fax: 02-9664 2103
Heritage-style seaside pub, nicely
renovated. Located opposite
picturesque Coogee Beach with
ocean views from the front rooms.
Bus to city takes about 40 mins,
taxi 15 mins.

The Grantham
1 Grantham Street, Potts Point
Tel: 02-9357 2377
Fax: 02-9358 1435
www.thegrantham.com.au
Many of these apartments have
great views across the city skyline
to the Botanic Gardens and Sydney
Harbour. Functionally designed, with
all the facilities you need, the
rooms are good value for money.

The Hotel Bondi
Corner of Campbell Parade and
Curlewis Street, Bondi Beach
Tel: 02-9130 3271
Fax: 02-9130 7974
www.hotelbondi.com.au
Bondi's landmark historic pub, right
on the main street, has undergone
a series of renovations and can now
offer a moderate standard of
accommodation, with five bars, café
and entertainment. The pub is a bit
raucous, so it is worth staying here
only if you get a front room with
ocean view; for these, you need to
book well in advance.

The Manhattan Park Inn
International Hotel
6–8 Greenknowe Avenue,
Elizabeth Bay
Tel: 02-9358 1288
Fax: 02-9357 3696
www.parkplaza.com.au
Various standards of rooms available
in an elegant Art Deco building, many
with water views and balconies.
Walking distance to fine restaurants
and cafés, short taxi ride to city.

Morgan's of Sydney
304 Victoria Street, Darlinghurst

Tel: 02-9360 7955
Fax: 02-9360 9217
www.morgans.com.au
One of the "boutique" hotels
fashionably located in the Kings
Cross/Darlinghurst area. Aimed at
successful young business people,
Morgan's is stylish and
comfortable; the downstairs bar is
a scene for the "beautiful" people.
Paid parking only.

Regents Court
18 Springfield Avenue, Potts Point
Tel: 02-9358 1533
Fax: 02-9358 1833
www.regentscourt.com.au
The friendly management set up
this "designer" hotel for a clientele
of arts-orientated professionals.
Nestled in a surprisingly peaceful
backstreet of otherwise seedy
Kings Cross, these huge sparse
rooms of ultra-modern design lack
views, but guests meet on the
garden rooftop at cocktail hour.

Victoria Court Hotel
122 Victoria Street, Potts Point
Tel: 9357 3200
Fax: 9357 7606
www.victoriacourt.com.au
Historic boutique hotel and B&B in
elegant Victorian terraced house.
Central, quiet location in the heart
of Sydney's gastronomic precinct.

Budget (A$55–85)

Budget accommodation is mainly
found in Kings Cross, the central

Sydney's Hotels

Sydney has an almost
overwhelming choice of hotels.
The best method for making a
decision, after budgetary
considerations, is where in Sydney
you would like to be. Most of the
deluxe hotels are located in the
historic Rocks and city area. This
has the major advantage of being
right on Sydney Harbour, but there
are other inner-city suburbs with
harbour views. Potts Point, for
example, has a wealth of
accommodation, much of it
moderately priced. It provides
quick access to the city and has
many fine restaurants and cafés.

business district, Bondi or Manly. Victoria Street in Kings Cross has a score of privately run hostels for backpackers; it's also the place to network with other travellers in arranging lifts, buying cheap flights, or buying a car for that extended road odyssey around Oz. A short trip from the city, through the eastern suburbs, will take you to beautiful Bondi Beach. Glebe is also an attractive student neighbourhood with inexpensive options. Manly is a quieter beach suburb with a more family feel, with ferry transport to and from the city.

For details of the huge range of B&Bs on offer in Sydney, log onto www.australianbedandbreakfast. com.au/

Australian Sunrise Lodge
485 King Street, Newtown
Tel: 02-9550 4999
Fax: 02-9550 4457
Newtown is a fairly bohemian student suburb, about 10 minutes' drive from the city, with great-value ethnic restaurants, pubs with live bands, and an interesting vibe. A modern hotel with sunny double, triple and family rooms.

Broadway University Motor Inn
25 Arundel Street, Glebe.
Tel: 02-9660 5777
Fax: 02-9660 2929
Opposite the University of Sydney, an area known for its alternative lifestyle and a wide range of cafés.

Cremorne Point Manor
6 Cremorne Road,
Cremorne Point
Tel: 02-9953 7899
Fax: 02-9904 1265
A ferry ride across the harbour connects the charming suburb of Cremorne Point to the city. This is a restored Federation mansion with excellent harbour views.

Hostels (A$25–55 per person)
Manly Beach Resort
6 Carlton Street, Manly (corner of Pittwater Road)
Tel: 02-9977 4188
Fax: 02-9977 0524
Spacious house with dorm and double accommodation. Ferry to city takes 30 minutes.

Standard Categories

- **International** Hotels, resorts or historic manor houses of unquestioned five-star standard
- **Premier** Four-star standard, including hotel chains, with a range of reliable services
- **Moderate** Comfortable, well-kept properties
- **Budget** Simple, clean and modest accommodation

Sinclairs of Bondi
11 Bennett Street, Bondi
Tel: 02-8399 2518
Fax: 02-9744 0664
500 metres/yards east of Bondi Junction. Cooking facilities.

YWCA (Y On the Park)
5–11 Wentworth Avenue
Tel: 02-9264 2451
Fax: 02-9285 6289
Great inner-city location, with over 100 beds. Safe, clean and good facilities. Close to Oxford Street, over the road from Hyde Park.

For backpackers, there are three **Jolly Swagman** hostels in Kings Cross (also called **Sydney Central Backpackers**), tel: 02-9358 6600; 02-9358 6400; fax: 02-9357 4733.

OUTSIDE SYDNEY

International (A$200–375)
Blue Mountains
Less than two hours' drive from Sydney, the Blue Mountains are a popular getaway destination with a choice of accommodation in the main towns.

Blueberry Lodge and The Loft
Waterfall Road, Mount Wilson
Tel/fax: 02-4756 2022
Chalet in historic Blue Mountains village.

Lilianfels Blue Mountains
Lilianfels Avenue, Katoomba
Tel: 02-4780 1200;
Freecall: 1800-024 452
Fax: 02-4780 1300
www.slh.com/lilianfels
Well-managed, tranquil resort located near most Blue Mountains attractions. Popular indoor pool/ health club. Wonderful restaurant in

early 20th-century guest house makes for a special evening.
Rural NSW
Milton Park
Horderns Road, Bowral
Tel: 02-4861 1522
Fax: 02-4861 4716
One and a half hours' drive from Sydney, in the Southern Highlands, Milton Park is an elegant estate, offering horse riding, golf, tennis, bush walking and peaceful solitude. Fine cuisine using fresh seasonal produce.

Premier (A$130–350)
Peppers Fairmont Resort
1 Sublime Point Road, Leura
Tel: 02- 4784 4144
Fax: 02-4784 1685
www.peppers.com.au
Large hotel complex with magnificent mountain views. The resort is known for its golf courses and other sporting facilities and is often the choice for large business conventions.

NORTH OF SYDNEY

International
Casuarina Country Inn
Hermitage Road, Pokolbin, Hunter Valley
Tel: 02-4998 7888
Fax: 02-4998 7692
Striking garden and vineyard views are provided from nine fantasy-themed suites.

Kim's Beach Hideaway
Charlton Avenue, on the Beach, Toowoon Bay
Tel: 02-4332 1566
Fax: 02-4333 1544
www.kims.com.au
Ninety minutes north of Sydney, Kims has been a much-loved resort for generations. Now more luxurious than ever, it offers private beach houses, many facing directly onto the bay. And Kim's tradition of fresh hearty seafood dishes prevails.

Pips Beach Houses
14 Childe Street, Byron Bay
Tel/fax: 02-6685 5400
For romantic beachfront privacy, these are cabins hidden in the bush on the dunes of Belongil Beach.

Rae's on Watego's
8 Marine Parade,
Watego's Beach, Byron Bay
Tel: 02-6685 5366
Fax: 02-6685 5695
Near the Queensland border and
designed after a 1920s
Mediterranean villa with Indonesian-
inspired interiors. Guests enjoy five-
star cuisine in a terraced restaurant
overlooking the beach. No children
under 13.

Premier (A$110–240)
Byron Bay Beach Resort
Beside The Beach
Bayshore Drive
Byron Bay
Tel: 02-6685 8000
Fax: 02-6685 6916
www.byronbaybeachresort.com.au
This resort offers 78 self-contained
cabins set among native gardens of
large beachfront property.

Pelican Beach Resort Australis
Pacific Highway, Coffs Harbour
Tel: 02-6653 7000
Fax: 02-6653 7066
www.australishotels.com
Several hours' drive north of
Sydney, this large, well-run
establishment often has package
specials. Guests love the massive
landscaped swimming pool.

Pepper's Convent
Halls Road, Pokolbin, Hunter Valley
Tel: 02-4998 7764
Fax: 02-4998 7323
www.peppers.com.au
Early 20th-century Roman Catholic
convent with guest rooms and
restaurant.

Peppers Guest House
Ekerts Road, Pokolbin,
Hunter Valley
Tel: 02-4993 8999
Fax: 02-4998 7739
www.peppers.com.au
The extensive gardens are ablaze
in spring and autumn, but Peppers
is perhaps most famous for its
restaurant – Chez Pok.

Eating Out

SYDNEY

Although great restaurants are
located all over Sydney, some
neighbourhoods or streets have
become more popular. In the city
centre, the wharf area of The Rocks
has a wealth of seafood restaurants.
Highly recommended are **The Wharf
Restaurant** and the **Quay
Restaurant**, while former rugby star
David Campese's **Rocks Canterbury
store** serves the best coffee.

Macleay Street in Potts Point is a
bustling scene of Modern Australian
bistros; in the same
neighbourhood, Victoria Street is
scattered with fashionable cafés.

Further up is trendy Darlinghurst.
Le Petit Creme serves amazing
quality café fare to a thronging
clientele (the Sunday brunch is a
classic). **Fez Cafe**, also on Victoria
Street, is a hip hangout for "Modern
Middle Eastern" food and around
the corner, **Bill's** is an airy
environment for tranquil breakfasts
the morning after the night before.

The *Sydney Morning Herald Good
Food Guide* and *Cheap Eats in
Sydney* are two of the best guides
to either end of the restaurant price
spectrum. It's a daunting task to
recommend a few restaurants from
so many excellent options. There
are hundreds more great places,
covering a wide range of cuisines
and prices – however, you won't go
wrong with any of the following.
Note: BYO means "bring your own
alcohol".

Modern Australian
Claude's
10 Oxford Street, Woollahra
Tel: 02-9331 2325
Licensed or BYO. Fixed-price three
courses from A$125 per person.
The atmosphere at this
continually acclaimed restaurant
is one of serene elegance. Like
the private dining room of a
tasteful manor house, one can
relax in tranquillity, enjoying as
fine French/Australian cuisine as
Sydney has to offer.

Cottage Point Inn
2 Anderson Place, Cottage Point.
Tel: 02-9456 1011
You can arrive by boat (or by car
through the national park) for bush
dining at this seafood-dominated
establishment.

Freshwater
On the beach, Moore Road,
Harbord.
Tel: 02-9938 5575
A restaurant in a gracious old
mansion, offering plenty of
Australian options including fresh
local seafood.

Guillaume at Bennelong
Sydney Opera House,
Bennelong Point
Tel: 02-9241 1999
Licensed. This award-winning
restaurant now offers modern
French cuisine, with main courses
around A$35. Booking essential.

Lotus
22 Challis Avenue, Potts Point
Tel: 9326 9000
Signature dish is soft squid stuffed
with couscous and chilli, seasonal
best fish, or grain-fed T-bone steak.
Main courses about A$26.

Rockpool
107 George Street, The Rocks
Tel: 02-9252 1888
Licensed. Main courses around
A$45, plus drinks. The cutting edge
of Modern Australian cuisine with
crowd-pleasing Asian/European
creations. Glamorous environment
in keeping with the bill.

Native Australian
Edna's Table
204 Clarence Street
Tel: 02-9267 3933
Crocodile, kangaroo, emu and
sundry real Aussie "bush tucker"
offer you a comprehensive choice
from the diets developed in
Australia over the past 60,000
years or so.

American
Burgerlicious
215 King Street, Newtown, Sydney
Tel: 02-9519 7401
BYO. Full meals under A$50.
Informal American-style burger
house. Locals love Burgerlicious for
its low prices, real ingredients and
generous servings. Eat in or
takeout.

Chinese
Golden Century
393–399 Sussex Street, Sydney
Tel: 02-9212 3901

Sydney's Restaurant Scene

Thanks to the surge of excitement about Modern Australian cuisine and native foods or bush tucker, Sydney now has a multitude of upbeat bistros, brasseries and cafés in addition to the already vast choice of ethnic restaurants. Many of these, in turn, are creating new genres they call "Modern Italian" or "Modern Asian" as they too incorporate Australian produce.

Licensed and BYO. A\$40 per person, plus drinks. The best Cantonese preparation of the best Aussie seafood. Talk to your waiter for valuable advice on the menu.

Fu-Manchu
249 Victoria Street, Darlinghurst
Tel: 02-9360 9424
BYO. Mains average A\$35. A designer noodle bar with no pretensions, but serving quality Cantonese, northern Chinese and Malaysian dishes. Great value for the variety and authenticity of the food.

Greek
Diethnes
336 Pitt Street, City
Tel: 02-9267 8956
Licensed. Main courses A\$15–18. One of Sydney's oldest Greek restaurants. Traditional favourites like moussaka, lamb casserole, cabbage rolls and taramasalata, complemented by Greek coffee and sticky sweet baklava. Busy but friendly atmosphere.

Indian
Oh! Calcutta!
251 Victoria Street, Darlinghurst
Tel: 02-9360 3650
BYO. A\$25 per person. Exciting range of dishes include modern innovations such as the popular Kangaroo Sahk Khada. Excellent Tandoori. Plenty of vegetarian choices.

Italian
Buon Ricordo
108 Boundary Street, Paddington
Tel: 02-9360 6729
Licensed. Main courses A\$35–45. This much-loved restaurant provides a thoroughly Italian experience, in the decor, presentation and superbly conceived Neapolitan and Tuscan dishes. Described as a night at the Italian opera – *I Pagliacci,* to be precise.

Japanese
Japanese Restaurant on 36
Level 36, ANA Harbour Grand Hotel, 176 Cumberland Street, The Rocks
Tel: 02-9250 6123
Licensed. A\$60 per person, plus drinks. Quintessential harbour views and great sushi.

Tsukasa
200 Crown Street, East Sydney
Tel: 02-9361 3818
Licensed and BYO. Main courses around A\$25 per person, plus drinks. A relaxing alternative to many prim Japanese interiors. Reasonable prices and extensive selection.

Modern Asian-Mediterranean
Bambu
Bay 4, Overseas Passenger Terminal, West Circular Quay
Tel: 02-9247 6044
Main courses around A\$30. Signature dish is pan-fried snapper on braised daikon. Great views of Sydney's vibrant maritime bustle.

Thai
Sailors' Thai
106 George Street, The Rocks.
Tel: 02-9251 2466
A good main course is A\$20–32. Voted best Thai by a respected Australian food guide.

Vegetarian
Iku Wholefoods
25a Glebe Point Road, Glebe
Tel: 02-9692 8720
Around A\$10 per person. This counter-style café has provided many years of squeaky fresh organic dishes to happy Glebian vegetarians. Outdoor seating area, generous servings and no smoking make for a thoroughly wholesome experience.

Coffee Bars
Dean's
5 Kellett Street, Kings Cross, Sydney
Tel: 02-9368 0953
Licensed. A legendary late-night coffee shop in the tree-lined sidestreets of Kings Cross. This quirky, loveable place has the relaxed bohemian feel of Kings Cross when it was the preferred address of Sydney's artists, night-owls and creative types. Serves great coffee and tasty economical meal like nachos. Generous servings.

Piccolo Bar
6 Roslyn Street, Kings Cross, Sydney
Tel: 02-9368 1356
LIcensed and BYO. An inner-city Sydney classic. The Piccolo is a truly miniscule Italian-style coffee bar in busy Kings Cross. Squeeze in and watch the locals wander by – Roslyn Street sees lots of uniquely Kings Cross-style street activity.

RESTAURANTS WITH A VIEW

Sydney's harbour and beaches mean there are some excellent restaurants with great views:

Bathers Pavilion
4 The Esplanade, Balmoral
Tel: 02-9969 5050
Licensed. Main courses about A\$30. At the base of winding roads lies picturesque Balmoral Beach and the original 1920s bathers' pavilion. Modern Australian cuisine in a light, exclusive setting and very good service. Uninterrupted harbour views and sea breezes.

Catalina Rose Bay
Lyne Park, off New South Head Road, Rose Bay (between ferry wharf and seaplane base)
Tel: 02-9371 0555
Licensed. Main courses about A\$30. The terrace of this glass-fronted harbourside restaurant is a great place to be on a fine day.

Doyles on the Beach
11 Marine Parade, Watsons Bay
Tel: 02-9337 2007
Licensed. Main courses about
A$40. It's an institution – and
although the views are great, and
all the tables occupied at sunset,
the seafood dishes are not as
interesting as many of the newer
harbourside restaurants.

Jonah's
69 Bynya Road,
Palm Beach
Tel: 02-9974 5599
Licensed. Main courses about A$30.
Possibly the best ocean view in the
world. Guests can drive here or arrive
by seaplane to spend a glorious
afternoon either in the restaurant or
on the private garden terrace. French-
Mediterranean dishes incorporate
Australian produce.

The Pier
594 New South Head Road,
Rose Bay
Tel: 02-9327 6561
Licensed. Main courses about
A$50. Idyllic location and the best
seafood dishes in town. Oysters are
shucked on the spot, Queensland
reef fish are served, and the
harbour views are spectacular.

The Summit
Level 47, Australia Square,
264 George Street
Tel: 02-9247 9777
A revolving restaurant with aerial
views of Sydney and surrounds. So
unforgettable that you wouldn't
even notice if the food were bad,
which it isn't.

Attractions

SIGHTSEEING

The Rocks

Sydneysiders have been referring to
the area under the Sydney Harbour
Bridge as "The Rocks" for more
than 200 years. Australia's first
European settlers landed here, and
it is still, in a way, the heart of
Sydney. A well-preserved
neighbourhood of cobbled streets
and historic buildings, The Rocks is
best explored by foot – starting at
the Visitor Centre at 106 George
Street North. Here you can obtain

information and a walking tour map
of the area. The old warehouses
have been restored and turned into
gift shop/café complexes, such as
the **Argyle Centre** and **The Rocks
Centre**. The main places of interest
in The Rocks are the **Argyle Cut**,
Millers Point, **Lord Nelson Hotel**,
Hero of Waterloo Hotel, **Colonial
House Museum**, **Cadman's
Cottage**, **Sydney Observatory** and
the **National Trust Centre**.

Sydney Harbour Bridge

At the base of The Rocks stands
one of the great pylons of the
Harbour Bridge. The "old coat-
hanger" was completed in 1932 at
a cost of A$20 million. From here
it's a pleasant harbour walk around
Circular Quay to the Opera House.
For a unique experience, you can
rope yourself to a group of fellow-
adventurers and a guide, and climb
the bridge's main arch for the
ultimate harbour view.

Sydney Opera House

This gracious splay of curving walls,
soaring to 67 metres (220 ft),
poised centre-stage in Sydney
Harbour, has become an
internationally recognised symbol of
Australia. The Opera House is a fine
sight from any angle, especially
from the harbour and North Shore.
To get a feeling for the building,
take a stroll around the exterior to
study its form and space. Then take
one of the guided tours which
operate regularly from 9am (except
Christmas Day and Good Friday),
tel: 02-9250 7111. On Sunday
there is often free outdoor
entertainment on the harbourside
forecourt – everything from street
theatre to jazz bands – and there is
a good choice of restaurants
nearby.

The Parks

The eastern section of Sydney's
Central Business District (CBD) is
dominated by three beautiful parks
– the Royal Botanic Gardens, The
Domain and Hyde Park. The Royal
Botanic Gardens, the most
pleasant, was established in 1816.
If you are visiting the Opera House

on foot, simply continue around the
harbour through the big iron gate to
the garden promenade. Stretching
back from the harbourfront, ancient
trees and more than 400 varieties
of plants grow throughout the
park's 27 hectares (67 acres). If
you stick to the harbour walk you
will eventually approach Lady
Macquarie's Chair, the next harbour
headland, from where another fine
panorama can be enjoyed. Open
from sunrise to sunset, the gardens
include a very good restaurant,
tranquil ponds and special botanic
displays such as the Tropical
Pyramid Glasshouse.

The Domain is an open stretch of
grassland where on Sunday after
2pm some of Sydney's orators
climb on their soapboxes to
entertain anyone who will listen.
Hyde Park is the inner-city park,
with the Archibald Fountain and
Anzac Memorial.

Sydney's biggest park of ponds,
natural grasslands, and bush is
Centennial Park, in the eastern
suburbs; it also has cycling and
horse tracks and both mounts can
be hired nearby.

Museums and Galleries

Art Gallery of New South Wales
Situated across from the Domain,
the Art Gallery mounts important
temporary exhibitions, has an
excellent bookshop and a
comprehensive permanent
collection of Australian, European
and Aboriginal paintings. Open daily
10am–5pm, Wed till 9pm; www.
artgallery.nsw.gov.au.

Museum of Contemporary Art
Right at Circular Quay, in the
attractive Maritime Services
building. The focus is on Australian
and internationally significant
contemporary art. The café in front
is a very "in" place to dine, and the
bookshop has good postcards. Open
daily 10am–5pm; www.mca.com.au.

Equally impressive is the exciting
Museum of Sydney, built on the
site of the first Government House.
With a strikingly modern exterior,
the museum is a showcase for
state-of-the-art museum
installations, which include many

Ticket Through Time

A number of the city's most interesting historical museums are managed by the Historic Houses Trust of New South Wales. If you intend to visit more than three of these nine attractions, it would be worth purchasing a Ticket Through Time, which entitles you to admission to all the properties. Visit: www.hht.net.au/visit

artefacts found on the site. It also has an excellent book, gift and card shop that is worth a visit in its own right. Open daily 10am–5pm.

Further up Macquarie Street is the **Hyde Park Barracks Museum**, focusing on the daily lives of the convicts and set in a beautiful convict-designed building. The **Justice and Police Museum** offers a popular insight into the world of Sydney crime. Other attractions are **Vaucluse House** and gardens, **Elizabeth Bay House**, **Elizabeth Farm**, **Susannah Place** in the Rocks, and the 1950s' **Rose Seidler House**.

The **Australian Museum** – located at the corner of College and William streets, across from Hyde Park – features Australian natural history and includes an extensive Aboriginal section. Open daily 9.30am–5pm; www.austmus. gov.au.

The **Powerhouse Museum** of applied arts and sciences on Harris Street, Ultimo, is a totally different (and very exciting) museum. Located in a spectacular modern building, it allows visitors to operate working models of engines and see exhibits of early aeroplanes, gramophones, keyboard instruments, cameras, model ships and clothing. Open daily 10am–5pm; www.phm.gov.au.

The Powerhouse Museum is just a part of the massive **Darling Harbour** development – a sort of tourist/leisure park set on a harbour inlet, featuring the huge **IMAX cinema** and full of restaurants, shops, arcades, parks, pubs and harbourside walks.

Further Attractions

Beyond the city's business district, you'll find other destinations worth visiting:

Kings Cross is Sydney's sin centre. Apart from strip joints and sex shops, it has many genuinely good restaurants and lots of hookers. The outdoor café beside the El-Alamein Fountain at the end of Darlinghurst Road serves great cocktails at a reasonable price, making it a popular meeting place on a warm evening.

The adjoining suburbs of **Potts Point**, **Elizabeth Bay** and **Darlinghurst** are less seedy, and are great neighbourhoods to explore historic houses in tree-lined streets, cafés and bistro life.

Paddington is a bit further out from the city centre – about 4 km (2½ miles) southeast of Circular Quay. Called "Paddo" by locals, this area has narrow streets lined with beautifully restored Victorian terraced houses, as well as restaurants, pubs, antique shops and galleries, and the famous Paddington Bazaar on Saturdays (held in the churchyard at the corner of Oxford and Newcombe). It's the place for bargains on jewellery, handicrafts and clothes.

Taronga Park Zoo is a short ferry ride from No. 2 jetty at Circular Quay and houses an impressive gathering of Australian and other animals. It has one of the most attractive settings of any zoo in the world. In fact, taronga in Aboriginal means "view over the water". On arrival choose from the walk up, or the aerial safari – an overhead cable ride. Open daily 9am–5pm.

Fox Studios at Driver Avenue, Moore Park. The studio entertains with a hands-on approach to TV and film making. There are also cinemas, restaurants, bars, shops, live music and a comedy store. Open daily 10am–midnight; www. foxstudios.com.au

The Beaches

Along the coast south of Sydney harbour are about 32 km (20 miles) of good beaches. The closest

(and most famous) is **Bondi Beach**, where many a Sydneysider congregates on warm days. About 45 minutes from the centre by bus, 30 by train/bus combination, or 10 minutes in a taxi, Bondi is not the easiest suburb to get to, but the beautiful beach is well worth it. An ideal place to spend the whole day, Bondi has a range of great new cafés and bistros. Around the corner from Bondi is equally pretty **Tamarama**, followed by **Bronte** beach. The best surfing beaches are further south: Maroubra and Cronulla.

One of Sydney's best-known northern beach areas is **Manly**, a family-orientated resort suburb with both harbour and ocean beaches. On West Esplanade, the **Manly Art Gallery & Museum** houses an interesting exhibition which includes the history of surfing and beach culture. At the end of the beach, **Oceanworld** (open daily 10am–5.30pm; www. oceanworld.com.au) has a very good oceanarium. Beyond Manly, a string of oceanfront suburbs stretch 40 km (25 miles) north to **Palm Beach** and the spectacular **Barrenjoey Head**.

There are many tiny bay beaches within Sydney Harbour which are sheltered and calm, often with an exclusive atmosphere generated by protective locals. On summer weekends they tend to be crowded. **Lady Jane Beach** near South Head is a nudist beach. Topless bathing is allowed on most Sydney beaches.

The National Parks

Two superb national parks are within easy reach of the city, where you can walk, swim or observe the wildlife. **Ku-ring-gai Chase National Park**, on the southern banks of the Hawkesbury River, is only 25 km (15 miles) north of Sydney; there are many excellent bushwalks in the park, and some magnificent Aboriginal rock carvings. West Head offers a beautiful view across Pittwater. About 30 km (19 miles) south of the city is the **Royal National Park**. This is the second-oldest national park in the world and offers excellent bushwalking as well as good surfing beaches.

Information on all the national parks in the area can be obtained from New South Wales National Parks and Wildlife Service, www.npws.nsw.gov.au.

Excursions from Sydney

West of Sydney lie three historic towns: **Parramatta**, **Windsor** and **Richmond**. Among Australia's earliest settlements, they contain buildings dating back to the late 18th and early 19th centuries. Most of the historic buildings are open to visitors.

Featherdale Wildlife Park

Doonside, near Parramatta, has a large collection of native birds and other wildlife. You can cuddle a koala here. Open daily 9am–5pm, tel: 02-9622 1644; www.featherdale.com.au. Entrance fee.

The Blue Mountains

Located 110 km (70 miles) by road west of Sydney, these mountains form part of the Great Dividing Range that runs along Australia's east coast, once creating an impenetrable barrier to expansion inland. Today they provide a popular vacation retreat for Sydney residents. Katoomba is the main resort centre and trains run there from Sydney's Central Station on a regular basis. Sydney tour companies also operate day-trips to the Blue Mountains.

Hunter River Valley (around

Cessnock and Pokolbin).

It takes 3 hours by car to drive the 160 km (100 miles) north from Sydney to the Hunter River Valley, noted for its wineries. Be prepared for hot and dry conditions during the summer months. Most of the wineries are open to visitors; several Sydney tour companies make day-trips here, and most of the wineries put considerable effort into making possible purchasers feel at home.

Theatre, Film & Music

The **Sydney Opera House** is a focal point of fine performances, including concerts, opera, ballet, theatre and films, but it isn't the only venue. Among the larger performance venues are the Capitol Theatre, the State Theatre, Her Majesty's Theatre and the Theatre Royal.

The Sydney Theatre Company has a harbourside home in the Wharf Theatre – a renovated old wharf in the Rocks – and presents an extensive schedule of productions. The Sydney Dance Company occasionally performs here. The **Seymour Centre** stages a variety of unusual shows and the **Belvoir Street Theatre** has a history of experimentation. Smaller venues include the **Bay Street Theatre** in Glebe, the **Rep Theatre** in Newtown, the **Footbridge Theatre** at Sydney University and the stunning **Ensemble Theatre** at Milsons Point.

For foreign films, art films and generally good films, go to the **Valhalla Cinema** in Glebe, the **Chauvel**, the **Verona** or **Academy** in Paddington and the **Dendy** in the city or Newtown. The more commercial films are shown at multi-cinema complexes on George Street in the city. The majestic old **State Theatre** in the city is the site of the annual Sydney Film Festival.

Whatever your taste in music may be, it can be satisfied in Sydney. The Sydney Symphony Orchestra is an international-class orchestra; it appears regularly with leading Australian and international conductors at the Opera House.

To listen to jazz, try the **Basement** (29 Reiby Place) or **Soup Plus**, at 383 George Street in the city.

What's On

The best guide to entertainment in Sydney is in the *Sydney Morning Herald's* Metro section every Friday.

Nightlife

In some of the city's clubs and rock pubs you will be uncomfortable if you are over 30; in others if you are under 30. Dress codes vary, from de rigueur designer fashion to "neat casual". Sloppy or dirty clothing will often keep you out on the street. If you are one of those who look eternally young, you must have ID to prove that you're over 18 (the minimum legal drinking age). For up-to-date listings, consult Friday's *Sydney Morning Herald* Metro entertainment supplement, or check out www.sydney. citysearch.com.au.

The band scene is nearly always in the pubs, which are scattered throughout the city and suburbs; almost every little place will have live music on Friday and Saturday nights – check the *Herald*'s Metro section on Fridays for the line-up. In general, the best rock-pubs are in Surry Hills, Newtown and Glebe: try the **Excelsior** and the **Harold Park** (115 Wigram Road). Also good bets are the **Metro Theatre** in the city centre and **Selina's** in the Coogee Bay Hotel, Coogee Bay.

Sport

PARTICIPANT

Yachting The yachting season runs September–March. Races and regattas are held nearly every weekend between the 18-footers. A spectator ferry leaves Circular Quay at 1.30pm every Saturday and occasionally on other days. Spectators also turn out in full force each year for the Sydney-to-Hobart Yacht Race, on 26 December.

Surfing Surfing carnivals are held at one of Sydney's ocean beaches on most Saturdays between October and March. These consist of swimming races, surfboat races and board-paddling events. There are also professional and amateur surfboard-riding competitions in the summer and autumn months, but the location is often not selected till the day of the contest to take advantage of the best surf.

Golf and Tennis There are more than 80 golf courses within Sydney, nearly all of them open to the public. And for the tennis player, Sydney has public courts and private tennis clubs.

Shopping

Sydney's main shopping district is bounded by Martin Place, George, Park and Elizabeth streets. Here you'll find large department stores like David Jones and Grace Bros, the elegantly restored Queen Victoria Building (QVB) on George Street, the Royal, Strand and Imperial arcades, and the four-level Centrepoint shopping arcade that runs between Pitt and Castlereagh streets. Bargains include opals and sheepskin products.

Sydney's busiest area is around Martin Place and Pitt Street Mall. These pedestrian plazas provide seating for weary shoppers and at lunchtime on weekdays, office workers and shoppers gather to hear free entertainment.

A visit to Paddington Markets is a Saturday afternoon ritual: they're at the corner of Oxford Street and Newcombe. The Rocks markets operate all weekend.

SPECTATOR

Horse Racing The city has six tracks. Randwick is the closest and principal track, but races are held throughout the year at Canterbury, Rosehill and Warwick Farm. Trotting (harness) races are held Friday nights at Harold Park Paceway, and greyhound races on Saturday nights at Wentworth Park.

Football Four types of football are played in Sydney, the most popular being rugby league. Games are played in winter months at the Sydney Football Stadium at Moore Park and at other ovals in Sydney.

Cricket One of Sydney's main summer sports is cricket. The season runs October–March with international and interstate matches. You can watch cricket at the Sydney Cricket Ground at Moore Park.

Australian Capital Territory

Canberra

In 1912 an American architect, Walter Burley Griffin, won first prize in a worldwide competition to undertake the design of Australia's new capital, which, unlike any other Australian city, would be set inland. The Depression and two world wars slowed development of the site, and it wasn't until the 1950s and '60s that progress was really made.

Burley Griffin's plan was based on a combination of the City Beautiful and the contemporary vogue for garden cities. But underlying these are the geomantic principles of sacred geometry used in Rome, Greece and Ancient Egypt. The heart of the plan was the "parliamentary triangle". At the apex, on Capitol Hill, stands Australia's Parliament House, while below it sits the long white structure of its predecessor. Nearer Lake Burley Griffin are the other major elements of the grand plan: the National Library; the High Court; the National Science and Technology Centre; and Australian National Gallery.

The population today is 310,000; about 40 percent are under 26 years of age. Canberra is principally a city of government, education, public services and tourism.

Getting Around

FROM THE AIRPORT

Canberra airport is 7 km (4 miles) from the city centre. An Airliner Shuttle bus charges A$5 each way; several other bus companies operate regular services into town. Alternatively, the taxi fare is about A$16.

FROM THE CITY CENTRE

Fast-moving circular highways radiate out to a network of satellite suburbs. These are a joy for Canberra motorists but a pedestrian's worst nightmare. The only way to get around Canberra safely is by bus, car or bicycle.

BY BUS

ACTION bus services are adequate and modern, but you need to study a map and timetable together. A red double-decker bus offers a 24-hour pass and you can get on and off as often as you like. Tel: 131-710.

BY BICYCLE

Cycling is perhaps the most pleasant choice for sightseeing in Canberra, as the terrain is flat and bike paths are extensive. Bicycles can be hired by the hour, by the day, or by the week. If you intend hiring a bike make sure to get a copy of the *Canberra Cycleways* map from the tourist office or bookshops.

Where to Stay

CANBERRA

Because Canberra is so spread out, location is important. While some hotels are close to the shopping

Tourist Information

The Canberra Tourism Visitor Information Centre is a 10-minute walk from the city centre, down Northbourne Avenue (tel: 02-6205 0044; open Mon–Fri 9am–5.30pm, weekends and public holidays 9am–4pm; www.visitcanberra.com.au) You can also tune the radio to 98.9 FM for tourist information.

and business district, others are within walking distance of the National Gallery and Parliament House. Each outer suburb has its own shopping complex and a number of restaurants.

International (A$200–350)
Hyatt Hotel Canberra,
Commonwealth Avenue
Yarralumla
Tel: 02-6270 1234
Fax: 02-6281 5998
www.hyatt.com.au
This is the place to stay in Canberra if your budget allows it, and well worth a visit if it doesn't. A part of the city's history, the Hotel Canberra is an elegant example of Australian Art Deco, restored by the Hyatt chain. Custom-designed 1920s carpets, period-outfitted staff and interior balconies. Set on extensive landscaped gardens and located within the Parliamentary Triangle. Easy walking distance from major tourist attractions.

Premier (A$110–260)
Canberra Rex Hotel
150 Northbourne Avenue
Braddon
Tel: 02-62485311
Fax: 02-6248 8357
www.canberrarexhotel.com.au
Reliable four-star hotel, popular with business people. An easy walk from the central business district, with an indoor pool, sauna, gymnasium and Millies Restaurant.
Olims Canberra Hotel
Corner of Limestone and Ainslie avenues, Braddon
Tel: 02-6248 5511;
Freecall: 1800 020 016
Fax: 02-6247 0864
Only about 1 km (⅔ mile) from the city centre and very close to the war memorial, this Heritage-listed property has split-level executive apartments designed around a central courtyard.
The Parkroyal Canberra
Binara Street, City
Tel: 02-6247 8999
Fax: 02-6257 4903
www.crowneplaza.com.au
Centrally located next to Canberra Casino and Convention Centre, close

to shopping, theatres, cinemas and restaurants, the Parkroyal has 24-hour room service, a health club and undercover parking.
Rydges Canberra
London Circuit
Canberra City
Tel: 02-6247 6244
Fax: 02-6257 3071
Closer to the commercial centre of the city, rooms provide great views of the lake and surrounding mountains. There are several pleasant bars in which to unwind.

Moderate (A$80–200)
Diplomat Boutique Hotel
Corner of Canberra Avenue and Hely Street, Griffith
Tel: 02-6295 2277;
Freecall: 1800-026 367
Fax: 02-6239 6432
www.flagchoice.com.au
Canberra's boutique hotel offers honeymoon packages in a Diplomatic Spa Suite. Large rooms, extensive facilities, 3 km (2 miles) from city centre.
Forrest Inn and Apartments
30 National Court, Forrest
Tel: 02-6295 3433
Freecall: 1800-676 372
Fax: 02-6295 2119
Close to Parliament House and National Gallery; in leafy surrounds. Some rooms have park views.
Oxley Court Serviced Apartments
Oxley and Dawes streets
Kingston
Tel: 02-6295 6216;
Freecall: 1800 623 960
Fax: 02-6239 6085
www.oxleycourt.com.au
A good choice for families and small groups. Spacious fully self-contained apartments a short drive from the city centre.

Budget (A$55–85)
Hotel Heritage
203 Goyder Street, Narrabundah
Tel: 02-6295 2944
Freecall: 1800-026 346
Fax: 02-6239 6310
www.hotelheritage.com.au
Hotel rooms and family apartments 12 minutes from the city centre and close to many of Canberra's tourist attractions.

Standard Categories
- **International** Hotels, resorts or historic manor houses of unquestioned five-star standard
- **Premier** Four-star standard, including hotel chains, with a range of reliable services
- **Moderate** Comfortable, well-kept properties
- **Budget** Simple, clean and modest accommodation

Hostels (A$15–25 per person)
Canberra YHA Hostel
Dryandra Street, O'Connor
Tel: 02-6248 9155
Fax: 02-6249 1731
www.yha.com.au
One of the best YHA Hostels in Australia. A short bus ride to the city centre, or rent one of the hostel bicycles. A travel desk provides help with future arrangements.
Victor Lodge
29 Dawes Street, Kingston
Tel: 02-6295 7777
Friendly place, close to the railway station, 5 minutes drive from Parliament House. Offers twins or bunk rooms with shared bathrooms. Breakfast included, and bicycles available to rent.

OUTSIDE CANBERRA

Premier (A$110–240)
Brindabella Station
Brindabella Valley Station
Brindabella
Tel: 02-6236 2121
Fax: 02-6236 2128
Historic homestead set in classic Australian bush, between two National Parks. A superior country retreat, with five comfortable rooms.

Eating Out

WHERE TO EAT

Top public servants need to be well fed, so there have always been a number of excellent but conservative restaurants serving the discreet business luncheon. Now Modern Australian cuisine is loosening up Canberra, adding upbeat cafés, breakfast hot-spots, espresso bars, and designer pizza parlours to many neighbourhoods.

Note: BYO means "bring your own alcohol".

Modern Australian
Aubergine
18 Barker Street, Griffith
Tel: 02-6260 8666
Griffith's unglamorous shopping centre has been dragged into culinary fame by a much-admired international chef. Main courses at A$30 offer international choices at suburban prices.
Jean-Pierre at Fringe Benefits
54 Marcus Clark Street
Capital Centre
Tel: 02-6247 4042
Licensed. Main courses about A$25. An oldie and a goodie. Famous wine cellar dictates the menu. Outdoor seating.

American Southwest
Tutu Tango Cafe and Bar
124 Bunda Street
Canberra City
Tel: 02-6257 7100
Licensed. Main courses about A$15–20. Funky Tex-Mex bistro with refreshingly upbeat crowd.

Chinese
The Chairman & Yip
108 Bunda Street, Civic Centre
Tel: 02-6248 7109
Licensed and BYO. East-meets-West fusion, upstairs and downstairs. Try the duck pancake with shiitake mushrooms and hoisin sauce.

Turkish
Ottoman Cuisine
Corner of Boughton and Blackall streets, Barton
Tel: 02-6273 6111
Licensed. Main courses about A$30. The only problem with this fabulous Turkish restaurant is getting a table. This is where Canberra's chefs eat on nights off. Separate cigar lounge.

Attractions

SIGHTSEEING

National Capital Exhibition
The National Capital Exhibition at Regatta Point on the north shore of Lake Burley Griffin helps put Canberra's development into perspective. Open daily 9am–5pm, it houses a collection of models, photos and diagrams to show how this planned city really works.

Black Mountain
For vistas, head for the top of Black Mountain or Mount Ainslie. From the Black Mountain summit, you can survey the Australian National University, the Civic Centre and Lake Burley Griffin, with the Captain Cook Memorial water-jet in the distance. There is also the 195-metre (640-ft) Telstra tower, with viewing galleries and revolving restaurant. The summit is open to the public daily 9am–10pm.

Mount Ainslie is closer to the city, and a popular spot for night visits. (Clear Outback skies are stunning for star-gazing.) From this summit, you can see central Canberra, including Parliament House, the National Library, Australian War Memorial and Lake Burley Griffin.

From either summit, it is easy to see how the twin hubs of Capitol Hill and City Hill dominate Canberra's design, and how Lake Burley Griffin neatly divides the city into two. The shoreline of the lake extends for some 35 km (22 miles); it's not recommended for swimming but is fine for boating.

There are also several places of interest around the lake. The Carillon, standing on Aspen Island and connected to the shore by a

United Nations

Canberra's abundance of foreign diplomats has helped create the wide selection of ethnic restaurants and cafés, with Chinese, Japanese, Malaysian, Mediterranean and Turkish food highly recommended.

footbridge, was built to mark Canberra's 50th anniversary and was presented by the British Government to the Australian people. It is one of the largest free-standing bell towers in the world and its 53 bells are either played by hand or automatically; recitals take place regularly.

Parliament House
The spectacular Parliament House on Capitol Hill was built for the 21st century, and occupies a 32-hectare (80-acre) site with landscaped gardens. Designed to preserve the original hill's shape, the building is underground, with its rooftop grassed over. The project cost A$1.1 billion and was completed in 1988 to mark Australia's Bicentenary. Open daily 9am–5pm daily; www.aph.gov.au.

National Gallery of Australia
One of the best reasons for visiting Canberra, this vast modern gallery located at the bottom of the parliamentary triangle houses a superb art collection on three levels. Opened in October 1982, the collection ranges from traditional Aboriginal art to contemporary works. It features Australian artists such as Tom Roberts, Arthur Streeton, Charles Conder, Albert Tucker and Arthur Boyd. The galleries have glass panels which unobtrusively incorporate surrounding parkland views. Open daily 10am–5pm daily; tel: 02-6240 6502; fax: 02-6240 6529; www.nga.gov.au.

National Library
Opened in 1968, the National Library is regarded by many as Canberra's most elegant building. Not a public lending library, it provides services for other libraries and researchers. Brilliant features in the foyer include three Aubussion tapestries and 16 coloured-glass windows by Australian artist Leonard French. Displays include rare books, manuscripts, special exhibitions and a cannon from Captain Cook's ship *The Endeavour*. The Library is open 9am–9pm

Captain Cook Memorial

Close to the Commonwealth Avenue bridge, the Captain Cook Memorial Jet hurls a column of water 140 metres (460 ft) up into the air. It is one of the world's highest and at any one time there can be up to 6 tonnes of water suspended in mid-air.

On the shore opposite the jet is a large metal globe on which are traced Cook's three great voyages of discovery.

Mon–Thurs, 9am–5pm Fri and Sat and 1.30pm–5pm Sun. Guided tours are available on Thursday at 12.30pm, tel: 02-6262 1111; fax: 02-6257 1703; www.nla.gov.au.

High Court

The High Court building is another impressive structure. Opened by the Queen in May 1980, the core of the design is a public hall 24 metres (79 ft) high, encircled by open ramps which rise to the courts. It is linked to the National Gallery by a pedestrian bridge. Open daily 9.45am–4.30pm; tel: 02-6270 6811.

Questacon – National Science and Technology Centre

This distinctive drum-shaped structure on the lake shore specialises in hands-on science and technology exhibitions. Allow at least 3 hours for a fascinating visit. Open daily 9am–5pm; tel: 02-6270 2800, freecall: 1800-020 603; www.questacon.edu.au.

Australia War Memorial

One of Canberra's biggest tourist attractions, the War Memorial draws over 1 million visitors a year. It houses a fascinating collection of dioramas, artefacts and pictorial exhibitions. The focus of the memorial is the Hall of Memory where, in 1993, the body of the Unknown Australian Soldier was brought home from France and entombed. Open daily 10am–5pm, tel: 02-6243 4211; www.awm.gov.au.

The Royal Australia Mint

Just about the only big factory in Canberra, the RAM on Denison Street, Deakin, is one of the largest and most modern mints in the world. Built at a cost of A\$9 million, it produces metal currency for a number of other countries besides Australia and houses a rare coin collection. Open Mon–Fri 9am–4pm (when you can watch the coins being produced), weekends and public holidays 10am–4pm; tel: 02-6202 6800 or 1300-652 020; fax: 02-6202 6953; www.ramint.gov.au.

National Botanic Gardens

On the lower slope of Black Mountain, the Botanic Gardens are devoted entirely to native Australian flora. Planting began in 1950, and the gardens were opened in 1970. The gardens include numerous species of eucalyptus, plants used by Aborigines, and a rainforest zone – achieved in Canberra's dry climate by a special "misting" system. Open daily 9am–5pm, Jan and Feb till 8pm; tel: 02-6250 9540; fax: 02-6250 9599; www.anbg.gov.au.

Embassies

Over 60 countries maintain diplomatic representatives in Canberra, and their buildings form a tourist attraction of their own. The British High Commission was the first diplomatic office in Canberra in 1936, followed in 1940 by the US Embassy.

The embassies are mostly south and west of Capitol Hill, scattered through the suburbs of Red Hill, Forrest and Yarralumla. Many of the buildings have been designed in the architectural style of the country the mission represents, such as the US Embassy in a red-brick Williamsburg Mission style and the Thai Embassy with its upswept roof corners and gold-coloured roof tiles. (See Useful Addresses, page 337.)

Nightlife

Because of Canberra's liberal licensing laws, quite a few bars are open 24 hours a day. The ageing **Canberra Casino** on Constitution Avenue opens at 10am on Fridays and closes at 4am the following Monday. The student community of the ANU (Australian National University) has live bands perform at the **ANU Union Bar** during term; big-name touring bands play at the **Refectory**.

The **Canberra Theatre Centre** on Civic Square contains a theatre, playhouse and gallery, and presents everything from Shakespeare to rock music. Apart from the cinema complexes around the Civic Square area and Manuka, the National Gallery and the National Library have scheduled films.

Tilley's Devine Café Gallery, Wattle Street, Lyneham, tel: 02-6249 1543, is one of Canberra's more bohemian venues, featuring national and local musicians, storytellers, poetry readings and art exhibitions. Originally set up as a "women only" centre, the outcry forced Canberra to change its sex-discrimination laws and it is now open to all.

Consult the Good Times section in the Thursday edition of the Canberra Times for what's on. Also the free monthly magazine BMA lists bands and other events.

Shopping

London Circuit is the civic and business heart of Canberra. A series of shopping complexes lie close to Civic Square, with department stores, boutiques, cafés and gift shops.

Each suburb has its own comprehensive shopping complex. South of the lake, **Manuka Shopping Centre** is an upmarket location, including a cinema centre, several bars and stylish eateries. Canberra's city shops are open Mon–Thurs 9am–5pm, Friday 9am–9pm and Saturday 8.30am–noon.

Victoria

Melbourne

Melbourne might not be as visually spectacular as Sydney, but it continues to lay claim to being the fashion, food, cultural and financial centre of Australia.

Don't let Melbourne's conservative appearance fool you – the city does hum. Its reputation for bad weather, however, is probably deserved: the climate is totally unpredictable, and it's possible to experience all four seasons in one day.

The heart of the inner city, the "Golden Mile", contains the administrative and commercial hub of Melbourne, its chief shopping streets, and the main hotels and theatres. The perimeters are the Yarra River on the south, Spencer Street on the west, La Trobe Street on the north and Spring Street on the east. For a bird's-eye view, go to the observation deck on level 55 of the Rialto Towers building at 525 Collins Street (the tallest office building in the Southern Hemisphere).

Information on Victoria can be obtained from Tourism Victoria, *see page 340*.

Getting Around
FROM THE AIRPORT

Melbourne's airport is 22 km (14 miles) from the city centre. A taxi costs about A$26–30; for about half that price, the Skybus departs every half hour.

PUBLIC TRANSPORT

Called the Met, Melbourne's public transport system is one of Australia's best. **Trams** form the basis of the system. There are about 750 trams and they operate as far as 20 km (12 miles) out of the city. **Buses** are the secondary form of public transport, often taking over when trams are out of service. **Trains** connect an underground city loop to the outer suburbs.

A good idea is to visit the Met Shop. Located at 103 Elizabeth Street in the city, it has a useful "Discover Melbourne" kit and provides all the information you could ever need. There is a wide choice of tickets that enable travel over various periods of time and throughout the various zones of the city (zone 1 is big enough to cover most visitors' purposes). There are daily and weekly options, and tickets for use on both trams and buses. A brochure from the Met Shop outlines the options and advises which are the best tickets for your plans.

Transport Information

For telephone information on all public transport call the **Met Public Transport Information Centre**, tel: 131-638; 6am–10pm daily or visit www.victrip.com.au.

BY TAXI

Melbourne's transport system tends to curl up and go to sleep around midnight, after which taxis are the only form of transport available. Melbourne City Taxis, tel: 03-9335 3536.

BY BICYCLE

Melbourne is fairly flat, which affords the cyclist a number of good long tracks. Bike paths lie along the Yarra River, the Maribyrnong and the Merri Creek. For general cycling information, contact **Bicycle Victoria** at Level 10, 446 Collins Street, tel: 03-8636 8888; www.bv.com.au.

Where to Stay

Melbourne has a wide range of accommodation dispersed throughout the city. There are a number of "designer" or "boutique" hotels with fashion-conscious interiors, as well as a range of apartment-style accommodation, which often provide more space and facilities for the same price as a hotel. The seaside suburb of St Kilda offers moderate accommodation. The classified columns of *The Age* newspaper on Wednesdays and Saturdays are also a good guide to new and off-beat places.

MELBOURNE

International (A$250+)
Crown Promenade Hotel
Yarra Bank
Tel: 03-9292 6688;
Freecall: 1800-776 612
Fax: 03-9292 6677
www.crownpromenadehotel.com.au
This 39-floor hotel towers above the Yarra River and a vast casino and entertainment complex that includes cinemas, restaurants and live entertainment.
Grand Hyatt Melbourne
123 Collins Street
Tel: 03-9657 1234 or 131-234
Fax: 03-9650 3491
www.melbourne.grand.hyatt.com
Ostentatious display of brass and marble right down to the huge black marble bathrooms. Popular with business conventions.
Hotel Como
630 Chapel Street, South Yarra
Tel: 03-9825 2222;
Freecall: 1800-033 400
Fax: 03-9824 1263
www.mirvachotels.com.au
Many of the rich and famous wouldn't stay anywhere else. The Como wins awards year after year for its attention to comfort and uniquely designed suites. In the fashionable South Yarra district, famous for its fine restaurants and boutiques.
Sheraton Towers Southgate
Southgate Avenue, Southbank
Tel: 03-8696 8888
Fax: 03-9690 6581

Standard Categories

- **International** Hotels, resorts or historic manor houses of unquestioned five-star standard
- **Premier** Four-star standard, including hotel chains, with a range of reliable services
- **Moderate** Comfortable, well-kept properties
- **Budget** Simple, clean and modest accommodation

www.sheraton.com
Central to the Southgate Development, this highrise promotes an almost English, aristocratic ambience, with a butler on each floor. Private promenade to the shopping district.

The Sofitel
25 Collins Street
Tel: 03-9653 0000
Fax: 03-9650 4261
www.sofitelmelbourne.com.au
Guest rooms start on the 36th floor and offer sweeping views across Melbourne and Port Phillip Bay. Le Restaurant has entered the American Express Restaurant Hall of Fame.

The Windsor
103 Spring Street
Tel: 03-9653 6000
Fax: 03-9633 6001
www.thewindsor.com.au
For the old wealth of Melbourne, there is no question about the Windsor's supremacy. This majestic National Trust building in the centre of Melbourne is one of the few in Australia originally built as a hotel. Intended in 1883 to provide the most luxurious accommodation in Melbourne, the Windsor in many respects still holds that title. Excellent service, old-world interiors and a famous high tea at 3pm.

Premier (A$150+)

Adelphi
187 Flinders Lane
Tel: 03-9650 7555
Fax: 03-9650 2710
An ultra-modern designer hotel in the heart of the city. Spectacular views from the roof-top bar and pool.

Le Meridien at Rialto
495 Collins Street
Tel: 03-9620 9111;
Freecall: 1800-331 330
Fax: 03-9614 1219
European-style hotel in historic building, within walking distance of the Casino, World Congress Centre and business district.

Manor House Apartments
36 Darling Street, South Yarra
Tel: 03-9867 1266
Fax: 03-9867 4613
www.manorhouse.com
Well-furnished apartments in the exclusive restaurant and shopping district of South Yarra.

Savoy Park Plaza International
630 Little Collins Street
Tel: 03-9622 8888;
Freecall: 1800-036 188
Fax: 03-9266 8877
www.parkplazamelbourne.com
An intimate 1920s hotel, recently restored and promoting an elegant, club-like atmosphere.

Moderate (A$80+)

Albert Heights Serviced Apartments
83 Albert Street
East Melbourne
Tel: 03-9419 0955
Fax: 03-9419 9517
Modern apartment units, all facing a central garden courtyard and spa pool. Functional but tasteful, the units include all expected facilities.

Batmans Hill Hotel
66–70 Spencer Street
Tel: 03-9614 6344;
Freecall: 1800-335 308
Fax: 03-9614 1189

www.batmanshill.com.au
Hotel named after Melbourne's founder with an elegant historic exterior; the style is old-fashioned and friendly.

Carlton Clocktower Quest Inn
255 Drummond Street, Carlton
Tel: 03-9349 9700;
Freecall: 1800-062 966
Fax: 03-9349 2542
www.clocktower.com.au
Stylish apartments in bustling Lygon Street area.

Downtowner on Lygon
66 Lygon Street, Carlton
Tel: 03-9663 5555;
Freecall: 1800-800 130
Fax: 03-9662 3308
www.downtowner.com.au
Carlton is the cosmopolitan location of this hotel near the University. Stylishly decorated rooms. Guests receive gold membership to the Melbourne City Baths.

Hotel Grand Chancellor
131 Lonsdale Street
Tel: 03-9656 4000;
Freecall: 1800-331 006
Fax: 03-9662 3479
www.grandhotelsinternational.com
Comfortable rooms, close to Melbourne Cricket Ground and shopping district.

Budget (A$55–85)

Georgian Court
21–25 George Street
East Melbourne
Tel: 03-9419 6353
Fax: 03-9416 0895
www.georgiancourt.com.au
Comfortable Bed & Breakfast situated on a tree-lined street,

March Means Festivals in Melbourne

March is usually the best time of year in Melbourne, packed with events taking a punt on the good weather. **Moomba**, one of Australia's largest outdoor festivals, is held in the first two weeks of March. Moomba is an Aboriginal word meaning "let's get together and have fun".

Over 200 activities include the world's best water skiers on the Yarra, the bizarre birdman contest

for amateur aviators, and games, music and rides in the Alexandra Gardens.

Later in March, the **Antipodes Festival** is Australia's largest ethnic celebration and reputedly the biggest Greek festival in the world.

Also look out for the **Food and Wine Festival**, the **International Dragon Boat Festival** and the start of the **Melbourne International Comedy Festival**.

Tourist Information

For the most comprehensive range of free brochures and information on Melbourne, visit the Tourist Information centre at Federation Square, corner of Swanston & Flinders streets, open daily 9am–6pm, or call 132-842.

across from beautiful Fitzroy Gardens and just a short walk to the city centre. Thirty-one rooms; dinner available most nights.

Olembia Guest House
96 Barkly Street, St Kilda
Tel: 03-9537 1412
Fax: 03-9537 1600
Cosy and friendly guesthouse with dorm rooms, singles and doubles. Very good facilities, heating, parking and a pleasant guest lounge.

The Victoria Hotel
215 Little Collins Street
Tel: 03-9653 0441;
Freecall: 1800-331 147
www.victoriahotel.com.au
Fax: 03-9650 9678
Budget, standard and superior rooms offered in this good standard hotel. Excellent location, within walking distance of the CBD.

The Nunnery
116 Nicholson Street, Fitzroy
Freecall: 1800-032 635
Converted Victorian building close to the city, with comfortable heated rooms at different price ranges, good facilities and a friendly atmosphere. Dormitory-style accommodation for under A$30.

Other budget-priced hotels are concentrated on the Spencer Street end of the city, around the bus and train terminal. The **Explorers Inn** at 16 Spencer Street, tel: 03-9621 3333, freecall: 1800-816 168; fax: 03-9621 1922, is a modern hotel with simple but good rooms.

Hostels (from A$20 per person)

Backpacker accommodation is mainly concentrated around St Kilda. Contact the **Backpacker's Travel Centre**, 250 Flinders Street, tel: 03-9654 8477; fax: 03-9650 3290, or the **Youth Hostels**

Association, tel: 03-9670 3802.
The Hotel Y
489 Elizabeth Street
Tel: 03-9329 5188
www.ywca.net
Old but comfortable, secure and well-maintained downtown complex. All rooms have showers and toilets.
Queensberry Hill YHA Hostel
78 Howard Street, North Melbourne
Tel: 03-9329 8599
Fax: 03-9326 8427
Huge property with fine facilities. Breakfast and dinner service available.

OUTSIDE MELBOURNE

International (A$200–400)
Lake House
King Street, Daylesford
Tel: 03-5348 3329
Fax: 03-5348 3995
www.lakehouse.com.au
Located in "Spa Country", 90 minutes from Melbourne, this is a luxurious retreat on the shore of Lake Daylesford with one of Victoria's finest restaurants. Everything from the pastries to the preserves are made on the premises. While you're there, you can visit local wineries, a sheep station and "Hanging Rock" (scene of the picnic in Peter Weir's film).
Mount Buffalo Chalet
Mount Buffalo
Tel: 03-5755 1500
Spectacularly situated atop an escarpment in Victoria's high country, the chalet has a wide range of summer and winter activities. Sweeping views of the Great Dividing Range, snow clad in winter, and the green valleys below.

Premier (A$140–200)
Comfort Inn Shamrock
Corner of Pall Mall and Williamson streets, Bendigo
Tel: 03-5443 0333
Fax: 03-5442 4494
www.powerscourt.com.au
Grandiose country hotel from the height of the gold-mining period. Ornate roof structure and surrounding balconies. Rooms range from inexpensive

"traditional" rooms to deluxe suites.
Cumberland Lorne
150 Mountjoy Parade, Lorne
Freecall: 1800-037 010
www.cumberland.com.au
A memorable scenic drive down the Great Ocean Road, and you're in one of Victoria's favourite seaside playgrounds. The Cumberland offers a variety of suites with wonderful views and complimentary recreational acitivities, right in the heart of the friendly town.
Hotel Pension Grimus
149 Breathtaker Road,
Mount Buller
Tel: 03-5777 6396
Fax: 03-5777 6127
www.pensiongrimus.com.au
This is a great place to stay at Mount Buller, Victoria's premier ski resort area. Legendary skiier hosts Hans and Lotte Grimus (Hans has a ski lift named after him) run a friendly, great-value lodge. All rooms have double spa baths. Families welcome; babysitting available.

Moderate (A$80–180)
Mt Ophir Estate
Stillards Lane
Rutherglen
Tel: 02-6032 8920
Fax: 02-6032 9911
www.mount-ophir.com
Historic winery buildings, plus two homesteads with four bedrooms in each. Emu and elk farm, vineyards and forests, as well as organic cropping farm.
Southern Grampians Cottages
35 Victoria Valley Road
Dunkeld
Tel: 03-5577 2457
Fax: 03-5577 2489

Standard Categories

- **International** Hotels, resorts or historic manor houses of unquestioned five-star standard
- **Premier** Four-star standard, including hotel chains, with a range of reliable services
- **Moderate** Comfortable, well-kept properties
- **Budget** Simple, clean and modest accommodation

www.grampianscottages.com.au
Attractive log-style cabins, self-contained with wood fires, spas and kitchens, in bushland setting. Located next to National Park full of wildlife and nature walks.

Budget (A$55–85)
Amaroo Caravan Park and YHA Hostel
Corner of Church and Osborne streets, Cowes
Tel: 03-5952 2548
Fax: 03-5952 3620
In the main town of Phillip Island, this is the best budget accommodation by far. Friendly hostel and caravan park with evening meals, bicycles for hire and organised tours to the Penguin Parade and Wilsons Prom.

Eating Out

Melburnians take their evening meal seriously: they make a real night of it. Good restaurants lie throughout the city, but certain streets have become concentrated restaurant rows.

Chapel Street, in exclusive South Yarra, is an ever-evolving centre for fashionable and pricey eateries, as is the Southgate Development on the Yarra River.

Fitzroy Street, St Kilda, is a young and lively scene of door-to-door cafés, bars and bistros of all cuisines, and the beachfront restaurants are chaotically popular on weekends. For the hippest scene, try Brunswick Street in Fitzroy: Melburnians head there with a bottle of wine or two tucked under their arms to promenade up and down before choosing one of the dozens of very reasonably priced café-restaurants.

Excellent Italian food can be found everywhere in Melbourne today. Lygon Street, Carlton, was for years the place to go, with its many casual bistros lining the streets; these days, although still retaining some local colour, Lygon Street can be a bit touristy. Similarly, Little Bourke Street was always known for its Chinese restaurants, but Modern Chinese and Asian restaurants can now be found in any suburb – as can

A City that Prides itself on its Food

Melbourne likes to think of itself as Australia's culinary capital, and many other Australian visitors to the city acknowledge its supremacy (at the very least, for Italian food). There is also an abundance of fine Modern Australian restaurants catering to the needs of Melbourne's well-heeled gourmets. The state of Victoria produces a range of excellent wines, meats and cheeses, the staples for serious foodies.

fine Japanese, French, Greek, Turkish, Lebanese, Indian, Vietnamese and Thai.

Melbourne is also famous for its high-quality produce markets. If you're staying in a self-contained apartment, take advantage of the celebrated Prahran or Queen Victoria markets, where you can purchase every Victorian speciality for your own gourmet creation. Even Melbourne's pub food is of high standard.

Many of Melbourne's less expensive restaurants use the BYO (bring your own alcohol) system. You can choose from a wide selection of excellent local wines in any bottle shop. Even with a small corkage fee, the result is a considerable saving.

Modern Australian
Ezard at Adelphi
187 Flinders Lane
Tel: 03-9639 6811
Licensed. Full meals A$75–115.
Gets good reviews every time. This chic, award-winning restaurant in central Melbourne serves up a spectacular combination of Japanese, Chinese and seafood dishes. The menu's wide selection is sure to please everyone, including the most fussy of diners.
Jacques Reymond
78 Williams Road, Windsor
Tel: 03-9525 2178
Licensed. Main courses A$38–45.
Housed in a glamorous Victorian mansion, this is French haute cuisine at its finest.
The Stokehouse, St Kilda
30 Jacka Boulevard
St Kilda
Tel: 03-9525 5555
Licensed. Main courses A$28–36.
Right on the beach, in the original bathing pavilion. The upstairs

restaurant is more formal and pricey, serving carefully prepared seafood, with great views of the bay. Downstairs attracts a casual and occasionally deafening young crowd on the weekend; it has less elaborate, but still good, food (try the seafood pizzas).
Vlado's Charcoal Grill
61 Bridge Road, Richmond
Tel: 03-9428 5833
Licensed. Full meals A$50–75.
Vlado's is a steak house institution, serving some of the best steaks in Melbourne. A good place for a hearty, filling meal after a busy day of out-and-about sightseeing.

Chinese
Bamboo House
47 Little Bourke Street
Tel: 03-9662 1565
www.bamboohouse.com.au
Licensed. Main courses A$20–30.
A long-running institution; the menu extends to Shanghai and Beijing dishes, and the waiters are very helpful.
Chine on Paramount
Shops 9–10, Paramount Centre
108 Bourke Street
Tel: 03-9663 6556
Cantonese cuisine in the city's Chinese eatery quarter. Main courses A$14–60
Flower Drum
17 Market Lane
Tel: 03-9662 3655
Licensed. Main courses A$30–60.
Regarded by many as the best Cantonese restaurant in Australia. Guests are welcome to choose from the menu, but usually discuss their options from the freshest available ingredients. Slightly Western presentation, without diluting the flavours.

Where to Eat

For a comprehensive listing and review of Melbourne restaurants, *The Age Good Food Guide* is available from bookshops and is excellent value for money.

Greek
Jim's Greek Tavern
32 Johnston Street
Collingwood
Tel: 03-9419 3827
BYO. Main courses A$20–30.
This courtyard restaurant specialises in seafood; your choice from the counter is chargrilled for you.

Italian
Becco
11–25 Crossley Street
Tel: 03-9663 3000
www.becco.com.au
Reliably authentic Italian fare. Main courses $25–30.
Cafe Di Stasio
31a Fitzroy Street
St Kilda
Tel: 03-9525 3999
Licensed. Main course A$30–50. A loyal crowd fills the attractive dining room and outdoor tables for the house specialities and operatic atmosphere.
Pellegrini's Espresso Bar
66 Bourke Street
Tel: 03-9662 1885.
Melbourne people have long known that the best coffee is served here. Stand, lean or perch on stools, Milano style.

Japanese
Akita
34 Courtney Street
North Melbourne
Tel: 03-9326 5766
Licensed and BYO. Main courses A$25. One of the best in Australia. Famous for sushi and tempura, but also has excellent specials list.
Kenzan
Lower Ground Floor
Collins Place, 45 Collins Street
Melbourne
Tel: 03-9654 8933
Licensed. Main courses A$20–30. The most formal Japanese

restaurant in the city, popular with visiting Japanese businessman, and with an excellent vegetarian banquet for lunch.

Lebanese
Abla's
109 Elgin Street
Carlton
Tel: 03-9347 0006
BYO. Main courses A$20–30. Where Lebanese choose to eat and a place where the worthwhile dishes go way beyond falafel.

Seafood
Toofey's
162 Elgin Street
Carlton
Tel: 03-9347 9838
Licensed. Main courses A$25–30. Seafood restaurant recommended by the *Age Good Food Guide.*

Thai
Lemongrass
176 Lygon Street
Carlton
Tel: 03-9662 2244
Main courses A$20–40. Authentic Royal Thai and regional dishes.

Attractions

State Library
This complex takes up the whole block between Russell and Swanston streets. The library has a domed octagonal reading room with a great atmosphere and is open daily.

Old Melbourne Gaol
A block further up Russell Street is the Old Melbourne Gaol and Penal Museum. Built in 1841, it is now owned and operated by the National Trust. This is where bushranger Ned Kelly was hanged and with its many penal relics on display, it is a gruesome reminder of Australia's early convict days. Open daily 9am–5pm.

The National Gallery
The Ian Potter Centre at the National Gallery of Victoria, situated in Federation Square, contains the finest and most comprehensive collection of Australian art

anywhere in the world. Open Mon–Thur 10am–5pm, Fri till 9pm, Sat, Sun till 6pm;
www.ngv.vic.gov.au.

Victoria Arts Centre
The Victoria Arts Centre is on St Kilda Road. This complex includes the excellent Melbourne Concert Hall and the State Theatre, Playhouse and George Fairfax Studio, as well as two exhibition spaces and a café. It can be readily identified by its 115-metre (350-ft) laser-lit spire. Tours of the complex, and of backstage areas, can be booked, tel: 03-9281 8000;
www.vicartscentre.com.au.

The Yarra River and Southbank
Murky brown though it may be, the Yarra is a much-loved feature of Melbourne. Many locations in the city afford pleasant views, which often include graceful rowing teams. There are park sites along the river for barbecues, beautiful historic bridges and a stylish walkway linking the city with the cosmopolitan Southgate development, which features upmarket restaurants, cafés, boutiques, the Sheraton Towers Hotel and sculptures.

The Gardens
Victoria calls itself the "Garden State", and, in Melbourne, it is easy to see why. Fully one-third of the city area is taken up by parkland. The **Royal Botanic Gardens**, between Alexandra Avenue and Domain Road, are simply the finest gardens in Australia. They cover 40 hectares (100 acres) and contain some 12,000 plant species. Open daily from sunrise to sunset, the Gardens are just a part of the larger park known as **The Kings Domain**, which contains the Shrine of Remembrance, La Trobe's Cottage and the Sidney Myer Music Bowl.

Alexandra Gardens is the popular lunchtime retreat for city office workers. **Queen Victoria Garden** has a 10,000-plant floral display clock as its focal point.

At the eastern end of Collins Street are **Fitzroy Gardens** and the adjacent **Treasury Gardens**, where magnificent English elms provide shade for a quiet picnic lunch.

In Fitzroy Gardens, surrounded by lawns and covered by ivy, is Captain Cook's Cottage, which was brought from Yorkshire and reassembled in 1934. Open daily 9am–5.30pm.

Queen Victoria Market

A Melbourne institution, this century-old market is the city's retail produce centre and a multi-cultural hubbub of stalls trading in poultry, fruit and vegetables. Located on the corner of Peel and Victoria streets, it opens at 6am (9am on Sunday) and continues until 2pm on Tuesday and Thursday, 6pm Friday, 3pm Saturday and 4pm Sunday (closed Monday and Wednesday); www.qvm.com.au.

Melbourne Cricket Ground

The MCG was the central stadium for the 1956 Olympics. It can hold over 100,000 spectators and remains Australia's biggest sporting venue. It also contains the Australian Gallery of Sport & Olympic Museum, which houses Aussie sporting memorabilia. Open daily 10am–3pm with hourly tours; www.mcg.org.au.

Melbourne Museum

Opened in 2000, this is Australia's largest museum and its many interactive attractions include displays on science and natural history and an Aboriginal Centre. The complex also features an IMAX cinema. Open daily 10am–5pm; www.melbourne.museum.vic.gov.au. Entrance fee.

Royal Melbourne Zoo

A famously well-designed zoo, and one of the oldest in the world. It lies just north of the city centre in Parkville and provides creative walk-through environments, a butterfly enclosure and an excellent gorilla forest. During January/February the zoo stays open until 9.30pm for Zoo Twilights. Open daily 9am–5pm; www.zoo.org.au. Entrance fee.

Scienceworks Museum

This collection of tactile displays aims to make science and technology fun, and includes a Planetarium and Pumping Station. Located at 2 Booker Street, Spotswood. Open daily 10am–4.30pm; tel: 03-9392 4800.

Day Tours Around Melbourne

While Melbourne's immediate setting is undramatic, there are regions of stunning beauty all around.

To the east of the city, the **Dandenong Ranges** are one of the most popular day-trip destinations. The hills are cool, green and packed with giant tree ferns that benefit from the altitude and heavy rainfall. One of the major attractions is **Puffing Billy**, a restored steam train that runs along a 13-km (8-mile) track from Belgrave in Melbourne to Emerald Lake Park. The round trip takes 2 hours.

Tucked away beneath the foothills of the Great Dividing Range some 65 km (40 miles) northeast of Melbourne, **Healesville** is an idyllic pleasure resort in the valley of the Watts River. The top attraction here is the **Healesville Wildlife Sanctuary**, internationally famous for its totally natural enclosures. Open daily 9am–5pm; tel: 03-5957 2800; www.zoo.org.au.

One of Melbourne's most popular excursions is to see the "Fairy Penguin Parade", when the flightless birds come ashore on **Phillip Island** every evening at dusk. The island is joined to the mainland by bridge and offers very good surf beaches. Tel: 03-9585 5730.

Private companies also run tours along the scenically spectacular Great Ocean Road to the famous **Port Campbell National Park** with its amazing natural rock formations known as the **Twelve Apostles**.

Theatre/Film/ Nightlife/Music

The best listings for Melbourne's lively arts scene can be found in the Entertainment Guide in every Friday issue of *The Age* newspaper.

Melbourne is noted for its high-quality live performances of comedy, theatre and music.

There are always theatre productions at the city's major arts venue, The **Victoria Arts Centre**, which has four theatres. Other major commercial theatres include the grand **Princess Theatre**, 163 Spring Street; **Her Majestys**, 219 Exhibition Street; the **Comedy Theatre**, 240 Exhibition Street and the spectacularly refurbished 2,000-seat **Regent Theatre**. The Melbourne Theatre Company is the major theatrical company, performing at the **Russell Street Theatre** and **La Mama**.

The Last Laugh was the birthplace of Melbourne's reputation as comedy capital and it is still going strong. Situated in the **Athaenum Theatre** at 380 Lygon Street, Carlton. The **Melbourne International Comedy Festival** offers three weeks of the best comedy in Australia *(see Events, page 335)*.

The peak months for the arts in general are March, during the **Moomba Festival**, and October for the **Melbourne International Festival of the Arts**, the **Fringe Festival** and the **Writers Festival**.

The Melbourne Symphony Orchestra performs at a variety of locations between March and October.

Quality art and independent films are shown at **Astor Cinema** in St Kilda and the **Kino** in Collins Street, the **Valhalla** in Northcote and both the **Carlton Moviehouse** and **Cinema Nova** in Carlton.

Much of Melbourne's rock and jazz scene is found in its thriving pub venues. Listen to the gig guide on the FM stations 3RRR, 3MMM and 3PBS for what's on. The **Esplanade Hotel** in St Kilda has been a good rock bet for years, as have the **Punter's Club** in Brunswick Street and the **Fitzroy** and the **Tote** in Richmond. A popular jazz venue is **Ruby Red** in Drewery Lane in the city. Cover charges vary widely depending on what night of the week and what band is playing. Shows are free on some nights, but generally cost from around A$8.

Melbourne offers a huge choice of nightclubs and wine bars offering cheap gigs. Just stroll along Brunswick Street, Fitzroy and take your pick. Melbourne also has a thriving Irish pub scene, from the more traditional **Molly Blooms** in Port Melbourne to the Guiness-inspired chain of **P.J. O'Briens** in Southgate. Most of the nightclubs in the "West End" King Street strip have been turned into table-top dancing and men's clubs.

Check out *The Age* for listings of gay and lesbian venues.

Shopping

Melbourne sees itself as Australia's major fashion centre. In fact, "shopping tours" have become one of the city's biggest tourist draw cards: they include lunch and an itinerary that takes in Melbourne's famous factory outlets and seconds shops. Try **Shopping Spree Tours**, tel: 03-9596 6600.

In the city centre, shoppers find many of the major department stores, such as Myer, David Jones and Daimaru. Other shopping centres include the **Melbourne Central** complex, with its multi-level glass atrium. **Collins Place** offers over 40 stores, all under a transparent roof, and hosts an "Australian-Made Art & Craft Market" every Sunday. The **Sportsgirl Centre** is an attractive and well-designed modern complex, and **Australia on Collins** features over 60 stores, many with imported fashions. Suburban shopping complexes are also huge. **Chadstone** shopping complex is the largest in the Southern hemisphere. In South Yarra and Toorak, **Chapel Street** and **Toorak Road** are for the

well-heeled only. Younger, cooler designers tend to congregate along **Brunswick Street, Fitzroy**. Richmond is a popular strip of factory outlets and bargain clothing shops where you can also buy clothes by young designers.

Melbourne also has several famous shopping arcades. The oldest, the **Royal Arcade**, dates from 1870 and, along with the intimate **Block Arcade**, it is one of Melbourne's landmarks. Street markets are also very popular in Melbourne: there's the lively **Queen Victoria Market**, while the comprehensive **Prahran Market** is where you'll find all the Melbourne gourmands.

Sports

To see the locals cast away their Victorian reserve, any major sporting event will do – but football and horse racing are the surest bets. Australian Rules Football – a mixture of rugby, soccer and Gaelic football – is at its best in Melbourne. Matches are held every Saturday, some Friday nights and Sundays during the April–September season. The finals pit the two top teams at the Melbourne Cricket Ground before more than 100,000 fanatical supporters.

Melbourne's other great passion is horse racing, held year-round on the metropolitan courses at Flemington, Caulfield, Mooney Valley and Sandown. Flemington is the home of the **Melbourne Cup**, an internationally famous racing event held on the first Tuesday in November. On this day, the entire nation stops to follow the race on radio or television. Meanwhile, all Melbourne is at the track where huge amounts of champagne and betting money flow. It's also the fashion event of the season.

December to February is the season for international test cricket matches played at the Melbourne Cricket Ground, where the Boxing Day test forms the year's highlight.

South Australia

Adelaide

Although its population is just over 1 million, Adelaide manages to retain many of the charms of a much smaller city. It is dignified and calm, with a superb setting: the city centre is surrounded by a ring of parks and, further out, the metropolitan area is rimmed by the Mount Lofty Ranges.

Adelaide is an easy city to get to know, since the streets are laid out in a rigid grid pattern. The main street through the centre of the town is King William Street, but the main shopping street is Rundle Street, with a mall closed to traffic. The Torrens River separates the city centre from North Adelaide, which has some of the finest residences in Australia.

The South Australian Visitor and Travel Centre is at 18 King William Street (open Mon–Fri 8.30am–5pm; 9am–2pm weekends). Call centre with full booking service, tel: 1300 655 276; www.southaustralia.com.

Getting Around

FROM THE AIRPORT

The international airport, 8 km (5 miles) from the city centre, has a Skylink shuttle bus, stopping at major hotels. The domestic airport (also used for flights to Kangaroo Island) is slightly further away. A taxi into the city centre costs about A$15.

PUBLIC TRANSPORT

Adelaide has bus and train services, plus one tram that runs between Victoria Square and the beach suburb of Glenelg. Concession, special-offer and one-day unlimited travel tickets are available. A free Bee Line bus follows the city shopping circuit from Victoria Square to the railway station along King William Street; it runs every 5 minutes from 7.40am–6pm daily except Friday when it continues to 9.20pm. The GGC or City Loop is another free bus – running every 15 minutes – it does a wider circuit of the city stopping at or near most main sights. Detailed maps are available from Tourism South Australia.

All information regarding the Adelaide transport system is available from the Office of Public Transport on the corner of King William and Currie streets, tel: 08-8210 1000.

BY BICYCLE

Running alongside the Torrens River is the 40-km (25-mile) long Linear Park Bike and Walking Track, one of the best in Australia. You can hire bikes from the Linear Park Bike Hire, tel: 08-8223 6271.

Where to Stay

ADELAIDE

Adelaide has been spaciously planned, so if you need to be within walking distance of the Festival Centre, South Australian Art Gallery, and lively East End neighbourhood, make sure to stay in the central business district. However, North Adelaide is just a short distance across the Torrens River and has a wealth of historic B&Bs with views of the Adelaide Hills. The suburb of Glenelg is an attractive beachfront community with many Mediterranean-style houses and restful ocean views.

International (A$200+)
Hyatt Regency Adelaide
North Terrace
Adelaide

Standard Categories

- **International** Hotels, resorts or historic manor houses of unquestioned five-star standard
- **Premier** Four-star standard, including hotel chains, with a range of reliable services
- **Moderate** Comfortable, well-kept properties
- **Budget** Simple, clean and modest accommodation

Tel: 08-8231 1234 or 131 234
Fax: 08-8231 1120
www.adelaide.hyatt.com
Luxurious tower accommodation and a casino housed in an historic railway station. Best location in the centre of town, right beside the Adelaide Festival Centre. Rooms provide excellent views of the city. Upper-floor guests receive "Regency Club" membership entitling them to free evening cocktails.
Stamford Grand
Jetty Road
Glenelg
Tel: 08-8376 1222;
Freecall: 1800-882 777
Fax: 08-8376 1111
Beautiful views of the ocean or the Adelaide Hills from this grand highrise resort in peaceful Glenelg. Award-winning hotel provides extra-large rooms and touches of the Victorian era.
Stamford Plaza Adelaide
150 North Terrace
Adelaide
Tel: 08-8461 1111;
Freecall: 1800-500 175
Fax: 08-8231 7572
www.stamford.com.au
Adelaide's original five-star hotel includes a delightful terrace garden for breakfasts and buffets. In the centre of town with city views.

Premier (A$120–250)
All Seasons Adelaide Meridien
21–37 Melbourne Street
North Adelaide
Tel: 08-8267 3033
Fax: 08-8239 0275
www.adelaidemeridien.com.au
Fashionable street in North Adelaide known for its cafés,

boutiques and parklands. Modern terraced structure comprises standard and executive suites.
North Adelaide Heritage Apartments & Cottages
109 Glen Osmond Road
Eastwood
Tel/fax: 08-8272 1355
www.adelaideheritage.com
Manages many B&Bs in Heritage-listed properties – including manor houses, early settlers' cottages, a fire station and iron-lace villas – in the historic boulevards of North Adelaide.

Moderate (A$80–180)
Chifley On South Terrace
226 South Terrace
Tel: 08-8223 4355
Fax: 08-8232 5997
www.chifleyhotel.com
With views of the attractive South Parklands directly opposite, this 4-star property is 15 minutes' walk to the city and close to the business centres of Parkside, Unley and Wayville.
International Hotel Adelaide
62 Brougham Place
North Adelaide
Tel: 08-8267 3444;
Freecall: 1800-888 244
Fax: 08-8239 0189
www.hoteladelaide.com.au
Scenic views of the city and surrounding gardens in a prime location in North Adelaide just a short stroll from the city centre. Good value.
Mercure Grosvenor Hotel
125 North Terrace
Tel: 08-8407 8888
Fax: 08-8407 8866
www.mercure.com.au
Opposite the Star City casino in the centre of town, this makes an ideal base for walking to all major attractions.

Budget (A$55–85)
Budget accommodation in central Adelaide is limited – a wider selection can be found in the attractive beachside suburb of Glenelg.
Glenelg Beach Resort
1–7 Moseley Street
Glenelg
Tel: 08-8376 0007

Standard Categories

- **International** Hotels, resorts or historic manor houses of unquestioned five-star standard
- **Premier** Four-star standard, including hotel chains, with a range of reliable services
- **Moderate** Comfortable, well-kept properties
- **Budget** Simple, clean and modest accommodation

www.glenelgbeachresort.com.au
120 beds, everything from eight-share dorms to family apartments

Princes Lodge
73 Lefevre Terrace
North Adelaide
Tel: 08-8267 5566
Fax: 08-8239 0787
www.princeslodge.com.au
Friendly management and good location in North Adelaide, within walking distance of the city. Light breakfast is served.

Hostels: (from A$20 per person)

Adelaide Backpackers Inn
112 Carrington Street
Tel: 08-8223 6635
www.tne.net.au/abackinn
Dormitories and annexe with singles and twins. Free hot apple pie and ice cream every night.

Adelaide Youth Hostel
135 Waymouth Street
Adelaide
Tel: 08-8414 3010;
Freecall: 1800-222 942
Fax: 08-8414 3015
www.yha.com.au
A modern YHA hostel with good facilities; movies every night.

OUTSIDE ADELAIDE

International (A$500–1,100)

Thorngrove Country Manor
Glenside Lane
Stirling
Tel: 08-8339 6748
Fax: 08-8370 9950
www.slh.com
About 20 minutes by car from

Adelaide, this is a Gothic fantasy complete with turrets and gables. Although it sounds tacky, the Manor offers five-star luxury, with large private suites furnished with valuable antiques, as well as a fine restaurant.

Premier (A$110–240)

Collingrove Homestead
Eden Valley Road
Angaston
Tel: 08-8564 2061
Fax: 08-8564 3600
www.collingrovehomestead.com.au
National Trust-listed homestead in the Barossa Ranges, with extensive English gardens and original antiques; ideal for a peaceful escape.

Lighthouse Keeper's Cottage
Kangaroo Island
Tel: 08-8559 7235
Fax: 08-8559 7268
Stay in one of the unique heritage cottages in Kangaroo Island's wilderness. Bookings handled by National Parks & Wildlife, South Australia, Flinders Chase National Park, Kangaroo Island.

Padthaway Homestead
Riddoch Highway
Padthaway
Tel: 08-8765 5039 or
08-8765 5555
Fax: 08-8765 5554
www.padthawayhomestead.com
Magnificent 19th-century mansion amid the Padthaway Estate vineyards, home of fine Australian champagne-style wines. Six rooms, cosy lounges with fireplaces and a relaxed friendly service.

Moderate (A$80–180)

Arkaroola Tourist Resort & Wildlife Sanctuary
Arkaroola, via Port Augusta
Tel: 08-8648 4848;
Freecall: 1800-676 042
Fax: 08-8648 4846
www.arkaroola.on.net
Part of the huge Arkaroola/Mt Painter Sanctuary, a rugged Outback landscape 600 km (373 miles) north of Adelaide, rich in native flora and fauna. Winner of SA Tourism Awards.

Desert Cave Hotel
Hutchison Street
Coober Pedy
Tel: 08-8672 5688;
Freecall: 1800-088 521
Fax: 08-8672 5198
www.desertcave.com.au
Deluxe underground hotel in Australia's most famous opal-mining outback community (2½ hours' flight from Adelaide; only one hour from Ayers Rock). All residents live below ground as an escape from the desert sun. Natural textures of naked rock walls and impressive skylit foyer.

Langmeil Cottages
89 Langmeil Road
Tanunda
Mobile: 0408-089722
Beautiful views from self-contained units, with the use of bicycles, barbecue and swimming pool.

Budget (A$55–85)

The Underground Motel
Catacomb Road
Coober Pedy
Tel: 08-8672 5324;
Freecall: 1800-622 979
Fax: 08-8672 5911
A more economical choice in (or under) Coober Pedy, also with natural rock walls; friendly comfortable place with a guest kitchen for self-catered breakfasts.

Eating Out

Adelaide easily compares with Sydney and Melbourne as a gastronomic centre. In fact, for price alone, it's number one – even the best restaurants charge less than A$30 for main courses, which would cost nearly twice that in Sydney. The city has always been a bastion of Modern Australian cuisine. Thanks to Adelaide's fine dry climate there are dozens of places to relax in the open air. And the "liquid lunch" becomes a tempting option when Australia's best wines, from the nearby Barossa Valley, are served at bargain rates on every corner.

Adelaide dining can be broken into three major areas:

Central City

Botanic Gardens Restaurant and Kiosk

Botanic Gardens
North Terrace, Adelaide
Tel: 08-8223 3526
Licensed. Two courses cost around
A$35. Lunch only, daily. On a fine
day there's no better choice for
lunch than the patio of this superb
restaurant. Black swans bob on the
lake by your table, while scents
from the gardens add to the
dreamlike setting. Wandering in the
rose garden after lunch provides an
ideal end to the meal.

MBC Bar & Restaurant

The Embassy, 96 North Terrace
Tel: 08-8124 9912
Chic restaurant with stylish décor
and excellent service, an emphasis
on local cuisine, with an average
main course at A$30–40.

Other restaurants in the city
area worth mentioning are
Rigoni's, 27 Leigh Street, tel: 08-
8231 5160, an Italian lunchtime
spot which is a real scene for
journos, politicians and hangers-
on; **Universal Wine Bar**, 285
Rundle Street, tel: 08-8232 5000,
slick and stylish with an
impressive wine list and ever-
changing menu; and **The Oxford
Hotel**, 101 O'Connell Street, tel:
08-8267 2652, a great bistro
offering excellent service and
outside dining.

Rundle Street East

This is where to head in search of
cheaper, more exciting meals. Ethnic
influences from Adelaide's Greek,
Italian, Indian and Thai communities
dominate the lively East End district
concentrated on Rundle Street
beyond the mall. At night, join the
throngs strolling past endless
upbeat eateries occupied by the

Worth Leaving Town

Outside Adelaide, **The Magill
Estate Restaurant**, at 78 Penfold
Road, Magill, tel: 08-8301 5551,
about 8 km (5 miles) from the
city at the historic Magill Estate
vineyard is highly recommended.

Hotel Kitchens

Bear in mind that the five-star
hotels in Adelaide are home to
excellent restaurants.

The Grange Restaurant at
the Hilton International (tel: 08-
8217 2000) flourishes under
the legendary Modern
Australian chef Cheong Liew
(credited with virtually founding
New Aussie Cuisine), while
Blake's at the Hyatt Regency
(tel: 08-8231 1234 or 131 234)
has one of the country's most
famous wine lists.

fashionable crowd; when the Fringe
Festival is happening, kitchens often
don't close before 3am.

Try **Austral Hotel** for Modern
Australian pub cuisine, or **Lemon
Grass**, an upmarket Thai downstairs
with teppanyaki Japanese upstairs.
It's noisy but fun. The best coffee
in the street is at *Al Fresco*, and
their outdoor tables are the ideal
spot for watching the curious mix of
people going by.

Amalfi Pizzeria Ristorante

29 Frome Street, Adelaide
Tel: 08-8223 1948
Amalfi's turns out authentic Italian
specials to its loyal supper crowd.
Here you'll find a real cross-section
of Adelaide nightlife, and the good-
natured staff add to the appeal.

Gouger Street

Lined with restaurants on both sides
and for several blocks, Gouger
Street has, as they say, the world on
a fork. There is a particular
abundance of Chinese restaurants
and Australian seafood cafés, plus
French, Greek, Thai and more.

Red Ochre Restaurant

War Memorial Drive, North Adelaide
Tel: 08-8211 8555
Main courses about A$18.
Specialising in bush tucker/native
Australian produce. The place to
sample smoked wallaby or emu
pâté. Sit outdoors, cooled by
overhead vines.

Ying Chow

114 Gouger Street
Tel: 08-8211 7998

One of the best-value restaurants in
town and a favourite of many young
Adelaidians, Ying Chow is a busy,
casual place serving first-rate
regional Chinese dishes at low
prices.

Attractions

SIGHTSEEING

Tourism S.A. has an excellent range
of maps and general guides to tours
and accommodation in Adelaide
and in other regions. They can tailor
information to suit particular
interests such as history, art and
culture, the great outdoors,
shopping or wine and food.

The **Adelaide Explorer** is a tram
replica that travels via tourist
attractions, including Glenelg. The
"tram" leaves from 38 King William
Street every two hours. A great fold-
out walking map – available from
the Tourism Office – takes you past
all the historic points of interest,
and a cassette with headphones
provides a good commentary.

Official Adelaide

The widest capital city street in
Australia is King William Street,
where you'll find the city's banks,
insurance offices and post office.
Another main tree-lined boulevard is
North Terrace. Important buildings
along this thoroughfare include
Parliament House, Holy Trinity
Church, Government House, South
Australian Museum, Art Gallery of
South Australia, State Library and
the University of Adelaide.

Art Gallery of South Australia

State-of-the-art gallery that shows
off one of Australia's best
collections of local art (including
some of Tom Roberts' colonial
classics). Art lovers should allow at
least a full day. Open daily
10am–5pm; www.artgallery.
sa.gov.au.

The Festival Centre

Just north of North Terrace on the
banks of the Torrens River is the
Festival Centre complex. The centre
was completed in 1973 as a home

What's On?

Check the Gig Guide in Thursday's edition of the *Advertiser* newspaper or the free publication *Rip It Up,* for what's on in Adelaide. The free magazine *Adelaide Review* also lists theatres and galleries.

for the Adelaide Festival, which takes place during March of every even-numbered year. It contains a 2,000-seat auditorium, a smaller drama theatre, a 360-seat experimental theatre, a 2,000-seat open-air amphitheatre, an art collection, restaurants and a bar. The Adelaide Symphony Orchestra and the State Theatre Company perform here, as well as international artistes.

Botanic Gardens

The Gardens comprise 40 hectares (100 acres) of parkland, including a wealth of native Australian vegetation, a wide variety of food and medicinal plants and a beautiful Victorian Palm House.

Adelaide Zoo

Located on Frome Road next to the Botanic Gardens, the zoo is noted for its Australian birds, including pelicans, penguins, lorikeets, and blue and gold macaws. There are also sea lions, big cats and a reptile house. Open daily 9.30am–5pm; www.adelaidezoo. com.au.

Glenelg

Leaving from Victoria Square, the vintage tram takes 30 minutes to reach this very attractive beach suburb, the oldest in Adelaide, with plenty of historic sites and colourful Mediterranean-style houses. In the summer when it's very hot, some of the locals sleep on the beach.

Day Trips from Adelaide

BAROSSA VALLEY

One of Adelaide's greatest attractions, Australia's most celebrated wine region is just 64 km (40 miles) northeast of the city. Every tour company in Adelaide has a Barossa Valley excursion on its books. Most trips last a day, take in a number of stops for wine tasting and include lunch. The South Australia tourist office *(see page 340)* can supply you with a full list of available tours.

Mount Lofty

A half hour's drive to the southeast of Adelaide, Mount Lofty (771 metres/2,529 ft) offers spectacular views; there are a number of parks in the hills with a wide variety of wildlife. Contact South Australian Tourism Commission, tel: 1300-655 276, fax: 08-8303 2249; www.southaustralia.com for details. The information centre and café bistro at the Mount Lofty summit take full advantage of their location and make an ideal starting point from which to explore nearby Mount Lofty Botanic Gardens and Cleland Wildlife Park.

Hahndorf

Just 29 km (18 miles) southeast of Adelaide, Hahndorf has the oldest surviving German festivals in SA. These include the Schuetzenfest Beer Festival, held in January, with street parades and beer and wine tastings. Details from the Adelaide Hills Information Centre on Main Street, open 10am–4pm, tel: 08-8388 1185.

Port Adelaide

Historic Port Adelaide is easily accessible by car, bus or train (20–30 mins). The Heritage walking tour takes in historic buildings and monuments, the Port Dock Railway Museum and Maritime Museum (both are open daily, 10am–5pm), and the Sunday Fisherman's Wharf market. River cruises are also popular. For more information contact the South Australia tourist office *(see page 340)* or the City of Port Adelaide Enfield, 63 St Vincent Street, Port Adelaide, tel: 08-8405 6600.

Kangaroo Island

Australia's third-largest island is rich in native wildlife thanks to its isolation from the mainland; there are also beaches, bushwalks and shipwrecks. Many private companies in Adelaide offer package trips – including transport by flight or ferry, accommodation and tours. The National Parks and Wildlife Service is located at 37 Dauncey Street in Kingscote, tel: 08-8553 2381, fax: 08-8553 2930. The service is open Mon–Fri 8.30am–5pm, and sells Island Passes that cover entry and guided tours.

Culture

The city comes alive during the Adelaide Festival – held every two years (2006, 2008, etc.) in February and March. Street theatre is everywhere, spontaneous and usually very funny, with non-stop partying. The festival includes a mainstream schedule of international performances in the Festival Centre, plus the ever-popular Fringe Festival – three weeks of stand-up comedy, alternative theatre and visual arts. Similar in concept and quality to the Edinburgh Festival, the Adelaide Fringe draws comedians and other acts from around the English-speaking world and is well worth a trip to Adelaide to experience its variety and fun.

At the same time, Writer's Week brings important scribblers from around the world and a huge audience of adoring listeners to hear them read and discuss their work. There is also a Visual Arts Festival, a showcase of cutting-edge artworks, which can take place in any form – even in the homes of artists.

During the festival, there are extra information booths in Rundle Mall and a number of free publications which give listings and information about the daily events.

Events/Nightlife

There is always something to be seen at the Adelaide Festival Centre, while many pubs offer rock, folk and jazz music.

Art films are shown at the **Nova** and the **Palace**, both in Rundle

Street, also at the **Trak** in Toorak Gardens, the **Picadilly** in North Adelaide and the **Capri** in Goodwood.

The grand old railway station on North Terrace now houses a **casino**, for those inclined. The "sin centre" of Adelaide is Hindley Street, although few will be shocked by it. Interspersed with excellent restaurants you'll find strip clubs, bars, porno bookstores and the usual persons of the night.

Shopping

Adelaide's main shopping area is the pedestrian mall of Rundle Street. Further east along Rundle Street, the **East End Markets** are a colourful maze of stalls selling alternative clothes and jewellery. Wines can be bought from the cellar doors of many wineries in the Barossa Valley, Clare Valley, McLaren Vale, Adelaide Hills and the Coonawarra. The **Retail Art and Craft** shop at the Tandanya National Aboriginal Cultural Institute sells a wide range of quality indigenous art, craft, books, music and clothing, as well as the essential didgeridoos and boomerangs.

Queensland

Brisbane

The city of Brisbane is just five degrees south of the Tropic of Capricorn. The best months to visit are the cooler, dry months from April–November, when daytime temperatures range between 20 and 27°C (68–80°F). Most of the rain (and occasionally cyclonic weather) occurs during the warmer months from November to March.

With a population of close to 1.5 million, Brisbane is Australia's third-largest city, and has seen more redevelopment in the past few years than any other. Previously considered little more than a "big country town", Brisbane's image has been transformed into a thriving young city with an upbeat yuppie culture and a swarm of fashionable new hangouts.

Brisbane is an ideal base from which to explore southern Queensland, and the string of beaches not far to the north identified as the Sunshine Coast. (Note that the Great Barrier Reef begins near Bundaberg – a 45-minute flight north of Brisbane – and stretches up the Queensland coast, Cairns being the most popular of several access points.)

Brisbane's main commercial streets follow a grid pattern. Streets running northeast have feminine names; those running northwest, masculine. The Parliament buildings and the Botanic Gardens are nestled on the bend of the river at the top of the peninsula, with the South Bank Parklands opposite the city.

Tourist information outlets include the **Queen Street Mall Information Centre** on the corner of Queen and Albert Street, tel: 07-

3229 5918. Open Mon–Thur 9am–5.30pm, till 7pm on Fri, and shorter hours on the weekend. Another helpful source is the **Greater Brisbane Tourist Association**'s information desk in the Brisbane Transit Centre, Level 2, corner of Roma and George streets, tel: 07-3236 2020. The Tourism Brisbane information counter in City Hall is another good place to start. Open Mon–Fri 8am–5pm, tel: 07-3221 8411.

Getting Around

FROM THE AIRPORT

The domestic and international airport terminals lie 13 km (8 miles) from the city centre. At any time when flights are arriving or departing, a combination of bus and fast rail transport options provides easy connections between Brisbane Airport, Brisbane city and the Gold Coast. The hub is the city coach/rail terminus, and the "Trans-info" service (tel: 131-230) or the information desks at the airport will help you identify the easiest and most convenient way to get from A to B.

BY BUS

For information on city buses, go to the underground bus station beneath the Myer Centre in the Queen Street Mall, open weekdays 8.30am–5pm. Apart from the regular city buses, there are Cityxpress buses, which connect certain suburbs to the city, and

Brisbane Ferries

Brisbane ferries provide pleasant river crossings to Kangaroo Point, South Bank Parklands and along the river to other locations.

They depart from Eagle Street Pier and Edward Street on the corner of the Botanic Gardens. They are fast, efficient, inexpensive – and under-appreciated by Brisbane folk.

Camping Out and About in Queensland

For an excellent guide to Queensland camping grounds, contact the Environmental Protection Agency, PO Box 155, Brisbane Albert Street, Queensland 4002, tel: 07-3227 8197, fax: 07-3227 8749; www.qld.gov.au. They publish a Queensland National Parks and Wildlife Service booklet entitled *Camping in Queensland*, detailing over 230 places to camp in national parks, state forests and water reserves. Bookings are recommended to avoid disappointment.

In addition, the Royal Automobile Club of Queensland publishes *Camping in South and Central Queensland*. To obtain a copy, call in at any RACQ office. Members of the association can order online at www.racq.com.au.

Rockets, which are peak-hour commuter services. Fares are based on a zone system and there are a number of special deals such as day or weekly passes.

BY TRAIN

The electric Cititrain services are very efficient. They all pass through the city stations of Roma Street, Central and Brunswick on their way out to the suburbs. The Public Transport Information Centre is located in Central Station. There are tickets that enable unlimited travel in one day.

Where to Stay

Queensland's coastline is a near-continuous strip of excellent beaches, with hundreds of holiday resorts. While Brisbane itself has no beaches, it is an excellent base or jumping-off point for exploring the south of Queensland. Cairns in the far north is the direct arrival point for visitors to the Great Barrier Reef and Cape York.

BRISBANE

International (A$275–1,240)
Hotel Conrad & Treasury Casino
William and George streets
Tel: 07-3306 8888
Freecall: 1800-506 889
(reservations only)
Fax: 07-3306 8880
www.conradtreasury.com.au
The Treasury building – which houses Brisbane's casino – is one of the finest 19th-century structures in the city. Accommodation is in individually decorated suites, featuring many original furnishings.
Quay West Suites Brisbane
132 Alice Street
Tel: 07-3853 6000
Freecall: 1800-672 726
(reservations only)
Fax: 07-3853 6060
www.mirvachotels.com.au
One- and two-bedroom apartment accommodation in the city centre, overlooking the Botanic Gardens. All suites have balconies.
Stamford Plaza Hotel
By the Botanic Gardens
Corner of Margaret and Edward streets
Tel: 07-3221 1999
Freecall: 1800-773 700
(reservations only)
Fax: 07-3221 6895
www.stamford.com.au
Brisbane's finest luxury hotel. Impressive oil paintings of early Queensland grace the lobby, which extends alongside a serene central courtyard. providing a haven from the inner city. Elegant rooms of generous country-style proportions overlook the winding Brisbane River. Located in the city centre beside the historic Botanic Gardens. Try the excellent "Siggi's at the Port Office" restaurant for special occasions.

Premier (A$95–650)
Albert Park Hotel
551 Wickham Terrace
Tel: 07-3831 3111
Freecall: 1800-777 702
(reservations only)
Fax: 07-3832 1290
www.albertparkhotel.com.au
Up-market hotel with European-style decor, located near Roma Street Parkland and Transit Centre.
Carlton Crest Hotel
King George Square
Tel: 07-3229 9111
Freecall: 1900-777 123
(reservations only)
Fax: 07-3229 9618
www.carltonhotels.com.au
City-centre location with a choice of four-star Crest Tower, or five-star Carlton Tower accommodation.
Dockside Apartment Hotel
44 Ferry Street
Kangaroo Point
Tel: 07-3981 6644
Freecall: 1800-775 005
(reservations only)
Fax: 07-3891 6900
www.docksidehotel.com.au
Spacious self-contained apartments, each with a sweeping view from a private balcony. Across the river from the city but there's a ferry at the bottom of the garden.
Mercure Hotel
85–87 North Quay
Tel: 07-3236 3300
Fax: 07-3236 1035
www.mercurebrisbane.com.au
Great location on the Brisbane River overlooking the Cultural Centre, Southbank Parkland, and the Brisbane Convention and Exhibition Centre. Comfortable accommodation just a few minutes walk from the Central Business District and casino.

Moderate (A$80–265)
The Chifley on George Hotel
103 George Street
Tel: 07-3221 6044
Fax: 07-3221 7474
www.chifleyhotels.com
Boutique 99-room hotel refurbished with a distinctive casual elegance. A 5-minute walk to the Southbank Parkland across the river.
Explorers Inn
63 Turbot Street
Tel: 07-3211 3488
Freecall: 1800-623 288
Fax: 07-3211 3499
www.explorers.com.au

Convenient budget-style accommodation in the Brisbane CBD, 150 metres/yards from the Queen Street Mall.

Ryans on the River
269 Main Street
Kangaroo Point
Tel: 07-3391 1011
Fax: 07-3391 1824
www.ryans.com.au
Attractive property in a great location in Kangaroo Point on the walking and cycle pathway.

Budget (A$20–105)
Acacia Inner City Inn
413 Upper Edward Street
Tel: 07-3832 1663
Fax: 07-3832 2591
Friendly inner-city facility with a range of accommodation choices, and a sociable environment. Continental breakfast inclusive.

Spring Hill Terraces
260 Water Street
Spring Hill
Tel: 07-3854 1048
Fax: 07-3852 2121
www.springhillterraces.com
Modern and comfortable self-contained apartments and budget rooms in a good location, about 5 minutes' drive from the city centre.

Hostels (From $20 per person)
Brisbane City YHA Hostel
392 Upper Roma Street
Brisbane
Tel: 07-3236 1004
Fax: 07-3236 1947
www.yha.com.au
Excellent facilities in this backpacker-orientated youth hostel. Located in trendy Paddington, close to the city, the hostel has an inexpensive restaurant for breakfast and dinner.

Palace Backpackers
308 Edward Street
Tel: 07-3211 2433
Freecall: 1800-676 340
(reservations only)
Fax: 07-3211 2466
www.palacebackpackers.com.au
Smack in the middle of the city, right opposite Central Station. Everything you need at your fingertips, including the famous Down Under Bar.

Southern Queensland

OUTBACK

International/Premier (A$185–500)
Talgai Homestead
Allora–Ellinthorp Road, Allora,
Southern Darling Downs
Tel: 07-4666 3444
Fax: 07-4666 3780
A small, friendly hotel with country-style cooking in a National Trust listed homestead furnished with antiques. The emphasis is on total relaxation.

CENTRAL QUEENSLAND OUTBACK

Premier (A$105–300)
Albert Park Motor Inn
Sir Hudson Fysh Drive
Longreach
Tel: 07-4658 2411
Fax: 07-4658 3181
Very comfortable with modern facilities, within walking distance of the Stockman's Hall of Fame and the Qantas Founders' Outback Museum.

Carnarvon Gorge Wilderness Lodge
Carnarvon Gorge, via Rolleston,
Queensland
Tel: 07-4984 4503
Freecall: 1800-644 150
(reservations only)
Fax: 07-4984 4500
www.carnarvon-gorge.com
Unique timber and canvas safari cabins have their own Outback charm, and make a good base for exploring the gorge with its ancient plant life and fossilised Aboriginal rock art.

Standard Categories

- **International** Hotels, resorts or historic manor houses of unquestioned five-star standard
- **Premier** Four-star standard, including hotel chains, with a range of reliable services
- **Moderate** Comfortable, well-kept properties
- **Budget** Simple, clean and modest accommodation

GOLD COAST

There are dozens of generic high-rises along this 35-km (20-mile) stretch of sand, which includes Surfer's Paradise, but most people who come here have their hotel already organised through package tours. There are also many small motels for the independent traveller. A couple of options:

International (A$590–3,310)
Sheraton Mirage Resort and Spa
Sea World Drive
Main Beach
Tel: 07-5591 1488
Freecall: 1800-073 535
(reservations only)
Fax: 07-5591 2299
www.sheraton.com
Beachfront low-rise luxury resort with comprehensive health club facilities. Restaurants highly rated.

Budget (A$75–120)
Motels such as **Sunset Court** in Surfers Paradise, tel: 07-5539 0266, are typical of the cheap Aussie vacation hangouts here – functional, often with a kitchen, and not far from the beach.

Broadwater Keys Quest Inn
125 Frank Street
Labrador
Tel: 07-5531 0839
Fax: 07-5591 3675
www.broadwaterkeys.com.au
About 100 metres/yards from the Broadwater, self-contained units available on daily and weekly rates.

SUNSHINE COAST

International/Premier (A$210–1,350)
Hyatt Regency Coolum Golf Resort & Spa
Warran Road
Coolum
Tel: 07-5446 1234
Freecall: 1800-266 586
(reservations only)
Fax: 07-5446 2957
www.coolum.hyatt.com
About 90 minutes' drive north of Brisbane, a championship golf-course resort set in natural

bushland with ocean beachfront, and its own lifeguard on duty.

Noosa Blue Resort
16 Noosa Drive
Noosa
Tel: 07-5447 5699
Fax: 07-5447 5485
www.noosablue.com.au
A stylish boutique resort perched high on Noosa Hill, with sweeping views of Noosa's coastline and hinterland, and only 450 metres/yards from its Hastings Street social and shopping centre. Luxury self-contained suites with spas and fine attention to detail.

FRASER ISLAND

International (A$180–450)
Kingfisher Bay Resort and Village
Tel: 07-4120 3333;
Freecall: 1800-072 555
Fax: 07-4120 3326
www.kingfisherbay.com
The only deluxe property on this stunningly beautiful World Heritage-listed island. (Arrive by car ferry or catamaran from Urangan, approx 3½ hours' drive north of Brisbane.) For a fee the resort provides tours to scenic sites, or you can rent a four-wheel drive.

LAMINGTON NATIONAL PARK

Moderate (A$100–295)
Binna Burra Mountain Lodge
Beechmont
Tel: 07-5533 3622
Freecall: 1800-074 260

Standard Categories

- **International** Hotels, resorts or historic manor houses of unquestioned five-star standard
- **Premier** Four-star standard, including hotel chains, with a range of reliable services
- **Moderate** Comfortable, well-kept properties
- **Budget** Simple, clean and modest accommodation

(reservations only)
Fax: 07-5533 3658
www.binnaburralodge.com.au
Award-winning eco-accredited lodge in world-heritage area with over 160 km (100 miles) of hiking tracks. Packages include rustic cabin accommodation, all country-style meals, abseiling, and flying fox, rainforest and bird-spotting walks. Camp sites also available.

O'Reilly's Rainforest Guest House
Via Canungra
Tel: 07-5544 0644
Freecall: 1800-688 722
(reservations only)
Fax: 07-5544 0638
www.oreillys.com.au
Friendly family-run guesthouse which has been providing accommodation, naturalist guide services, touring and special events in this beautiful world-heritage region for over 80 years. About 2 hours' drive southwest from Brisbane.

Far North Queensland

International (A$260–1,825)
Sebel Reef House & Spa
99 Williams Esplanade, Palm Cove
Tel: 07-4055 3633
Fax: 07-4055 3305
www.reefhouse.com.au
Elegant tropical resort only 25 minutes north of Cairns on Palm Cove's golden beach. The design is refreshingly light and spacious.

Sheraton Mirage Port Douglas
Davidson Street
Port Douglas
Tel: 07-4099 5888
Freecall: 1800-818 831
(reservations only)
Fax: 07-4099 5354
www.sheraton-mirage.com.au
The glitziest resort in the fast-developing town of Port Douglas. All the man-made five-star luxury you can imagine, including 2 hectares (5 acres) of swimmable blue lagoons and an 18-hole international-standard golf course.

Sofitel Reef Hotel Casino
Corner of Wharf and Spence streets, Cairns
Tel: 07-4030 8888
Freecall: 1800-808 883
Fax: 07-4030 8788

www.reefcasino.com.au
This luxury development in Cairns includes a 1930s-style nightclub, rainforest conservatory, five restaurants and a casino. All suites have balconies and modern woodgrain furnishings in a vaguely tropical Queensland fashion.

Premier (A$95–200)
Archipelago Studio Apartments
72 Macrossan Street
Port Douglas
Tel: 07-4099 5387
Fax: 07-4099 4847
www.archipelago.com.au
Self-contained apartments right on Macrossan Street and only 50 metres/yards from Four Mile Beach. Proprietors Christel and Wolfgang are a goldmine of local knowledge.

The Lakes Resort & Spa
2 Greenslopes Street
Cairns
Tel: 07-4053 9411
Freecall: 1800-666 614
Fax: 07-4053 9401
www.thelakescairns.com.au
Adjoining the Botanical Gardens and close to the city action without complete immersion, a thoughtfully designed resort in natural surroundings.

Sovereign Resort Hotel
128 Charlotte Street
Cooktown
Tel: 07-4069 5400
Fax: 07-4069 5582
www.sovereign-resort.com.au
A relaxed "plantation-style" resort hotel in the heart of Cooktown. Excellent balcony restaurant, and the air-conditioning is welcome at the end of a warm day. Airport courtesy pick-up by arrangement.

Budget (A$25–170)
Gilligan's Backpackers Hotel & Resort
57–89 Grafton Street
Cairns
Tel: 07-4041 6566
Fax: 07-4041 6577
www.gilligansbackpackers.com.au
Cairns' newest and best backpacker facility, right in the heart of town and with all the services you're likely to look for.

Lake Eacham Hotel
Yungaburra
Tel: 07-4095 3515
Fax: 07-4095 3202
www.yungaburrapub.com.au
A fine example of Federation-style architecture in the quiet village of Yungaburra, a comfortable base for exploring the rolling hills of the Atherton Tablelands. The rooms are simple but pleasantly decorated, good pub food, and staff are friendly.

Port O'Call Lodge
Corner of Craven and Port streets
Port Douglas
Tel: 07-4099 5422
Fax: 07-4099 4595
www.portocall.com.au
YHA associate. The best option for budget accommodation, about 1 km ($^2/_3$ mile) from the town. Four-share and private rooms, cooking facilities, bar and bistro, a pool and courtesy bus to and from Cairns (Mon–Sat, conditions apply).

The Reef Retreat
10–14 Harpa Street
Palm Cove
Tel: 07-4059 1744
Fax: 07-4059 1745
www.reefretreat.com.au
Good-value resort accommodation in Palm Cove, 20 minutes' north of Cairns. Natural tropical setting, idyllic beach, bars and alfresco dining.

Far North Eco Resorts

For a more natural and unspoilt environment, the following resorts provide a glimpse of real North Queensland.

International (A$320–1,680)
Bloomfield Wilderness Lodge
PO Box 966, Cairns
Tel: 07-4035 9166
Fax: 07-4035 9180
www.bloomfieldlodge.com
Remote and beautiful location abutting Cape Tribulation National Park. Private cabins hidden in the rainforest, overlooking the Coral Sea. Possible to continue by four-wheel drive to historic Cooktown and surrounds. Minimum two-night packages include all meals and flight transfers from Cairns.

Reef Resorts

A number of the more up-market island resorts – Lizard, Bedarra, Dunk, Silky Oaks, Heron and Brampton – are owned by P&O Resorts and accessed by road/sea or (more commonly) by air. Their freecall number in Australia is 1800-812 525; fax: 07-3360 2453/2436. In the USA or Canada call 1800-227 4411; in Europe and Japan, contact any international Qantas office. Their website is www.poresorts.com.

Coconut Beach Rainforest Lodge
Cape Tribulation Road
Cape Tribulation
Tel: 07-4098 0033
Freecall: 1300-134 044 (reservations only)
Fax: 07-4098 0047
www.voyages.com.au
Hideaway accommodation nestled in the rainforest, and only minutes to the beach from its Cape Restaurant. A "canopy crane" is an innovative way to view the rainforest treetops from above, and the resort has its own boat for reef trips.

Daintree Eco Lodge & Spa
Daintree Road, Daintree
Tel: 07-4098 6100;
Freecall: 1800-808 010
Fax: 07-4098 6200
www.daintree-ecolodge.com.au
Comfortable lodges set in the rainforest opposite the tropical Daintree River. Only 90 minutes' north of Cairns on a sealed road – no ferry crossing. Winner of 2002/3 award for ecotourism that incorporates indigenous culture.

Kewarra Beach Resort
Kewarra Beach
Tel: 07-4057 6666
Fax: 07-4057 7525
www.kewarra.com
Private deluxe bungalows hidden in tropical beachfront property 20 minutes from Cairns. Quiet relaxation after busy North Queensland day trips. Fine collection of Aboriginal and

Torres Strait art and historical artefacts.

Premier (A$220–420)
Cape Tribulation Exotic Fruit Farm B&B
Lot 5 Nicole Drive, Cape Tribulation
Tel: 07-4098 0057
Fax: 07-4098 0067
www.capetrib.com.au
A fruit-tasting and farm tour in a permaculture orchard,will add another dimension to your rainforest experience.

The Horizon at Mission Beach
PO Box 150, Mission Beach
Tel: 07-4068 8154
Fax: 07-4068 8596
www.thehorizon.com.au
South of Cairns and high above historical Tam O'Shanter Point, surrounded by rainforest, with commanding views of Dunk and Bedarra Islands. Spacious verandas look out to sea and a short stroll leads to a private beach.

Silky Oaks Lodge
Finlayvale Road
Mossman River Gorge
Tel: 07-4098 1666
Freecall: 1800-737 678
Fax: 07-4098 1983
www.poresorts.com
Some 27 km (17 miles) from Port Douglas, this rainforest hideaway lies on the edge of Mossman Gorge, which adjoins Daintree National Park. The treehouses and river houses have all the creature comforts you need, plus a spa, restaurant,

The Far North

While this region of Queensland includes an amazing wealth of natural beauty for visitors, the city of Cairns – and, an hour further north, the village of Port Douglas – offer the widest range of accommodation. Both are used as bases for Great Barrier Reef trips, but Port Douglas is smaller, more charming and more convenient (it also has the Four Mile Beach, while Cairns faces mudflats).

and rainforest excursions and canoe trips on the Mossman River.

Budget (A$25–170)

The Beach House
Cape Tribulation Road
(38 km/24 miles from the ferry)
Tel: 07-4098 0030
Fax: 07-4098 0120
www.capetribbeach.com.au
Dormitory and family cabins as close to the beach as the National Parks Authority will allow. Kitchen/laundry facilities, swimming pool and bistro/bar.

Red Mill House
11 Stewart Street, Daintree Village
Tel/fax: 07-4098 6233
www.redmillhouse.com.au
Excellent B&B in an old Queenslander house set in spacious gardens near the Daintree River – catering especially to keen birdwatchers and nature lovers.

Undara Lava Lodge
Mount Surprise
Tel: 07-4097 1411
Fax: 07-4097 1450
www.undara.com.au
Accommodation is in quaint refurbished railway carriages on the edge of the Undara Volcanic National Park. Savannah Guides conduct interpretive tours through ancient caverns. Also has a camping area.

Cape York

Punsand Bay Safari & Fishing Lodge
Via Bamaga, Cape York
Tel: 07-4069 1722
Fax: 07-4069 1403
This lodge, which offers camping facilities and serviced accommodation for Cape York's annual influx of four-wheel drive adventurers as well as air travellers (via Bamaga or Horn Island), provides access to some of the remotest, most historic and beautiful sites on the Cape York Peninsula – virgin rainforest, clear, fast-flowing streams, and endless unpopulated beaches. Camping sites also available.

Great Barrier Reef & Whitsunday Islands

International (A$585–4,200)

Bedarra Bay Resort
Bedarra Island, via Mission Beach
Freecall 1800-812 525
www.poresorts.com.au
Bedarra Bay Resort has created a mystique surrounding its rich and famous guests. Privacy is the draw, since only 15 individual luxury villas are nestled into beachfront foliage. Guests (no under-15s) are free to explore the island by motor dinghy and find their private beach to settle down with their champagne-filled picnic hampers.

Hayman Island Resort
Great Barrier Reef
North Queensland
Tel: 07-4940 1234
Freecall: 1800-075 175
Fax: 07-4940 1567
www.hayman.com.au
One of the Whitsunday Islands, located between the coast and the Great Barrier Reef, Hayman Island is another "total luxury" resort. A modern, three-level complex overlooks a vast pool and the sea. Unlike some luxury resorts, young children are welcome and a crèche and babysitting are available. Even so, it's a popular honeymoon venue.

Lizard Island
Via Cairns
Tel: 07-4060 3999
Freecall: 1800-737 768
Fax: 07-4060 3991
www.poresorts.com.au
Thoroughly exclusive atmosphere on the most deluxe resort island of the Barrier Reef. The northernmost Reef island, Lizard's natural beauty includes excellent dive sites and idyllic calm waters with a colony of giant clams. Sophisticated cuisine and world-class game fishing. No facilities for children under six.

Premier (A$240–850)

Daydream Island Resort and Spa
Whitsunday Islands
Mackay
Tel: 07-4948 8488
Freecall: 1800 075 040
(reservations only)
Fax: 07-4948 8499
www.daydream.net.au
Family-style resort on a smallish, pretty tropical island with wide range of free activities including outdoor cinema. Day trips to Outer Reef and Whitehaven Beach.

Green Island Resort
PO Box 898, Cairns
Tel: 07-4031 3300
Freecall: 1800-673 366
Fax: 07-4052 1511
www.greenislandresort.com.au
Forty-five minutes by fast catamaran from Cairns, Green Island Resort is a luxury ecotourist development built on a coral cay. Also popular with large numbers of day visitors.

Heron Island Resort
Via Gladstone
Tel: 07-4972 9055
Freecall: 1800-812 525
(reservations only)
Fax: 07-4972 0244
www.poresorts.com
A coral cay located right on the Great Barrier Reef and one of the world's top dive sites, the island is a pristine national park, bird sanctuary and turtle rookery. Turtles come in summer to lay their eggs, and tiny hatchlings emerge from December to April. Whales arrive in August and September. During the mating season hundreds of indigenous birds are joined by migrating species to nest and rear their young in the lush forest of pisonia trees. No telephones or TV in the rooms. High standard of tropical cuisine; fishing trips; guided walks; sunset wine and cheese cruises; overnight camping trips to uninhabited Wilson Island.

Standard Categories

- **International** Hotels, resorts or historic manor houses of unquestioned five-star standard
- **Premier** Four-star standard, including hotel chains, with a range of reliable services
- **Moderate** Comfortable, well-kept properties
- **Budget** Simple, clean and modest accommodation

Orpheus Island Resort
Private Mail Bag 15
Townsville
Tel: 07-4777 7377
Fax: 07-4777 7533
www.orpheus.com.au
Designed as an intimate, secluded resort, with only 21 beachfront rooms available. Emphasis on couples and romantic picnics. Surrounded by national park on an island 11 km (7 miles) long and 1.5 km (1 mile) wide.

Moderate (A$135–390)

Brampton Island
Via Mackay
Tel: 07-4951 4499
Freecall: 1800-737 678
Fax: 07-4951 4097
www.poresorts.com
Intimate resort on an island which is almost entirely on national parkland, and where you can take the mini-train to the daily fish feeding. Located 32 km (20 miles) northeast of Mackay (a 20-minute flight or 50-minute launch trip). Activities include golf, catamaran sailing and plenty of other sports. Reef trips and seaplane flights additional.

Dunk Island
Via Townsville
Tel: 07-4068 8199
Freecall: 1800-737 768
(reservations only)
Fax: 07-4068 8528
www.poresorts.com
Almost completely rainforested, Dunk is home to richly diverse native flora and fauna. It has walking trails, an Australian farm and game fishing, and is 45 minutes by ferry from Mission Beach. Good for families with a full range of activities, four levels of accommodation and child-minding facility.

Fitzroy Island Resort
Fitzroy Island
PO Box 2120, Cairns
Tel: 07-4051 9588
Fax: 07-4052 1335
www.fitzroyisland.com.au
A continental or "high" island reached by catamaran from Cairns, Fitzroy features beach cabins with private facilities and beach

bunkhouses with communal facilities.

Great Keppel Island Resort
Via Rockhampton
Tel: 07-4939 5044
Freecall: 1300-305 005
Fax: 07-4939 1775
www.gkeppel.com.au
A Contiki "party resort" aimed at the the 18–35 age group with 25 km (15 miles) of white sandy beach and land- and water-based activities, ranging from water-skiing and sailing to tandem skydiving.

Island Leisure Resort
4 Kelly Street, Nelly Bay
Magnetic Island
Tel: 07-4778 5000
Fax: 07-4778 5042
www.islandleisure.com.au
A short ferry ride from Townsville, a family-style resort comprising 17 self-contained units in a tropical village garden setting only 50 metres/yards from the beach.

Pumpkin Island
South of North Keppel Island
PO Box 1151, Kenmore, Qld 4069
Tel: 07-4939 4413
www.pumpkinisland.com.au
Five large cabins are available; each accommodates five or six people and has solar power and gas appliances. You'll need to bring food and linen. Transport to the island is by charter boat arranged when you book.

Hostels (from A$20 per person)

Great Keppel Youth Hostel
Great Keppel Island
Tel: 07-4933 6416
Fax: 07-4933 6429
Camping, safari tents and on-site cabins. Book well ahead for this popular location. Snorkel gear for rent, bushwalks and other activities. Facilities include café and shop.

Where to Eat

BRISBANE

Modern Australian

Cha Cha Char
Eagle Street Pier
1 Eagle Street
Tel: 07-3211 9944
An à la carte wine bar and grill by

the Brisbane River, specialising in Australian beef. Main courses about A$30.

E'cco Licensed Bistro
100 Boundary Street
Tel: 07-3831 8344
Licensed and BYO. Main courses about A$32. Set in what was once an old tea warehouse, this restaurant has consistently been one of Brisbane's best. Closed Sunday and Monday.

French

Anise
697 Brunswick Street, New Farm
Tel: 07-3358 1558
Licensed. Among the best wine collections in Brisbane, with special attention to matching your menu choice with something from the international wine list, and a bit of theatre thrown in. Main courses around A$35.

Bruno's Table
85 Miskin Street, Toowong
Tel: 07-3371 4558
Modern French with multicultural nuances. Even the bread is made in-house. Licensed. Main courses around A$28.

Italian

Il Centro
Eagle Street Pier
1 Eagle Street
Tel: 07-3221 6090
Licensed. Main courses about A$28. One of the many happening places in this riverfront location. The house speciality is a superb sand crab lasagne.

Seafood

Brett's Wharf Seafood Restaurant
449 Kingsford Smith Drive
Hamilton
Tel: 07-3868 1717
Licensed. Main courses average A$35. Riverfront eatery and veranda constructed from original wharf timbers. Specialises in Queensland seafood and Tasmanian lobster. The CityCat will get you there and back.

Pier Nine Oyster Bar & Seafood Grill
Eagle Street Pier
Tel: 07-3226 2100
Sit indoors or find a table outdoors

Totally Tropical

Thanks to its many Modern Australian restaurants and lively late-night bistros, Brisbane's culinary scene is comparable to the southern capitals. Chefs have the added advantage of immediate access to tropical produce such as reef fish, crabs, prawns, mangos, paw-paws (papaya) and avocados.

and watch the river while enjoying freshly shucked oysters and fine wine. Main courses around A$32.

Japanese
Oshin
1st floor, Koala House, corner of Adelaide and Creek streets
Tel: 07-3229 0410
Popular with both Japanese businessmen and tourists. Highlights are the Sushi Bar and the friendly service. Main courses around A$22.

Vietnamese
Green Papaya
898 Stanley Street
East Brisbane
Tel: 07-3217 3599
Main courses A$18–35. Authentic and aromatic menu includes green papaya salad; spicy prawns in coconut juice, lemongrass and chilli, and their black rice pudding.

Sporting Club Nightlife
Broncos' Leagues Club
Fulcher Road, Red Hill
Tel: 07-3858 9000
Just 10 minutes' drive from the CBD, adjacent to the rugby club's training ground, the club offers an all-you-can-eat three-course buffet for around A$20, entertainment, and gambling. Visitors need to be signed in to collect their winnings, but it's an easy procedure.

NOOSA

This resort town is now one of the best restaurant centres in Australia thanks to amazing local produce, especially seafood.

French
berardo's on the beach
On the beach
Hastings Street
Tel: 07-5448 0888
In the heart of swishy Hastings Street, this is cutting-edge modern Australian cuisine; try a "six course degustation" while enjoying the fabulous ocean views. Main courses around A$26.

Italian
Lindoni's
13 Hastings Street (almost opposite the Sheraton)
Tel: 07-5447 5111
Traditional Italian cuisine and atmosphere, and everything on the menu's a house speciality. Your dining backdrop is the nightly atmosphere created by Noosa's "beautiful people" in relaxation mode. Mains around A$28.

SUNSHINE COAST HINTERLAND

The Ginger Factory
Yandina
Tel: 07-5446 7100
Fifteen minutes from Coolum, a Devonshire tea (or lunch) with a difference – ginger scones and ginger tea, a huge choice of ginger products, and the world's largest confectionery ginger plant is a tourist attraction in itself (open daily 9am–5pm).

The Terrace Seafood Restaurant of Maleny
Cairncross Corner
Maleny
Tel: 07-5494 3700
A short drive from Noosa. Spectacular views of the coast and Glasshouse Mountains. Licensed or BYO. Award-winning seafood dining and fresh local seafood banquets.

Far North Queensland

CAIRNS

There are many quite decent restaurants in the large Cairns hotels, including fine sushi bars. Dozens of small cafés and eateries

line the back streets, but few are exceptional. Try the waterfront eateries like **Pescis**. Nearby Shields Street and Spence Street, both leading to Cairns Central shopping centre, offer a wide choice of reasonably priced restaurants, including the **Hog's Breath Cafe** and the **Indian Taj**.

Red Ochre Grill
43 Shields Street
Tel: 07-4051 0100
"Creative Native Australian cuisine" is offered on an inventive menu that uses up to 40 different native ingredients to enhance dishes such as emu, kangaroo, crocodile, tropical fruit and seafoods. Try the kangaroo sirloin with quandong chilli glaze, and for dessert, wattle seed pavlova with mango sauce. Main courses A$22–30.

PORT DOUGLAS

Catalina
22 Wharf Street
Tel: 07-4099 5287
Three ancient mango trees dominate the open veranda of this classic colonial building, awash with old Port Douglas charm. The food is Australian, with French and Asian influences. Main courses around A$29.

Nautilus
17 Murphy Street
Tel: 07-4099 5330
A Port Douglas institution: totally tropical with an island-architecture entrance and coconut-palm canopy, and a semi-al fresco dining experience. Modern Australian cuisine; mains around A$40, dinner only.

On the Inlet
3 Inlet Street
Tel: 07-4099 5255
"Sunset Special" between 4 and 6pm offers oysters or a bucket of prawns while you're watching the sun go down over the jungle-clad ranges behind Mossman Gorge. This innovative pier-front restaurant then resumes its role as one of the "Port's" premier restaurants, with a strong emphasis on fresh seafood

caught locally. Open daily noon–late. Mains around A$32

Attractions

BRISBANE

City Hall
Although dwarfed by high-rises, the City Hall Tower still has the best views to begin a tour of Brisbane. The City Hall, built in 1930, is one of the biggest in Australia; it has a museum and art gallery on the ground floor. Three tours daily, with free lunch-hour concerts. RSL Headquarters and underground shrine are in Anzac Square. The viewing platform and clock tower are open Mon–Fri 10am–3pm, Sat 10am–2.30pm.

Parliament House
At the corner of Alice and George streets, overlooking the Botanic Gardens, Parliament House was opened in 1868. This imposing example of French Renaissance architecture has a newer annexe that towers above the original structure. Tours are given five times a day unless Parliament is in session.

The Old Windmill and Observatory
Standing on Wickham Terrace, this is one of Brisbane's earliest buildings, dating from 1828. Built by convict labour, it was originally designed to operate as a windmill but a design error prevented its use. It was later turned into a signal post and finally a meteorological observatory.

What's On?

Pick up a copy of the two free entertainment guides – *Time Off* and *Rave* – from any café, as well as the Thursday edition of Brisbane's daily newspaper *The Courier Mail*, for an up-to-the-minute guide to what's on.

A useful website containing lots of information on events, accommodation and attractions is **www.ourbrisbane.com.**

Taking a Tour of Brisbane's Heritage

As in other Australian cities, Brisbane has a continuous tour bus that stops at each attraction. This "City Sights" tram-style bus departs at 45-minute intervals from Post Office Square, and you can get on and off all day.

For a tour of Brisbane's historic buildings, take a copy of the Brisbane City Council's Heritage Trails brochure from the National Trust at Old Government House, 2 George Street, tel: 07-3229 1788, or from any one of the tourist information booths.

The Queensland Cultural Centre
Spanning two blocks of riverfront directly across from the city, this complex is the cultural heart of Brisbane. It incorporates the Performing Arts Complex, Queensland Art Gallery, Queensland Museum, and State Library, plus several great cafés. Most attractions are free. For information and guided tours, tel: 07-3840 7444;

Parks and Gardens
Brisbane's main parks and gardens, scattered through the city and inner suburbs, have lately been enhanced by the addition of the Goodwill Walking Bridge, which links the old Botanic Gardens with the South Bank so you don't have to negotiate the hectic traffic; and by the Roma Street Parkland, 16 hectares (40 acres) of subtropical garden right in the heart of Brisbane. Ever-changing horticultural displays include unique specimens of some of the world's most endangered botanical species.

South Bank Parklands
Across the winding Brisbane River, this extensive redevelopment faces the city squarely. Created after the 1988 World Expo was held here, it includes a man-made tropical beach (a good idea, since Brisbane is one of the few places in Queensland with no natural swimming spots). There is also a boardwalk through a lush tropical rainforest. Other attractions include a Nepalese Pagoda, the Queensland Maritime Museum, a piazza with free entertainment for kids and adults, and a plethora of restaurants and cafés, tel: 07-3867 2051. Also see www.south-bank.net.au

The Casino
Housed in the six-storey atrium of the Brisbane colonial Treasury building, the casino has a fine location overlooking the Brisbane River. The building includes gaming emporium, restaurants and deluxe accommodation.

Lone Pine Koala Sanctuary
One of Brisbane's top attractions at Fig Tree Pocket, 11 km (7 miles) south of the city. As well as its colony of more than 100 koalas, the sanctuary has wombats, emus, Tasmanian devils, platypuses and other Australian animals. Open daily 8am–5pm.

The sanctuary is often included on longer Cityxpress bus or river cruises. Bus tours often stop at Mount Coot-tha Reserve, 8 km (5 miles) from the city. From here, you can look out over Brisbane and the surrounding countryside to Moreton Bay. Within the park are the Mount Coot-tha Botanic Gardens, a Tropical Display Dome and the Sir Thomas Brisbane Planetarium.

Shopping

Every Sunday, the vast **Riverside (Eagle Street) Market** is held at the Riverside Centre, with 150 craft stalls and many cafés. The **South Bank Markets** also offer craft and clothing on Friday evenings and weekends.

The main shopping centres are located around the Queen Street Mall, with the **Myer Centre** being the most comprehensive. The best selection of native handicrafts and artefacts can be found at **Queensland Aboriginal Creations** on George Street. Other souvenir items include rugs, garments and bags made from hides and skins, and jewellery fashioned from local gemstones (such as rubies, sapphires and opals). Large arcades include Wintergarden on the Mall, T&G, Rowes and Post Office Square.

Nightlife

The busy late-night spots in Brisbane are the Riverside Centre, Elizabeth Street, Petrie Terrace and Fortitude Valley. New eating places are constantly cropping up in New Farm.

Brisbane's main theatre company is the **Queensland Theatre Company**, based at the Performing Arts Complex. The **Powerhouse Centre for Live Arts** on the river at New Farm also offers regular performances and exhibitions, and downtown you'll find a plethora of new acts playing in pubs, clubs and restaurants.

Northern Territory

The Northern Territory is one of the world's last frontiers. It is commonly divided into the "Red Centre" and "Top End" by its residents.

When planning a trip to Darwin and the rest of the Top End, take into account that it only has two seasons: the Wet or monsoon season from December–April, and the Dry, from April–November. The latter is the more pleasant, but the wildlife attractions of the Wet Season draw many nature lovers.

In the Red Centre (where Alice Springs is the base), April–November mark the cooler months – again, much more pleasant than summer, when the heat can be blistering.

Getting Around

FROM THE AIRPORT

Darwin airport is 12 km (7½ miles) from the CBD, and a taxi costs around $24. For the 15-km (9-mile) journey to Alice Springs, the fare is around $25-30. Both cities are serviced by airport shuttles.

BY BUS

Both Darwin and Alice Springs have town bus services that connect accommodation precincts with the CBD. Darwinbus Tourcards allow unlimited travel for one or seven days. Buses connect the three central attractions – Darwin, Alice Springs and Ayers Rock. Services are frequent, comfortable and fast.

McCafferty's Greyhound (Tel: 132 030) runs daily services between Alice Springs and Yulara (It's 460 km/286 miles each way.)

BY TRAIN

There's only one railway in the Northern Territory. The recently extended **Ghan** (tel: 132147) runs straight through the middle of the country, from Adelaide in South Australia through Alice Springs and now on to Darwin. The two-night, 3,000-km (1,864-mile) trip can be broken in Katherine for short sightseeing tours by boat or helicopter, and Alice Springs for longer stopovers.

BY CAR

It is usually a long distance between attractions, but rental cars, camper vans and four-wheel drive vehicles are plentiful *(see page 342)*. But if you're getting around the bush independently, you must constantly remind yourself that you're in seriously frontier country.

Carrying adequate water, notifying people of your intentions, using reliable vehicles and protecting yourself from sunburn should be high on your list. Picking up hitch-hikers is, in general, a bad idea.

Independent travellers should also be aware that significant tracts of the Northern territory are designated as Aboriginal land, and a permit may be required to enter them.

BY AIR

The three main attractions – Darwin, Alice Springs and Ayers Rock are connected by an efficient airline service.

Where to Stay

DARWIN/TOP END

Darwin is spread over a large area and although many hotels can be found in the city centre, a number of pleasant options are located a short drive away. Keep in mind that the rates are often significantly higher during the dry season of May–October.

Since Darwin is the starting point for so many adventure travel options, there is a good selection of accommodation for backpackers and the budget-conscious. Many of these are conveniently located near the Transit Centre.

International (A$190–1,300)
Crowne Plaza Darwin
32 Mitchell Street
Darwin
Tel: 08-8982 0000
Fax: 08-8981 1765
www.crowneplaza.com.au
Centrally located high-rise, views of the harbour and city. Spa and health club.
MGM Grand Darwin
Gilruth Avenue
Darwin
Tel: 08-8943 8888
Freecall: 1800-891 118
Fax: 08-8943 8999
www.mgmgrand.com.au
A beachside casino hotel on 7 hectares (18 acres) adjoining a golf course and the Botanic Gardens.

Premier (A$155–500)
Marrakai Luxury All Suites
93 Smith Street
Darwin
Tel: 08-8982 3711
Freecall: 1800-653 732
Fax: 08-8981 9283
www.marrakai.com.au
Located in the city area, this is a high-rise of balcony apartments close to the Mall. Barbecue area, ideal for families or groups. Secure underground car park.
Novotel Atrium Darwin
100 The Esplanade
Darwin
Tel: 08-8941 0755
Fax: 08-8981 9025
www.noveldarwin.com.au
On the Esplanade in downtown Darwin, just a short walk from the city centre, with its own indoor tropical rainforest. Spacious hotel rooms and two-bedroom suites.
Parap Village Apartments
39–45 Parap Road
Parap
Tel: 08-8943 0500
Fax: 08-8941 3465
Five minutes' drive from the city

Standard Categories

- **International** Hotels, resorts or historic manor houses of unquestioned five-star standard
- **Premier** Four-star standard, including hotel chains, with a range of reliable services
- **Moderate** Comfortable, well-kept properties
- **Budget** Simple, clean and modest accommodation

centre and 10 from the airport, standard or deluxe large apartments overlooking two swimming pools.
Saville Park Suites
88 The Esplanade
Darwin
Tel: 08-8943 4333
Freecall: 1800-681 686
Fax: 08-8943 4388
www.savillesuites.com.au
On the Esplanade overlooking Darwin Harbour, foreshores, tropical parklands and the city skyline. Adjacent to the Transit Centre. Apartment style or traditional hotel services.

Moderate (A$100–340)
Botanic Gardens Apartments
17 Geranium Street
Stuart Park, Darwin
Tel: 08-8946 0300
Fax: 08-8981 0410
www.botanicgardensapts.com.au
High on a hill overlooking the Botanic Gardens and the Arafura Sea.
Mirambeena Resort Darwin
64 Cavenagh Street
Darwin
Tel: 08-8946 0111
Freecall: 1800-891 100
Fax: 08-8981 5116
www.mirambeena.com.au
In the heart of the city, with lush tropical pool area. Treetops restaurant, poolside bar and café, minigolf and gym.
Palms City Resort
64 The Esplanade
Darwin
Tel: 08-8982 9200
Freecall: 1800-829 211
Fax: 08-8981 9575

www.palmscityresort.com
Modern motel rooms or tropical-style villas with balcony barbecues.

Budget (A$90–130)
Steeles at Larrakeyah
4 Zealandia Crescent
Darwin
Tel: 08-8941 3636
www.steeles-at-larrakeyah.com.au
Private, quiet B&B close to shops, tourist facilities, Mindil Beach markets and Botanic Gardens. Hosts Janette and Roger are knowledgeable long-term Territorians.

Hostels (from A$20 per person)
Frogs Hollow Backpackers Lodge
27 Lindsay Street
Darwin
Tel: 08-8941 2600
Freecall: 1800-068 686
Fax: 08-8941 0758
www.frogs-hollow.com.au
Popular spacious hostel in city, 10-minute walk to Transit Centre. Spas, travel info. Clean, friendly; off-season rates.

TOP END/OUTSIDE DARWIN

International (A$140–310)
Gagudju Crocodile Holiday Inn
Flinders Street
Jabiru (Kakadu)
Tel: 08-8979 9000
Fax: 08-8979 9098
www.gagudju-dreaming.com
Shaped like a giant crocodile, with the swimming pool as its stomach, this is the only deluxe hotel in the Kakadu National Park.
Seven Spirit Bay Wilderness Lodge
Garig Gunak Barlu National Park
Coburg Peninsula
Tel: 08-8979 0281
Fax: 08-8979 0284
www.sevenspiritbay.com
A 45-minute scenic flight from Darwin transports you to the sea breezes, sights, sounds and natural harmony of the tropics – day and night. Guests stay in free-standing, airy, hexagonal "habitats", each with an open-air bathroom, set in a tropical garden. Located in Garig Gunak Barlu

National Park in Aboriginal Arnhem Land, where entry is by permit only and extremely limited.

Moderate (A$105–240)
Gagudju Lodge
Cooinda
Tel: 08-8979 0145
Freecall: 1800-500 401
Fax: 08-8979 0148
www.gagudju-dreaming.com
Situated on the Yellow Water Billabong, 1 km (½ mile) from the Warraadjan Cultural Centre. Provides both comfortable units and budget rooms.
Mercure Inn Katherine
Cypress Street (off Stuart Highway)
Katherine
Tel: 08-8972 1744
Fax: 08-8972 2790
www.mercure.com.au
A 3-hour drive from Darwin brings you to this historic town. Tours of the stunning Katherine Gorge. Two levels of accommodation.

RED CENTRE/ALICE SPRINGS/ ULURU (AYERS ROCK)

Alice Springs is the rather characterless service town for the whole Central Australian desert area, although many striking attractions within a short driving distance make it worth considering as part of your itinerary. Uluru (Ayers Rock) is about six hours' scenic desert drive away; and the small village of Yulara caters for its visitors.

International (A$145–500)
Crowne Plaza Alice Springs
Barrett Drive
Alice Springs
Tel: 08-8950 8000
Fax: 08-8952 3822
www.ichotelsgroup.com
Low-rise luxury resort with spectacular views of the MacDonnell ranges.
Sails in the Desert Hotel
Yulara Drive
Yulara
Tel: 02-9339 1040
Freecall: 1300-139 889
Fax: 02-9339 4555

Standard Categories

- **International** Hotels, resorts or historic manor houses of unquestioned five-star standard
- **Premier** Four-star standard, including hotel chains, with a range of reliable services
- **Moderate** Comfortable, well-kept properties
- **Budget** Simple, clean and modest accommodation

www.voyages.com.au
The premier hotel at Yulara, famous for its soaring white "sails", which shelter outdoor areas from the intense desert sun.

Premier (A$180–395)
Alice Springs Resort
34 Stott Terrace
Alice Springs
Tel: 08-8951 4545
Fax: 08-8953 0995
www.alicespringsresort.com.au
Five minutes' walk to town, quality rooms, oasis-style pool area and à la carte restaurant.
Kings Canyon Resort
Luritja Road
Kings Canyon Watarrka
National Park
Tel: 08-8956 7442
Freecall: 1300-139 889
Fax: 08-8956 7410
www.voyages.com.au
Six kilometres (4 miles) from the spectacular canyon, providing all levels of accommodation.
Outback Pioneer Hotel and Lodge
Yulara Drive
Yulara
Tel: 02-9339 1040
Freecall: 1300-139 889
Fax: 02-93394555
www.voyages.com.au
Ayers Rock location with both comfortable private rooms and dormitory-style accommodation.

Moderate (from A$110)
Desert Palms Resort
74 Barrett Drive
Alice Springs
Tel: 08-8952 5977
Fax: 08-8953 4176
www.desertpalms.com.au

One kilometre (⅔ mile) from town, great-value air-conditioned villas with private verandas and lush tropical pool area.

Budget (from A$60)
Todd Tavern
1 Todd Mall
Alice Springs
Tel: 08-8952 1255
www.toddtavern.com.au
The only traditional pub left in Alice. Meals are served 7am–9pm.

Hostels (from A$25 per person)
Pioneer Youth Hostel
Corner of Parsons Street and Leichhardt Terrace
Alice Springs
Tel: 08-8952 8855
Fax: 08-8952 4144
www.yha.com.au
Built within the walls of a heritage-classed outdoor movie theatre; close to shops, cafés and pubs.

Eating Out

Darwin has a fair range of restaurants for a city of its size, and its many immigrants have educated the locals towards the pleasures of a curry lakhsa over the more traditional Aussie stale meat pie. Just go to the Mindil Beach Market on Thursday night or the Parap Market on Saturday morning for a sampling of Darwin's Asian offerings. Around dusk, many Darwinians head for the Wharf Precinct where you can buy fish and chips and a beer and take a seat by the water. **Note:** BYO means "bring your own alcohol".

Modern Australian
Café Twilight
2 Lindsay Street
Darwin
Tel: 08-8981 8631
BYO. Main courses A$18 lunch, A$24 dinner. Always full of Darwin locals, the dishes are Australian with a fusion of Asian and European influences. Set downstairs in a classic old-style Darwin house. Mosaic-floor courtyard and tropical gardens.
Cornucopia Museum Cafe

Conacher Street
Fannie Bay
Darwin
Tel: 08-8981 1002
Licensed. Main courses A$15–25.
Great salads. Located in front of
the excellent NT Museum,
overlooking the harbour. Daily
9am–5pm. Need to book for the
popular Sunday brunch.

Katie's Bistro
At the Knotts Crossing Resort,
corner of Giles and Cameron
streets, Katherine
Tel: 08-8972 2511
Main courses from A$20–26. The
setting alone is delightful. Dine in a
tropical garden under coconut palms
at this remote tropical resort – the
best deals are the local seafood, in
particular the succulent barramundi.

Rorke's Drift Bar & Café
46 Mitchell Street, Darwin
Tel: 08-8941 7171
Popular with hungry backpackers.
Great steaks. Open 7 days till late.

The Sounds of Silence Dinner
Yulara
In the desert sunset, enjoy a
gourmet meal of barbecued
barramundi and kangaroo, with an
astronomer to guide you around the
glittering stars. Book in Yulara.
Around A$40 per adult.

Asian/International
The Hanuman
28 Mitchell Street
Tel: 08-8941 3500
Licensed. Main courses about
A$20. Intimate al fresco dining on
famous Nonya dishes such as
ginger-flower barramundi and their
signature dish of Hanuman oysters.

**Mindil Beach Sunset Market
Association**
Mindil Beach
Tel: 08-8981 3454
Dishes A$6–10. Open from 5pm
Thur evenings, late April–October. If
you pass through Darwin on a
Thursday, there's no prettier spot
than this beach with its huge craft
market and sensational
international food stalls.

Nirvana
6 Dashwood Crescent
Darwin
Tel: 08-8981 2025

Licensed restaurant specialising in
Indian, Thai and Malaysian food.

Cantonese/Sichuan
Dragon Court
MGM Grand Darwin Casino
Gilruth Avenue
Darwin
Tel: 08-8943 8888
Licensed. Main courses about
A$20–25. Rave reviews for the most
authentic Cantonese in Darwin –
many say in Australia. Most popular
are the seafood dishes.

Malaysian
Rendezvous Cafe
Star Village, 32 Smith Street Mall,
Darwin
Tel: 08-8981 9231
Well known for the best curry
lakhsa in town, served in a simple
café with tables and booths. Main
courses around A$10.

Seafood
Crustaceans on the Wharf
Stokes Hill Wharf
Tel: 08-8981 8658
Licensed and BYO. Mains
A$27–60. Fascinating views from
this outdoor setting on the end of
a working wharf. Included in the
range of seafood dishes are
lobsters, prawns, crabs, mussels,
scallops, crayfish and bugs (a type
of crayfish).

Attractions

SIGHTSEEING

Museum and Art Gallery of the Northern Territory
This is essential viewing for the first-
time visitor to the Top End. Among
the exhibitions are a comprehensive
collection of Aboriginal artworks, a
memorial exhibition of Cyclone Tracy,
and others covering natural
sciences, history, and culture.
Mon–Fri 9am–5pm, Sat and Sun
10am–5pm. Admission free.

Uluru (Ayers Rock)
Although many people think Uluru
overshadows Alice Springs, the
world's largest monolith actually
lies some 440 km (250 miles)

away – a distance that usually
takes about six hours to drive. You
can fly directly to the Rock these
days. Climbing is still permitted,
although the traditional Aboriginal
owners are trying to stop the
practice, which they see as
dangerous and a desecration of
the sacred site. For more on the
Rock, *see page 279*.
Note: the Aboriginal-owned
company Anangu Tours operates
from Yulara with a variety of
unusual tours, tel: 08-8956 3138.
Other sites of interest within easy
striking distance from Alice Springs
are **The Olgas (Kata Tjuta)** and
King's Canyon; tour operators
advertise widely in hotels. It's also
popular to take camel treks and
balloon rides in the desert.

Nightlife

Darwin pubs are popular meeting
places for the locals, with a varied
nightlife ranging from rowdy live-
band performances to the relative
sophistication of imported casino
entertainers. Although the city's
hard-drinking, macho/sexist
culture is on the wane, pubs are
still the centre of social life. A
good start is the **Tourist &
Entertainment Precinct**, running
the length of Mitchell Street.

Shopping

Darwin and Alice Springs are two of
the best places in Australia to buy
Aboriginal artefacts.

In Darwin, try the **Arnhem Land
Gallery** in Cavenagh Street and
Aboriginal Fine Arts, corner of
Mitchell and Knuckley streets.
Darwin also offers unique
opportunities to buy locally
produced gems – Paspaley pearls
and Argyle diamonds.

In Alice Springs, there are
Aboriginal art stores at every turn.
The **CAAMA Shop** at 101 Todd
Street, run by Central Australian
Aboriginal Media Association, on
Hartley Street, is worth checking
out, as is **Gallery Gondwana**
situated at 43 Todd Mall.

Western Australia

Perth

With a population of 1.4 million, the capital of Western Australia lies astride the Swan River some 19 km (12 miles) inland from the seaport of Fremantle. It is a very relaxed, spacious, well-designed city, and enjoys a year-round average of 8 hours sunshine per day.

The **WA Tourist Centre** is in Albert Facey House on Forrest Place, next to the GPO, tel: 1300-361 351. Open Mon–Thur 8.30am–6pm, Fri 8.30am–7pm. Winter (May–July) Mon–Thur 8.30am–5.30pm, Fri 8.30am–6pm. Sat 8.30am–12.30pm. It has a good selection of publications covering tourism and entertainment throughout WA.

Getting Around

FROM THE AIRPORT

Taxis from the domestic and international airports cost around A$25 and A$35 respectively. A shuttle bus runs between Fremantle and the airport. Book with Fremantle Tourist Bureau, tel: 9431 7878. The cost is around A$20 single, A$25 double; home or hotel pick-up A$5.

PUBLIC TRANSPORT

Perth has five bus routes aboard the Central Area Transit (CAT). The "Perth Tram" (actually a bus) operates a circuit of tourist attractions. Regular bus services have fares based on a zone system, with discount passes. For maps and on-the-spot information, a

Transperth office is in the Plaza Arcade (off the Hay Street Mall), tel: 136 213, www.transperth.wa.gov.au.

Where to Stay

PERTH, FREMANTLE AND ENVIRONS

International (A$200–500)
The Loose Box
6825 Great Eastern Highway
Mundaring
Tel: 08-9295 1787
Fax: 08-9295 3111
www.loosebox.com
Located in the ranges 35 km (20 miles) east of Perth, private cottages are available to guests of the restaurant, acknowledged as one of the finest in Australia *(See Where To Eat page 384)*.
Radisson Observation City Hotel
The Esplanade, Scarborough Beach,
Tel: 08-9245 1000
Fax: 08-9224 7788
www.rendezvous.com.au
Ultra-modern hotel complex overlooking the Indian Ocean, on white sandy beaches just 15 minutes from city. Includes many restaurants, bars and deluxe facilities.
Sheraton Perth
207 Adelaide Terrace, Perth
Tel: 08-9224 7777
Fax: 08-9224 7788
www.sheraton.com/perth
Deluxe and centrally located; all rooms have breathtaking views of the Swan River or the city skyline.

Premier (A$110–240)
Esplanade Hotel – Fremantle
Corner of Marine Terrace and Essex Street, Fremantle
Tel: 08-9432 4000
Fax: 08-9430 4539
www.esplanadehotelfremantle.com.au
In the heart of Fremantle, a grand gold rush-style building with continuous verandas divided into private balconies.
Pier 21 Resort
7–9 John Street
Fremantle
Tel: 08-9336 2555
Fax: 08-9336 2140
www.pier21club.com.au

Peaceful location on the banks of the Swan River in Fremantle. All rooms offer panoramic views.
Sebel of Perth
37 Pier Street
Tel: 08-9325 7655
Fax: 08-9325 7383
www.mirvachotels.com.au
The Sebel is a boutique hotel featuring a large heated swimming pool in a spectacular courtyard overlooked by bar and café. Ideally located close to the best shopping and the Swan River.

Moderate (A$80–180)
Bel Eyre Motel
285 Great Eastern Highway
Tel: 08-9277 2733
Fax: 08-9479 1113
www.beleyremotel.com.au
Convenient location, courtesy airport transfers available and swimming pool.
Hotel Ibis Perth
334 Murray Street
Tel: 08-9322 2844
Fax: 08-9321 6314
In the centre of Perth, with popular restaurants and bars.
Kings Hotel
517 Hay Street
Tel: 08-9325 6555
Fax: 08-9221 1539
www.kingshotel.com.au
Central location near the Mall and Swan River; good value.
Ocean Beach Hotel
Corner of Eric Street and Marine Parade, Cottesloe Beach
Tel: 08-9384 2555
www.obh.com.au
Much loved by locals, the hotel is right on the beachfront. Spacious rooms and great counter meals.

Budget (A$65–90)
Adelphi Hotel Apartments
130A Mounts Bay Road
Tel: 08-9322 4666
Fax: 08-9322 4580
Excellent-value family-style accommodation only two minutes' walk from Perth City Centre.
Flag Motor Lodge
129 Great Eastern Highway
Rivervale
Tel: 08-9277 2766
Fax: 08-9479 1304

Standard Categories

- **International** Hotels, resorts or historic manor houses of unquestioned five-star standard
- **Premier** Four-star standard, including hotel chains, with a range of reliable services
- **Moderate** Comfortable, well-kept properties
- **Budget** Simple, clean and modest accommodation

www.accom@flagmotorlodge.com.au
Inexpensive units, some with cooking facilities. Restaurant and room service; swimming pool, bus to city.
The Witch's Hat
148 Palmerston Street
Perth
Tel: 08-9228 4228
Near bus terminal and Perth railway station. Refurbished Victorian residence with a lfresco dining and Internet café.

Hostels (from A$20 per person)
YMCA Jewell House
180 Goderich Street
Perth
Tel: 08-9325 8488
www.ymcajewellhouse.com
Large, with clean, comfortable rooms. A 15-minute walk to the city, or catch the Red Clipper bus, which passes outside.

MARGARET RIVER/ SOUTHWEST

International (A$310–485)
Cape Lodge
Caves Road
Margaret River
Tel: 08-9755 6311
Fax: 08-9755 6322
www.capelodge.com.au
Stunningly beautiful and tranquil country retreat between Yallingup and Margaret River, an ideal base to visit the area's famous boutique vineyards and beaches. Mansion within a plantation and gardens, overlooking a private lake and featuring 15 luxurious rooms and suites, seven with spas.

Moderate (A$100–150)
Margaret River Holiday Cottages
Lot 2, Boodjioup Road
Margaret River
Tel/fax: 08-9757 2185
Homestyle two-bedroom cottages in tranquil park setting; fully equipped and ideal for families. Bushland walks to see kangaroos and native flowers.

BROOME/KIMBERLEY

International (A$25–1,700)
Cable Beach Club Resort
Cable Beach Road
Broome
Tel: 08-9192 0400
Fax: 08-9192 2249
www.cablebeachclub.com
Located on beautiful Cable Beach. Deluxe bungalows reflect Broome's Asian heritage: designs are in keeping with the traditional style of pearling-masters' houses, with wide verandas and lattice screens. The grounds comprise lush tropical gardens, waterfalls and swimming pools.
El Questro
Gibb River Road
Kununurra
Tel: 08-9169 1777
Fax: 08-9161 4320
www.elquestro.com.au
A vast cattle station in the Kimberley, on the edge of the Chamberlain Gorge, El Questro offers many classic Outback activities like barramundi fishing, bathing in natural springs, night crocodile spotting and mustering by helicopter. There are also trips to an impressive rock gallery of Aboriginal paintings in the Chamberlain Gorge. Accommodation ranges from inexpensive campsites to luxurious homestead suites. Gourmet cuisine at the main homestead. Packages available.

Eating Out

WA has won several Australian culinary awards, and the State is now considered a force to be reckoned with. Both Perth and the Margaret River region have an excellent choice of Modern Australian, French and Italian restaurants. Bistro life is thriving in Fremantle with many waterside seafood eateries. Perth's café scene is centred on Hay Street, Subiaco, and King Street, City. Ethnic eateries are concentrated in the Northbridge area of the city.
Note: BYO means "bring your own alcohol".

Modern Australian
Coco's Restaurant
85 The Esplanade, South Perth
Tel: 08-9474 3030
Beef and fresh seafood are the specialities. Seafood is filleted and beef hung on the premises. Fully licensed, Main courses in the A$26–35 range.
Flutes Café
Brookland Valley Vineyard
Caves Road, Willyabrup
Tel: 08-9755 6250
Licensed. Main courses about A$30–35. A must for all visitors to the Margaret River region, this café has picturesque views, wine tastings, great coffee and cakes – not to mention a fine set lunch and dinner menu.
44 King Street
44 King Street
Perth
Tel: 08-9321 4476
Licensed. Main courses about A$22. Open all day, serving everything from Asian brunch to late-night Italian suppers. Noted for its excellent coffee and cakes.
Fraser's Restaurant
Fraser Avenue, King's Park, West Perth
Tel: 08-9481 7100
Licensed. Main courses about A$25. One of the most popular restaurants in Perth with great views of the city and imaginative dishes. Great outdoor area, seats 100.
Jackson's
483 Beaufort Street, Highgate
Tel: 08-9328 1177
Surprisingly delicate, Euro-accented food in a friendly semi-suburban environment.

Asian
Joe's Oriental Diner
Hyatt Hotel, 99 Adelaide Terrace

Perth
Tel: 08-9225 1268
Licensed. Main courses about A$20.
Classy Asian-theme restaurant
producing good-quality and
inexpensive dishes from Thailand,
Indonesia, Malaysia and Singapore.

French

The Loose Box
6825 Great Eastern Highway
Mundaring
Tel: 08-9295 1787
Licensed. Open Wed–Sat, Sun
lunch. Four-course set menu around
A$88. One of the best restaurants
in Australia, this superb French
chalet complex is a 30-minute drive
from Perth. Avoid the weekend
throng of adoring Perth locals and
visit during the week, or stay over:
six cottages available.

Italian

Perugino
77 Outram Street
West Perth
Tel: 08-9321 5420
Licensed. Main courses about
A$40. Exquisite Italian cuisine with
contemporary influences.
Exceptional seasonal produce is
used to produce sensational food.
Professional and informed service
in a classical atmosphere.

Seafood

**The Oyster Bar Mead's Mosman
Bay**
15 Johnson Parade
Mosman Park
Perth
Tel: 08-9383 3388
Licensed. Main courses about
A$35. This attractive venue is the
place to be on a sunny day. The
freshest possible seafood is
carefully yet simply prepared.

Attractions

SIGHTSEEING

Astronaut John Glenn looked down
on Perth during one orbit and
declared it "The City of Lights", and
Perth's clear skies also offer a
breathtaking vista of the stars. The
Southern Cross and Milky Way are
sparkling features of the night sky
and you can get an expert guided
tour at the **Perth Observatory**, just
outside Perth. Book well in advance
on 08-9293 8255,
www.wa.gov.au/perthobs.

A perfect way to spend the
daylight hours is to take a picnic
into the bush or even the city's
Kings Park. Find all-Western fine
produce and Lamont's Swan Valley-
grown wines at King Street Food
and Wine shop, Shop 1, Newspaper
House, 125 St Georges Terrace.

King's Park

A lush 400 hectares (990 acres) of
natural bushlands within Perth, with
attractions including sculpted
gardens and wildflowers.

London Court

Perth's central city shopping arcade
recreated as a 16th-century English
street (believe it or not).

The Western Australian Museum

Situated on Francis Street with fine
displays of whales and a variety of
Aboriginal cultural artefacts. Open
daily 9.30am–5pm; www.museum.
wa.gov.au.

The Art Gallery

Located at 47 James Street,
featuring contemporary and original
Australian painting.

The Old Mill

Restored as a pioneer folk museum
in South Perth.

Western Australian Maritime Museum (Fremantle)

Recognised as a world leader in
maritime conservation, this new
museum provides visitors with a
unique view of early visits by
European sailing ships to the
Australian continent. It sits in the
midst of historical buildings and near
the fishing harbour – home of some
of the best fish and chip shops in the
country. Open daily 9.30am–5pm;
www.mm.wa.gov.au. The original
museum now known as **Shipwreck
Gallery** and featuring Dutch wrecks,
is in nearby Cliff Street.

Fremantle Chocolate Factory

This gourmet attraction entices you
to over-indulge on chocolate, fudge,
biscuits and sweets, by allowing you
to watch them being manufactured.
Open daily 10am–5pm daily;
312–314 South Terrace, Fremantle,
tel: 08-9335 5529.

Culture

Perth has a vibrant cultural life
and is the proud home of
Australia's longest-running arts
event, the Perth International Arts
Festival, which takes place in
February and March
(www.uwa.edu.au/festival).
Outstanding drama is regularly
presented by the **Black Swan
Theatre Company**, **Perth Theatre
Company** and **Deckchair Theatre**.

Children's events, including the
Awesome International Children's
Festival in November–December,
includes contributions by **Barking
Gecko Theatre** and **Spare Parts
Puppet Theatre**. Given Perth's
Mediterranean climate, outdoor
concerts and performances are
popular in the summer months.

Art galleries worth visiting
include **Craftwest**, 357 Murray
Street; **Gomboc Sculpture Gallery**,
James Street, Middle Swan, open
Wed–Sun 10am–5pm; and the
Fremantle Arts Centre, 1 Finnerty
Street, Fremantle. Perth is also
home to a surprising number of
international best-selling authors,
including Booker Prize winner Tim
Winton, and Elizabeth Jolly.

Perth's multitude of theatres
and concert venues offer year-
round entertainment. **The Perth
Concert Hall** is the performance
home for the West Australian
Symphony Orchestra; **His
Majesty's Theatre** houses the
West Australian Ballet and Opera
companies, and the **Playhouse** is
the base for the Perth Theatre
Company. Other city-based venues
offering plays, musicals and
cabarets are the **Burswood
Casino's Showroom**, the Art Deco-
style **Regal Theatre** and the
Subiaco Theatre Centre. Bookings
and enquiries on Perth's two

booking services: BOCS Ticketing, 08-9484 1133; Freecall: 1800-193 300; www.bocsticketing.com.au, and Ticketmaster7, tel: 136-100, www.ticketmaster7.com.au.

Day Trips from Perth

Boats leave the city, Fremantle and Hillarys Boat Harbour for **Rottnest** for days of walking, cycling and swimming on this small paradise just off the coast. Package tours are available for visits to the **Pinnacles Desert** north of Perth, which is well worth a trip. On the way, stop-offs to examine roadside bush are very rewarding in the wildflower season of July–November.

The **Swan Valley** is another worthwhile day-trip. Historic wineries, top restaurants and cafés and some fine galleries can all be found in this fertile river plain. Recognised for its fortified wines, the Swan Valley also produces good reds and memorable whites.

Nightlife

A variety of publications including *Scoop* and *Perth's Cultural Guide* are available from hotels and the Western Australian Visitor Centre. Daily updates are available in the entertainment segment of the *West Australian* newspaper and every Thursday in *X-Press*, a free magazine with details of bands, exhibitions and clubs.

Shopping

Distinctive local products to shop for are opals, Aboriginal crafts and iron-ore jewellery. For lively market shopping go to the **Subiaco Pavilion** and the **Wanneroo Markets**.

Hay Street Mall is Perth's most enjoyable place to shop. Branching away from this central mall are the other traffic-free shopping arcades: **Piccadilly**, **City**, **Trinity**, **Plaza** and **Carillon**.

Tasmania

Many of this island state's 474,000 residents think of themselves as Tasmanians first and Australians second, with the mainland often referred to as "the big island".

Tasmania is unlike the rest of Australia, thanks to its high rainfall and dense vegetation. Picturesque Hobart, with a population of 180,000, is the island state's capital. Surrounding one of the world's finest deep-water harbours, the city covers the broad lower valley of the Derwent River. Mount Wellington provides a spectacular backdrop to the city and the 1,270-metre (4,166-ft) summit provides a fine view of the city, and a good portion of south and central Tasmania as well.

The first stop for visitors should be the **Tasmanian Travel & Information Centre**, on the corner of Elizabeth and Davey streets in Hobart. Tel: 03-6230 8233. Open Mon–Fri 8.30am– 5.30pm; weekends and holidays 9am–5pm.

Here bookings can be made for tours and accommodation around Tasmania. Information is also available from Mures Fish Centre at Victoria Dock.

Where to Stay

HOBART

International (A$200–500)
Hotel Grand Chancellor
1 Davey Street
Hobart
Tel: 03-6235 4535;
Freecall: 1800-625 138
Fax: 03-6223 8175
This deluxe hotel is situated in the historic Docks area, within walking distance of popular restaurants. Panoramic river views.

Premier (A$110–240)
Lenna of Hobart
20 Runnymede Street
Battery Point
Tel: 03-6232 3900;
Freecall: 1800-030 633
Fax: 03-6224 0112
Award-winning colonial hotel ideally located in Battery Point, the historic headland above Salamanca Place which is the home of Hobart's trendy restaurants and cafés.
Quest Serviced Apartments
Hobart Brooker Avenue (corner of Davenport Street)
Tel: 03-6236 9656
Spacious, immaculately finished apartments, five minutes' drive from city centre.
Rydges Hobart
Corner of Argyle and Lewis streets, North Hobart
Tel: 03-6231 1588;
Freecall: 1800-801 703
Fax: 03-6231 1916
www.rydges.com
Grand historic hotel in leafy North Hobart, minutes from the city centre, offering luxury antique suites or contemporary decor.

Moderate (A$80–180)
There are many small, historic B&Bs in the Battery Point area. Although quite a few have succumbed to Ye Olde Twee and are decked out with throw-pillows and beaming hosts, the location is excellent.
Crelin Lodge
1 Crelin Street
Battery Point
Freecall: 1800-030 776
Fax: 03-6223 3995

Standard Categories

- **International** Hotels, resorts or historic manor houses of unquestioned five-star standard
- **Premier** Four-star standard, including hotel chains, with a range of reliable services
- **Moderate** Comfortable, well-kept properties
- **Budget** Simple, clean and modest accommodation

Fully self-contained one- and two-bedroom holiday apartments.

Tantallon Lodge Edwardian B&B Guest House
8 Mona Street
Battery Point
Tel/fax: 03-6224 1724
Grand Edwardian house; many rooms have river or mountain views.

Budget (A$55–85)
Hobart Tower Motel
300 Park Street
Newtown
Tel: 03-6228 0166
Fax: 03-6278 1056
One of the best-value options in Hobart. The rooms are spacious and provide a high standard of comfort and facilities. Family units available.

Montgomery's Private Hotel
9 Argyle Street, Hobart
Tel: 03-6231 2660
Clean, bright and comfortable with some shared facilities.

Hostels (from A$20 per person)
Central City Backpackers
138 Collins Street
Tel: 03-6224 2404
Massive building, with a maze of rooms, sparse but clean. Dormitories and private rooms.

Adelphi Court YHA
17 Stoke Street
Newtown
Tel: 03-6228 4829
Fax: 03-6278 2047
Hostel as well as guesthouse accommodation.

OUTSIDE HOBART

Wherever you go in Tasmania, you're never far away from quality historic accommodation. In popular destinations, such as Launceston, Strahan, Stanley and the Tasman Peninsula, there are a number of beautiful cottages and a spattering of luxury lets in larger homes.

International (from A$240)
Cradle Mountain Lodge
Cradle Mountain
Tel: 03-6492 1303;
Freecall: 1800-737 678
Fax: 03-6492 1309

Standard Categories

- **International** Hotels, resorts or historic manor houses of unquestioned five-star standard
- **Premier** Four-star standard, including hotel chains, with a range of reliable services
- **Moderate** Comfortable, well-kept properties
- **Budget** Simple, clean and modest accommodation

www.cradlemountainlodge.com.au
Wilderness retreat with secluded cabins and alpine spa at the entrance to the Cradle Mountain–Lake St Clair National Park. There are over 20 walking tracks and the chance to breathe what the Australian scientists claim is some of the purest air in the world.

Franklin Manor
The Esplanade, Strahan
Tel: 03-6471 7311
Fax: 03-6471 7267
www.franklinmanor.com.au
Situated at the edge of Macquarie Harbour with a range of accommodation, including rooms within the historic mansion and in the old stables. Franklin is known for its excellent restaurant.

Freycinet Lodge
Freycinet National Park
via Coles Bay
Tel: 03-6257 0101
Fax: 03-6257 0278
Environmentally sensitive resort development in unspoilt coastal setting. Comfortable private bush cabins lead down to tiny beach areas. Restaurant and bar overlook Great Oyster Bay. Seasonal whale watching, diving with seals, hiking and special tour programmes available.

Premier (A$110–240)
Piners Loft
The Esplanade, Strahan
Tel: 03-6471 7036
Fax: 03-6471 7588
Amazing pole-house construction overlooking Macquarie Harbour. Features innovative design in timber using recycled huon pine, celery-top

pine and other prized local timbers. This is a place where travelling groups of two to six people can experience luxury at a reasonable cost.

Moderate (A$80–180)
Boat Harbour Beach Resort
Tel: 03-6445 1107
Fax: 03-6445 1027
www.boatharbourbeachresort.com
An exceptionally picturesque, European-style holiday beach-stay between the tulips of Wynyard and history of Stanley. Comfortable, unit-style accommodation with excellent restaurant and very pretty bush and beach surrounds.

Bronte Park Highland Village
Bronte Park, 6 km (4 miles) north of the Lyell Highway (Lake Country)
Tel: 03-6289 1126
A half hour's drive from Lake St Clair, this utterly peaceful holiday village features converted hydro-electric workers' huts, originally built to accommodate fishermen. Well-designed private cottages and an inexpensive restaurant serving simple but excellent fish dinners. Access by Tasmanian Wilderness Transport from Launceston or Devonport.

King Island Holiday Village
Grassy, King Island
Tel: 03-6461 1177;
Freecall: 1800-359 993
Fly from Wynyard or Melbourne; hire cars available. This clean, green Bass Strait island is well worth holidaying in. It produces Australia's finest beef and cheese and is the shipwreck capital of the Southern Hemisphere, with more than 60 wrecks in the past 200 years. An ex-mining town, Grassy has a population of around 50. Look out over gorgeous empty beaches and experience three coasts within an hour's drive.

Penny Royal Motel & Apartments
147 Paterson Street
Launceston
Tel: 03-6331 6699;
Freecall: 1800-060 954
Fax: 03-6334 4282
www.leisureinns.com.au
Historic watermill renovated to a hotel with rooms or self-contained

apartments, restaurant and tavern. Five minutes' walk to the Cataract Gorge.

Port Arthur Lodge
Arthur Highway
Port Arthur
Tel: 03-6250 2888
Fax: 03-6250 2999
www.portarthurlodge.com
Award-winning natural-design log cabins all with log fires, overlooking Stewarts Bay; a short walk from the Port Arthur Historic Site.

Silver Ridge Retreat
46 Rysavy Road, Mount Roland, via Sheffield
Tel: 03-6491 1727
Fax: 03-6491 1925
www.silverridgeretreat.com.au
Idyllic rural getaway featuring self-contained accommodation located right at the foot of breathtaking Mount Roland. There are great walks, especially to Roland summit. It is also only a 40-minute drive to Cradle Mountain.

Eating Out

HOBART

Most good restaurants are concentrated in the waterfront area, particularly in the restored Salamanca Place, at the base of Battery Point. Further around the waterfront in the Dock area are more touristy seafood restaurants. **Note:** BYO means "bring your own alcohol".

Modern Australian
Mummaluka
89 Salamanca Place
Tel: 03-6224 2929
Licensed. An original menu specialises in steaks, fresh Tasmanian seafood, home made gnocchi and a vegetarian dish or two, all prepared with flare and novelty. Main courses around A$23.

Retro Cafe
Corner of Salamanca Place and Montpelier Retreat
Tel: 03-6223 3073
BYO. Main courses about A$15. The best coffee in Hobart and a great place for breakfast with all the trimmings included.

Moorilla Estate
Moorilla Estate
655 Main Road, Berriedale
Tel: 03-6277 9900
www.moorilla.com.au
Licensed. Main courses about A$20. Just a short drive to the outskirts of Hobart takes you to this vineyard and a great opportunity to sample excellent wines with a menu designed to complement them. Take a stroll around the vineyard after lunch.

Asian
Vanidol's
353 Elizabeth Street
North Hobart
Tel: 03-6234 9307
BYO. Main courses A$20. Extremely popular; mostly Thai dishes as well as Indian and Indonesian, very reasonably priced. The laksa is legendary.

Japanese
Orizuru Sushi Bar
Victoria Dock
Tel: 03-6231 1790
Licensed. Main courses from about A$20. A casual Japanese dockside restaurant overlooking Victoria Dock. Still popular with fishermen, the range and freshness of the seafood is of the highest standard. Outside tables.

Seafood
Kelley's Seafood Restaurant
5 Knopwood St, Battery Point
Tel: 03-6224 7225
Licensed. Full meals A$50–75. Located in an old sail-maker's cottage in Battery Point, Hobart's most historic waterside suburb, Kelley's speciality is seafood. Friendly service, classic seafood fare and the freshest ingredients.

Mure's Upper Deck Restaurant
Victoria Dock
Tel: 03-6231 1999
Licensed. Main courses about A$30. An institution in Tasmania, with an idyllic location. All the seafood is superb, from the Pacific oysters to the Tasmanian salmon.

Prossers on the Beach
Beach Road
Sandy Bay
Tel: 03-6225 2276
The perfect lunchtime spot, facing the Derwent River.

Vegetarian
Sirens
6 Victoria Street
Tel: 03-6234 2634
Licensed. Full meals A$50–75. Classy vegetarian cuisine, lush decor and relaxed atmosphere. Sirens donates part of their profits to ecologically sound charities.

WEST COAST

Franklin Manor
The Esplanade
Strahan
Tel: 03-6471 7311
Licensed. Two fixed-price menus A$45 and A$85, as well as à la carte. This charming manor hotel restaurant presents a fastidiously designed menu of locally produced ingredients which changes daily.

Ormiston House
Strahan
Tel: 03-6471 7077
www.ormistonhouse.com.au
Exclusive accommodation: only five rooms, four of which are named after ex-owner and founder of Strahan, Frederick Ormiston Henry. Close to Macquarie Harbour with fine in-house dining.

Attractions

SIGHTSEEING

Places of interest in Hobart are included in a self-guided walking tour organised by the National Trust, in a booklet called *An Architectural Guide to the City of Hobart*. It takes in the finest examples of Georgian architecture – many of which are located in **Davey** and **Macquarie streets**, **Battery Point** and **Salamanca Place**. Other places you'll want to visit are the **Waterfront Dock** area, **Maritime Museum**, **Anglesea Barracks**, the **Tasmanian Museum and Art**

Gallery, and **Cascade Brewery** – Australia's oldest.

Nightlife

Hobart nightlife is fairly quiet. Most of the action is in the Docks area and Salamanca Market. Quality pubs with good live music are the norm, the best are: **Knudwoods**, **Brooke Street Bar** and, in the City, the raucously Irish **New Sydney Hotel**. **Wrest Point Hotel Casino** was Australia's first casino – it also houses a restaurant, accommodation and a nightclub. The casino opens at 1pm and operates Sun–Thurs until 3am, Friday/Saturday until 4am.

For other entertainment – cinemas, pub bands and the like – check the *Mercury* newspaper for a guide to what's on.

Shopping

Salamanca Place has a number of good-quality souvenir stores. Look for local gemstones, wooden products made from Huon Pine or Sassafras, shellcraft and antiques.

Language

Aussie Slanguage

Despite the stereotype, Australians don't actually wander around yacking at each other like cockney parodies. However, there are some definite peculiarities in the vernacular, often called "Strine". The term derives from saying the word "Australian" through both closed teeth and the nose – a local accent that some scholars claim arose out of a need to keep the trap (mouth) shut against blowies (blow flies).

The lingo has a laconic, poetic originality ("he was flash as a rat with a gold tooth…") and can be colourfully coarse ("…and as thin as a streak of pelican shit").

Following are a few oddities and words unique to Australia worth knowing:

A

ABC Australian Broadcasting Corporation
ACT Australian Capital Territory (Canberra)
ACTU Australian Council of Trade Unions
ALP Australian Labor Party
ASIO Australian Security Intelligence Organisation
Across the ditch Across the Tasman Sea: i.e. New Zealand
Alf Stupid Australian
Alice, The Alice Springs
Amber fluid Beer
Ankle-biter Young child
Anzac Australian & New Zealand Army Corps (World War I)
Arvo Afternoon
Avago Have a go (popular at sporting events: as in "avagoyamug!")

B

BHP Broken Hill Proprietary, a mining corporation
Back of Bourke Far Outback
Back of beyond Further Outback
Bag of Fruit Suit
Bail up To rob, hold up
Banana bender Queenslander
Barbie Barbecue
Barrack To cheer for, encourage
Bastard Term of endearment (when it's not a term of dislike)
Bathers Swimming costume
Battler One who struggles for a living
Beaut Short for "beautiful" (very good, great, fantastic)
Bible basher Religious preacher
Biker Non-gang motorbike rider
Bikey Biker gang member
Billabong Waterhole in semi-dry river
Billy Tin container used for boiling water to make tea
Bitser Mongrel dog ("bits a this and bits a that")
Black Stump, The Where the back of Bourke begins (as in the phrase "beyond the black stump")
Blind Freddie could have seen it Something obvious
Bloody Universally undeleted expletive, as in "shootin' kanga-bloody-roos"
Blowie Blowfly
Bludger Slacker
Blue A fight
Bluey A redhead
Bomb A bad car
Bonzer Terrific
Boomer Huge kangaroo
Boomerang Aboriginal hunting instrument
Bottler Terrific (esp Beauty Bottler!)
Bottlo Liquor Shop
Buckley's Chance One chance in a million
Bug Small edible crustacean, as in Balmain Bug/Moreton Bay Bug
Bullamakanka Mythical, far distant place
Bull Dust Bullshit
Bunyip Australia's Yeti, Big Foot or Loch Ness monster. Lives in a billabong
Burl A try (give it a burl)
Bush The countryside
Bushranger Highwayman, outlaw

Bushweek Traditionally a period of licence when rural folk hit the towns. Now used when you think someone is putting something over on you (in the expression, "What do you think this is...bushweek?")
BYO Bring Your Own (liquor to a restaurant)

C

Cask Boxed bag of cheap wine
Chips Crisps (unless hot and fried)
Chook Chicken
Chuck a U-ey Do a U-turn
Chunder Vomit. (Other quaint expressions – pavement pizza, curbside quiche, technicolor yawn)
Cobber Antique version of "mate"
Cockie Farmer
Come a gutser Make a bad mistake
Compo Workers' Compensation
Coolabah Box eucalyptus tree
Cop it sweet To take the blame or the loss agreeably
Corroboree Aboriginal ceremonial gathering
Cow Cockie Cattle grazier
Counter Lunch A pub lunch
Crissie Christmas
Crook Broken, sick or no good
Cut lunch A lunch mainly consisting of sandwiches

D

Dag Mild term for fool or unfashionable person; the popular adjective is daggy
Daks Trousers
Damper Unrisen bread, usually cooked in a campfire (a staple of bush tucker)
Dero Derelict person
Didgeridoo Aboriginal droning instrument
Digger Australian soldier, or any old male character
Dill Idiot
Dingo Australian native dog
Dinkie die The truth
Dinkum Genuine or honest
Do yer block Lose your temper
Dob To report on someone. ("To dob in")
Don't come the raw prawn Don't try and fool me

Doona Quilted eiderdown (duvet)
Drongo Idiot
Dumper A roundly crashing wave, unsuitable for bodysurfing
Dunny Toilet ("Useless as a glass door on a dunny")

E–F

Esky Portable cooler for drinks, food
Fair dinkum Same as "Dinkie die" and "dinkum," above
Figjam F★★★ I'm good, just ask me (used derogatively as in "He's figjam")
Flash as a rat with a gold tooth Showing off
Footpath Pavement or sidewalk
Footy Aussie Rules football
Fossicking To search for gold in abandoned works, rummage

G–H

G'day Good day
Galah Fool or idiot (after the parrot of same name)
Garbo Garbageman
Give it the flick Get rid of it
Gong, The Wollongong
Good on ya Well done
Greenie A conservationist
Grog Alcoholic drink
Gurgler, down the Down the toilet, wasted
Heart starter First drink of the day
Hoon Loudmouth young motorised hooligan
Hotel Some hotels are pubs, some hotels are hotels, some are both
Humpy Aboriginal shack

I–J

Icey-pole Store-bought frozen ice confection on a stick
Jackaroo Male managment trainee on an outback station
Jillaroo Female same
Job To punch
Jocks Men's underpants
Joe Blake Snake
Joey Baby kangaroo
Jumbuck Lamb

K

A kangaroo short in his top paddock A bit crazy
Karked it Died
Kip To sleep. Also an instrument used to toss pennies in the gambling game "two-up"
Knuckle To punch

L

Lair A show-off
Lamington Aussie dessert: cubes of sponge cake, covered in chocolate and desiccated coconut
Larrikin Previously a street hoodlum. Now a cheeky or mischievous youth
Loaf To do nothing ("just loafing about"). Also means a head ("use yer loaf")
Lob Arrive ("To lob in")
Lolly Candy or sweet
Lurk A racket, a "dodge" or illegal scheme

M

Mad as a cut snake Particularly crazy
Mick A Roman Catholic
Middy 285 ml/10oz glass of beer (in NSW)
Mob A group of persons or things (not necessarily unruly)
Mozzie Mosquito
Mug A gullible fool

N

Neck oil Beer
Nervy A nervous attack (To "chuck a nervy")
Never-never Far off in the Outback
Nick Steal
Nit Fool, idiot
No-hoper Same as above, but worse
Nong Fool

O

O.S. Overseas
Ocker Quintessential Aussie bumpkin-loudmouth, a favourite target of comedians

Outback The bush; uncivilised, uninhabited country
Oz Australia

P

Panic merchant Chronic anxiety case
Pashing Kissing
Perve To ogle at an attractive person
Pie Floater A meat pie in a bowl of pea soup
Pie-eyed Drunk
Pinch Arrest, or steal
Pissed Off Angry
Plonk Cheap wine
Poker machine Slot machine (a.k.a. "pokie")
Pom English person
Postie Mail person
Private school For fee-paying pupils
Public school State school, not "private"

Q–R

Quarts Pints, but only in Queensland
RSL Returned Servicemen's League, known for their entertainment clubs
Ratbag Trouble-maker (also a friendly term of abuse)
Ratshit Lousy, ruined. Abbreviation "RS" also used
Rid Insect repellent
Ridgi-didge Genuine, true
Ringer Stockman or woman on an outback station
Ripper Good
Road train Outback truck with up to three trailers
Roo Kangaroo
Roof rabbits Possums or rats in the attic
Root Sexual intercourse
Rooted Exhausted
Ropable Very angry
Running round like a chook with its head cut off useless, frenetic activity

S

Salvo Member of the Salvation Army
Sanger Sandwich

Scab Technically a strike-breaker; often used to describe someone who's cheap and/or underhanded; can also be used to mean borrow ('Can I scab a dollar off you?')
Schooner Large beer glass (NSW)
Scrub Bushland
Scunge A dirty, untidy person
Semi-trailer Articulated truck
She'll be apples It'll be right
She's sweet Everything is all right
Sheila Female (derogatory)
Shoot through Leave unexpectedly, escape
Shonky Unreliable
Slats Ribs
Smoke-o Work break (archaic)
Snags Sausages
Speedos Nylon swimming trunks
Sprog Baby
Spunk Good-looking person
Squatter Large landholder in early colonial times
Station Large farm or ranch
Stickybeak Busybody
Stinger Box jellyfish
Stirrer Trouble maker
Stockman Cowboy, station hand
Stonkered Exhausted
Strain the potatoes (or spuds) Urinate
Strides Trousers
Strine Vernacular Australian
Stubby Small bottle of beer, kept cold in a "stubby holder"
Stunned Mullet Someone who looks shocked
Swagman Vagabond, rural tramp
Sydney or the Bush All or nothing

T

TAB Totalisator Agency Board, legal offtrack betting shop
Tall poppies High achievers (as in the expression "tall poppy syndrome", to describe Australians' habit of attacking anyone who has achieved something)
Tassie Tasmania
Taswegian resident of Tasmania
Telly Television, also the *Sydney Telegraph Mirror*
Thongs Flip-flop sandals and, increasingly, string knickers
Tinnie Can of beer, also a small aluminium boat

Togs Swimsuit (sometimes called "bathers")
Top End Northern Territory
Too Right! Absolutely!
Troppo Unhinged by tropical weather
Tube Can of beer or innermost section of breaking surf wave
Tucker Food
Turps Any form of alcohol ("On the turps" – to be drinking)
Two-pot screamer Person unable to hold their drink
Two up Popular gambling game involving two pennies thrown in the air

U

Uni University
Unit Apartment, flat
Urchin Baby or small child
Ute "Utility" truck – a pickup truck

V–W

Vegemite Brown yeast sandwich spread which Australians grow up on but is regarded by most foreigners as semi-toxic
Walkabout Travelling on foot for long distances – an Aboriginal tradition – usually involves disappearing entirely for long periods at a time
Wheeties Weetbix or most other breakfast cereals
Whinge Complain (often used in relation to "whingeing Poms")
Wharfie Dockworker
Wog Minor disease or flu
Wowser Killjoy, prude

X–Y

XXXX Beer
Yabber Chatter
Yabbie Small freshwater crayfish
Yack To talk
Yahoo An unruly type
Yakka Work
Yobbo Hoon, loudmouth – Pacific redneck
Your blood's good enough to bottle I like you

Further Reading

General

Australian Dreaming: 40,000 Years of Aboriginal History. Compiled and edited by Jennifer Isaacs. Sydney: Lansdowne Press, 1980.
The Heritage of Australia: The Illustrated Register of the National Estate. Melbourne: Macmillan, 1981.
Australia's Living Heritage: Arts of the Dreaming by Jennifer Isaacs. Sydney: Lansdowne Press, 1984.
Wilderness Australia by David McGonigal. Sydney: Reed Books, 1987.
Australian Geographic Book of the Kimberley by David McGonigal. Sydney: Australian Geographic, 1990.
Australia. The Greatest Island by Robert Raymond. Sydney: Lansdowne Press, 1982.
Wine Western Australia by Mike Zekulich. Perth: St George Books, 1994.

History

A Shorter History of Australia by Geoffrey Blainey. Random House, 1994.
A New History of Australia by F.R. Crowley. Melbourne: William Heinemann, 1974
Turning Points in the Making of

Travel

The Songlines by Bruce Chatwin.
Explore Australia by Four-Wheel Drive by Peter & Kim Wherrett. Viking O'Neil.
Tracks by Robyn Davidson.
One for the Road by Tony Horwitz.
The Ribbon and the Ragged Square by Lindas Christmas.

Social History

History as it Happened by L. Kepert. Melbourne: Nelson.
Life on the Australian Goldfields by Derrick I. Stone. Sydney: Methuen.
The New Gold Mountain: The Chinese in Australia by C. Young. Richmond: S.A. Raphael Arts.

Australia by Michael Page. Adelaide: Rigby, 1980.
A Secret Country by John Pilger. London: Vintage, 1990. (An inside view by the respected journalist.)
The Explorers edited by Tim Flannery: Text Publishing, 2000.
Terra Australis introduced by Tim Flannery: Text Publishing, 2001.
The Spirit of Kokoda by Patrick Lindsay: Hardie Grant Books, 2002.
The Floating Brothel by Sian Rees. A perspective on the First Fleet; Thorndike Press, 2002.

Natural History

Australia, the Wild Continent by Michael Morcombe. Sydney: Lansdowne, 1981.
Australian Wildlife: Best-Known Birds, Mammals Reader's Digest.
Wild Australia Sydney: Reader's Digest.
Australia's Natural Wonders by Michael Richardson. Sydney: Golden Press, 1984.

Aboriginal History

Ethnographic Studies of Northwest Central Queensland by W.E. Roth.
Triumph of the Nomads by Geoffrey Blainey; Penguin 1982.
Aboriginal Australians by Richard Broome, 1982.
A Change of Ownership by Mildred Kirk. Jacaranda 1986.
My Place by Sally Morgan.
The Fringe Dwellers by Nene Gare: Heinemann 1961.
Prehistory of Australia; John Mulvaney and John Kamminga: Smithsonian Books 1999.
Why Weren't We Told? by Henry Reynolds, an authority on Aboriginal relations with white Australians: Penguin Australia 2000.
Songman by Allan Baillie: Puffin 1995.

Australian Language

The Macquarie Dictionary. Sydney: Macquarie University: 1981.
Let's Talk Strine by Afferbeck Lauder. Sydney: Lansdowne Press.
New South Wales Aboriginal Place Names by F.D. McCarthy. Sydney: Australian Museum, 1971.
Dictionary of Australian Colloquialisms by G.A. Wilkes. Sydney: University Press, 1996.

Fiction/Poetry

There are many excellent choices from Australia's recognised writers:
The Man from Snowy River (and other collected poems from this 19th-century master of the bush ballad) by Banjo Paterson.
Short Stories by Henry Lawson. (the classic bush lyricist).
For the Term of His Natural Life by Marcus Clarke. Rip-roaring adventure set in convict era.
A Fortunate Life by Albert Facey. A digger's life in the early 20th century.
The True History of the Kelly Gang by Peter Carey. Tale of the Kelly Gang told through the eyes of Ned Kelly.
The Sound of One Hand Clapping by Richard Flanagan. Moving account of the hard life of Tasmania's immigrant workers.
Matthew Flinder's Cat by Bryce Courtenay.
Dirt Music by Tim Winton.
Morgan's Run by Colleen McCullough.
Territory by Judy Nunn
Bliss, Illywhacker or Oscar and Lucinda by Peter Carey. An unusual love story set in mid-nineteenth century Australia from the Booker prize winner.
Other authors to check out include: Helen Garner, Thomas Keneally, Beverley Farmer, Kate Greenville, Elizabeth Jolley, Thea Astley and Kaz Cooke.

Children's Books

The Magic Pudding by Norman Lindsay, 1918.
Snugglepot & Cuddlepie by May Gibbs, 1918.
Possum Magic by Julie Vivas & Mem Fox, 1983.

Other Insight Guides

Other titles in the Insight Guide range that highlight destinations in this region include **Insight Guides** to **Melbourne** and **Sydney**,

the **Insight Pocket Guides** to **Sydney**, **Perth**, and **Brisbane and the Gold Coast**,

and the **Insight Compact Guide** to **Sydney**.

Feedback

We do our best to ensure the information in our books is as accurate and up-to-date as possible. The books are updated on a regular basis, using local contacts, who painstakingly add, amend and correct as required. However, some mistakes and omissions are inevitable and we are ultimately reliant on our readers to put us in the picture.

We would welcome your feedback on any details related to your experiences using the book "on the road". Maybe we recommended a hotel that you liked (or another that you didn't), as well as interesting new attractions, or facts and figures you have found out about the country itself. The more details you can give us (particularly with regard to addresses, e-mails and telephone numbers), the better. We will acknowledge all contributions, and we'll offer an Insight Guide to the best letters received.

Please write to us at:
Insight Guides
PO Box 7910
London SE1 1WE
United Kingdom
Or send e-mail to:
insight@apaguide.co.uk

ART & PHOTO CREDITS

AFP/Getty Images 85, 102, 103
Apa Photo Agency 209R, 218
Australian Tourist Commission spine, back cover left & top left, 66, 143T, 156, 161, 180, 203, 214B, 249, 257T, 279T, 280T, 293, 295, 297, 317L, 325
Bill Bachman 68, 76, 169, 183, 275, 324T
Ian Beattie/Auscape 243T
Brendan Beime/Auscape 79
John Borthwick 254
David Bowden 208
Linda Carlock 204L
Sylvia Cordaiy Photo Library 120
David Curl/Anca 83
Andy Dalton/FootPrints 252T
Jerry Dennis 23, 88, 99, 105, 172, 186, 193, 195T, 210, 211, 213, 231, 243, 247, 276T, 283, 297T, 324
Jeff Drewitz/Wildlight 278
Edifice/Corbis 296
Emmler/laif/Katz 145, 258
John Fairfax Features 58
John Farmar/Sylvia Cordaiy 117L, 221, 224, 234, 251
Jean-Paul Ferrero/Auscape 158T, 324T, 328T
Getty Images 94, 100, 101
Glyn Genin/Apa 70, 135, 142
Graeme Goldin/Sylvia Cordaiy 10/11, 178/9, 181
Manfred Gottschalk back flap top, 19, 124/5, 165, 170, 205, 229, 280, 282, 300, 304
David Gray/Reuters/Corbis 60
Great Southern Railway 276
Nick Hannah/FootPrints 262/3
Gary Hansen/Auscape 168
D. & J. Heaton front flap top & bottom, 16/17, 114, 116, 246R
Heeb/laif/Katz 189
Peter Hendrie/Image Bank 201
Dave G. Houser/Corbis 173
Phil Jarratt 126/7, 245
A. B. Joyce 175, 329
Catherine Karnow 67, 69
Alan Keohane/Impact 281, 284
Nan Kivell Collection/NLA 31
Kobal Collection 92, 93
Ford Kristo/Planet Earth 251T
Dennis Lane 74
Lansdowne Picture Library 8/9, 27, 33, 35, 36, 49, 50, 54, 82, 117R, 159, 207, 209L, 212, 265, 301, 309, 315

Lodestone Press 56
Phil Lyon/Sylvia Cordaiy 303
David McGonigal 81, 149, 160, 230, 286, 299, 302, 307, 328, 330
Robert Mort/Getty Images 279
NHPA/ANT 119, 121, 236
Robbi Newman 47
Stewart Owen Fox 162, 244T
Ozsport 98
D. Parer & E. Parer-Cook 205T
D. Parer & E. Parer-Cook/Auscape 317R
Tony Perrottet bc right, 2/3, 12/13, 14, 20, 59, 62/3, 64/5, 71, 77, 78, 86/7, 107, 108, 112/3, 128/9, 134, 137, 138, 139, 143, 144, 145T, 146, 147, 148, 150/1, 154, 164, 184/5, 187, 191, 192, 194, 195, 204R, 216/7, 219, 223, 227, 238/9, 241, 244, 246T, 248, 252, 253, 255, 256, 257, 259, 267, 285, 287, 288, 289, 312/3, 314, 318, 319, 320, 321, 322, 323, 326, 327
Martin Philbey 95
Planet Earth Pictures 115
Steve Pohlner/Apa 246L
Alain Proust/Cephas 228T
Carl & Anne Purcell/Corbis 237
Philip Quirk/Wildlight 306
Nick Rains/Sylvia Cordaiy 153, 171, 235, 261, 264
Mick Rock/Cephas 214T
Jean-Marc La Roque/Auscape 75, 190T, 210T
Photo Simons 166, 167, 228
South Australian Tourist Commission 225, 233
David Stahl 6/7, 21, 91, 177
Paul Steel 200
Tony Stone bc bottom, 18, 80, 260
Oliver Strewe/Wave Productions back flap bottom, 130, 163, 198/9, 206, 215, 273, 290/1, 292, 305, 310, 311
Sydney Symphony Orchestra 90
Andrew Tauber/Apa 106

Tom Till/Auscape 250
Norman Tomalin/Alamy 272
Tourism New South Wales 155, 174, 176, 222
Alexander Turnbull Library 51
Penny Tweedie 22, 26, 73
Voscar 211T
Murray Walmsley 158
Patrick Ward/Corbis 277
Steve Watkins/Natural Exposure 308, 310T
Dave Young/Planet Earth 109

Picture Spreads

Pages 96/7 Tony Perrottet, except shell painting, top left, and tortoise (Jerry Dennis), and Muntja Nungurayai and Tjakamarra brothers (Steve Watkins/Natural Exposure).
Pages 110/11 Bins of grapes: Joy Skipper/Anthony Blake Photo Library. Hunter Valley signs and winemaker Neil Pike: J. Topps/Anthony Blake. Cooper, Rutherglen barrels and Karadoc: Mick Rock/Cephas. Mountadam and Yeringberg: Andy Christodolo/Cephas. Red wines: Cephas/Wine magazine.
Pages 122/3 Bilby, Tasmanian devils, mole and spider: NHPA/ANT. Koala sign: Norbert Wu/Planet Earth. Tortoise: John Farmar/Sylvia Cordaiy. Kangaroo and bower bird: Ford Kristo/Planet Earth. Platypus: D. Parer & E. Parer-Cook/Auscape. Copperhead: NHPA/Pavel German.
Pages 140/1 Jerry Dennis, except Trade Wall (Gary Warner/Museum of Sydney) and interactive exhibit (Marinco Kojdanovsky/Powerhouse).
Pages 196/7 Jerry Dennis, except Windsor Hotel (Tony Perrottet).
Pages 270/1 All FootPrints. Shark: Emma Jane Lonsdale. Lobster and cod: Adam Powell. Flower coral, clown fish, staghorn coral and crown-of-thorns: Andy Dalton. Moray eel: Alex Misiewicz. Sea fan: Carlos Lima.

Map Production: Polyglott Kartographie, Berndtson and Berndtson Publications, Elsner & Schichor
© 2005 Apa Publications GmbH & Co. Verlag KG, Singapore.

INSIGHT GUIDE
australia

Cartographic Editor **Zoë Goodwin**
Design Consultants
Klaus Geisler, Graham Mitchener
Picture Research **Hilary Genin**

Index

Note: page numbers in *italics* refer to illustrations

www.insightguides.com

✕ INSIGHT GUIDES

The World Leader in Visual Travel Guides & Maps

As travellers become ever more discriminating, Insight Guides is using the vast experience gained over three-and-a-half decades of guidebook publishing to create an even wider range of titles than before. For those who want the big picture, Insight Guides and Insight City Guides provide comprehensive coverage of a destination. Insight Pocket Guides supply personal recommendations for a short stay. Insight Compact Guides are attractively portable. Insight FlexiMaps are both easy to use and rugged. And specialist titles cover shopping, eating out, and museums and galleries.

INSIGHT GUIDES

The classic series that puts you in the picture

Alaska
Amazon Wildlife
American Southwest
Amsterdam
Argentina
Arizona & Grand Canyon
Asia's Best Hotels & Resorts
Asia, East
Asia, Southeast
Australia
Austria
Bahamas
Bali
Baltic States
Bangkok
Barbados
Barcelona
Beijing
Belgium
Belize
Berlin
Bermuda
Boston
Brazil
Brittany
Brussels
Buenos Aires
Burgundy
Burma (Myanmar)
Cairo
California
California, Southern
Canada
Caribbean
Caribbean Cruises
Channel Islands
Chicago
Chile
China
Colorado
Continental Europe
Corsica
Costa Rica
Crete
Croatia
Cuba
Cyprus
Czech & Slovak Republic
Delhi, Jaipur & Agra
Denmark

Dominican Rep. & Haiti
Dublin
East African Wildlife
Eastern Europe
Ecuador
Edinburgh
Egypt
England
Finland
Florence
Florida
France
France, Southwest
French Riviera
Gambia & Senegal
Germany
Glasgow
Gran Canaria
Great Britain
Great Gardens of Britain
   & Ireland
Great Railway Journeys
   of Europe
Greece
Greek Islands
Guatemala, Belize
   & Yucatán
Hawaii
Hong Kong
Hungary
Iceland
India
India, South
Indonesia
Ireland
Israel
Istanbul
Italy
Italy, Northern
Italy, Southern
Jamaica
Japan
Jerusalem
Jordan
Kenya
Korea
Laos & Cambodia
Las Vegas
Lisbon
London

Los Angeles
Madeira
Madrid
Malaysia
Mallorca & Ibiza
Malta
Mauritius Réunion
   & Seychelles
Mediterranean Cruises
Melbourne
Mexico
Miami
Montreal
Morocco
Moscow
Namibia
Nepal
Netherlands
New England
New Mexico
New Orleans
New York City
New York State
New Zealand
Nile
Normandy
North American &
   Alaskan Cruises
Norway
Oman & The UAE
Oxford
Pacific Northwest
Pakistan
Paris
Peru
Philadelphia
Philippines
Poland
Portugal
Prague
Provence
Puerto Rico
Rajasthan

Rio de Janeiro
Rome
Russia
St Petersburg
San Francisco
Sardinia
Scandinavia
Scotland
Seattle
Shanghai
Sicily
Singapore
South Africa
South America
Spain
Spain, Northern
Spain, Southern
Sri Lanka
Sweden
Switzerland
Sydney
Syria & Lebanon
Taiwan
Tanzania & Zanzibar
Tenerife
Texas
Thailand
Tokyo
Trinidad & Tobago
Tunisia
Turkey
Tuscany
Umbria
USA: The New South
USA: On The Road
USA: Western States
US National Parks: West
Venezuela
Venice
Vienna
Vietnam
Wales
Walt Disney World/Orlando

INSIGHT GUIDES

The world's largest collection of visual travel guides & maps